The first edition of the *Politics of India since Independence* argued that the Indian state, society, and economy were in the midst of a systemic crisis produced by the centralizing drives of a national leadership determined to transform the country into a modern, industrialized, militarily strong state. In the three years since this edition was published, this crisis has intensified, revealing itself in secessionist movements and in increased inter-caste conflicts. The country has witnessed the rise of Hindu nationalism and the worst communal massacres since Independence following the destruction of the mosque in Ayodhya. The issue before the country now is whether or not it can find within its own traditions the moral and material resources and the leadership to restore a political and communal balance in state and society.

THE NEW CAMBRIDGE HISTORY
OF INDIA

*The politics of India since
Independence*

THE NEW CAMBRIDGE HISTORY OF INDIA

General editor GORDON JOHNSON

President of Wolfson College, and Director, Centre of South Asian Studies,
University of Cambridge

Associate editors C. A. BAYLY

Vere Harmsworth Professor of Imperial and Naval History, University of Cambridge,
and Fellow of St Catharine's College

and JOHN F. RICHARDS

Professor of History, Duke University

Although the original *Cambridge History of India*, published between 1922 and 1937, did much to formulate a chronology for Indian history and describe the administrative structures of government in India, it has inevitably been overtaken by the mass of new research published over the last fifty years.

Designed to take full account of recent scholarship and changing conceptions of South Asia's historical development, *The New Cambridge History of India* is published as a series of short, self-contained volumes, each dealing with a separate theme and written by a single person, within an overall four-part structure.

The four parts are as follows:

I The Mughals and their contemporaries

II Indian states and the transition to colonialism

III The Indian empire and the beginnings of modern society

IV The evolution of contemporary South Asia

A list of individual titles already published and in preparation will be found at the end of the volume.

THE NEW CAMBRIDGE HISTORY OF INDIA

IV·1

The politics of India since Independence

SECOND EDITION

PAUL R. BRASS

PROFESSOR OF POLITICAL SCIENCE
AND SOUTH ASIAN STUDIES
UNIVERSITY OF WASHINGTON

CAMBRIDGE
UNIVERSITY PRESS

Published by the Press Syndicate of the University of Cambridge
The Pitt Building, Trumpington Street, Cambridge CB2 IRP
40 West 20th Street, New York, NY 10011–4211, USA
10 Stamford Road, Oakleigh, Melbourne 3166, Australia

First published 1990
Reprinted 1991
Second edition 1994
Reprinted 1995, 1996, 1997

Printed in Great Britain at the University Press, Cambridge

A catalogue record for this book is available from the British Library

Library of Congress cataloguing in publication data

Brass, Paul R.
The politics of India since independence / Paul R. Brass. – 2nd ed.
p.   cm. – (The New Cambridge history of India : IV, 1)
Includes bibliographical references and index.
ISBN 0 521 45362 3. – ISBN (invalid) 0 521 45990 2 (pbk.)
1. India – Politics and government – 1947–   I. Title. II. Series.
DS480.84.B67 1994
320.954 – dc20   93–30782 CIP

ISBN 0 521 45362 3 hardback
ISBN 0 521 45970 2 paperback

CE

For SU,
with my love

CONTENTS

FIGURES AND TABLES

PREFACE

The first edition of this book was written between 1986 and 1989. It built upon my own work of the previous twenty-seven years on Indian politics, ethnicity and nationalism, and political economy as well as that of my colleagues who had written on these subjects during the previous three decades. The central theme of the first edition concerned the consequences of increasing efforts by the country's national leaders to centralize power, decision making, and control of economic resources in one of the most culturally diverse and socially fragmented agrarian societies in the world. These centralizing drives, intensified in the post-Nehru era, had increasingly contrary effects. The effectiveness of political organizations had been eroded, ethnic, religious, caste, and other cultural and regional conflicts had heightened, and the ability of the central government to implement in the states and localities economic plans and programs designed in New Delhi had declined. These consequences suggested the existence of a systemic crisis in the Indian polity which, I argued, would not be easily resolved. I had, however, also argued that alternative paths toward such a resolution existed within Indian political and economic thought and political practices and that an alternative leadership might yet arise to seek such a resolution, basing itself on India's own traditions.

In the four years since the final revisions on the original manuscript were made, the several crises evident then have intensified to that turning point signified by the Greek meaning of the term crisis. That is, the Indian polity has reached a turning point in its post-Independence history. The old political order dominated by the Congress and parties sprung from it is in decay. These parties lack effective or popular leadership, compelling ideals, and local organization.

An alternative leadership has indeed arisen in the intervening years, self-consciously basing itself on India's Hindu traditions while pursuing even more relentlessly a Western ideal model of building a strong, centralized, militarily powerful state, possessing nuclear weapons, able

xiii

to bring order to the country while commanding the respect of the great nations of the contemporary world. Unlike its decaying rivals, the RSS family of organizations including the BJP and the VHP have effective leadership, dedicated party cadres, and a coherent ideology of "Hindutva" or militant Hindu nationalism. Moreover, it has demonstrated an ability to mobilize large masses of the Hindu population around its subsidiary goals, principally the removal of the mosque at Ayodhya and its replacement by a temple to the Hindu god Ram. In the process, the movement led by the RSS family of organizations has also deliberately contributed to the communalization and political polarization of the Hindu and Muslim populations of the northern and western parts of the country, brought to a peak by the destruction of the Babari Masjid on December 6, 1992 and its violent aftermath.

Despite its negative, destructive consequences for national unity, its positive message of militant Hindu nationalism has left hardly any middle or upper class or educated Hindus in northern and western India untouched, virtually all of whom accept at least some aspects of the Hindu nationalist ideology. On the other hand, a spirit of dejection and fear has overtaken the large Muslim population of the country, whose leaders have themselves contributed significantly to the communal crisis. Among the Muslims, as among the Congress/Janata family of organizations, there is no effective leadership.

Thus, the BJP, the political party spokesman for militant Hindu nationalism, appears to be ascendant, heading relentlessly toward the achievement of its goal of attaining national power. Yet, there remain numerous obstacles in its way. The first is the persistent regional, cultural, ethnic, and linguistic diversity of the country which continues to pose formidable obstacles to its capturing of power at the Center. The RSS ideology has not yet had a major impact in the eastern and southern parts of the country. The Tamil-speaking, non-Brahman population of Madras is not likely to be swayed by the ideology of a northern party devoted to the spread of Hindi whose top leadership contains a high percentage of Brahmans. In the north itself, the Janata group of parties seeks to combine the backward castes, the Muslims, and the low castes, who comprise the majority of the northern population of the country against the BJP coalition of mostly upper caste groups. The hope is that this Janata coalition will be able to head off a north Indian sweep by the BJP, which would carry it to power in the next election.

Yet, the opposition to the BJP lacks a compelling counter-message. Against the RSS ideology of Hindu unity, it presents a negative image of divisiveness rather than a positive image, which would somehow convey the virtues of Indian cultural diversities and translate them into a view of a new Indian political order which represents these diversities faithfully. Until such an alternative political order can be projected by the Congress, the Janata group of parties and their regional allies and rivals in West Bengal and the south, the country as a whole will lack a meaningful alternative to the unifying ideology of the BJP. The ability of the Congress and the organizations sprung from it to obstruct the rise to power of the BJP will then have only a temporary character whose end result could well be further disintegration in the Indian political order, which will itself facilitate the rise of the BJP to power in the longer run.

In the meantime, a minority Congress government with fragile and ineffective leadership continues to grapple with other aspects of the crises in the Indian political, economic, and social orders. A brutal and violent police campaign against Sikh militants in Punjab seems at length to have brought these groups under control, but the popular insurrection against continued Indian rule in Kashmir has persisted in the face of an equally brutal and violent campaign of state repression. In the aftermath of the December–January riots and pogroms in Bombay and other cities and towns in northern and western India, there is a momentary lull in the violence between elements from the Hindu and Muslim communities.

In the face of this ethnic and communal turmoil and political fragmentation, the one strongly positive feature has been the decisive efforts taken by the Congress government under Prime Minister Narasimha Rao to transform the Indian economy, to remove the stifling system of semi-socialist, bureaucratic controls over industry, and to open the economy to internal and international market forces. It is too soon to tell how effective these changes will be in dismantling the Nehruvian socialist system, which had contributed so much to the transformation of India, like its Socialist models, into a corrupt bureaucratic state. Nor do these changes contain any design for the overwhelming majority of the population who continue to depend on agriculture for a livelihood and who live in abysmal conditions of poverty and degradation both in the rural areas of the country and in the most horrific – and ever-proliferating – urban slums the world has ever seen.

My revisions for this edition have focused on the deepening crises of national unity which have affected the Indian state in the past four years, the intensified inter-caste conflict, the proposed transformations in the Indian economy, and the political/electoral changes in the party system, especially those associated with the continuing decline of the Congress and the rise of the BJP. Limitations of space have meant that I have had to reduce or eliminate some material from the first edition in order to accommodate a full account of these aspects of India's deepening crisis, especially – to my regret – sections on tribal politics and on migrant–non-migrant conflicts. It is likely that these sections will have to be re-introduced and updated in the third edition of this book.

I have tried to take account of criticisms of the first edition of the book published in various reviews and conveyed to me personally by several colleagues, though several of the criticisms could not be answered fully without vastly increasing the size of this book. I especially hope that the new index will satisfy critics of the previous one. Finally, I want to thank again Irene Joshi, our University of Washington South Asia librarian, for her invaluable and timely bibliographic assistance in helping me prepare both the first and second editions of this book.

PAUL R. BRASS

New Delhi
India International Centre
June 4, 1993

ABBREVIATIONS

AASU	All Assam Students' Union
ABSU	All-Bodo Students' Union
AD	Akali Dal
ADMK	Anna Dravida Munnetra Kazagham
AGP	Asom Gana Parishad
AIADMK	All India Anna Dravida Munnetra Kazagham
AICC	All India Congress Committee
AMU	Aligarh Muslim University
BJP	Bharatiya Janata Party
BJS	Bharatiya Jana Sangh
BKD	Bharatiya Kranti Dal
BLD	Bharatiya Lok Dal
CLM	Commissioner for Linguistic Minorities
CPI	Communist Party of India
CPM	Communist Party of India (Marxist)
CPML	Communist Party of India (Marxist-Leninist)
CPP	Congress Parliamentary Party
CSRE	Crash Scheme for Rural Employment
DM	District Magistrate
DMK	Dravida Munnetra Kazagham
DMKP	Dalit Mazdoor Kisan Party
DPAP	Drought Prone Areas Program
EPW	*Economic and Political Weekly*
HYV	High Yielding Variety
HYVP	High Yielding Variety Program
HPU	Hill People's Union
IAAP	Intensive Agricultural Area Program
IADP	Intensive Agricultural District Program
IAS	Indian Administrative Service
ICS	Indian Civil Service
INC	Indian National Congress
INCI	Indian National Congress (Indira)

INCJ	Indian National Congress (Jagjivan Ram)
INCS	Indian National Congress (Socialist)
IPS	Indian Police Service
IRDP	Integrated Rural Development Program
ISS	Islamic Sevak Sangh
JD	Janata Dal
JDG	Janata Dal (G)
JNP	Janata Party
JNPS	Janata Party (Secular)
JP	Jayaprakash Narayan
KMPP	Kisan Mazdoor Praja Party
LD	Lok Dal
LKDB	Lok Dal (B)
LTTE	Liberation Tigers of Tamil Eelam
MFAL	Marginal Farmers and Agricultural Laborers Agency
MG	Maharashtrawadi Gomantak
MGR	M. G. Ramachandran
ML	Muslim League
MLA	Member, Legislative Assembley
MNF	Mizo National Front
MP	Member of Parliament
M. P.	Madhya Pradesh
MPP	Manipur People's Party
NC-F	National Conference (F)
NCO	Indian National Congress (O)
NEP	New Economic Policy
NNO	Naga Nationalist Organization
NPC	Nagaland People's Council
NREP	National Rural Employment Program
NTR	N. T. Rama Rao
PIREP	Pilot Intensive Rural Employment Project
PM	Prime Minister
PR	President's Rule
PSP	Praja Socialist Party
RLEGS	Rural Labor Employment Guarantee Scheme
RSS	Rashtriya Swayamsevak Sangh
SFDA	Small Farmers Development Agency
SGPC	Shiromani Gurdwara Prabhandak Committee

SHS	Shiv Sena
SJP	Samajwadi Janata Party
SKSP	Sikkim Sangram Parishad
SOC	Socialist Party
SP	Superintendent of Police
SSP	Samyukta Socialist Party
SWA	Swatantra Party
TADA	Terrorist and Disruptive Activities Act
TDP	Telugu Desam Party
TPS	Telangana Praja Samiti
ULFA	United Liberation Front of Assam
U.P.	Uttar Pradesh
VHP	Vishwa Hindu Parishad

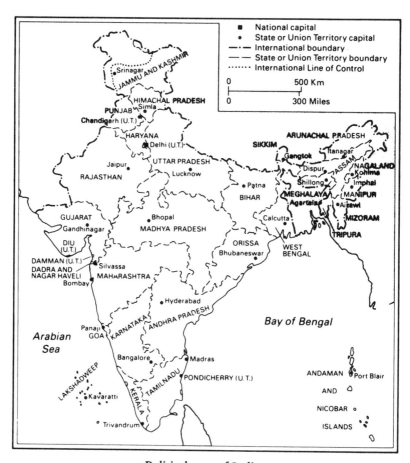

Political map of India
Based on Ashok K. Dutt and M. Margaret Geib, *Atlas of South Asia*
(Boulder, CO: Westview Press, 1987)

CHAPTER 1

INTRODUCTION: CONTINUITIES AND DISCONTINUITIES BETWEEN PRE- AND POST-INDEPENDENCE INDIA

India arrived at Independence after a long struggle and with a multiplicity of heritages and legacies which influenced its post-Independence course in complex ways. Among the legacies were the long experience of British rule itself, which extended back more than two centuries, and of the various institutions, ideas, and practices, introduced by the British. Of particular importance at Independence was the Government of India Act of 1935, which was the most recent framework of rule under which the country was governed and which included a considerable measure of responsible government for Indians in the provinces. A second legacy was that provided by the shared experience of those Indians who participated in or identified with the nationalist movement and its great leaders. A third was the existing social order, the social structure and social conflicts which surrounded and influenced political movements, ideas, and practices. Finally, there was the great body of traditions and cultural practices which preceded British rule in a civilization of great depth, complexity, and diversity.

THE CONSTITUTION AND THE COLONIAL LEGACY

In some ways, it is possible to view Independence and the adoption in the early years after Independence of a new Constitution as another stage in the evolution of India toward representative government in a process that dates back to the Indian Councils Act of 1861 and continues through the Morley–Minto Reforms of 1909, the Montagu–Chelmsford Reforms of 1919, and the Government of India Act of 1935. At each of these reforms, the participation of Indians in the central and state legislatures and in the executive councils was increased and the franchise was extended to ever larger numbers of people.

It has often been noted especially that there was a considerable degree of continuity between the Government of India Act and the Constitution of India. The features of continuity included the adoption of a federal system of government with three legislative lists of powers to be exercised exclusively by the Union, exclusively by the states, or concurrently, and a combination of a considerable degree of provincial autonomy with extensive powers left to the Center,[1] including emergency powers which made it possible to convert the federal system into a unitary one. Similarly, the Constitution of independent India is federal, but contains strong unitary features, including a strong central government which retains not only extensive emergency powers but the residuary powers of the Union as well. The states are normally supposed to function autonomously, but the Center retains the ultimate power to control, even take over the direct administration, of the states under certain conditions.

In several respects, however, the Constitution of India makes a sharp break with the British colonial past, though not with British political practices. Firstly, the Constitution adopts in total the Westminster form of parliamentary government rather than the mixed parliamentary–bureaucratic authoritarian system which actually existed in India. Secondly, fundamental rights were included in the Constitution of India, but not in the Government of India Act of 1935. Thirdly, the Constitution introduced universal adult suffrage.

The Constitution also contains some unique features that reflect a desire to depart from strict British parliamentary practices and to introduce into the charter of the country a program of social and economic reform. Most notable in this respect is the presence in the Constitution of a list of both Fundamental Rights of the People and Directive Principles, a combination of protections for the people against the encroachments of state authority with directives to the state to introduce specified reforms to make those rights effective. This

---

[1] "Center" is the most common term used to refer to the Union government in New Delhi. It carries the same sense as in the United States practice of referring to the national government in Washington, D.C. as the "federal government." However, in addition, the term is also used sometimes to allude to actions and decisions which flow from leadership circles in New Delhi as opposed to the state capitals.

peculiar combination, however, was later to lead to a great struggle between the government and Parliament, on the one side, and the judiciary, on the other, as to which have priority, rights or directive principles.

The simultaneous presence in the Constitution of these two sets of principles and guidelines reflected some of the tensions which existed in the minds of the leaders of the country at Independence. While they respected the British–American traditions of parliamentary practice and personal liberty, some, particularly Nehru, also were influenced by the Soviet model and the Socialist traditions of Western Europe and Britain as well. They wished to extend the liberties of the people of India, but they wished also to bring about rapid social and economic change and they wanted no obstacles to stand in the way of their so doing.[2]

There was also the idea that fundamental rights were not enough, would not be meaningful in a land where the mass of the people were extremely poor, illiterate, tied to traditions, and perceived as exploited by merchants, moneylenders, and landlords. It was feared that such rights might be used to protect the exploiters rather than the exploited. In a society based on hierarchy, caste inequality, and blatant discrimination, equality of opportunity such as existed in Britain and the United States would not be enough to provide the means for enhancing the well-being of the poor. Instead, special measures would be required, such as reservations of places in representative institutions, government agencies, and public institutions for backward and disadvantaged classes and groups. There was a desire also not merely to protect the rights of the people, but to eliminate certain features of social practice, such as untouchability and *begar* or forced labor, which were explicitly abolished in the Constitution. And, finally, there was a desire to limit the role of private enterprise in India and a feeling that the protection of property provided in the Constitution

---

[2] This contradiction has been noted increasingly by recent writers on civil liberties issues, including Kuldeep Mathur, who has remarked: "The Indian Constitution gives enough opportunities to the Executive and Legislature to enact laws that negate the very rights the Constitution is supposed to confer on the people." See his "The State and the Use of Coercive Powers in India," *Asian Survey*, xxxii, No. 4 (April, 1992), 341. Jean-Alphonse Bernard has made a similar point, remarking that the extraordinary powers available to the government under Part xviii [Emergency Provisions] and other articles" constitute "a kind of 'second constitution'." See his "The Presidential Idea in the Constitutions of South Asia," *Contemporary South Asia*, i, No. 1 (1992), 49.

might prevent the Indian state from attaining goals of economic justice, which some thought could be achieved only through the establishment of social ownership of the means of production, then identified with state ownership. So, the Constitution recognized the right to hold property as a fundamental right, but also included directive principles of policy which stated that the material resources of the country must be distributed and operated in such a way as to promote the common good and avoid excessive concentration of wealth.

Those who argue that India's Independence should not be seen as marking a great break with the past also point to the preservation of such characteristic features of British autocratic rule in India as the Indian Civil Service (ICS), renamed as the Indian Administrative Service (IAS) at Independence. The small, enormously powerful, elite cadre of ICS officers was seen as the "steel frame" that had held the British Empire in India together. Authority and responsibility were concentrated in their hands in the districts, where they acted simultaneously as heads of the administration and of the judicial institutions, maintaining law and order and collecting the revenue. Yet, the leaders of independent India felt the need for maintaining that "steel frame" to help preserve order in the country, which was undergoing so much turmoil at Independence. It was not long, however, before a contradiction was perceived between the predominant functions of the old ICS and the developmental goals of the independent Indian state, which required a different type of administrative structure. Since Independence, there have been numerous attempts to devise structures of local self-government, administration, and development institutions more suited for these development goals, which would also provide for popular participation at the local level without undermining the older structures of state authority which the leadership of the country was unwilling to give up.

At Independence, therefore, the leaders of the country quite self-consciously maintained many features of the colonial legacy. They also adopted some new features derived from the political practices of Great Britain and the United States. However, most of the specific features of the Constitution of India and the administrative structure retained or adopted at Independence represented borrowings from abroad, which had to be adapted to the social structure, traditions, and practices of an entirely different society.

4

SOCIAL STRUCTURE: THE COMMUNAL AND
CASTE BASES OF INDIAN POLITICS

It was commonly argued by the British rulers of India that parliamentary democracy was unsuited to a society intensely divided into religious and other communal groupings, whose social structure also was imbued with an ideology of hierarchy rather than equality. The rise of the Muslim League and the Pakistan movement which led to the bitter catastrophe of partition of the subcontinent was seen by such persons as proof of the inherent incompatibility of Western parliamentary institutions and Indian communal realities. Indian nationalists, however, argued strongly against such ideas and insisted that Hindu–Muslim communalism itself was a British creation and that, left to themselves, Hindus and Muslims would work together in a secular political order and would divide internally on economic and class, rather than religious lines. The British, operating on a set of assumptions that treated Hindus and Muslims as distinct peoples, introduced mechanisms, notably separate electorates, which served to keep them apart. At Independence, however, the framers of the Constitution eliminated separate electorates and established only general electorates in which members of all castes, religions, and communities would vote.

It was also argued that caste Hindus and untouchable and other low castes could hardly be expected to work together as equals in a democratic political order, that the former would maintain the rigidity of traditional hierarchies and caste discriminations which would prevent the poor and disadvantaged low castes from participating effectively in politics. Congress leaders themselves were painfully aware that they had been unable before Independence to recruit successfully most low caste and disadvantaged groups. So, at Independence, though they resisted any efforts to create separate electorates for the low castes, the Constitution and government policies instituted mechanisms and procedures to ensure their full participation as equal citizens in the new order. These mechanisms and procedures included reservation of seats in the legislatures and other bodies, the maintenance of a list of low caste groups on a schedule (hence the name Scheduled Castes) entitling them to special privileges and preferential policies of all sorts, the abolition of untouchability, and the like.

The division between caste Hindus and untouchables was not the only kind of problem posed by the caste order for the effective functioning of parliamentary institutions in post-Independence India. In most villages in India, one or two large elite castes control most of the land and other resources, constituting what anthropologists call "dominant castes." After Independence, these dominant castes often were able to control and deliver the votes of their clients among the low castes, who were considered to constitute "vote banks."

Divisions among the elite and middle status land-controlling castes in large parts of India also existed at Independence. In some parts of India, particularly Tamil Nadu and Maharashtra, non-Brahman movements had been launched to displace the dominant Brahman castes in those states from their disproportionate control over jobs in the public services and other advantages in society. Backward caste leaders had argued before Independence that their place was insecure under a parliamentary system which the elite castes could turn to their advantage and that they too, like the Scheduled Castes, required special protections. Since Independence, the spread of conflict between these elite and backward caste groups has become a major source of social tension in many other states of the Union besides Tamil Nadu and Maharashtra and has precipitated considerable violence in some states such as Bihar and Gujarat.

These issues of Hindu–Muslim communal relations, of the integration of the low castes as effective participants in a democratic political order, and of caste conflict between the backward castes and the elite castes have persisted throughout the post-Independence period up to the present and have posed recurring challenges to the maintenance of an integrated society, an equalitarian polity, and non-violent mechanisms of conflict resolution.

IDEAS DERIVING FROM THE NATIONALIST MOVEMENT

Three-quarters of a century of thought and struggle over defining the Indian nation, over freeing the country from alien occupation, and over the desirable shape of the social and economic order in a future independent India had provided the nationalist leadership at Independence with a set of ideas and goals that helped to structure their responses to the problems of governing the newly independent country. At the top of their goals, the *sine qua non* for everything else was an abiding faith in and determination to preserve the national unity and integrity of the country against all potential internal and external threats to it. The very fact that this first priority, the center of the dreams of the Congress nationalists, had to be sacrificed at Independence itself, with the partition of the country, reenforced the determination of the leaders never to make such a sacrifice again.

Since Independence, therefore, two strict rules have been followed in all dealings with dissident domestic ethnic, religious, linguistic, and cultural group demands. The first is that no secessionist movement will be entertained and that any group which takes up a secessionist stance will, while it is weak, be ignored and treated as illegitimate, but, should it develop significant strength, be smashed, with armed force if necessary. All secessionist demands in post-Independence India which acquired any significant strength have been treated in this way, especially in the northeastern part of the country and lately in the Punjab and Kashmir. Secessionist demands have also been headed off in other places such as Tamil Nadu in the 1950s by the clear under-standing that force would be used against the groups who promoted such demands if they persisted.

The second rule has been a prohibition against the concession of demands for any form of political recognition of a religious commu-nity. Muslims, Sikhs, and other religious minorities are free to preserve their own personal law, to practice their religion as they see fit, to seek protection for their language and culture, but not to demand either a separate state for their community even within the Indian Union or separate electorates or any form of proportional representation in elected or appointed government bodies.

In the transformation of the Congress from a mass movement claiming to represent the entire nation into a political party engaged in free and open competition with other parties for dominance in a democratic political system, however, the Congress leaders had to make a number of changes and compromises in relation to other groups whose demands were neither secessionist nor communal relig-ious. They had to decide how to treat dissident movements and forces of all sorts. During the Independence struggle, Congress leaders had shown little tolerance for any kind of dissent which seemed in any way

7

to threaten the unity of the movement against the British authorities. Yet, the leaders themselves knew that some groups, despite their own desires to the contrary, had been left out of the movement and that some potentially divisive problems had been put aside and now had to be dealt with. In dealing with internal and external dissident forces after Independence the leaders of the Indian National Congress followed hegemonic policies of absorption in relation to some groups, deliberately set out to destroy others, and adopted tolerant and conciliatory stances in relation to still others.

Scheduled Castes had largely been left out of the Congress during the nationalist movement. Congress set out to rectify this situation quickly after Independence by such measures as giving Dr. Ambedkar, the great untouchable leader, a central role in the Constitution-making process, by seeking to provide other Scheduled Caste persons with positions as ministers in the central and state governments, and by pursuing a variety of preferential policies designed to improve their social standing and ameliorate their economic deprivations.

Other groups, such as the former landlords and princes, were treated quite differently. They were considered collaborators with the British, representatives of an outdated feudal order, and exploiters of the peasantry who provided the bulk of the political support for the Congress in the countryside. The Congress had, for the most part, avoided supporting direct class confrontations between the tenants and landlords in British-ruled India in order to preserve maximum unity in the fight against the British themselves. However, once Independence was achieved, Congress governments in most states moved to expropriate the former princes and landlords through the passage of various land reform measures such as abolition of all intermediaries between the cultivator and the state and land ceilings legislation.

In relation to political opposition groups, the Congress was prepared to allow free and open competition. This did not, however, stop the Congress from adopting quite ruthless political tactics to defeat such early opposition parties as the Socialists who split from the Congress in 1948, the left wing of the Communist party in the 1960s, and, from time to time, adopting repressive measures against parties considered to be communal, both Hindu and Muslim. Moreover, in general, the Congress has sought to absorb political dissident movements it could not defeat in the electoral arena, the terms always being that any political group so absorbed must give up all vestiges of an independent political organization and its members join the party as individuals.

Congress leaders also arrived at Independence ready to tolerate considerable internal factionalism, provided no groups formed permanently with ideological goals that differed from the official party policy. And it was always clear before and after Independence that there was a "High Command" of Congress leaders, who exercised final authority in the country in relation to state and local factional conflicts that threatened to damage the party in any large part of the country.

The Congress had arrived at Independence largely by pursuing a non-violent path. Terrorist groups, though sometimes acknowledged as true patriots, were not condoned within the Congress. Nor did it tolerate the military style of nationalism promoted by the famous Bengali political leader, Subhas Chandra Bose, who resigned from the Congress presidency in 1939 in the face of total opposition to him and his policies from Mahatma Gandhi.

On the other hand, Gandhi's tactics of non-violent resistance to untruth and injustice, which included a variety of individual and mass protest techniques, had become embedded in Congress ideology and practice. Some even argued in the Constituent Assembly that *satyagraha*[3] was a fundamental right of the people. Other Congress leaders, however, argued that now that India was independent and functioning with a competitive parliamentary system, such techniques no longer had a legitimate place. In practice, the Congress governments at the Center after Independence have followed an ambiguous policy toward such extra-constitutional, non-violent forms of protest. On the one hand, they were often allowed; on the other hand, the Constitution armed the state with several measures, most notably, preventive detention, which allowed the government of the day to deal effectively, even in advance, with any protest that threatened to become violent or was too inconvenient for the ruling party to tolerate. This exemplifies the adaptation of parliamentarism and constitutionalism in India to the particular practices of Indian society – here, in the institutionalization

[3] *Satyagraha*: Gandhi's terms for active, non-violent persistence in the pursuit of truth and justice in the face of the exercise of alien or unjust authority.

of a process of extra-constitutional confrontation between the state and dissident groups in which both sides use as a matter of course measures that are uncommon in Western parliamentary systems.

THE LEADING IDEAS OF THE NATIONALIST ELITE AT INDEPENDENCE

The leading ideas of the nationalist elite at Independence can be summarized under these headings: sovereignty, unity, order, a strong state, secularism, democracy and parliamentarism, economic self-sufficiency, and the need for social and economic reform. The nationalist leaders at Independence were determined to declare for all the world to hear and for any internal dissidents who had a different view that India was to be a sovereign independent republic. In the Constituent Assembly, speakers denounced and ridiculed Winston Churchill who had cast doubts on the sovereign representative character of the Assembly, invited the leaders of the Muslim League to join its deliberations but insisted that if they did not the Assembly meant to speak for the nation without them, and warned the former princes that they had no divine right to rule any longer and that power in India now came from the people and its representatives in the Constituent Assembly of the country. Other speakers in the Assembly also saw India's sovereignty and independence in terms of the emergence of India not merely as an ordinary independent state but as the new leader of Asia, indeed of the world.

Unity was the second assumption of the nationalist elite. They had reluctantly accepted the partition and communal division of the country but were not reconciled to it. Many speakers in the Constituent Assembly expressed the belief that the unity of India would ultimately be restored. The partition experience also led the nationalist leaders, some of whom had previously been sympathetic to some kinds of regional cultural and linguistic demands, to reject sharply in the Constituent Assembly and in the early years after Independence any other potential division that seemed to threaten the country's unity, such as a north–south division implied in the Dravidastan[4]

---

[4] The term Dravidastan refers to the idea that the peoples of south India are Dravidians, of a different stock and culture from northern Indo-Aryans, and that they ought to comprise a separate political unit.

slogan of the Tamil regional nationalist party, the DMK, or even the linguistic reorganization of states, which had been an implicit part of the Congress program since the 1920s.

The nationalist leaders had always feared the potential for violence and disorder in Indian society. Gandhi's non-violence was not something that simply arose out of an indigenous tradition of peace and spirituality, but rather was a tactic which acknowledged the enormous potential for violence which existed in a highly fragmented and culturally heterogeneous society. The disintegration of public order in the Punjab, in Calcutta, and in the national capital of Delhi itself, whose streets were littered with dead bodies during the riots that accompanied partition, strengthened the determination of the nationalist elite to enforce authority in independent India, to instill discipline in its people, and to maintain order at all costs. That determination was also applied to any efforts on the part of revolutionary leaders to promote violent revolution in any part of India, a major instance of that determination being the suppression of the Communist-led insurrection in the Telangana region of Andhra between 1947 and 1951.

The early nationalist leaders believed wholeheartedly in democracy and parliamentarism. They wanted the British out, but were prepared to adopt their institutions. The leaders of the Constituent Assembly studied carefully both British and American political institutions and practices and adopted the conventions of the British parliamentary system as well as some features of American political practice such as the establishment of a Supreme Court with powers of judicial review. Advocates of the development of a set of political institutions and practices derived from Indian traditions were notable for their absence in the Constituent Assembly, where Gandhian ideas of non-party government, decentralization of power and authority, and the adoption of village self-government hardly challenged the predominant consensus which favored rather the adoption and adaptation of foreign political models.

The nationalist leaders also felt strongly that political and economic independence were interrelated, that India could not retain control over its political destiny if it remained economically dependent on Britain and the other industrialized states of the West. Economic independence and self-sufficiency were associated with industrialization, which required foreign economic aid in the short term, but which would soon enable India to free itself from dependence on foreign imports and from further need for foreign aid.[5] These considerations were behind the drive which was launched especially at the beginning of the Third Five Year Plan in 1961 to create a massive industrial base in the country and to promote the policy of import substitution to eliminate India's dependence on foreign countries, particularly in the durable capital goods sector of the economy.

The nationalist elite held the view that India's social and economic progress had been retarded by centuries of British rule, that the country had been kept agrarian, its industrial potential arrested, its people kept backward, illiterate, and bound to outmoded forms of agricultural production. Consequently, it was necessary and urgent for the state itself to undertake the modernization of Indian society and to institute economic reforms that would free the country from feudalism and archaic social practices. These ideas implied centralized economic planning and direct state intervention through legislation for the removal of institutions and practices – such as landlordism, untouchability, and the giving of dowry – deemed unsuited to a modern state and society in a modern world.

Secularism was another widely shared and deeply felt value of the Indian nationalist elite at Independence. Secularism had negative and positive aspects. It meant that communalism and political demands of any sort based on religion would no longer be tolerated in independent India. It meant that separate electorates had to be replaced by joint electorates so that all communities could discuss issues of economic well-being and advancement on a common ground. Positively, it meant that every cultural group in India was to be entitled to promote, preserve, and protect its cultural life, its language and script. Most important, it involved an assertion that nationalism and the nation, based on the loyalty of individuals to the state before their community, was the basis for modern politics and not religion, the deceptive slogan of the Pakistan elite.

All these leading ideas held by the nationalist elites converged to provide overwhelming justification in their minds of the need for a strong, centralized state. Once the partition decision had been reached, in the midst of deliberations in the Constituent Assembly on

---

[5] See especially on this point Baldev Raj Nayar, *The Modernization Imperative and Indian Planning* (Delhi: Vikas, 1972), pp. 99, 125.

a federation that would be flexible enough to accommodate the Muslim-majority as well as the Hindu-majority provinces, discussions in the Assembly took an immediate about-face in which speaker after speaker emphasized the imperative necessity for India to have a "strong Center" and a "strong state." The state was perceived as the instrument which would establish India's sovereign independent presence in the world, would preserve its unity against foreign enemies and internal secessionists, ensure authority, order, and discipline in a society perceived as always on the brink of disorder and violence, promote economic development through centralized planning which would bring India out of the backwardness of agrarian life and free it of a social order dominated by feudal institutions and practices and by religious superstitions, and make it possible for Indians also to maintain an effective parliamentary system.

INDIA'S POLITICAL CULTURE: RHETORIC VERSUS REALITY

It was commonly remarked at Independence that Indian leaders were bent upon adopting the political conventions, ideas, and practices of Western democratic societies, but that those institutions and ideas could not be separated from the societies from which they had organically evolved. India, it was argued, had an entirely different social order not suited for parliamentary institutions and egalitarian ideologies and would do better to search its own traditions for institutions more in consonance with its own culture. Those arguments were largely ignored in the Constituent Assembly, even though some of them came from Gandhi himself and his followers, mostly outside the Assembly. It became apparent very quickly after Independence, however, that fundamental transformations were occurring in the actual functioning of the institutions and practices borrowed from the West. Adjustments were made that reflected indigenous cultural and behavioral patterns, but without any conscious modeling on India's own traditions.

Some observers attempted to encapsulate the process of contradiction and adjustment that was going on by arguing that there were several "idioms" or "cultures" in fundamental conflict with each other – a modern or Western idiom, centered in the ideas of the nationalist

13

elite and in the institutions in Delhi, a traditional idiom or culture, rooted in the kin, caste, and communal relations of village, locality, and province, and a "saintly" idiom characteristically Indian, associated with Gandhi and his disciples involving selfless devotion to constructive work for the good of society and immune from the mimicking of foreign models or from contamination by the archaic superstitions and feudal practices of Indian society.[6]

These useful attempts to categorize the basic contradictions between Indian politics and society, however, left many adjustments, adaptations, and everyday practices not satisfactorily explained. Little attention, for example, was paid to indigenous traditions of princely rule and their effects upon contemporary political practices, demonstrated every day in the morning and evening *darbars* or audiences held by every prominent politician in the land, in the duty of prominent people to provide support and protection for their clients, in the responsibility of those political leaders who achieved power and control over public resources to distribute them lavishly to their followers, and in the practice of dynastic succession to leadership in India.

It soon became evident also that there was a massive contradiction between the rhetoric of Indian public discourse and the reality of political practice, which expressed itself in many forms. For example, although the secular ideology of the Indian National Congress became dominant politically in India after Independence and the newly independent Indian state proclaimed secularism as the official state ideology, the post-Independence Indian state leadership has nevertheless felt compelled to make official distinctions between the Hindu population and the non-Hindu populations of the country by such measures as the passage of the Hindu Code Act, which established a uniform civil code for all "Hindus" (including Sikhs) in the country, while leaving Muslims with their own system of Personal Law. It has often also been alleged that many of the politicians of the country who proclaim their adherence to secularism as a state ideology actually harbor Hindu communal sentiments. The persistence of explicitly Hindu political organizations and movements in contemporary Indian politics also has been widely noted.

[6] Myron Weiner, "India's Two Political Cultures," in Myron Weiner, *Political Change in South Asia* (Calcutta: Firma K. L. Mukhapadhyay, 1963), and W. H. Morris-Jones, *The Government and Politics of India* (London: Hutchinson University Library, 1964, ch. 2).

One of the great, enduring games of political analysts of India has been to assert the tacit dominance and to predict the ultimate emergence of a militant Hindu nationalist political category which will overwhelm the Indian state and establish its mastery over the Indian population. Since the late nineteenth century, there have been numerous movements of "Hindu" political mobilization, which have taken a variety of forms. These include the Gaurakshini (Cow Protection) Sabhas formed in the 1890s, which have agitated for laws preventing cow slaughter in India from time to time and have launched a major mass movement as recently as the 1960s; the movement to promote the development and spread of a standardized Hindi language written in the Devanagari script, rather than Urdu in the Persian–Arabic script, as the official language of education and administration in north India and ultimately as the official language of the country; and the Hindu Mahasabha which worked to create a Hindu political community and to define the Indian nation through symbols drawn exclusively from "Hindu" texts, beliefs, and practices and from non-Muslim history.

This Hindu "revivalism" or militant Hindu nationalism has persisted up to the present and has manifested itself in various political organizations and movements and politicized religious movements. Such organizations and movements include: the Rashtriya Swayamsevak Sangh (RSS), a Hindu "cultural" organization organized into cells, whose members practice martial arts, and which promotes also an exclusively Hindu definition of the Indian nation; the Jan Sangh, originally the main political party offshoot of the RSS, but now a rump of quite extreme anti-Muslim supporters of Hindu nationalism; the Bharatiya Janata party (BJP), the more broadly based descendant of the original Jan Sangh; and such other organizations as the Vishwa Hindu Parishad, which has led for several years a campaign to "liberate" alleged Hindu religious sites from their occupation by Muslim mosques built on top of them with a focus especially on the Babari Masjid (Babur's mosque) at Ayodhya.

There is also presumed to exist a Hindu "vote" in India which can be mobilized for the sake of national unity against the secessionist or otherwise excessive demands of minorities such as Sikhs and Muslims. It has been noted that in the 1984 parliamentary elections, held in the aftermath of the assassination of Mrs. Gandhi by two of her Sikh bodyguards, the issue of national unity was communalized and made into the central issue in Rajiv Gandhi's landslide election victory.[7] In the two succeeding national elections in 1989 and 1991, the BJP exploited the Ayodhya issue, recaptured the Hindu vote lost to the Congress, and brought Hindu electoral consolidation to a higher level of unity in north India than ever before. The demolition of the mosque at Ayodhya on December 6, 1992 has further enhanced the support of the BJP among militant Hindus and has been followed by intensified efforts on the part of its leaders to consolidate the Hindu vote with a view to capturing power in the country in the next elections.

Nevertheless, there remains in India today considerable ambiguity concerning the use of the word "Hindus" to define any clearly demarcated group of people in the subcontinent and considerable doubt about the existence of a Hindu political community.[8] On the one hand, the historic problem of a split between so-called "caste" Hindus and untouchables persists in contemporary Indian politics, as do divisions among the "caste" Hindus themselves. On the other hand, there has also been a historic tendency to subsume Sikhs, Jains, and others in the "Hindu" fold. While this tendency is bitterly resented by some groups, such as most Sikhs especially, and is considered to be part of the absorptive quality of "Hinduism," it also suggests the continued indefiniteness of its religious, social, and political boundaries.

Revivalist or militant Hinduism nevertheless remains a pervasive and politically important presence in contemporary Indian politics. The tendency among militant nationalist organizations such as the RSS and the BJP to insist that Hindu and Indian are virtually interchangeable categories has spread beyond the organizational confines of these two organizations. Even more pervasive and subtle has been the more recent tendency to secularize the meaning of the term Hindu by going back to its earlier meaning of "native of India" and identifying India as

[7] Ranbir Singh, "Changing Social Bases of Congress' Political Support in Haryana," in Richard Sisson and Ramashray Roy (eds.), *Diversity and Dominance in Indian Politics*, Vol. 1: *Changing Bases of Congress Support* (New Delhi: Sage, 1990), pp. 306–307 and Paul R. Brass, *Caste, Faction and Party in Indian Politics*, Vol. 11: *Election Studies* (Delhi: Chanakya Publications, 1985), pp. 318–321.

[8] For the development of the use of the terms "Hindu" and "Hinduism" in modern India, see Robert E. Frykenberg, "The Emergence of Modern 'Hinduism' as a Concept and as an Institution: A Reappraisal with Special Reference to South India," in Gunther Sontheimer and Hermann Kulke (eds.), *Hinduism Reconsidered* (Heidelberg: South Asia Institute, 1988), pp. 1–29.

the nation of Hindus without, however, eliminating from it all the religious associations which are offensive to true Muslim, Sikh, and other believers.

A second example of a contradiction between rhetoric and reality in contemporary Indian politics concerns the disjunction between the language of planning, equality, socialism, and social justice spoken by party leaders in the country and the practices of day-to-day politics. Immediately after Independence, the leading opposition parties were the Communists and the Socialists, promoting variants of the wholly Western ideologies associated with those labels. Yet, those ideologies bore little relation to the social structure of Indian society, which lacked the class distinctions and contradictions upon which the ideologies were based. None of the political parties in India proved able to imitate the European political party traditions of disciplined behavior in the legislatures to which they were elected. Instead, Indian politicians began early to display, indeed had been practicing at the local levels since the nineteenth century, a strong penchant for opportunistic behavior in pursuit of personal ambition to achieve high office and control public resources for personal advantage and for distribution to one's followers.

The reason for this persisting disjunction between public political party discourse and actual political practice, which renders meaningful comparisons between Indian and Western political parties difficult, is that the issues and social forces which impinge upon party politics in India today are entirely different from those which have confronted either contemporary or nineteenth-century Europe and America. There are three such sets of issues, social forces, and aspects of social structure that contribute to the distinctiveness of Indian politics: the issues of control over agrarian resources, including control over land and the work force; social fragmentation; and center–locality relationships. The primary economic, social, and political resources in India today continue to be the land and its products and the primary struggles in the districts and localities of the country concern access to the inputs necessary to increase productivity and control over the produce from the land. Land being inherently a local resource and rural social classes being notoriously difficult to recruit into permanent extra-local organizations, the importance of land control and issues relating to it necessarily impart a local and personal character to politics. Governments in India may pass laws abolishing landlords and intermediaries, establishing land ceilings, and protecting tenants, but their implementation depends upon local patterns of domination and control by land controllers over land, resources, and people.

Those who get elected to state legislatures from rural constituencies in India themselves either come from important local land controlling communities or depend for support upon them. What matters most to such people is local influence with government departments that dispense resources for agriculture, adjudicate land matters, or control the local population, particularly the police. These local politicians do not care much for party manifestoes, policy pronouncements, and development goals. They will vote as disciplined members of ruling parties in the legislatures as long as such behavior gives them access to ministers in the state government who can control local resources and the local administration and as long as there is no better alternative. When there is a better alternative, particularly one that gives them a place in a ministry where they can exercise direct control themselves over local resources, they will defect and switch to another party or coalition.

The second great feature of Indian society that imparts a distinctive character to Indian politics is the social fragmentation associated with caste. Caste too, in some of its most fundamental aspects, permeates Indian politics with local and personal features. Success in elections in rural constituencies depends primarily upon the ability to establish a base in one of the locally dominant, land controlling castes and then combining that support with an effective approach to one or more other important local caste groups or a low caste group or the local Muslim minority. Influence in the bureaucracy and in public agencies generally depends upon personal networks of kinship and caste. Legislators and politicians generally who depend upon such local support bases and are themselves part of such personal networks again are not moved or inspired by party manifestoes and pronouncements, but are moved by what benefits they can get to distribute to their supporters, friends, and relations.

These two great features of Indian political economy and social structure – land control and caste – also contribute to a third political characteristic that imparts distinctiveness to Indian politics, namely, the necessity for those who wish to build power in state and national contexts to maintain direct or indirect links with those who can control local structures of power. Since government now provides or controls the greatest share of external resources of use in the local environments and since government also can threaten the hold of powerful local groups through land laws or police harassment, it is equally important for locally powerful persons to maintain connections with those who wield power in the state and national governments. These relations once again do not concern ideology, policy, and programs but concern control over resources and people, protection from harassment by the bureaucracy and the police, and the trading of political support and votes for such resources, protection, and other services. It should hardly be surprising, therefore, that the public politics of Indian political parties and legislatures, which are modeled after the British pattern and in which a language familiar to students of European politics is spoken, should in fact be dominated by faction, personal and local interest networks, struggles over patronage and distribution of resources, and political opportunism.

Indian politics have lacked the ideological underpinnings of European political traditions. In common with American political traditions, however, there is a strong moral streak in Indian commentary on politics which is displayed in constant condemnation of the corruption of the politicians and the bureaucrats and of the relentless pursuit of power. Such moralism, usually drawing inspiration from Gandhian ideals, gives force from time to time to mass mobilizations to bring down the ruling party. However, these mobilizations have not so far been as effective as the recurrent reform movements which every now and then have transformed American institutions and political practices. Nor has it been possible for most political parties in India to adhere to a consistent ideology in the manner of many European parties which formulate manifestoes, whose programs they actually implement when they achieve power. Rather, Indian politics have been characterized by an all-pervasive instrumentalism which washes away party manifestoes, rhetoric, and effective implementation of policies in an unending competition for power, status, and profit.

If American political traditions have continued to emphasize the importance of limiting the role of the state while Western Europe has adopted the model of the welfare state and the former Socialist countries the model of a socially transforming state, India has adopted the model of the state which exists for its own sake. It is a good in itself and the source of all goods. It exists to provide everything that Indians need and require: sovereignty, unity, welfare, jobs for all, social justice. It is the duty of the state and the holders of its offices, moreover, to provide these goods and services directly to the people, irrespective of any ideology or any notion of a broad common good. It is there to serve everybody's interests, not just an abstract "public interest." Of course, no state can serve everybody's interests and the Indian state has not succeeded in doing so. The contradictions between the foreign models adopted, the Indian traditions which have permeated the actual practices within the Western-derived institutions, and what can actually be achieved in an agrarian society, a caste-dominated social order, and a heterogeneous civilization have been of the essence of Indian politics since Independence.

POLITICAL LEADERSHIP, MOBILIZATION AND STATECRAFT IN PRE- AND POST-INDEPENDENCE POLITICS

One of the persisting disjunctions in pre- and post-Independence Indian politics is that between mobilization and "statecraft," between the bases for mass mobilization of the people and the actual political goals of the leaders. This disjunction was introduced into Indian politics with the rise of Gandhi and his famous mass movements, beginning from 1920–21. The mass of the people who flocked to see and hear Gandhi as he toured the country and who participated in the great movements launched by him from time to time were moved more by traditional religious beliefs, including the belief that Gandhi himself was a saint or god upon earth who would bring miraculous changes in their present or future well-being and happiness, than by the specific political and economic demands made in the Congress charter of demands.[9] There was in the Congress itself a clear division between Gandhi's leadership role and the parts played by other leaders such as Sardar Patel and Jawaharlal Nehru among others. Gandhi himself kept aloof from statecraft – though not from practical politics

[9] See Shahid Amin, "Gandhi as Mahatma: Gorakhpur District, Eastern UP, 1921–2," in Ranajit Guha (ed.), *Subaltern Studies III: Writings on South Asian History and Society* (Delhi: Oxford University Press, 1984), pp. 1–61.

– and left the day-to-day functioning of the Congress and later the government of the country to Patel and Nehru.

This tradition of a disjunction between mobilization and statecraft did not always imply, however, a division among the persons performing the separate tasks. Jinnah, for example, who was an early opponent of the mass mobilization techniques of Gandhi, which he saw as nothing but rabble-rousing, and who was in his early career oriented exclusively toward statecraft, at the end of his life performed both roles. In the great mobilization of the Muslim population of the subcontinent, Jinnah roused the Muslim masses behind the slogan of "Islam in danger," around a theme that implied the creation of an Islamic state, a land of the pure and the faithful when, in fact, he had no more in view than the creation of a modern, liberal, secular state in which Muslims would be in a majority.

In modern Sikh politics as well, there has been a division of roles and leadership between institutions and persons closer to the religious beliefs of the masses, on the one hand, and the politicians oriented toward party leadership and control of government in the Punjab, on the other. The secular leaders of the Sikh political party, the Akali Dal, are not equal to the task of mass mobilization and, therefore, require political alliance with a *sant*, a preacher or holy man, in order to preserve their own leadership, consolidate their control over the Akali Dal, or lead a successful political movement in pursuit of a set of political goals.

This division of roles or disjunction of political practices is, in fact, widespread in Indian politics. Even those politicians who deliberately set out to avoid the use of such techniques or even condemn it cannot escape the popular mentalities which attribute to them religious or other more-than-human, charismatic qualities essential to successful leadership in contemporary Indian politics. Nehru condemned every sort of "casteism, communalism, provincialism" and parochialism in his public speeches everywhere in India and was rewarded by the devotion of the Brahmans throughout north India and the adulation of the Hindu masses who probably saw him as they saw Gandhi, as a living god on earth. We have no studies of mass perceptions of Mrs. Indira Gandhi, but it is certain that she was widely perceived in the image of the female goddess and mother of the people of India and was, in fact, often called late in life "*Mataji*" or "mother" with somewhat more reverence than that ordinarily due to an older woman and mother of children in India.

Contemporary Indian politics have also witnessed the rise of film stars to the leadership of two south Indian states, Tamil Nadu and Andhra. In both cases, these film stars were of a different sort from Ronald Reagan, for their film roles were of mythopoeic characters and their audiences identified them with the heroes and gods whom they played on the screen. In these cases, however, there has been a reunion of roles in which the mass mobilizer and the master of statecraft merge into a single demagogic type.

The irony, however, is that this type of disjunction is not the kind which Gandhi himself could have sought. It is more likely, rather, that Gandhi himself sought to maintain a distance between the exercise of moral authority, on the one hand, and political action and the practice of statecraft, on the other. There was an implicit assumption in Gandhi's stance that power and political responsibility in state institutions were inherently corrupting and an explicit statement that freedom from British rule was less important than self-mastery. Indeed, most of the techniques adopted by Gandhi during his mass movements involved abstention, non-cooperation, and withdrawal from participation in institutions designed for India by the British. He left the definition of the means of gaining control of such institutions for the statesmen of the Congress.

This disjunction between moral and political authority has also continued to play its part in post-Independence Indian politics.[10] Like the other disjunction, it has sometimes involved a division of political roles and responsibilities or of institutions, but it has often also involved the same person attempting to adopt both stances. One form it has taken has been the disavowal by the acknowledged leader of a party of any desire for public office. Rammanohar Lohia, the famous radical Socialist leader who died in 1969, adopted this form, refusing to accept any formal leadership in his party and disavowing any desire for high political office beyond his membership in Parliament. Jayaprakash Narayan adopted the different strategy of withdrawal from the political arena into constructive work in the villages, while acting at the same time as a moral critic of political authority and moral adviser

[10] Partha Chatterjee, "Gandhi and the Critique of Civil Society," in Ranajit Guha (ed.), *Subaltern Studies III*, pp. 186–187.

to practicing politicians until his own sense of moral outrage against Mrs. Gandhi's authoritarian and perceived corrupting leadership of the country led him to take the lead as mass mobilizer in a movement to displace her from power. The third form in which this disjunction between moral and political authority has expressed itself has been in the attempt by some politicians to play crusading roles without withdrawing from politics and without renouncing political ambitions. For such politicians, their constant refrain is the need to cleanse Indian politics of its corruption and of their corrupt rivals.

In 1988, in preparation for the Ninth General Elections anticipated in 1989, a political struggle was waged between Vishwanath Pratap Singh, a former Congress minister in the central government and former chief minister of Uttar Pradesh (U. P.), and Rajiv Gandhi. The former resigned from office in 1987 in disgust over the alleged gross corruption by the holders of high office in connection with defense contracts which, it was implied, had not left the Prime Minister himself unsullied. In his initial resignation, he also stated explicitly his intention to avoid in future the acceptance of any office of state. However, in victory, he failed to adhere to his vow, and conform to the role established by Gandhi and repeated by Jayaprakash Narayan after the Janata victory in the 1977 elections of remaining aloof from the actual exercise of power in order to retain the purity of moral authority.

A third legacy of Gandhi which has become even more attenuated than the other two concerns the proper role of leadership in relation to the masses. Gandhi was a mass mobilizer of unprecedented skill in India who was using his skill to build a movement to expel the British from India. Yet, he distrusted the people and, by one account, even considered them at bottom a "mob," subject to immoral behavior and prone to violence.[11] Mobilization required simultaneously moral uplift and leadership to prevent the transformation of mass political action into criminal activity and violence.

Gandhi also was clearly aware that contemporary Indian society was internally divided into castes and religious communities. Effective mobilization of the heterogeneous fragments of Hindu society required, therefore, the use of transcendent Hindu symbols to emphasize Hindu unity while at the same time making special appeals for

[11] Chatterjee, "Gandhi and the Critique of Civil Society", p. 185.

Hindu–Muslim unity. It has often been pointed out that there was a problem of contradiction between the two goals, which Gandhi never resolved himself, though he was prepared to risk his own life for the second goal and did, in the end, become a martyr to it at the hands of a fanatical Hindu assassin.

In the post-Independence era, numerous variations on Gandhi's techniques of mass mobilization have been applied countless times in movements small and great. Increasingly, however, mass mobilization has become associated more with competitive demagogy, with the manipulation of symbols for the sole purpose of building a political following to win an election or to achieve some other purpose and with scant regard for any moral goal.

INTRA-PROVINCIAL POLITICS AND CENTER–PROVINCIAL RELATIONS BEFORE AND AFTER INDEPENDENCE

The difficulties of constructing all-India social movements and political organizations and of mobilizing the mass of the people around all-India symbols of unity or opposition arise partly out of the inherent cultural diversity of the peoples of India, partly out of the significance of local issues of land control, but also out of the dynamics of intra-provincial politics and center–provincial relations in India's multi-level political system. Those dynamics have operated repeatedly in similar ways. The main patterns are the following.

Firstly, at every level of the system, factionalism, personalism, and opportunism rather than ideology, party ties, nationalism, or communalism have structured routine conflict and alliance patterns. Factional conflicts are sometimes suppressed or attenuated at the bottom and the top of the system: at the bottom, when some local leader or leaders have overwhelming power; at the top, where it is hard to maintain the links in the chain of support that lead to a leader's local structures of power. At the middle levels, particularly at the provincial levels, factionalism is generally rampant.

The second feature is the principle of interference or intrusion of politics from higher levels into lower levels. This principle has had two bases. It has operated because of the absence of any doctrine of the autonomy of local bodies or "states' rights" and the presence instead of a presumed right of higher authority to intervene to maintain order at lower levels. The second basis has lain in the need either for support at lower levels in the system to build power at higher levels or for a transcendent appeal to overcome or bypass the essentially local character of politics and structures of power in Indian politics.

The third feature of routine politics in India has been the pervasiveness in provincial and local politics of intra-communal political divisions and inter-elite cooperation across communal boundaries. The fourth feature follows from the other three and may be called the principle of division, a variation on the theme of "divide and rule." In routine politics in India, power at each level and especially across levels is attained by dividing the opposition, not by oppressing it. One offers "inducements": ministerships, patronage, non-interference in a leader's local base, cash.

The fifth feature, however, runs counter to the others to some extent. It is the principle of hierarchical loyalties, which is based on the existence in India of ascending levels of loyalty running from *jati* (the local caste group) to nation, with many intermediate stages in between, that can be called upon by leaders and movements to build support through communal unity rather than through division of the opposition. It operates at the mass level and influences popular allegiances at moments of choice, such as elections, mass movements, or communal riots. It presents itself in the form of dichotomous oppositions between caste groups, religious communities, nationalists against British rulers, and occurs whenever structures of opportunity – such as the establishment of electoral constituencies or institutions at levels which correspond approximately to actual or potential levels of group loyalty – are created to facilitate or precipitate such oppositions.

The sixth feature is the premium on charismatic or demagogic leadership that can call upon the appropriate loyalties at critical moments to transcend the features of routine politics identified above, particularly at the mass level. The strategy of dealing with local leaders then becomes one not of dividing leadership groups, but of threatening to undercut the leader's local bases of support with an appeal that will move his local supporters and break temporarily local links and allegiance. There have been several kinds of leaders in South Asian political history with this kind of capacity. One type, of which Gandhi was the preeminent example, rose to prominence through both mass leadership achieved through struggle and effective liaison with provincial leaders. He retained no local political base for himself and sought no national power for himself.

A second type, represented by the Nehru family, achieved national power through direct anointment by Gandhi, in the case of Nehru, or through their own parents, as in the cases of Mrs. Gandhi and Rajiv. Father and daughter, however, retained their powers in different ways, the father by maintaining bargaining relations with provincial leaders, the daughter by destroying them. Both, however, maintained direct popular or demagogic links with the masses. Rajiv, who oscillated between the methods of his grandfather and his mother and and lacked any distinctive leadership qualities of his own, survived until his assassination in May, 1991 largely on the basis of divine right. The third type is exemplified by Jinnah, who built upon personal reputation rather than mass leadership, who was not really anointed by anyone but himself for the leadership role he ultimately adopted but who, at last, his own personal dispositions to the contrary notwithstanding, had to take up the same dual role that both Gandhi and the Nehrus adopted: plebiscitary or demagogic appeals directly to the masses combined with direct bargaining with political leaders.

It is a recurring feature of Indian political history that only a charismatic leader with a simple appeal can unite the subcontinent or any of its larger peoples for a political purpose. While the prevailing tendencies in normal times are towards disaggregation of power, regionalism, and opportunism, the desire to centralize power in India leads to efforts to nationalize issues, which also means their simplification and symbolization in slogans, which in turn places a high premium on charismatic or demagogic leadership. However, such mobilization is evanescent; power so aggregated soon crumbles, and defection and the scramble for places reemerge immediately the dust settles. From Gandhi's first great mass movement, the Non-cooperation/Khilafat movement of 1920–21 to the Hindu nationalist movement of the late 1980s and 1990s, Indian politics have oscillated between the sordid, everyday, patronage politics of the provincial and local politicians and the enthusiasms aroused by mass popular leaders.

A great new wave of enthusiasm has been spreading in India in the

1980s and 1990s as the RSS family of organizations[12] have sought to capture power with an appeal to Hindu nationalism. The Hindu nationalist organizations have spawned a multiplicity of leadership types and roles in one of the most complex and innovative movements seen since before Independence.[13] At its core is the shadowy presence of the supreme RSS leader, a Wizard of Oz who rarely shows his face but pulls the strings from the inner sanctum of the RSS headquarters. The BJP leaders present the moderate face of statecraft and political bargaining. The VHP leaders make use of powerfully emotive demagogic appeals designed at once to instill pride amongst Hindus in their identity and enmity against the Muslim "other." *Sadhus* and *shankaracharyas* are called upon to appeal to the faith of Hindus in the cause of rebuilding temples demolished by Muslim conquerors and rulers in centuries past.

An array of new mobilizing tactics also have been brought forth: the *rath yatra* (journey by chariot) conjuring up an image of Ram as a warrior riding forth to restore Hindu pride and protect Hindu faith. Bricks are consecrated and carried by the faithful to Ayodhya to build a grand new temple to Ram. *Kar sevaks* (voluntary workers) are called upon to come in tens of thousands to participate in the work itself. The ashes of "martyrs" killed in police confrontations at Ayodhya are carried in urns and spread around the country to sanctify the Hindu Indian earth.

This formidable movement promises fundamental changes in Indian political practices by changing the Hindu psyche. However, it propagates a different lesson from that taught by the greatest of all Indian mass mobilizers, Mahatma Gandhi. Instead of Swaraj defined as self-mastery, Hindu nationalists offer communal pride; instead of love for an alien oppressor who must nevertheless be fought, they offer hatred and pogroms against a weaker minority; instead of constructive work

[12] On the RSS family of organizations, see Walter K. Andersen and Shridhar D. Damle, *The Brotherhood in Saffron: The Rashtriya Swayamsevak Sangh* (New Delhi: Vistaar, 1987).

[13] The emotive power of the rituals and symbols used to appeal to Hindu nationalism are brought out especially well in two unpublished papers by Peter Van der Veer, Riots and Rituals: The Construction of Violence and Public Space in Hindu Nationalism, prepared for a volume to be edited by Paul R. Brass, Riots and Pogroms, forthcoming, and Richard H. Davis, The Iconography of Ram's Chariot, prepared for the Social Science Research Council Conference on South Asian Cultural Studies and the Subject of Representation, Durham, NC, February 4–6, 1993.

to improve the lives of the ordinary people of the country, they propose to create a great military industrial state and to build nuclear weapons to intimidate neighboring countries and gain the respect of foreign powers.

PART I

POLITICAL CHANGE

INTRODUCTION

Most theoretical models of political change and development applied
to the post-colonial states of Asia and Africa have emphasized the
critical role of "state-building" – stabilizing, extending, and strengthening the institutions of the centralized state – as a virtual precondition
for "modernization," national integration, and economic development. The central issue in these models of state-building concerns
"penetration" of the institutions of the centralized state into "empty
territories" or peripheral areas and into culturally and economically
diverse regions which have undergone uneven economic and social
development. It also involves establishing the authority of state laws
and values over the traditional laws, customs, and values of autonomous religious, tribal, and other local communities. It includes as well
the implementation of state goals of urban industrial development,
increased agricultural production using advanced technologies, and
agrarian reform in societies whose populations are overwhelmingly
rural, agrarian, and dominated by peasant cultivators.[1]

One influential model of state-building has been woven around the
argument that there is a basic tension between the needs for strong
state authority and the increased demands for participation by populations mobilized by nationalist leaders, party politicians, and others
in pursuit of a multiplicity of goals which ultimately come into conflict
with each other and with the broader public interest which only an
institutionalized and autonomous state can pursue effectively.[2] This
view magnifies such demands for participation into a developmental
"crisis," threatening to state authority and civil order.[3]

---

[1] Joseph LaPalombara, "Penetration: A Crisis of Governmental Capacity," in Leonard
Binder *et al.*, *Crises and Sequences in Political Development* (Princeton, N.J.: Princeton
University Press, 1971), pp. 220–227; cf. Gabriel A. Almond and G. Bingham Powell, Jr.,
Comparative Politics: System, Process, and Policy (2nd edn, Boston: Little, Brown, 1978),
p. 22 on the importance of penetration.

[2] Samuel P. Huntington, *Political Order in Changing Societies* (New Haven: Yale University Press, 1968), e.g., p. 24.

[3] See Myron Weiner, "Political Participation: Crisis of the Political Process," in Binder *et
al.*, *Crises and Sequences.* Weiner discusses the "participation crisis" in general, but does not
share Huntington's views on it.

All these views tend to exalt the centralized state, to assume its inevitable triumph in one way or another, and to give it an anthropomorphic shape while assigning only a secondary role to the specific actions of the wielders of state authority. It is sometimes suggested that the state may adopt federal features and may decentralize power to local institutions, but these are rarely seen as anything but measures to make more effective the capacity of the central state itself.[4] Political leaders, especially the nationalist leaders, and some of the more dynamic contemporary military leaders, have generally been seen as playing the important, but secondary role of transferring their charisma to state institutions and thereby imparting legitimacy to them. The "overloads" and crises which may lead to the collapse or functional irrelevance of "differentiated modern [state] structures" do not arise from the actions of the leaders but occur "when environmental strains become too great."[5]

The view taken here of the role of the Indian state since Independence is different in most respects from the dominant theoretical models. This study emphasizes the struggle for power among competing elites and individuals which often cuts across the functional differentiation and specialization of state institutions, bending them to the wills of the principal contenders for power. The Indian state does not mainly respond to and resolve or manage crises arising from the environment, but is, through the actions of its leaders, the principal agency directly and indirectly responsible for their occurrence in the first place. The Indian state, in common with all other states, does not merely respond to crises produced by uneven economic development and social change, but is itself the leading force providing differential advantages to regions, ethnic groups, and classes.

Although it is true that the entrance of new groups into the political process in post-Independence India has often been accompanied by intensification of conflict and violence, it is of no scientific value to attribute these consequences to an objectified participation crisis. More specific explanations are required and will be provided in the three parts of this study.

It will be noted in part I that there have been two alternative models for political development in post-Independence India: the over-

[4] Almond and Powell, *Comparative Politics*, pp. 160ff.
[5] Almond and Powell, *Comparative Politics*, p. 22.

whelmingly dominant model of a strong centralized state held by virtually all Congress leaders since Independence and a much less prominent model derived from Gandhi's ideas not for a merely federal, decentralized state, but for a state built up from the village, with the latter as the central political focus and with the satisfaction of the basic needs of its people as the aim of all social and political institutions. Contrary to the role assigned to charismatic leaders in most theories of political development, Gandhi, the preeminent leader of Indian nationalism, refused to transfer his charisma to the new Indian state.

Disregarding Gandhi's views, however, India's other national leaders framed a constitution providing for a federal but highly centralized state. India's federal system, though centralized, contains so many points of potential power which must be controlled in order to remain in command in New Delhi that political competition appears to be an endless process which never reaches equilibrium.

A second general argument of part I is that the drives toward centralization of power in Delhi have intensified markedly since the death of Nehru and the grand succession struggle which followed. The consequences have been to produce fundamental changes in the structure and functioning of the central government, in the form and character of party political competition, and in the relationships among central, state, and local institutions of governance and of politics. Those changes, discussed in detail in chapters 2, 3, and 4 are summarized briefly here.

The struggle for power in Delhi has not only become more competitive and more ruthless but has been marked since the Emergency period from 1975 to 1977 by a tension between authoritarian and democratic political tendencies. In the process, the office of Prime Minister has emerged as the central focus of all authority and struggle in the country, with the result that most other institutions have declined in authority and effectiveness.

However, as the drive to centralize political power in New Delhi has intensified, the political support to sustain it has declined. The highly factionalized, but once mighty Congress, with its strength based on the districts and in the state capitals, was reduced by Mrs. Gandhi in many states and districts to bodies of persons oriented more toward the favor of her emissaries from New Delhi than toward local support bases and state political leaders.

Opposition forces for their part have become increasingly regionalized. In many states, the Congress no longer competes effectively against dominant regional parties or can do so only when the central Congress leadership and the Congress Prime Minister make a massive effort, using instruments of central power and patronage, to displace such parties and shore up the regional Congress organization.

Indeed, the weakening of the Congress has led to a situation in which the central government increasingly uses and abuses central instruments of control over state government and politics. As Congress support bases have disintegrated, the functioning of state institutions, notably in those states where the Congress is ostensibly in power, has come to depend upon the wishes of the central leadership in New Delhi.

In the face of these disintegrative tendencies, the Congress nevertheless remains the strongest force in the country and the only party which has been able both to win national elections and produce stable leadership. Its successes in this regard, however, came to depend more and more on the persons and personalities of the Nehru family rather than upon the institutional strength of a functioning party organization with stable bases of support in the districts and localities of the country.

"State-building," therefore, has been leading in India not to political centralization but to regionalism and loss of effective control in large parts of the country. It has produced a systemic crisis, which arises less from failures of penetration or obstacles to it than from the subordination of goals associated with the term "penetration" to the narrow struggle for political control of the country from New Delhi. Nor are the rising demands and expectations of new groups of mobilized participants in politics responsible for the crisis. Where intense and violent conflicts between segments of the population have taken place, they are usually associated either with specific types of economic or other forms of competition or with struggles for political power in which state and central government and party elites are directly involved and are not merely responding to demands for increased participation from new participants in the political process.

CHAPTER 2

POLITICAL CHANGE, POLITICAL STRUCTURE, AND THE FUNCTIONING OF GOVERNMENT

PARLIAMENTARY DEMOCRACY IN INDIA

There has been a basic tension in the post-Independence political order, arising in part out of features of the Indian Constitution itself, between authoritarian and democratic tendencies. These in turn overlap with the tension between forces favoring centralization and those favoring decentralization. During the Nehru era, a balance was struck between these opposing tendencies and forces. British parliamentary conventions were adapted to Indian extra-parliamentary practices.

Although the Center's supremacy was rarely challenged, politics in the states were largely autonomous. The exercise of direct political control of state government and politics from the Center was quite infrequent. Indian parliamentarism functioned freely, openly, and competitively. A balance was also struck between the use of extra-constitutional methods by opposition groups and the state's use of extraordinary powers such as laws permitting preventive detention.

Since Nehru's death, the succession crisis that followed, the imposition of the Emergency regime of 1975–77, the increasing difficulties faced by national political leaders in aggregating power throughout this vast country and maintaining it for long, and the recent rise of violent and terrorist movements have unsettled the balance. The use of violence by protest groups has become more common as has the state's use of extreme force. Although Emergency rule was followed by the defeat of Mrs. Gandhi and the restoration of normalcy, the armory of coercive powers available to the state for use against its citizens remained very great and has been reinforced in recent years with the passage of new legislation providing extraordinary powers to the state and limiting those of its citizens in areas where violent secessionist movements are in progress. The use of coercive state powers has increased during the past decade and there has been as well a great growth in the number, size, and deployment of various police and semi-military forces to quell domestic disorder and suppress political dissent.[1] In the process, the autonomy of state politics has been further eroded and the balance of powers in India's federal system has shifted to the Center.

The Nehru period

Jawaharlal Nehru, the first Prime Minister of India, was not formally selected either by the Congress party organization or by the Congress party in Parliament. He was simply the natural choice as the acknowledged leader of the Congress and the designated political heir of Mahatma Gandhi. However, the party organization in the early years after Independence was dominated by Sardar Patel, who was also the most powerful minister in the Cabinet after Nehru and recognized as Nehru's equal in all other respects.

Numerous differences developed between Patel and Nehru in the Cabinet and a great struggle for control over the party organization culminated in a victory for Patel's candidate, Purushottamdas Tandon, as party President in 1950. However, after Patel's death in December, 1950, Nehru moved quickly to take over the party organization, forcing Tandon to resign the presidency, which Nehru then assumed himself for the next four years. After the overwhelming victory of the Congress under Nehru's leadership in the 1952 elections, there was no longer any doubt about Nehru's supremacy in the party and the government and he remained the unchallenged leader of both until his death in 1964.

Nehru's personality, attitudes, and style of leadership influenced profoundly all aspects of the functioning of the Indian political system during the period of his dominance. Nehru asserted effectively and decisively the primacy of the office of Prime Minister against challenges from the President and from the Congress organization. He was determined also that the Indian National Congress should rule the country and achieve power not only in Delhi but in all the Indian states. In a few cases, the attainment of that goal involved considerable political manipulation and the use of the power of the central government to undermine the positions of opposition parties and dissident

[1] Kuldeep Mathur, "The State and the Use of Coercive Power in India," *Asian Survey*, xxxii, No. 4 (April, 1992), 337–349.

Congress factions in states such as Punjab and Kerala. However, from the position of strength which Nehru established for the Congress, he then acted generously toward most opposition parties and their leaders, though not always so toward parties he considered to be of the extreme Right and toward the Communists. In some respects, Nehru himself was the leader of the opposition,[2] for he was constantly haranguing and berating subordinate leaders and the rank and file for not being faithful to Congress ideals and for failing to implement Congress policies.

During the Nehru period, state and central politics were largely autonomous, though the central leadership of the Congress, known as the High Command, often played arbitrating and mediating roles between competing factions in the state Congress parties. Moreover, under Nehru, a strong central government coexisted with strong states and powerful state leaders in a mutual bargaining situation in which ultimate authority existed in Delhi.

Nehru and his Cabinet also exercised firm control over both the civilian and military bureaucracies. Although the elite civil service established by the British was maintained, Nehru and his principal ministers provided clear and firm policy guidance. Similarly, the supremacy of civilian control over the military also was strongly asserted.

Finally, Nehru articulated a clear set of ideological and policy goals, which included a commitment to a non-dogmatic form of socialism, to secularism, economic development through state-directed planning, and non-alignment in international affairs. Success in achieving specific policies included under these broad goals was often limited, but they provided always a clear social and economic orientation, direction, and cohesion to state policies.

Toward the end of Nehru's life, the central party organization, with Nehru's acquiescence, reemerged as a powerful force, initially in support of Nehru's own desire to gain firmer control of both party organization and government in all the states of the Union. Kamaraj Nadar, former chief minister of the state of Tamil Nadu, was elected President of the Congress in 1963 and, along with four other party

---

[2] Ashish Nandy, "Indira Gandhi and the Culture of Indian Politics," in Ashish Nandy, *At the Edge of Psychology: Essays in Politics and Culture* (Delhi: Oxford University Press, 1980), p. 120.

Table 2.1. *Prime Ministers of India*

Jawaharlal Nehru	Congress	1947–64
Lal Bahadur Shastri	Congress	1964–66
Indira Gandhi	Congress	1966–77
Morarji Desai	Janata	1977–79
Charan Singh	Janata (S)	1979–80
Indira Gandhi	Congress	1980–84
Rajiv Gandhi	Congress	1984–89
Vishwanath Pratap Singh	National Front	1989–90
Chandrashekhar	Janata Dal (S)	1990–91
P. V. Narasimha Rao	Congress	1991–

"bosses" from different states, took control of the party organization. Upon Nehru's death in 1964, this group, known as the Syndicate, and especially Kamaraj as party President, played the critical roles in the succession to Nehru by Lal Bahadur Shastri and of Mrs. Gandhi to Shastri two years later.

The rise of Indira Gandhi

The entire period between Nehru's death in 1964 and the consolidation of power in the country under Mrs. Gandhi's leadership in 1971–72 constituted a prolonged succession crisis and struggle for power, with the period of Lal Bahadur Shastri's prime ministership from May, 1964 to January, 1966 but a brief interregnum between Nehru and Mrs. Gandhi, the two dominant leaders of India since Independence (see table 2.1). The period is marked by five critical steps in the rise of Mrs. Gandhi and the defeat of all her potential rivals.

The first step was her own succession to power in 1966 after the sudden death of Shastri. The 1967 defeat of Morarji Desai in the Congress Parliamentary Party (CPP) was the second critical step in Mrs. Gandhi's consolidation of power, which established her pre-eminence against her only serious rival, despite severe losses suffered by the Congress in the 1967 elections under her leadership.

Once again an unexpected death in office, this time of the President of India, Zakir Husain (table 2.2), had the effect of speeding up a struggle that was, in any case, already in progress. The Congress split

Table 2.2. *Presidents of India*

Election	President
1950	Rajendra Prasad
1952	Rajendra Prasad
1957	Rajendra Prasad
1962	S. Radhakrishnan
1967	Zakir Hussain (died 1969)
1969	V. V. Giri
1974	Fakhruddin Ali Ahmed (died 1977)
1977	Neelam Sanjiva Reddy
1982	Zail Singh
1987	R. Venkataraman
1992	Shankar Dayal Sharma

of 1969 over the Congress nominee for the presidency of India was the third critical point in Mrs. Gandhi's consolidation of power. Mrs. Gandhi won the battle for the presidency with the election of her candidate, V. V. Giri, against the official Congress nominee, Sanjiva Reddy. However, in the process, she was expelled from the Congress and lost control over the party organization since most of the entrenched state party bosses remained in the Congress (O), while Mrs. Gandhi's strength was more in the CPP than in the state party organizations.

Mrs. Gandhi decided to call national parliamentary elections in March, 1971. The people of India were, in effect, asked to settle the struggle for power that had been going on since Nehru's death, to choose between Mrs. Gandhi and her opponents, between the old Congress and the new. The results of the 1971 elections were an overwhelming victory for Mrs. Gandhi, whose Congress (R) won a two-thirds majority in the Lok Sabha. Mrs. Gandhi was now unquestionably the preeminent leader of the country.

Shortly after the March, 1971 election, the civil war and secessionist movement in East Pakistan began. Mrs. Gandhi's attentions had now to be turned to this conflict, which occupied her and the country until December, 1971, when the Indian Army invaded East Pakistan, defeated the Pakistan Army in the Third Indo-Pakistan War, and became the crucial factor thereby in the foundation of the new state of

Bangladesh. With this triumph behind her, the Congress (R) and Mrs. Gandhi were able to go to the polls in the March, 1972 legislative assembly elections with confidence and gain large majorities in all the major states in the Indian Union. At this point, one can say that the first succession crisis in post-Independence India had been decisively ended in favor of Mrs. Gandhi, who now occupied a position of centrality and dominance in the Indian political system that appeared to equal or even surpass that of her father.

Mrs. Gandhi established a distinctive strategy of rulership between 1972 and 1975 that was highly personalized and centralized and that involved unprecedented assertions of executive power in the Indian political system. Within the Congress organization also, Mrs. Gandhi established personal control, the dominance of the ministerial wing of the party over the organization, centralized direction of lower units, and authoritarian rather than democratic procedures for recruitment of party officers.[3]

Mrs. Gandhi's centralizing actions also transformed the character of center–state governmental relations in the states controlled by the Congress. Unlike her father, who preferred to deal with strong chief ministers in control of their legislative parties and state party organizations, Mrs. Gandhi set out to remove every Congress chief minister who had an independent base and to replace each of them with chief ministers personally loyal to her and without an independent base. Even so, stability could not be maintained in the states and factional manoeuvering to replace each appointed chief minister continued, the principal difference in such manoeuvering now being that the decisions could not be taken in the state capitals but only in New Delhi.

Threats to Mrs. Gandhi's dominance and the imposition of the Emergency

Threats to Mrs. Gandhi's dominance

A personalized strategy of rulership has the effect of focusing attention on the ruler, who receives the blame when things go wrong. In 1973–74, food shortages and rising prices combined with local political

[3] Stanley A. Kochanek, "Mrs. Gandhi's Pyramid: The New Congress," in Henry C. Hart (ed.), *Indira Gandhi's India: A Political System Reappraised* (Boulder, CO: Westview Press, 1976), pp. 95–102.

grievances to produce major popular demonstrations and movements that turned violent in the states of Gujarat and Bihar and that could not be handled effectively by the chief ministers appointed by Mrs. Gandhi in those states. Inside the Congress, a small group of MPs were becoming discontented with Mrs. Gandhi's economic policies.

Then, in March, 1974, a new and ominous development occurred when Jayaprakash Narayan (JP) took the leadership of the Bihar agitation and offered also to lead a countrywide movement against corruption and what he considered to be Mrs. Gandhi's increasingly authoritarian rule. JP offered a direct, personal challenge to Mrs. Gandhi's authority, legitimacy, and character from a personal position of moral authority.

In the midst of these and other developments threatening Mrs. Gandhi's dominance, the Allahabad High Court precipitated matters by finding Mrs. Gandhi's 1971 election invalid on the grounds of corrupt practices in an election petition filed by Raj Narain and decided on June 12, 1975. This event brought new hope and vigor to the opposition, which began to join forces and to plan a mass mobilization campaign to demand the resignation of Mrs. Gandhi.

The Emergency

In the early morning hours of June 26, 1975, Mrs. Gandhi moved decisively to put an end to all opposition to her continuance in office. All her principal opponents, not only in the opposition but in the CPP itself, were arrested. At her request, the President of India declared an Emergency under Article 352 of the Constitution. A twenty-point economic program was announced, emphasizing reforms for the poor and landless. Parliament moved swiftly to pass new electoral laws superseding the laws under which Mrs. Gandhi was found guilty and her election voided.

Within a few months, President's Rule was imposed in the two non-Congress-ruled states of Gujarat and Tamil Nadu, thereby bringing the entire country under direct dictatorial rule from Delhi. Parliamentary elections scheduled for March, 1976 were postponed and the terms of both Parliament and the state legislative assemblies extended. Mrs. Gandhi's young son, Sanjay, came forward as the principal defender of the Emergency, acquiring dictatorial powers himself because of his identification with his mother, which he exercised in an arbitrary, arrogant, and capricious manner.

Although Mrs. Gandhi initially announced that the imposition of the Emergency was to be a temporary measure to restore discipline and order in the country, she nevertheless took steps to institutionalize some of its features through laws and constitutional amendments. These included enhancements in the power and prestige of the offices of Prime Minister and chief minister, the institutionalization of procedures for censoring the press, the imposition of discipline in the workplace and in public life and of restrictions and limits on the civil liberties of the people, the reduction of the independent powers of the courts to review acts of Parliament and the state assemblies and to protect the rights of citizens, and extension of the terms of state legislative assemblies, among other actions.

Tens of thousands of local-level party workers were jailed and press censorship made it difficult for other than local and very limited political protests to be made publicly by regime opponents who were not in jail. It was not long, however, before considerable discontent at the mass level, though veiled, began to develop as a consequence of specific acts of the Emergency regime. The most notable set of such acts was the sterilization program of birth control introduced at the prompting of Sanjay Gandhi. Under this program, government employees with more than three children were expected to have vasectomies or be denied perquisites such as government housing. In some states, they were also given quotas to fulfill to have ordinary members of the public sterilized. Under these pressures, instances of forced sterilizations began to be reported and rumors spread across north India that instilled fear among villagers in the countryside that they might also have vasectomies imposed upon them.[4]

Discontent also began to develop among Muslims as a consequence of projects for slum clearance and elimination of pavement squatters for the sake of "beautification of Delhi." Slum residents and squatters were ordered to move and were provided new housing, usually miles away from the city, making it difficult for residents to find work in Delhi. Houses and markets were razed to the ground. Many of the demolitions and forced resettlements affected Muslims especially. The

[4] Myron Weiner, *India at the Polls: The Parliamentary Elections of 1977* (Washington, D.C.: American Enterprise Institute, 1978), pp. 39–40.

most controversial were in the Turkman Gate area of old Delhi, where six Muslims were killed in a police firing, and in the environs of the Jama Masjid, which offended the Imam of the great mosque.[5] As with the sterilization campaign, press censorship could not stop the spread of the news of these incidents by word of mouth among the Muslim population across north India.

Finally, all those persons who were affected by the demands for increased discipline in the workplace, by the pressures to procure sterilizations, and by freezes on wage increases also became disaffected with the Emergency regime. Most prominent in these categories were urban workers, government employees, and teachers.

The 1977 elections and return to normalcy

The 1977 elections

In the face of these simmering discontents, which were evidently not known to Mrs. Gandhi because of the distortions in the flow of information and communication produced by fear and sycophancy among Congressmen and government officials, Mrs. Gandhi suddenly announced in December, 1977 a call for new parliamentary elections and a relaxation of the Emergency restrictions on the press and the opposition, including the release from jail of most political prisoners. Mrs. Gandhi and Sanjay probably believed that the opposition would not have sufficient time to mobilize and gather the necessary resources to fight an effective election campaign in the few weeks available to them.

The results confounded any reasonable expectations that Mrs. Gandhi and Sanjay could have had. The Janata party achieved a great victory, winning 295 seats, a bare majority in the Lok Sabha, but the opposition as a whole secured more than two-thirds of the seats, reducing the Congress to 153 seats, only 28 percent of the seats in the House.

The return to normalcy

The Janata government that came to power with Morarji Desai as Prime Minister had promised to restore normalcy if it succeeded at the polls and it set out to do so immediately after taking office. Civil

[5] Weiner, *India at the Polls 1977*, p. 40.

liberties of the people were fully restored, press censorship was eliminated and the independence of the press from government interference reestablished, and all remaining political prisoners were released. The Janata government restored the main features of parliamentary democracy in India and made the future imposition of an emergency somewhat more difficult.

The Indian parliamentary system, since its restoration in 1977, has survived numerous political crises to be discussed in later chapters of this volume. They include the fall of the Janata government in 1979 and the return of Mrs. Gandhi to power thereafter, the threats to Indian unity posed by the Punjab and Kashmir crises, the assassination both of Mrs. Gandhi in 1984 and of her son Rajiv, in 1991, and the alternation in power since 1985 of Congress and non-Congress governments from Rajiv Gandhi to the National Front government of V. P. Singh to the Congress under P. V. Narasimha Rao (table 2.1). The Congress government, despite its relatively weak leadership and slim majority in Parliament, introduced in 1991–93 significant steps to promote economic vitality by virtually jettisoning the system of centralized economic planning and markedly opening the economy to domestic and international market forces.

Thus, India's parliamentary regime has persisted both in the negative sense of weathering major crises and in the positive sense of introducing major new policy changes. It would be unwise to assume that the parliamentary regime is now strong enough to weather all authoritarian challenges and present and future crises, but it does seem clear that parliamentary practices – however much adapted to Indian conditions and however much they depart from India's own constitutional design – have become deeply embedded in Indian political culture. It seems less clear, however, that Indian political elites are any longer capable of providing effective government, implementing social policies, resolving regional and local ethnic, caste, and communal conflicts, or even ensuring the safety of the people in several areas of the country from the depredations of criminal gangs, terrorist groups, and even the police and state security forces.[6] Moreover, state and

---

[6] *Cf.* Atul Kohli's argument that India's governing institutions have so declined in authority and effectiveness that there is a "crisis of governability"; *Democracy and Discontent: India's Growing Crisis of Governability* (Cambridge: Cambridge University Press, 1990) and Myron Weiner's description of the contradiction between India's maintenance of a "democratic political system" amid the persistence of a "high level of political violence" as

local elites with the tacit approval or malign neglect of national party and government leaders have on numerous occasions in the past decade resorted to deliberate provocation of violent incidents and rioting to embarrass or displace duly elected state and national governments.[7]

PATTERN AND STRUCTURE OF GOVERNMENT

The President

The Constitution of India formally vests virtually all the executive powers of government in the President. In fact, however, it is understood that the President's powers are to be exercised, with only rare exceptions, upon the advice of the Prime Minister and the Council of Ministers. Nevertheless, there have been persistent concerns from the time of the deliberations of the Constituent Assembly up to the present that a President might misuse or abuse – in effect, actually *use* – the powers formally granted to him in the Constitution or might, under certain circumstances, be in a position to exercise discretionary powers.

The most persistent concerns have centered around the degree of freedom the President may have to select a Prime Minister in an unstable House. Because of such concerns, ever since the 1967 elections and the split in the Indian National Congress in 1969, as a consequence of which the political dominance of the Congress at the Center has not been assured and inter-party political competition for the prime ministership has become more intense, the election of the President has become a highly politicized matter.

However, it was not until Sanjiva Reddy's term of office (1977–82) that the anticipated difficulties surrounding the exercise of presidential discretion in selecting a new Prime Minister and dissolving the House and calling a new election in a divided House arose: in July, 1979, after the resignation of Morarji Desai and a month later after Charan Singh, Desai's successor, also lost his majority. In three instances, precedents were established for the exercise of discretion by the President: in rejecting Morarji Desai's request to form a new government after his

"the Indian paradox" in *The Indian Paradox: Essays in Indian Politics* (New Delhi: Sage, 1989), p. 9.
[7] On this point also, Kohli's *Democracy and Discontent* provides ample evidence.

initial resignation, in insisting that his successor, Charan Singh, seek a vote of confidence in the Lok Sabha by a specific date, and in his insistence, after Charan Singh's resignation with a recommendation for calling a new election, upon consulting other party leaders before making the decision himself to call a new election. Although all three actions by the President were controversial, none was inconsistent with parliamentary conventions nor did they betray a desire for the exercise of personal power by the President.[8]

In 1989 and 1991, President R. Venkataraman was faced with situations comparable to those dealt with by Sanjiva Reddy a decade earlier. In December, 1989, he appointed V. P. Singh as head of a minority National Front government, but required him to demonstrate his majority support by a vote of the House. Then, in March, 1991, the second non-Congress government having fallen like its predecessor twelve years before, the President appointed Chandrashekhar as a minority Prime Minister with the support of the Congress in the Lok Sabha. When differences arose between Chandrashekhar and Congress leader, Rajiv Gandhi, the President followed the advice of his Prime Minister and dissolved the House with a call for new elections. Thus, two precedents have been established with regard to this crucial and necessary exercise of presidential power: the President may appoint a Prime Minister from a minority party, but may also require him to seek a vote of confidence; second, the President may follow the advice of an outgoing Prime Minister in a House without a clear majority and call for new elections.[9] However, in the latter case, the President may also first consult other party leaders before accepting the advice of his Prime Minister.

In other matters, the exercise of even the limited discretionary powers available to the President has occurred so infrequently that each such exercise has occasioned extensive public comment and some controversy. In 1987, for example, Giani Zail Singh made use for the first time since Independence of the President's power to return a bill to Parliament – the Indian Post Office (amendment) Bill, authorizing the Post Office to open private mail for intelligence purposes. The

---

[8] For a contrary view, see Barun Sengupta, *Last Days of the Morarji Raj* (Calcutta: Ananda Publishers, 1979), ch. 10.

[9] Jean-Alphonse Bernard, "The Presidential Idea in the Constitutions of South Asia," *Contemporary South Asia*, 1, No. 1 (1992), 43.

employment of this power and the President's written complaints to the Prime Minister at the same time that he was not even being kept briefed on major issues precipitated a public controversy and much speculation on the President's motives and intentions, including the possibility that he might exercise his formal power to dismiss the Prime Minister. Further speculation concerning the President's intentions appeared later in 1987 when a major government scandal involving alleged "kickbacks" to high government and party officials on weapons procurements from the Swedish arms manufacturer, Bofors, broke with the resignation from the government of former Defense and Finance Minister Vishwanath Pratap Singh. It has since become known that the President did, in fact, hold extensive consultations with Congress and opposition party leaders to consider the dismissal of the Prime Minister.[10] The latter situation notwithstanding, the actual constitutional reality has been that the President can function effectively only if he has the confidence of the Prime Minister and not vice versa.

There appear, therefore, to be few real grounds for concern that the President of India represents a potential political counterweight to the Prime Minister, the Cabinet, and the elected leadership of the country as long as there is a stable government in power. Nor has misuse of the office of the President for political purposes occurred even when there has been unstable government at the Center. Nevertheless, the desire of the leader of the party in power at the time of a presidential election to ensure the election of a President whose actions will not go against his or her interests has meant that presidential elections have become integrated into partisan politics. Efforts to reach inter-party consensus on the selection of a president have generally failed, as they did in 1992 when the Congress unilaterally selected Shankar Dayal Sharma as its nominee,[11] who was elected ninth President of the country thereafter (table 2.2).

Prime Minister and Cabinet

The framers of the Constitution adopted the conventions of British Cabinet government as it had evolved up to that time, including the leading position given to the Prime Minister and the collective

---

[10] *India Today*, April 15, 1988.   [11] *India Today*, July 15, 1992.

responsibility of the Cabinet.[12] During the Nehru period, from the time of the death of his chief political rival, Sardar Patel, in 1950, to 1964, the Cabinet functioned in conformity with the basic norms of "Prime Ministerial government," but one in which individual cabinet ministers were still allowed to play important political roles and of whom some were persons with substantial political followings.

Under Nehru's successor, Lal Bahadur Shastri, the Prime Minister's Secretariat emerged as an alternative source to the Cabinet of advice, influence, and power in the executive branch of government.[13] Following Shastri's example, Mrs. Gandhi used the PM's Secretariat as an independent source of advice, but she enlarged its role significantly. However, the influence of the Secretariat also declined, especially during the Emergency between 1975 and 1977, when Mrs. Gandhi came to rely heavily for both policy advice and political counsel upon her son, Sanjay.

The restoration of parliamentary government by the Janata coalition which came to power with Morarji Desai as Prime Minister in 1977 did not succeed in restoring the significance of the Cabinet as an institution. The divisions in his government were too great, the collective responsibility of the Cabinet disintegrated in open warfare, and Desai himself had to resign in July, 1979.

The pattern of prime ministerial dominance of a weak Cabinet was restored by Mrs. Gandhi after her electoral victory in 1980. After the death of her son Sanjay, in 1981, Mrs. Gandhi relied upon other relatives and former retainers of the Nehru household and turned increasingly also to her second son, Rajiv. Rajiv as Prime Minister continued his mother's pattern of consulting his own personal circle of advisers – dubbed the "coterie" by the press – irrespective of their position inside or outside the Cabinet.

In the pattern followed by Mrs. Gandhi and Rajiv, the close advisers of the Prime Minister may come from the political sphere, business, former school associates, his immediate family, distant relatives, or family retainers. Although it is more comparable to the White House staff than to the British Cabinet, the closest parallel is to the Indian

[12] M. V. Pylee, *Constitutional Government in India* (New York: Asia Publishing House, 1965), pp. 345, 370–371.
[13] Michael Brecher, *Succession in India: A Study in Decision-Making* (London: Oxford University Press, 1966), pp. 115–118.

institution of the *darbar* which, in one meaning, refers to the inner circle of advisers to the ruler. Members of the inner circle are dependent upon the ruler's favor for their positions. They may receive the ruler's patronage or dispense it on his behalf, but they may also be dismissed or find themselves disregarded and have no recourse for their positions are informal, not institutionalized. Moreover, most members of the inner circle lack an independent political base. The ruler, therefore, depends upon the members of this inner circle but is not dependent upon them. He can change them at will.

Since the defeat of the Congress in 1989 and the assassination of Rajiv Gandhi in 1991, India has had three Prime Ministers, of whom one, Chandrashekhar, was in power only briefly. Both V. P. Singh, National Front Prime Minister from 1989 to 1991, and P. V. Narasimha Rao, Congress Prime Minister after 1991, had to reckon with severe internal divisions within the governing party and the Cabinet. V. P. Singh was criticized by many of his former Cabinet colleagues for failing to consult them.[14] Nor did he develop any systematic procedures for consultation with Cabinet members or administrative officers.

Narasimha Rao at first reverted more to the pattern of Lal Bahadur Shastri, relying heavily upon senior bureaucrats in the Prime Minister's office more than upon either members of his Cabinet or senior Congress leaders.[15] However, frequent consultations were said in press reports to have occurred among senior Cabinet members before and after the Ayodhya crisis in December, 1992, though it was also widely reported that there were serious divisions among them. Therefore, in the midst of the national crisis of the years since 1989, the pattern of prime ministerial dominance of weak cabinets has been replaced by weak and ineffective prime ministerial leadership of divided cabinets.

The role and powers of Parliament

In principle in India, as in Britain, the Prime Minister is chosen by Parliament and he and his Cabinet are "collectively responsible" to it, that is, they must retain the confidence of a majority of the members of the lower House of Parliament or resign and give way to an alternative Congress. On only a few occasions, however, has there actually been a

[14] Personal interviews.   [15] *India Today*, September 15, 1992.

contested election in the ruling parliamentary party in India. In fact, even though the CPP played an important role in maintaining support for Mrs. Gandhi in her struggles with her rivals, it is the MPs who have been in the dependent role, following a popular leader to what they have considered their best hope for power for themselves as well rather than actually selecting a leader from among alternatives.

There have, however, been several occasions in the post-Independence period when the persistence of a government in power has depended in fact upon the confidence of the House as a whole. The first occurred in 1969, after the party split in the ruling Indian National Congress when Mrs. Gandhi retained a majority in Parliament. The second occasion was in July–August 1979, when the ruling Janata coalition split and Morarji Desai lost his majority in Parliament and had to resign. After the defeat of the Congress in the 1989 elections, three minority governments followed which depended upon uncertain majorities in the House: the National Front government of V. P. Singh, the tenuous and short-lived government of Chandrashekhar, and the government of P. V. Narasimha Rao, which came to power without a majority in Parliament following the indecisive result of the 1991 elections.

Individual MPs and opposition groups in the Indian Parliament also have played roles that are equivalent in importance to those played by their counterparts in Britain in the question hour, the amendment process, and debate. Equally important in India, however, have been dramatic gestures, defiance of parliamentary procedure, and other forms of demonstrative behavior designed to express total opposition to government policies.[16] Only during the Emergency was such opposition to Parliament stifled. On the other hand, some of the normal prerogatives of the legislature in India have been encroached upon by the Cabinet on numerous occasions, most notably the very frequent passage of legislation by Ordinance of the President (that is, in effect, by the Cabinet or the Prime Minister's Secretariat).

Although the Lok Sabha (House of the People) is the lower house and the supreme legislative body in India, the Rajya Sabha (Council of States) is not without importance. While the Rajya Sabha does not normally obstruct legislation passed in the Lok Sabha, it has occasionally done so, particularly on constitutional amendments which

[16] Pylee, *Constitutional Government*, pp. 445–446.

require a two-thirds majority in both houses. The second important power of the Rajya Sabha is its coequal role with the Lok Sabha as an electoral college, which includes also the state legislative assemblies, for the election of the President of India. The significance of these two powers taken together is that the Rajya Sabha must also be controlled before a government can consolidate its power in Delhi.

The Judiciary

The powers of the Indian Supreme Court are comparable to those of its United States counterpart, including broad original and appellate jurisdiction and the right to pass on the constitutionality of laws passed by Parliament.[17] In the exercise of its powers, however, the Court has been at the center of major controversies concerning the constitutional and political order in India. Two such controversies have been especially persistent and have had broad ramifications. One concerns the efforts by the Court to give priority to the Fundamental Rights provisions in the Constitution in cases where they have come into conflict with the Directive Principles, which specify the broad ideological and policy goals of the Indian state and to which the executive and legislature have often given priority. The second concerns the court's powers of judicial review of legislation passed by Parliament, which have on numerous occasions led to stalemates that point to a constitutional contradiction between the principle of parliamentary sovereignty and that of judicial review. Although the contradiction has not been satisfactorily resolved, with the two institutions each asserting an incompatible priority, the Court has retained an imprecisely defined power of judicial review which at its broadest, according to the judgment in the landmark 1973 case of *Keshavananda Bharati* vs. *State of Kerala*, prohibits Parliament from passing even constitutional amendments which violate "the fundamental features" or the "basic structure" of the Constitution.

During the Emergency, the Court's powers were severely eroded when both Fundamental Rights and judicial review were suspended. The Court even failed to uphold the hallowed common law right of *habeas corpus*. Although many of the Court's powers have since been

[17] Pylee, *Constitutional Government*, pp. 467, 500; Gerald E. Beller, "Benevolent Illusions in a Developing Society: The Assertion of Supreme Court Authority in Democratic India," *The Western Political Quarterly*, xxxvi, No. 4 (December, 1983), 516.

restored, the executive assertion of the primacy of the Directive Principles has been largely sustained and the principle of judicial review has not been established as firmly in India as it has in the United States.

Nevertheless, the Court has become a centrally important institution in the Indian political system, deeply and directly implicated in the political process in ways which have rarely if ever occurred in the United States. A 1975 decision of the High Court of Allahabad (the highest court in the province of Uttar Pradesh), overturning the election of Mrs. Gandhi while she was Prime Minister, was reviewed by the Supreme Court in a judicial process that precipitated the Emergency. When the Emergency ended and the Janata government came to power, the Court passed on the constitutional validity of the following actions of the new government designed to consolidate its power in the country and to keep Mrs. Gandhi on the defensive: the dismissal of nine state governments before the end of their terms and the calling of new elections in those states (the Dissolution Case, 1977) and the appointment of Special Courts to try Mrs. Gandhi for alleged excesses and criminal acts committed by her during the emergency (the Special Courts Reference Case, 1978).

Government in the states

In India's federal parliamentary system, the structures and institutions of the central government have their counterparts at the state level. Each state has a Governor who is the official head of state, a bicameral legislature in which the directly elected Lower House is generally called the Vidhan Sabha and the Upper House, whose members are elected under a variety of different types of franchises, is generally called the Rajya Sabha, a Chief Minister and his Council of Ministers or Cabinet, and a High Court.

These state institutions, however, have not functioned in the same way as their central models. The politics of the state legislatures have been much more fluid than politics in Parliament and there is often no clear majority in the legislature. As the agents of the central government, appointed by the President acting on the advice of the Prime Minister, it has been common since the late 1960s for the governors to intervene in such situations of instability in the states in ways which clearly indicate that they are following the explicit directives or the tacit desires of the central government rather than simply implementing their constitutional mandate to give formal approval to the decisions of the chief minister and Cabinet and to report impartially to the Center the situation in the states.

During the early post-Independence period in some states, a form of "chief ministerial" government developed, but the more common patterns were Cabinet instability and struggles for power even within the ruling Congress parties, which have always been highly factionalized, leading in many states to frequent changes in the office of the chief minister. Two factors have prevented the establishment in most states of governments dominated by the chief ministers: the fluidity of party loyalties and alignments in the legislatures and the unwillingness in the post-Nehru period of the leadership of the ruling party or coalition at the Center to permit strong chief ministers. Increasingly, therefore, many state legislatures have lost their powers to choose the chief ministers and cabinets, a function which has been taken up by the governing group at the Center. The primary activities of the state legislators consist of plotting to overthrow the government of the day and seeking patronage to distribute to followers in their constituencies.

The High Courts in the states, like the Supreme Court, have become involved in issues of fundamental rights and in matters of judicial review. Many of the constitutional issues which ultimately reached the Supreme Court were originally adjudicated in the High Courts.

In general, however, there have been marked differences in the actual practices of state and central government institutions.

LOCAL GOVERNMENT

The Constituent Assembly made only a modest concession to Gandhian ideology by establishing as a principle of state policy in the Directive Principles of the Constitution the goal of decentralizing power and participation to the subprovincial level.[18] However, the whole structure of the new Indian state ran contrary to the ideology of Gandhian decentralization, which not only was meant to provide for direct participation by the people in planning for their own economic

---

[18] Granville Austin, *The Indian Constitution: Cornerstone of a Nation* (Oxford: Clarendon Press, 1966), p. 38.

improvement but to minimize the role of the centralized state and its bureaucratic "agencies in the ordering of the economy."[19]

While the District Magistrate is no longer the sole focus of state administration and authority in the district and does not have the full freedom of his district ICS predecessors, he remains the central focus. At the district level, the Superintendent of Police (SP) has become nearly coequal in authority with the District Magistrate.

Alongside the pre-Independence system of administrative and police control in the districts, the post-Independence Indian state introduced a new administrative hierarchy to implement rural development plans. The community development block, whose jurisdiction comprises usually around 100 villages, is the pivotal administrative unit in the system, staffed by a multiplicity of technical administrative personnel, with the emphasis on agriculture, but also including other aspects of rural development, whose central purpose was to bring economic development and an enhanced quality of life generally to the villages.

In order to provide popular participation in development planning, a parallel system of local government in tiers from the village to the district level, called *panchayati raj*, was introduced in many states in several different forms. There were considerable differences, for example, in the extent of powers granted to *panchayati raj* institutions and in the tiers at which the powers granted were most concentrated. In some cases, these institutions were not adopted at all. In practice, moreover, *panchayati raj* "institutions came to be dominated by the socially or economically privileged sections in the local community."[20]

In the face of the failure and the decline of *panchayati raj* institutions of democratic decentralization in most of the Indian states and the persisting influence of rural elites in most aspects of rural development activities, there has been a renewed call from some sources and a renewed public debate on the desirability of countering the centralizing drives of the modern Indian state with a new dose of more effective decentralization. These issues will be discussed in chapter 4 below.

[19] Charan Singh, *Economic Nightmare of India: Its Cause and Cure* (New Delhi: National, 1981), p. ix.
[20] Shriram Maheshwari, *Rural Development in India: A Public Policy Approach* (New Delhi: Sage, 1985), pp. 54–55.

ADMINISTRATION AND DEFENCE OF THE INDIAN STATE: THE BUREAUCRACY, THE POLICE, AND CIVIL–MILITARY RELATIONS

The bureaucracy

The British ruled India through a bureaucratic system, whose primary functions were the maintenance of law and order and the collection of revenue. The fear of disorder and disintegration of the new Indian state at Independence, occasioned by the partition of the country, communal violence, and the problems involved in integrating the princely states into the Indian Union caused the leadership of independent India to rely heavily on the existing bureaucratic apparatus and to put aside any ideas of reform. At the highest levels of government in India, in fact, senior officers of the Indian Administrative Service (IAS), especially those in the Prime Minister's Secretariat created under Prime Minister Lal Bahadur Shastri, have at times become more influential than Cabinet ministers. Mrs. Gandhi especially relied upon a few senior officers in her Secretariat to carry out her political bidding as well as to provide her with policy advice. Many of the senior bureaucrats welcomed her Emergency regime. Consequently, when the Janata Government came to power, most of the senior officers closely identified with the Emergency regime were transferred to undesirable postings or suspended from service under charges of corruption. The post-Independence structure of political–bureaucratic relationships has consequently been fundamentally transformed in the direction of a patrimonial regime in which the political leadership selects officers who are personally loyal, who serve their narrow political interests, and who expect reciprocal preferments in return.[21]

The highest levels of the state administration, as well as of the central government, are staffed by IAS officers. Below the elite all-India services, there are several layers of bureaucracy in both the central and provincial governments, including the higher state civil services as well as vast armies of clerks, peons, and messengers at the lower levels. The numbers of government employees in central, state, quasi-government, and local bodies quadrupled from approximately

---

[21] Bhagwan D. Dua has used the term patrimonialism also to apply to the selection and dismissal of chief ministers in "Federalism or Patrimonialism: The Making and Unmaking of Chief Ministers in India," *Asian Survey*, xxv, No. 8 (August, 1985), 793–804.

four million in 1953 to more than sixteen million in 1983.[22] At the end
of 1988, the total had reached nearly 18.5 million.[23] The pay and
emoluments of government servants constitute a major drain on state
revenues and resources to such an extent that they constitute a leading
cause of the deficiency in resources needed to increase public sector
capital investment in the economy.

The decision to retain the IAS system of bureaucratic control was
associated also with the decision of the Constituent Assembly in favor
of a predominantly centralized system of government with federal
features. The proponents of an alternative, "Gandhian" tradition have
succeeded from time to time in having institutional reforms enacted to
introduce measures of decentralization. In fact, however, the planning
process, including the articulation of goals, the allocation of resources,
and the systems of bureaucratic control and accountability everywhere
in India have remained highly centralized.

Below the IAS level and the level of the senior officers in other
branches of administrative service, the bureaucracy is generally ineffective and non-cooperative in most areas of policy implementation.
Although there remains some doubt about the extent to which corruption has penetrated the IAS officer cadres, there is universal agreement
that bribe-taking on a small scale at the lowest levels and extensive,
massive corruption at the middle and higher levels up to and including
some IAS officers is endemic and pervasive. In order to serve the needs
of the people, therefore, "middlemen," "fixers," and "brokers" have
sprung up in the countryside to serve as intermediaries between
villagers and bureaucracy to make actually available to the people the
agricultural, medical, and other services that are supposed to be provided under myriad government programs.[24]

Thus, both at the top and the bottom, the Indian administrative
system that has evolved since Independence departs significantly from
"Weberian" criteria of a rational legal system.[25] The mechanisms, ties,
and attachments that make the system work are based rather on

[22] David C. Potter, *India's Political Administrators: 1919–1983* (Oxford: Clarendon
Press, 1986), p. 159.

[23] Calculated from Government of India, Ministry of Planning, Department of Statistics,
Central Statistical Organisation, *Monthly Abstract of Statistics*, XLIII, No. 12 (December,
1990), 4.

[24] G. Ram Reddy and G. Haragopal, "The Pyraveekar: 'The Fixer' in Rural India," *Asian
Survey*, xxv, No. 11 (November, 1985), 1149.

[25] Reddy and Haragopal, "The Pyraveekar," p. 1152.

personal and social obligations to patrons and clients, kin and caste fellows, on informal connections, and on illegal fee-for-service cash payments. Although they are subordinate at the highest levels to the most powerful political leaders and at the lower levels to powerful local politicians, the higher grades of the Indian bureaucracy dominate routine decision making and, in the frequent absence of ministerial leadership, general policy making in both the central and state governments. They are no longer the elite "rulers of India" but the leading elements of a vast dominant class, whose members are the principal beneficiaries of the benefits and resources produced and distributed through the agency of the Indian state.

The police

The central government maintains several large police forces including, among others, the Central Bureau of Intelligence, the Central Reserve Police, the Border Security Force, the Central Industrial Security Forces (who maintain order at public sector industrial enterprises), and the Indo-Tibetan Border Police (see table 2.3). The domestic police force proper, however, is under the control of the state governments. In 1983, it comprised 709,743 men (civil and armed). The percentage increase in the police strength (table 2.4) has roughly kept pace between 1953 and 1983 (plus 87 percent) with the percentage increase in the total population of the country (plus 89 percent), but these figures did not include a number of other special duty police forces. Also, the state police forces are supplemented by Provincial Armed Constabularies, which are often called out for duty during riots and other major disturbances. Their numbers are estimated at 250,000 (table 2.3).

The administrative structure of the Indian Police Service (IPS) is similar to that of the IAS. It is an all-India service, divided into state cadres. The IPS officers constitute an elite corps whose members fill virtually all the senior state and district police administrative positions. Officers advance from assistant superintendent of police (SP) in a district to district SP and ultimately to a deputy inspector-general or to an inspector-general position in the state capital in charge of an entire branch of state police administration. During the British period and into much of the post-Independence period, the SP was under the control of the district magistrate, but the SPs are now directly

Table 2.3. *Military, paramilitary, and provincial armed force levels in India, 1990–91*

Force	Number
Armed forces	1,265,000
Army	1,100,000
Navy	55,000
Air Force	110,000
Paramilitary Forces	449,800
Border Security Force	140,000
Central Reserve Police Force	100,000
Railway Protection Forces	60,000
Central Industrial Security Forces	55,000
Defense Security Force	30,000
Indo-Tibetan Border Police	22,000
Assam Rifles	15,000
Special Frontier Force	10,000
National Rifles	10,000
National Security Guards	5,000
Coastguard	2,800
Provincial Armed Constabularies	250,000

Source: The Military Balance, 1991–1992 (London: The International Institute for Strategic Studies, 1991), pp. 162–164.

responsible for the police administration in their districts to the state inspectors-general and are no longer considered to be subordinate to the district magistrates. Below the IPS cadre is the rank of deputy SP, which is recruited by the state public service commission; below that rank are the inspectors and sub-inspectors, recruited at the district level; and at the bottom are the constables recruited by the district SP. The pay and service conditions of the IPS are comparable to those of the IAS, but those of the constables are wretched, below those of peons in civil administration.

In addition to the ordinary police establishment which carries out the routine police work and maintenance of public order on a daily basis, each state also has a substantial armed police force, known as the Provincial Armed Constabulary, which is a reserve force whose units remain in barracks most of the time, to be called out on special duty to deal with large-scale disturbances to public order.

Table 2.4. *Growth in strength of police force, 1953–83*

Year	Police strength	Percent increase	Total population (in millions)[a]	Percent increase
1953	379,130		361	
1963	473,603	25 ⎤	439	22 ⎤
1973	566,902	20 ⎬ 87	547	25 ⎬ 89
1983	709,743	25 ⎦	684	25 ⎦

Source: Government of India, Ministry of Planning, Department of Statistics, Central Statistical Organization, *Statistical Abstract of India*, 1987, 1975, 1967, 1955–56 (New Delhi: Government of India Press, 1988, 1976, 1968, 1957), tables on strength and cost of civil police.
[a]Figures in this column are for nearest censuses of 1953, 1963, 1973, and 1983, respectively.

The Indian police have become increasingly politicized in the past two decades from the local up to the national level. The more powerful district politicians want pliable and responsive SPs and Deputy SPs, who in turn require the support and patronage of the politicians. The principal sanctions which the politicians have to influence the police are the power to transfer constables to remote parts of their districts and senior officers to undesirable districts, protect corrupt police from criminal prosecution, and influence promotions. At the local level, protection from police victimization and the use of the police to harass one's rivals have become critical elements in the powers of local politicians. Politicians in the districts of India who wish to build a stable political base for themselves, therefore, must not only be able to distribute money and patronage, but must also be able to control the police.[26] The police in turn must have powerful political allies if they are to be effective and to advance their own careers.

Political involvement of the police in contemporary political controversies reached a peak during and after the Emergency when the police at all levels were called upon to arrest most of the important

[26] Bayley, "The Police and Political Order in India," *Asian Survey*, XXIII, No. 4 (April, 1983), 487, and Paul R. Brass, "National Power and Local Politics in India: A Twenty-Year Perspective," in Paul R. Brass, *Caste, Faction and Party in Indian Politics*, Vol. 1: *Faction and Party* (Delhi: Chanakaya, 1984), pp. 191–226.

opposition leaders in the country and to keep under surveillance many others, including leading figures in the ruling Congress (I) itself. After the Emergency, the Janata government replaced senior police officers who had acted partially and, allegedly, overzealously in supporting the Emergency.

The persistence in post-Independence India of Gandhian techniques of mass mobilization and the spread of group violence in communal riots, student agitations, and massive political demonstrations against the government of the day have increasingly involved the police in confrontations with the people. Police firings on unarmed crowds, participation of the police in brutal attacks on minorities, and pro-vocative actions against peaceful demonstrators that provoke them to commit acts of violence have become commonplace in contemporary India. During the past decade in Punjab, the police along with other security and armed forces have been engaged in an extremely bitter and bloody internal war in which even the families of police officers and of suspected terrorists have been deliberately killed in mutual retaliations.

The combination of increased group violence, decline of legitimate political authority in the countryside, politicization and criminali-zation of the police, and their involvement in incidents of violence has contributed to an increasingly pervasive Hobbesian state of disorder, unpredictability and fear of violence among ordinary people in the rural areas of India. The overall contemporary performance of the police in India, therefore, can no longer be considered appropriate to a free, democratic, impartial political order. In many parts of urban and rural India, the police are not in fact maintaining order, but are them-selves among the most dangerous and disorderly forces in the country.

The military and civilian–military relations[27]

India has one of the largest military forces in the world (see table 2.3) and one that has been continuously active since Independence in a wide range of actions, including the fighting of four wars, the takeover of Goa from the Portuguese in 1961, the intervention in the Sri Lankan civil war in 1987, and numerous domestic operations in support of the civil authorities.

[27] This section relies heavily on the works of Stephen P. Cohen. Specific references are given in the footnotes below.

The politicization that has so affected the bureaucracy and the police services and which has contributed to a decline in the effectiveness of their performance has not affected the functioning of the Indian military to the same degree.

The British reproduced in India the Anglo-Saxon pattern of civilian control over the military, whose officers were taught that the military must remain a politically neutral arm of the state. The values of senior Congress leaders also fostered military subordination to civilian leadership. In contrast to the pattern in many other developing countries, including neighboring Pakistan where an alliance of the civilian and military bureaucrats developed against the politicians, in India an early alliance developed between the politicians and the civilian bureaucracy to control the military. Specific steps taken to reduce military influence and to ensure civilian control included the removal of the Commander-in-Chief from the first Cabinet in independent India, followed by the abolition of the position itself, leaving no overall commander of all the armed forces other than the civilian head of government; the subordination of all three military chiefs to the civilian Defense Minister, who has usually been either a confidant of the Prime Minister or a powerful politician; and, in recent years, the use of the more doubtful practice of appointing only politically acceptable persons as commanders of the several armed forces.[28]

There is an alternative tradition of militarization of politics and of the infusion of nationalism with military values, represented in the nationalist period by Subhas Chandra Bose, the founder of the Indian National Army which fought against the British in Asia during World War II.[29] Since Independence, political leaders have emphasized the indispensability of a strong military for the maintenance of India as a powerful and respected country and have at times introduced into Indian nationalism a military element.

Military leaders have resented the extent of civilian control over their actions, the lack of specialized military knowledge of the civilian leadership, and their own limited role in the making of military

---

[28] Stephen P. Cohen, *The Indian Army: Its Contribution to the Development of a Nation* (Berkeley: University of California Press, 1971), p. 171, and "The Military and Indian Democracy," in Atul Kohli (ed.), *India's Democracy: An Analysis of Changing State–Society Relations* (Princeton, N.J.: Princeton University Press, 1987), pp. 115–121.

[29] Stephen P. Cohen, "The Military," in Hart (ed.), *Indira Gandhi's India*, pp. 210–211.

policies.[30] Internal discontents also have developed in the Indian army in recent years over pay, status, and declining opportunities for promotion. The potential for military intervention in Indian politics nevertheless remains low. There has never been an attempted *coup* in India. Even if the will to intervene were present, the obstacles to effective intervention are formidable. The military itself is too large and divided to imagine the possibility of a united leadership implementing a *coup*. The conditions which have led to or been used as a justification for military intervention in other Asian and African countries – such as political instability, widespread corruption, absence of electoral legitimacy of the civilian politicians, politicization of the military – have either not been present in India or have not been present in the same combination or else have not progressed to the same extent. With the exception of the period just before and during the Emergency, the legitimacy of the political leadership has never been seriously questioned. A *coup* remains highly unlikely, the subordination of the military to civilian leadership remains firm, and the government in Delhi continues to be led by legitimately elected authority.[31]

The more serious problems concerning the contemporary role of the military in Indian society pertain to the increasing use of the army – on the average 40 to 50 times per year – by the political authorities in domestic disturbances of all sorts, particularly to deal with major incidents of violence.[32] The increased use of the army to quell domestic violence is reflected in the figures showing the number of occasions on which it was called upon for this purpose between 1951 to 1970 and 1979 to 1984. In the earlier twenty-year period, the army was called out 476 times. In the later five-year period, the army was called out 433 times.[33]

Several paramilitary forces were created in the 1950s and 1960s specifically to handle situations that were beyond the capabilities of the local police. However, the army has had to be called in on several occasions to restore order within these forces themselves. In addition to its use to deal with specific disturbances, the army has also been

[30] Cohen, "The Military and Indian Democracy," p. 117.
[31] Cohen, "The Military and Indian Democracy," pp. 138–139.
[32] Cohen, "The Military and Indian Democracy," pp. 124–127.
[33] Mathur, "The State and the Use of Coercive Power in India," pp. 345–346.

stationed permanently or for long periods in several Indian states, continuously in Kashmir since 1947 and for long periods since 1983–84 in the troubled states of Assam and Punjab. One long-term danger to the Indian political system, therefore, is of a militarization of politics and a politicization and demoralization of the army arising from its widespread use as a mechanism of political control in a society tending towards anomie.

CENTER–STATE RELATIONS

India today is a Union of twenty-five states. The leadership of the Congress and the Constituent Assembly at Independence was firmly in the hands of those who believed in the necessity for a strong, centralized state in India. In the Indian federal system, therefore, there is a considerable array of central powers in relation to the states and numerous unitary features. They include the following: 1) separate lists of legislative powers for the Center and the states, but with a concurrent list in which the Center may claim priority, with residuary powers left to the Union, and with the power held in reserve in emergencies and other situations for the Center to legislate on matters contained in the state list; 2) the power of the Center to create new states and to revise the boundaries of or even eliminate existing federal units; 3) the retention by the Center of control over the most lucrative sources of taxation and the authority to collect certain taxes on behalf of the states and to distribute the revenues among them; 4) the power of the Center to take over the administration of a state and declare President's Rule under specified conditions that have been interpreted very broadly; 5) the power to declare a national emergency that, in effect, may convert the country into a unitary state.

In practice, however, despite strong centralizing drives by Congress governments in Delhi, especially during Mrs. Gandhi's leadership, there have been recurring problems in center–state relations and long-term trends that favor regionalism, pluralism, and decentralization.[34] For one thing, the states retain sole or primary constitutional authority over several important subjects, particularly agriculture (including

---

[34] Paul R. Brass, "Pluralism, Regionalism, and Decentralizing Tendencies in Contemporary Indian Politics," in A. J. Wilson and Dennis Dalton (eds.), *The States of South Asia: Problems of National Integration* (London: C. Hurst, 1982), pp. 223–264.

taxation of agriculture) education, law and order and the police, health, welfare, and local government. By action or non-action in these areas, the states may prevent the adoption of uniform policies for the country which the national leadership considers essential for the general processes of economic growth, development, and social justice. For example, the central leadership of the Congress insisted throughout the 1960s and into the 1970s that more substantial agrarian reforms through land ceilings and redistribution were important to reduce social and economic inequalities in the countryside. However, it is generally recognized that such reforms have been very limited in most states. The central policies themselves have, in consequence, been abandoned. Similarly, since the early 1960s, the Planning Commission has pleaded for increased agricultural taxation, but the state responses have often been quite in the opposite direction.

Moreover, even the effective use by the Government of India of central agencies such as the Finance Commission and the Planning Commission to implement national goals has often proved impossible because of the resistance of powerful state leaders. The Finance Commissions, for example, which are responsible for the distribution to the states of centrally collected taxes, have done little to rectify regional imbalances among states. The Planning Commission, which was designed to introduce a system of centralized economic planning, has never been able to ensure implementation of its goals by the states and has in general declined in influence during the past two decades. Although the Center has several times used the emergency provisions of the Constitution, especially during the 1975 to 1977 period, and has often imposed President's Rule on individual states, both of which allow it to exercise considerable direct control over the administration of the states, these measures are symptomatic of an overall weakening of effective central and state government in India rather than indications of permanent centralization.

Moreover, there have been recurring problems arising out of India's enormous cultural diversity. During Nehru's tenure in office, most linguistic, regional, and minority conflicts and controversies were ultimately resolved through pluralistic mechanisms. During Mrs. Gandhi's periods in office, however, especially in the 1980s, several issues developed into major challenges to the unity of India and to amicable relations among its major ethnic and religious communities.

By the end of the 1980s and the early 1990s, the Government of India was confronted with three open secessionist movements in Kashmir, Punjab, and Assam (see chapter 6) against which its police and armed forces were heavily engaged. Some of these problems were exacerbated by the centralizing drives of and the involvement of the central leaders themselves in political manipulation in the states in contrast to the Nehru period when the central government preferred to stand back from such problems as far as possible and adopt arbitrating and mediating roles (see chapters 5–7 below).

ADAPTATION, CHANGE, AND STRAINS IN INDIA'S FEDERAL PARLIAMENTARY SYSTEM

With the exception of the two-year Emergency period from 1975 to 1977, India has maintained a fuctioning parliamentary system modeled upon the British pattern. Like the British system itself, the Indian has developed in the direction of prime ministerial dominance, although both Parliament and the Cabinet have become less significant in India than in Great Britain. The Indian adaptations of the British system of prime ministerial government, however, have involved more than a strengthening of the office of Prime Minister at the expense of Parliament and the Cabinet. Rather, the sytem has been adapted to two distinctive sets of Indian political practices. The predominant one may be characterized as a patrimonial system centering around the Nehru family. A secondary one which has emerged at the Center on those occasions when the Congress has been defeated is a pattern of politics which prevails at the state and local levels in India, centering around personal ambition, inter-personal conflict, and political opportunism.

Federalism also has been adapted in particular ways to Indian conditions. Federalism is a system of government commonly designed to ensure a significant measure of autonomy to state units in continental and/or culturally diverse societies. Though India is both a sub-continental state and the most culturally diverse country in the world today, the federal system adopted has had from the beginning more unitary features than most other large federal systems, more notably that of the United States. Then, during the period of Mrs. Gandhi's preeminence, the states, expecially those in which the Congress remained the dominant party and which had retained political autonomy during the Nehru period, gave up much of it to a highly directive central leadership. Yet, at the same time, a counter-tendency was at work resisting the increased central control, taking the form – primarily in those states not ruled by the Congress – of increased articulation of regional political identities. In some cases, as in Andhra, the enhancement of central power *vis-à-vis* the states itself precipitated the new assertion of regional political and social forces.

These counter-tendencies and struggles between centralizing and regionalizing tendencies and social forces have also contributed to feelings not always openly expressed that the system ought to be changed formally in one direction or the other. One view favors the transformation of India's federal parliamentary system into a presidential government, more of the French than the American type, which would increase central authority. The justification for this view is the need for greater powers to bring order to disturbed areas of the country, to get rid of corruption, and to bring about more rapid social and economic change. On the other hand, the political elites in several states have from time to time expressed the opposite view that what is needed is to reduce the power of the Center and give the states greater autonomy, to reduce the meddling of the center in state politics and allow the states to use their own tax resources to develop their economies in their own ways.

In a curious twist, which has for some advocates a deep emotional significance and for others is merely a political tactic, persons with both centralizing and regionalizing views have called for a thoroughgoing decentralization of Indian politics to the local level, to the districts and villages of the country. Those who want more regional autonomy suspect any such moves initiated by the Center as merely a device to undermine state authority whereas the centralizers remain suspicious of demands coming from state political leaders which will remove state and local institutions ever further from central control. Complicating the clear expression of alternative views still further is the association of terms such as "regional autonomy" with demands made by insurrectionary and secessionist groups in Punjab, Kashmir, and the northeastern part of the country.

CHAPTER 3

PARTIES AND POLITICS

Party politics in India display numerous paradoxical features, which reveal the blending of Western and modern forms of bureaucratic organization and participatory politics with indigenous practices and institutions. India's leading political party, the Indian National Congress, is one of the oldest in the world, yet it has not succeeded in providing the nucleus for an institutionalized party system which can be fitted easily into any one of the conventional categories of party systems known in the West. There has been a strong Marxist and Communist revolutionary tradition in modern Indian political history. However, unlike other such traditions in most parts of Asia, its dominant parties and movements have neither succeeded in threatening the stability of the Indian state nor been threatened with physical extinction as in Indonesia, but have instead been integrated in the form of reformist political parties within routine politics in the country. The diversities and social fragmentation of Indian society have produced a proliferation of regional and other political parties which often give to each state in the Indian Union a unique party system imperfectly integrated into the "national party system." Some characteristically Indian features pervade virtually all parties in the country – factionalism, dynastic succession to leadership, and the presence of ideological differences among the parties without ideological cleavage in the party system.

Indian politics are distinctive among contemporary developing societies in having had forty-five years of nearly continuous – excepting the brief Emergency period – competitive electoral politics in which also alternation in power has occurred in all the Indian states and at the Center as well. Here, also, there are numerous paradoxical features and indigenous adaptations of an essentially British electoral system. These include: varying, but often quite high turnout rates among a population still overwhelmingly agrarian and illiterate; a special form of representation for "untouchables" or Scheduled Castes; electoral arenas not yet fully dominated and controlled by organized political parties; and the critical importance of the electoral process as a mechanism for the successive introduction of groups of voters, particularly caste groups, into politics, which impart to the Indian electoral process a quality which is quite different from the classic ideal of the electoral arena as a place where the "independent intelligence of the individual voter"[1] is exercised.

A diversity of interest associations also exists in Indian politics, which give the impression that India is a pluralist society, like the United States, in which the parties "aggregate" the interests of a multiplicity of private associations into public policies and in which the groups also exercise some independent influence over policy making. The impression, however, is only partly correct for, with Indian interest groups as with the parties, there are substantial differences in the types of interests, their organizational form, and their manner of operation. These differences include, among others, the limited sectors in Indian society in which formally organized interest associations operate, the considerable importance of informal movements which arise from time to time claiming to represent large unorganized sectors of society, the existence of specifically Indian types of interest associations, including revivalist movements and caste associations, the importance also of a wholly different type of "representation" in the form of intermediaries between the people and the bureaucracy, and the far greater importance of interest groups and intermediaries in the implementation as opposed to the formation of public policy. Moreover, in recent years, there has been a proliferation of non-party movements which are rare in stable representative systems, that is, explicitly violent secessionist and protest movements of various types. In the ensuing confrontations between such groups and state security forces, new interest associations have come into being to monitor, protest, and condemn violence and atrocities committed by both sides.

Thus, the tensions between authoritarian and democratic, centraliz-

---

[1] James Bryce, "Preface," in M. Ostrogorski, *Democracy and the Organization of Political Parties*, trans. by Frederick Clarke, Vol. 1 (New York: Macmillan, 1922). Bryce's statement reflects an ideal, which few would claim has been anything but imperfectly realized even in Western representative systems, but the ideal nevertheless underlies much, if not most, public discussion and scholarly analysis of the electoral process, for example especially in currently fashionable "rational choice" modeling of voting behaviour as well as other types of decision making in representative systems.

ing and decentralizing tendencies are evident in the party and associational sectors of Indian political life as well as in the formal institutional sector. These tensions find expression in the struggle among organized political parties, among which some focus on national, others on regional power. They find expression also in voting where the major parties and leaders contending for power at the Center seek to find general, transcendent, national issues to appeal to large categories of voters across regional boundaries while other parties focus on regional issues and many voters continue to be concerned primarily with the local affairs of their village and caste group. These tensions occur most dramatically nowadays in direct confrontations between central government security forces and secessionist and other organized groups making free use of violence to advance their regional and local aims and causes.

PARTIES AND PARTY SYSTEMS

The Indian National Congress

Parties, elections, and representative government came gradually to India during British rule. The Indian National Congress, the party which led the nationalist movement and took power after Independence, was founded in 1885. In the intervening years, the Congress went through several transformations. It began as a pressure group petitioning the government for political and administrative reforms. After the 1920s, the Congress became a mass membership party alternating between the use of strategies of mass mobilization under the leadership of Mahatma Gandhi and contesting elections to provincial and national legislatures. From 1935, with the introduction of provincial self-government, the Congress began the third change toward a governing party in the majority of provinces of British-ruled India, culminating in its emergence as the ruling party of the country at Independence in 1947.[2] The Indian National Congress is formally a mass party with a dues-paying membership divided into two categories of primary and active members and with an elaborate, hierarchical organizational structure extending from local to district to

[2] This paragraph has been borrowed from Paul R. Brass, "Democracy and Political Participation in India," in Myron L. Cohen (ed.), *Asia: Case Studies in the Social Sciences, A Guide for Teaching* (New York: M. E. Sharpe, 1992), p. 283.

state to all-India committees culminating at the top in a Working Committee, the executive committee of the national party, with an elected President as its head (figure 1). Other important structures during the Nehru period were the state and central Parliamentary Boards, which played the decisive roles in the allocation of party nominations to Congressmen to contest elections to the state legislative assemblies and to Parliament.

Although the formal structure was important in Nehru's days, more important was an informal structure of factional linkages and relationships from the local to the national level. Factions contested for control of the important committees at each level through formal elections preceded by membership drives in which competing faction leaders attempted to enroll, even if only on paper, as many member-supporters as possible. Although the factional conflicts which developed often became intense and bitter and were accompanied by frequent charges of "bogus enrollments," they also served to keep the party organization alive and to compel party leaders to build support in the districts and localities throughout the country.

Factional conflicts within the Congress ultimately culminated in struggles for control of the state governments themselves, with most states in the country divided between a ministerial wing, the faction which dominated the government and sometimes, but not always, the party organization as well and a dissident wing which struggled to gain control of the party organization in order to use it as a base to gain control of the government. Occasionally groups formed within the Congress to articulate general or particular points of view on public policy issues, but most factions – and the structure of the system as a whole – were non-ideological in nature.

Although the Congress organization, therefore, was in the 1950s and 1960s a highly factionalized, internally competitive party, ruled by personal opportunism rather than ideology, factional conflict terminated at the highest levels where, from 1950–51 onward, Nehru remained in complete mastery of policy and politics. Indeed, the national leadership of the party in those days was called the "High Command." It consisted of the trusted political confidants of Nehru who would also act as his mediators and arbitrators of factional conflicts at the state level, which threatened to get out of hand and, therefore, threatened the ability of the Congress to retain power in a state.

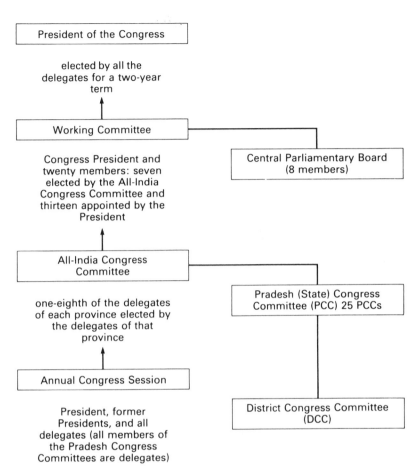

Figure 1   Indian National Congress, organization chart

Adapted from Stanley A. Kochanek, *The Congress Party of India*
(Princeton, N.J.: Princeton University Press, 1968), p. xxii and Myron
Weiner, *Party Building in a New Nation: The Indian National Congress*
(Chicago: University of Chicago Press, 1967), p. 41.

After the death of Nehru, and in the course of the grand succession struggle which followed between 1965 and 1972, Mrs. Gandhi emerged as the unchallenged leader of the dominant Congress party, which came to be called Congress (R) for Requisitioned – referring to a requisitioned party meeting summoned by Mrs. Gandhi during the split – but later meaning Ruling Congress. After a second split in the party in 1977, following an unsuccessful challenge to her leadership from Congressmen discontented with the effects of her leadership on the Congress organization during the Emergency, the Congress of Mrs. Gandhi became known as Congress (I) for Indira. The adoption of the designation Congress (I) also symbolized what had happened to the Congress organization under Mrs. Gandhi's leadership. It had become, in effect, her personal party, dependent upon her populist, sometimes demagogic leadership rather than on local party organization, to win elections.

Though factional conflict between ministerialist and dissident wings of the state party organizations continued, they were not usually allowed to run their course. Most decisions concerning the selection of the chief ministers of the states, the councils of ministers in the states, and the important leaders of the appointed PCCs were made by Mrs. Gandhi herself in consultation with a clique of personal advisers, some of whom were initially important politicians from different states in the country. Gradually, however, the party came to be controlled by personal retainers of the Nehru family and by members of the immediate family, including especially Sanjay Gandhi until his death in 1981.

The extent to which a great national movement had become converted into a Nehru family patrimony was indicated by the immediate and unquestioning acceptance of Rajiv Gandhi as Prime Minister of the country and leader of the Congress upon his mother's assassination on October 31, 1984. Rajiv began his tenure with a resolve to reform and democratize the Congress organization. He called in 1985 for the holding of party elections early in 1986.[3] However, in the face of his rapid decline in popularity and the prospect of further threats to his power that appeared to emerge as the date for party elections approached, Rajiv cancelled the plan for elections. The Congress continued under his leadership to be highly centralized, with state and

---

[3] Atul Kohli, *Democracy and Discontent: India's Growing Crisis of Governability* (Cambridge: Cambridge University Press, 1990), pp. 340–350.

local leadership fragmented, and with an absence of organizational vitality. What vitality was provided was of an ugly sort, in which the hooligan element in the party, recruited by Sanjay Gandhi during the Emergency, again began to play prominent roles.[4]

The dependence of the Congress on the Nehru family appeared even more evident, and pathetically so, after the assassination of Rajiv Gandhi on May 21, 1991. With no mature Nehru descendants left to take up the leadership of the party, a group of Rajiv's closest followers sought to persuade his mourning Italian-born wife, Sonia Gandhi, who had never played any important role or shown any interest in politics beyond helping her husband at election time, to accept the presidency of the party. Upon her refusal, a struggle took place among top leaders of the Congress from which P. V. Narasimha Rao emerged triumphant as the first Congress leader and Prime Minister not from the Nehru family since the brief interregnum of Lal Bahadur Shastri.

Lacking the authority of membership in the Nehru dynasty and facing challenges to his leadership and policies from senior Congress politicians with bases in their home states, notably Arjun Singh from Madhya Pradesh and Sharad Pawar from Maharashtra, Narasimha Rao sought to legitimize and strengthen his leadership by calling for party organizational elections for the first time in two decades. Elections at the local and state levels of the party organization were held in several states, but in others the state party leaders preferred instead to have Narasimha Rao himself appoint the state party Presidents, continuing the practice of Indira and Rajiv Gandhi.[5] Elections were held for the Working Committee at the AICC session held in Tirupathi in April, 1992.[6] Narasimha Rao was himself elected President of the Indian National Congress, the first elected President of the party in twenty years.[7] However, it is not clear whether or not the reopening of the Congress organization to competitive election procedures constitutes a step toward full restoration of the practices which prevailed during Nehru's time or a temporary measure in a developing succession struggle for supreme leadership of the party.

The Congress, therefore, though it remains formally a mass party became in the 1970s and 1980s a cadre party with a prominent popular

[4] Kohli, *Democracy and Discontent*, pp. 350–352.
[5] *India Today*, March 15 and April 30, 1992.
[6] *India Today*, October 15, 1992.   [7] *India Today*, April 30, 1992.

leader at its head while the organization at the local level was dominated by notables who maintained strong local structures of power
within their caste groups or in the remnants of old landed estates, or
through control of educational institutions, cooperative societies, or
other government or private organizations. In many districts, the
Congress lacked even locally powerful or popular leaders and became
a collection of appointees whose local influence depended on their ties
with persons connected to the Nehru family. In effect, the Congress
organization as an institutionalized force disintegrated at the local
level in large parts of the country, if not universally.[8]

In most states, particularly in north India and in Maharashtra, the
Congress leaders come from the elite – or at least middle status –
land-controlling, dominant castes in the countryside. In only a few
states, notably Karnataka and Gujarat, have Congress leaders been
recruited from the lower castes.

Popular support for the Congress, however, has been much broader
than its leadership. A basic, somewhat paradoxical, coalition was put
together early after Independence and strengthened under Mrs.
Gandhi, consisting of strong support from the extremes of the social
order, from the elite, land-controlling castes at the top, on the one
hand, and from the low castes, the poor, and disadvantaged, including
many minority groups, on the other hand.

The existence of this formidable coalitional support base combined
with the enormous popularity of the Nehru family leaders made the
Congress the center of the party system, which scholars came to label a
one-party dominant system to indicate at once the centrality of the
Congress in the system and the peripherality of the opposition to the
Congress in the country. In fact, however, the label has always been
something of a misnomer. It was always obvious that, since the
Congress itself rarely polled a majority of votes in most states and only
once since Independence, in 1984, nearly did so at the Center, Congress

---

[8] These remarks are based especially upon my own resurvey in 1982–83 of five districts of
north India which I first visited in 1961–63 and on a similar resurvey by Atul Kohli of five
districts around the country initially visited by Myron Weiner in 1961–62. See Paul R. Brass,
"National Power and Local Politics in India: A Twenty-year Perspective," in Paul R. Brass,
Caste, Faction and Party in Indian Politics, Vol. 1: *Faction and Party* (Delhi: Chanakya,
1983), esp. p. 194 and *passim*; Kohli, *Democracy and Discontent*, pt. 11; Paul R. Brass,
Factional Politics in an Indian State: The Congress Party in Uttar Pradesh (Berkeley:
University of California Press, 1965); and Myron Weiner, *Party Building in a New Nation:
The Indian National Congress* (Chicago: University of Chicago Press, 1967).

dominance was only partly a result of its own electoral strength. Equally important was the disunity of the opposition which, if it could be overcome, as it was in 1977, could lead to the displacement of the Congress from power at the Center (see tables 3.1, 3.2, and 3.3). Many opposition parties were quite serious about building counter-movements to challenge the Congress and several gradually developed strong support bases in different regions of the country. Finally, there has never really been a single, national party system but instead each region of the country has had its own distinctive party system in most of which the Congress was the dominant party, but itself had a distinctive social base and pattern of relationship with opposition parties in each state.

In the aftermath of the death of Rajiv Gandhi, the Congress is weaker electorally and organizationally than at any time since the 1977 elections. Moreover, it can no longer be said that the Congress is a strong force in every major state of the Indian Union, for it has been reduced to third position electorally in two of the largest states, Uttar Pradesh and Tamil Nadu. Although, therefore, the Congress remains the preeminent party in the country, the system itself can no longer be considered a "one-party dominant" system.[9] Congress preeminence is indicated by the still considerable interval between its popular vote and seat shares – even in 1989 and 1991 – and that of the next largest party, which was 22 percent in 1989 and 17 percent in 1991 for vote shares and 10 and 22 percent, respectively, for seat shares (table 3.3). On the other hand, the Congress has now failed to win a majority of seats in the Lok Sabha in three of the five most recent elections held between 1977 and 1991.

After the last two elections, the national "party system," as reflected in the distribution of seats by party and in the alliance patterns among the parties, took on the form of a loose three/four coalition system in which "national" parties combined with regional and other small parties in Alliances or Fronts to enhance their positions and to coordinate their policies and actions in the House. After the by-elections held in November, 1991, Congress stood at the center of the largest such coalition in which its own representation of 227 was increased to

<hr>

[9] For a technical discussion of this issue, see Giovanni Sartori, *Parties and Party Systems: A Framework for Analysis*, Vol. 1 (Cambridge: Cambridge University Press, 1976), pp. 192–200.

Table 3.1. *Distribution by party of votes polled in Lok Sabha elections 1952–91 (in percentages)*

Year	INC/ INCI	NCO/ INCU/ INCJ/ INCS	CPI	CPM	SOC	PSP/ KMPP	SSP	SWA	BJS/ BJP	JNP/ SJP	JD	JNPS/ LD/ DMKP/ LKDB	Other parties	IND
1952	45.0	—	3.3	—	10.6	5.8	—	—	3.1	—	—	—	16.4	15.9
1957	47.8	—	8.9	—	—	10.4	—	—	5.9	—	—	—	7.6	19.4
1962	44.7	—	9.9	—	2.7	6.8	—	7.9	6.4	—	—	—	10.4	11.1
1967	40.8	—	5.0	4.4	—	3.1	4.9	8.7	9.4	—	—	—	10.1	13.7
1971	43.7	10.4	4.7	5.1	—	1.0	2.4	3.1	7.4	—	—	—	13.8	8.4
1977	34.5	1.7	2.8	4.3	—	—	—	—	—	41.3	—	—	9.8	5.5
1980	42.7	5.3	2.6	6.1	—	—	—	—	—	19.0	—	9.4	8.5	6.4
1984	48.1	1.6	2.7	5.7	—	—	—	—	7.4	6.7	—	5.6	14.1	8.1
1989	39.5	0.3	2.6	6.5	—	—	—	—	11.4	1.0	17.8	0.2	15.5	5.2
1991	36.4	0.4	2.5	6.3	—	—	—	—	20.2	3.4	11.6	0.1	15.3	3.9

INC: Indian National Congress
INCI: Indian National Congress (Indira)
NCO: Indian National Congress (Organization)
INCU: Indian National Congress (Urs)
INCJ: Indian National Congress (Jagjivan Ram)
INCS: Indian National Congress (Socialist)
CPI: Communist Party of India
CPM: Communist Party of India (Marxist)
SOC: Socialist Party
PSP: Praja Socialist Party
KMPP: Kisan Mazdoor Praja Party

SSP: Samyukta Socialist Party
SWA: Swatantra Party
BJS: Bharatiya Jan Sangh
BJP: Bharatiya Janata Party
JNP: Janata Party
SJP: Samajwadi Janata Party
JD: Janata Dal
JNPS: Janata Party (Secular)
LD: Lok Dal
DMKP: Dalit Mazdoor Kisan Party
LKDB: Lok Dal (B)
IND: Independent

Source: V. B. Singh and Shankar Bose, *Elections in India: Data Handbook on Lok Sabha Elections, 1952–85*, 2nd edn (New Delhi: Sage, 1984), pp. 25 and 650; 1989: David Butler et al., *India Decides: Elections 1952–1991* (New Delhi: LM Books, 1991), p. 90; 1991: *Lok Sabha Poll: An A.I.R. Analysis* (New Delhi: Government of India, News Services Division, All India Radio, 1991), pp. 187–188.

Table 3.2. Distribution by party of seats won in Lok Sabha elections, 1952–91

Year	INC/ INCI	NCO/ INCU/ INCJ/ INCS	CPI	CPM	SOC	PSP/ KMPP	SSP	SWA	BJS/ BJP	JNP/ SJP	JD	JNPS/ LD/ DMKP/ LKDB	Other parties	IND	Total
1952	364	—	16	—	12	9	—	—	3	—	—	—	47	38	489
1957	371	—	27	—	—	19	—	—	4	—	—	—	31	42	494
1962	361	—	29	—	6	12	—	18	14	—	—	—	34	20	494
1967	283	—	23	19	—	13	23	44	35	—	—	—	45	35	520
1971	352	16	23	25	—	2	3	8	22	—	—	—	53	14	518
1977	154	3	7	22	—	—	—	—	—	295	—	—	52	9	542
1980	353	13	11	36	—	—	—	—	—	31	—	41	35	9	529
1984	415	5	6	22	—	—	—	—	2	10	—	3	74	5	542
1989	197	1	12	33	—	—	—	—	85	—	143	—	46	12	529
1991	227	1	14	35	—	—	—	—	119	5	56	—	53	1	510

Source: V. B. Singh and Shankar Bose, *Elections in India: Data Handbook on Lok Sabha Elections, 1952–85*, 2nd edn (New Delhi: Sage, 1984), pp. 26–27 and 66c; 1989: David Butler et al., *India Decides: Elections 1952–1991* (New Delhi: LM Books, 1991), p. 90; 1991: *Lok Sabha Poll: An A.I.R. Analysis* (New Delhi: Government of India, News Services Division, All India Radio, 1991), pp. 187–188.

Table 3.3. *Vote and seat shares for Congress and second place party in ten parliamentary elections, 1952–91*

| | Vote | | | Seats | | | | |
| | Percentage | | | Number | | Percentage | | |
Election	Congress	2nd party	Interval	Congress	2nd party	Congress	2nd party	Interval
1952	45	11	34	364	16	74	3	71
1957	48	10	38	371	27	75	5	70
1962	45	10	35	361	29	73	6	67
1967	41	9	32	283	44	54	8	46
1971	44	10	34	352	25	68	5	63
1977	35	41	−6	154	295	28	54	−26
1980	43	19	24	353	41	67	8	59
1984	48	7	41	415	30[a]	77	6	71
1989	40	18	22	197	143	37	27	10
1991	37	20	17	227	119	45	23	22

[a] The TDP (Telugu Desam Party), a regional Andhra party not shown in table 3.1 and 3.2, actually won the second largest number of seats in this Lok Sabha.
Source: As for tables 3.1 and 3.2.

251 through an alliance with the AIADMK of Tamil Nadu (eleven seats) and four other small parties. The BJP alliance with the Shiv Sena of Maharashtra accounted for another 123 seats. A third coalition comprised two groupings: the Janata Dal-led National Front and the CPM-led Left Front, whose combined strength in the House was 140.[10] The Congress, therefore, remained the predominant party in the leading coalition, which provided support to P. V. Narasimha Rao sufficient only to form a minority government.[11] Although the government could count for some time on the likelihood that the two other Alliance/Fronts would not soon combine to vote it out of office, the position in which this placed the Congress was far removed from that which it occupied in 1984 after its landslide victory under Rajiv Gandhi's leadership.

[10] M. L. Ahuja and Sharda Paul, *1989–1991 General Elections in India (Including November 1991 By-Elections*, (New Delhi: Associated Publishing 1992), p. 150.
[11] The Congress position was enhanced after the postponed Punjab elections for the Lok Sabha held in February, 1992 in which the Congress gained an additional twelve seats. *India Today*, March 15, 1992.

Non-Congress parties

Radical and revolutionary parties and movements[12]

Radical parties and politics have constituted a second important style of politics of differing degrees of importance in different parts of the country. The Left itself has been broadly divided since the 1930s into two main streams – Socialist and Communist.

After Independence, both broad movements split into numerous new parties, sometimes merging for a brief time only to split again. In the end, the result of the post-Independence history of splits and mergers has been the virtual disappearance of the non-Communist Left as a major political force anywhere in India and the division of the Communist movement into two chief parties, one of which, the Communist Party of India (Marxist) or CPM, has achieved dominance in the state of West Bengal, was also dominant for a decade in the small adjacent state of Tripura, and retains considerable importance in the state of Kerala, while the other, the Communist Party of India (CPI), has important regional strength in Kerala, West Bengal, and Bihar.

Aside from the usual opportunistic reasons and leadership conflicts that have contributed to or been dominant factors in party splits among most parties in India, there has been a single principal theme which caused divisions in both the Socialist and Communist movements, namely, the stance to be taken toward the ruling Congress. Division on that issue, rather than divisions in the international Communist movement, were principally responsible for the split in the CPI in 1964, which led to the formation of the CPM, and for the splintering off from both Communist parties after 1969 of a number of romantic revolutionary and terrorist movements. The CPI, throughout most of its post-Independence history, has favored a strategy of alliance with the Congress or at least with "progressive elements" within the Congress, whereas the CPM has favored a more militant policy of opposition to the Congress. Both parties, however, have adhered to a parliamentary and reformist rather than to a violent, revolutionary path.

A similar division occurred among the non-Communist Left parties in the 1960s and constituted the principal ideological division between

---

[12] This section draws heavily from Paul R. Brass, "Political Parties of the Radical Left in South Asian Politics," in Paul R. Brass and Marcus F. Franda (eds.), *Radical Politics in South Asia* (Cambridge, MA: MIT Press, 1973), pp. 3–118.

the more militant Socialist wing led by Dr. Rammanohar Lohia and the less militant Praja Socialist Party. However, the Socialist parties ultimately disappeared as organized entities and their various leaders ended up in several political parties which no longer bore a Socialist label.

The Communist movement also experienced two prolonged periods of debate on the question of political tactics, that is, whether to pursue parliamentarism or revolution. The first period, in which the central focus of debate was the famous Communist-led insurrection in the Telangana region of Andhra, saw the "anti-capitalist strategy" of revolutionary confrontation with state authority defeated by 1950 both in theoretical debate and in practice by the intervention of the Indian army. From 1950 to 1967, despite the split in the CPI in 1964, there was a broad consensus on the pursuit of parliamentarism and a multi-class strategy.

If the first debate was precipitated by the Telangana insurrection, the second was inspired by the split from the CPM in Bengal of a local group of party activists who were leading a violent agitation in the Naxalbari subdivision of Darjeeling district. The incidents in Naxalbari were followed by the spread of revolutionary romanticism among numerous Communist splinter groups, using terrorist tactics in widely dispersed pockets of the Indian countryside. Although the Communist parties, particularly the CPM, were initially shaken by these developments, neither of the two established parties diverged from their essentially parliamentary and reformist paths.

Revolutionary movements, represented by such formations as the Communist Party of India (Marxist–Leninist) and various fragments of it, the People's War party, and numerous other small groups in Andhra Pradesh and elsewhere have not been able to mobilize large segments of the population at the national or state levels. They have failed to do so partly because of the police and military power of the Indian state and partly because of deficiencies in their ideology and tactics. Nevertheless, numerous local movements, some using violence, have continued to arise from time to time in several regions of the country.[13]

[13] Bhabani Sen Gupta, "Communism Further Divided," in Henry C. Hart (ed.), *Indira Gandhi's India: A Political System Reappraised* (Boulder, CO: Westview Press, 1976), pp. 158–159 and 163–164, and Ghanshyam Shah, "Grass-Roots Mobilization in Indian

Several other ideological issues have distinguished or divided the parties of the Left from each other and from the Congress. The Socialist parties tended to favor Gandhian economic proposals for labor-intensive, small-scale industrial development and decentralization of the planning process whereas the Communists have continued to demand an even more single-minded heavy industrialization strategy than that pursued by the Congress. The Socialist parties tended to adopt distinctive positions on contemporary international issues focusing on the role of India as an independent actor in South Asia and in the world as a whole, whereas the Communist parties were far more oriented toward the superpower struggle and toward a policy of alignment with the Socialist camp in that world struggle.

There has always been a high degree of regionalization of support for the Communist parties, whose strength was originally concentrated in Kerala, West Bengal, and Andhra. However, since the 1950s, the Communists have disintegrated organizationally in Andhra, have been confronted in Kerala with a powerful Congress-led counter-coalition, and have remained strongest primarily in West Bengal. The Communist parties have been strongest in areas where Congress dominance of the nationalist movement was weakest. Their regional strength, therefore, derives more from political-historical than from economic factors.

The bastions of the Socialist movement were Bihar and U. P. where the young Socialists took the lead in the 1942 Quit India movement. Socialist strength in north India, therefore, like Communist strength elsewhere, is explained best by political-historical rather than economic factors.

The lack of clear differentiation among India's rural classes combined with the continued economic-political predominance at the local level of the elite and middle status landed castes has led most Left parties to pursue multi-class strategies rather than focusing solely on the poor peasantry and the landless. Both Communist parties have developed considerable strength among industrial workers in the major cities in India, the CPM in Kerala has considerable strength among the rural proletariat, but both the CPI and the CPM have

Politics," in Atul Kohli (ed.), *India's Democracy: An Analysis of Changing State–Society Relations* (Princeton, N.J.: Princeton University Press, 1988), pp. 287, 291–293, and *passim*.

drawn broad support from the landed peasantry as well in areas where they have been strong.

India has been distinctive among non-Communist countries in the extent to which Communist parties have actually held power at the state level. In Kerala, the CPM leads a counter-coalition against a Congress-dominated coalition, with whom it alternates in power. In West Bengal, the CPM has become the dominant party and has been in power at the head of a Left coalition in which it is overwhelmingly dominant since 1977. Compared with the Congress, the Communist parties have tended in power to be more serious about and more effective in implementing measures of agrarian reform such as land ceilings, land redistribution, protection of tenants and sharecroppers, and programs for the poor to provide them with employment opportunities and income-producing assets.

Although the Communist parties are allowed to control state governments, there are limitations on the performance that can be expected from them in a federal system where so much power remains with the Center. Other factors limiting the ability of the Left parties to introduce more radical change have been the absence of Left unity, the threat of political repression by the Center if the radical parties attempt to do too much too fast, and the fact that one of the leading communist parties has often been in alliance with the ruling Congress party. The prospects for further radical change in the future also are limited because the Left parties lack the necessary popular support outside of their areas of regional strength. Finally, the disintegration of the Soviet Union and the decline of Marxist ideology and practice throughout the world has left the Communist parties of India disconcerted. These great changes are likely to strengthen still further their historic integration as non-revolutionary parties in India's parliamentary political order.

Right-wing, agrarian, and militant nationalist parties

The Swatantra Party. The only authentic party of the traditional Right, as that term would be understood in Europe, was the Swatantra party, a coalition of urban big business and rural aristocratic and landlord elements in which the latter were dominant. The Swatantra party, which drew together a number of regional parties such as the Ganatantra Parishad in Orissa, the Janata party of the Raja of Ramgarh in Bihar, a coalition of landed groups in Gujarat, some of the former princes in Rajasthan, and scattered discontented former landlords in other parts of the country, was formed on an all-India basis in 1959. The Swatantra party was of consequence nationally only in three general elections, in 1962, 1967, and 1972. In 1967, it succeeded in winning forty-four seats in the Lok Sabha, emerging as the second largest party in the House after the Congress (see table 3.2 above). During its heyday, Swatantra was the leading secular party of the Right offering a full-scale critique of the Congress policies of centralized planning, nationalization of industries, agrarian reform, and non-alignment.

Lok Dal. The second major agrarian-based party which succeeded in achieving broad support in north India after its foundation in 1969, which played a central role in the Janata coalition against the Congress in 1977, and which subsequently emerged as the second largest party in the Lok Sabha in 1980 was the Lok Dal. The Lok Dal began life in U. P. under the leadership of a prominent former Congressman, Charan Singh, who left the Congress to form the first non-Congress government in that state in 1967. Charan Singh drew his agrarian supporters together, most of whom came from the so-called backward or middle-status cultivating peasant proprietor castes, into a new political party called the BKD, which emerged as the second largest party after the Congress in that state in its first electoral contest in the 1969 mid-term legislative assembly elections. In 1974, the largest section of the radical Socialists in both U. P. and Bihar, consisting primarily of those leaders whose support bases came from the backward classes in those states, joined forces with Charan Singh's BKD, which was thereafter called the BLD. In 1977, the BLD in turn merged into the Janata coalition. When that coalition itself fell apart, largely as a consequence of Charan Singh's aspirations to displace Morarji Desai and become Prime Minister himself, the old BLD reemerged as the Lok Dal. After the death of Charan Singh in 1987, the Lok Dal split, with Charan Singh's son Ajit leading the larger remnant. Both segments merged into the Janata Dal of V. P. Singh in 1989, after which only a tiny fragment of the old party persisted as the Lok Dal (B) (tables 3.1 and 3.2).

Jan Sangh. A major political tradition in modern Indian history that carried forward into the post-Independence period had drawn its central ideas and symbols from Hindu traditions and culture. Although the Jan Sangh was considered by its detractors to be a Hindu communal, even anti-Muslim party with fascist inclinations, its members would vehemently deny such charges and would accept only that they are militant nationalists in a Hindu country which, as such, ought legitimately to draw its symbols of nationalism from the predominantly Hindu traditions of the country.

The Jan Sangh aspired to become a national party and it did succeed in winning significant representation in the Lok Sabha in several elections from 1952 onwards, reaching a peak of thirty-five seats in the 1967 elections, making it the third largest party in the House after Congress and Swatantra. However, the overwhelming bulk of its support always came from the north Indian Hindi-speaking states of U. P., Bihar, M. P., Rajasthan, and Haryana. The Jan Sangh was a formidable force in north India not only because of the appeal of its ideology but because it was able to call upon a disciplined body of political workers from a militant Hindu cultural organization known as the Rashtriya Swayamsevak Sangh (RSS), who always provided the most vigorous canvassers at election time.

Party manifestoes emphasized the maintenance of traditional Hindu institutions of family, caste structure, and law. They demanded the displacement of English by Hindi as the sole official language of the country. They opposed concessions to the Muslim minority on matters of language and education. On economic issues, they opposed excessive state control over the Indian economy and were in favor of more liberal policies toward business and industry.

The leadership and the principal support bases of the Jan Sangh came mainly from merchants, shopkeepers, and businessmen in the towns, from big landlords in the countryside, and from some of the middle and rich peasant groups in the countryside. Although it drew support in some areas from middle status cultivating castes, its dominant leadership generally came from elite castes, particularly Brahmans.

The rise and fall of the Janata party and the Janata Dal

All the leading parties of the non-Communist Left, of the Center and of the Right, with the later addition also of some defectors from the

Congress, joined forces during and toward the end of the Emergency to form a new political formation called the Janata party.

The program and policies of the Janata party drew primarily from the agrarian ideas of Charan Singh for the promotion of agriculture, a self-sufficient peasantry, and labor-intensive small-scale industry. Similar ideas and an emphasis on a decentralized approach to planning also were contributed by the Socialist participants in the coalition. During the Janata period in power, a significant shift was made in the direction of increased allocations in the Sixth Five Year Plan for agriculture especially.

Structurally, the Janata party never succeeded in becoming anything other than a loosely knit coalition of ambitious political leaders and political parties which attempted to retain their previous organizational and social support bases. A struggle for preeminence developed within the central government itself, especially between Charan Singh and Morarji Desai, with Charan Singh seeking to displace Morarji and become Prime Minister himself. In July, 1979, the coalition broke apart, Charan Singh became Prime Minister for three weeks only until his resignation and the calling of a new election, which led in 1980 to the return of Mrs. Gandhi and the Congress to power.

After the disintegration of the Janata coalition, the political parties which initially joined it either re-formed themselves with new names or disintegrated. The principal remnants of the original Janata coalition until 1988 were the Lok Dal (divided after the illness and death of Charan Singh in 1987 into two separate parties, Lok Dal [A] and Lok Dal [B]), the Janata party led by a former Congressman of moderate Socialist inclinations, Mr. Chandrashekhar, and the Bharatiya Janata Party, which consists primarily of former Jan Sangh leaders and members.

Between 1987 and 1989, a new Janata coalition came on the scene under the leadership of Vishwanath Pratap Singh, who sought to duplicate the unity and victory of the Janata party of 1977. V. P. Singh had been a central government minister and close adviser of Rajiv Gandhi and had previously also been chief minister of U. P., the largest and politically most important state in the Indian Union. While he was finance minister in the central government, he instituted an inquiry into corruption involving "kickbacks" to middlemen in connection with a huge defence procurement contract with the Swedish Bofors company.

As his investigations began to implicate highly placed persons in the Congress organization and in the central government, V. P. Singh was transferred to the defense ministry. He chose instead to resign from the cabinet. His resignation was accepted, after which a smear campaign was directed against him by prominent Congressmen in government and in the Parliament and he was expelled from the Congress in August, 1987. Thereafter, he began an extensive and extended attempt to create a united opposition and gather public support to defeat the Congress in the 1989 elections.

At the end of 1988, V. P. Singh's own group of former Congressmen who had been expelled from the Congress or who had left the Congress to join him merged with the rump Janata party of Chandrashekhar, the factions of the Lok Dal, and another splinter group from the Congress – known as Congress (S) – into the Janata Dal. The latter in turn joined forces in early 1989 with three regional parties into a National Front of opposition parties pledged to work together to fight unitedly against the Congress in the 1989 elections. The three regional components of the National Front were the exclusively state parties in the southern states of Tamil Nadu and Andhra, the DMK and the Telugu Desam, respectively, and the Asom Gana Parishad of Assam. In addition, agreement was reached between the Janata Dal and the BJP for a partial adjustment of seats in north India to avoid dividing the anti-Congress vote.

Although the National Front failed to win a majority of seats in Parliament, it was able to form a government under V. P. Singh with the support of other parties in the House, namely, the BJP and the CPM. However, the BJP withdrew its support of the V. P. Singh government in October, 1990 on issues relating to reservations of Central Government-controlled public sector jobs for backward castes and the temple/mosque controversy in the city of Ayodhya in north India. The National Front government was then replaced by another minority government headed by a faction from the Janata Dal led by Chandrashekhar, supported in Parliament by the Congress. In the general elections held in May–June, 1991, in the midst of which the Congress leader, Rajiv Gandhi, was assassinated, the Congress was nevertheless returned to power with a minority government under its new leader, P. V. Narasimha Rao.

The rise of the BJP in the 1989 and 1991 elections

Between 1989 and 1992, the BJP became the most dynamic political force in the Indian party system. In the 1989 elections, it emerged as the third largest party in the Lok Sabha after the Janata Dal and the Congress (I), winning eighty-five seats and 11.4 percent of the vote in the country (tables 3.1 and 3.2). In state legislative assembly elections held thereafter in 1990, the BJP won a majority of seats in Madhya Pradesh and Himachal Pradesh and the largest number of seats in Rajasthan, becoming the ruling party in the first two states and the leader of the ruling coalition in Rajasthan. It also made major gains in Gujarat.

Then, in the Lok Sabha elections of May–June, 1991, riding on the wave produced by the *rath yatra* of its leader, L. K. Advani, and the movement to construct a temple to Ram in Ayodhya, the BJP achieved its greatest electoral victory since its formation, becoming the second largest party in the Lok Sabha with a strength of 119 seats in the House and a popular vote share of 20.2 percent. The BJP also won a majority of seats in the U. P. legislative assembly elections, after which it took power alone for the first time in the largest state in the country. In U. P., the BJP's success was achieved more at the expense of the Congress (I) than of the Janata Dal, as a consequence of which the Congress was displaced to a very weak third place in the state's party system.

The BJP also made substantial gains in both vote share and seats won in Gujarat. However, in other states, it lost some ground gained in 1989 in either vote share or seats won. In a few states, the BJP gained in both vote share and seats won mainly because it ran a much larger number of candidates than ever before. Overall, while the results of the 1991 elections appeared on their face to constitute a major step forward in the BJP's drive for national power, they were less favorable than the BJP leaders had expected.

The BJP's drive for national power is based upon an explicit appeal to Hindu nationalism. Its leading slogans are that India is a Hindu country and that Hindus have a right to be proud of their history and culture and to draw the central symbols of national identity from them. They claim that the large Muslim minority in the country has been "pampered" too long to the detriment of Hindus and the country's unity. They favor a strong hand to repress the militant and secessionist movements in Punjab, Kashmir, and the northeast.

Although the BJP and its allied organization, the Vishwa Hindu Parishad (World Hindu Society), have focused their appeal to Hindu identity around the creation of a new cult of Ram centered upon the drive to build a temple to Ram in Ayodhya, it is mistaken to consider the BJP a "fundamentalist" religious party. Hindu religious beliefs and symbols serve the BJP as a focus for creating a national identity, but the party's goals are secular: to transform India into a modern, industrial, military power with a united nation and a disciplined work force. The party favors the dismantling of India's public sector industries and bureaucratic controls and the transformation of the economy into one based on the market and private enterprise.[14] Its second rank of leaders come from the most modern sectors of society and the economy: from English-educated "intellectuals, retired army generals, ex-civil servants and prominent businessmen,"[15] as well as teachers, professional people, and engineers.

In the 1991 elections, the BJP broadened its electoral support base considerably. It retained strong support from its traditional voters in the urban business and commercial sectors of the economy and from the descendants of 1947–48 refugees from Pakistan. It increased sharply its strength among upper castes angered by the decision of the V. P. Singh government to implement the Mandal Commission Report recommendations for reservation of 27 percent of jobs in public sector enterprises under the control of the central government. It also gained some support among segments of the backward castes.

However, the BJP failed to make substantial inroads among the Scheduled Castes and it drove most Muslim voters in each constituency, particularly in north India, into the arms of any party which appeared to be in the strongest position to defeat it. Moreover, the election campaign in north India was preceded and accompanied by months of Hindu-Muslim communal tension and severe rioting as a direct consequence of its movement and that of its ally, the VHP, to build the temple to Ram and remove the Babari Masjid from the alleged site of Ram's birthplace. Therefore, the BJP's drive for national

[14] Yogendra K. Malik and V. B. Singh, "Bharatiya Janata Party: An Alternative to the Congress (I)?" *Asian Survey*, XXXII, No. 4 (April, 1992), 328.
[15] Malik and Singh, "Bharatiya Janata Party," p. 327.

consolidation has been inseparable from its opposite: an intensification of bitter communal conflicts.

The BJP must be seen as the latest and currently the most vital political force striving to build a united Indian nation, a dynamic economy, and a strong state. It seeks to overcome the heterogeneity and caste divisiveness of Indian society by consolidating a sense of Hindu nationalism around symbols common to all who claim to be Hindus. Unlike most other secular parties in post-Independence Indian history, it does not shrink from dividing Indian society in the short term in pursuit of the longer-term goal of national unity. No party or movement in Indian history, including the Congress at its height, has been able to create a lasting integral nationalism of this type. The BJP's drive for national power is based on the belief that the time is coming soon when such a nationalism can at last be achieved.

Regional parties

In several states in India, the largest non-Congress political parties are specific to a single state and have little or no strength outside their home state. The most important such parties have been the AIADMK and the DMK in Tamil Nadu, the Telugu Desam in Andhra, the Akali Dal in Punjab, the National Conference in Jammu & Kashmir, the Asom Gana Parishad in Assam, and the Shiv Sena in Maharashtra. In fact, in all these states, the regional parties either won majorities in legislative assembly elections held between 1985 and 1992 (see table 3.4) and formed governments thereafter, or became the principal opposition party to the Congress. In two states undergoing violent insurrectionary movements at the time, Punjab and Jammu & Kashmir, the regional governing parties were later dismissed and President's Rule imposed. In elections held in Punjab in 1992 under circumstances described below, the Congress was returned to power with a massive majority of dubious authenticity.

These single-state parties are distinguished by their adoption of a regional nationalist perspective, by their political desire for greater regional autonomy of states in the Indian Union, for their focus on issues specific to their states, or for their base within a religious minority.

Thus, the DMK and AIADMK, which trace their origins to the Dravidian movement of the nineteenth century and to the Self-Respect

Table 3.4. *Number of seats won by Congress and principal opposition party in 1987–92 state legislative assembly elections*

State	Congress	Principal opposition		Date of election
Andhra Pradesh	181	74	(TD)	1989
Arunachal Pradesh	37	11	(JD)	1990
Assam	66	19	(AGP)	1991
Bihar	71	120	(JD)	1990
Goa	20	18	(MG)	1989
Gujarat	33	70	(JD)	1990
Haryana	51	16	(SJP)	1991
Himachal Pradesh	8	44	(BJP)	1990
Jammu & Kashmir	27	39	(NC-F)[a]	1987
Karnataka	170	11	(JP)	1989
Kerala	55	29	(CPM)	1991
Madhya Pradesh	56	219	(BJP)	1990
Maharashtra	141	52	(SHS)	1990
Manipur	26	12	(MPP)	1990
Meghalaya	22	19	(HPU)	1988
Mizoram	23	14	(MNF)	1989
Nagaland	36	24	(NPC)	1989
Orissa	10	123	(JD)	1990
Pondicherry	15	6	(AIADMK)	1991
Punjab	87	3	(AD[K])	1992[b]
Rajasthan	50	85	(BJP)	1990
Sikkim	0	32	(SKSP)	1989
Tamil Nadu	61	163	(AIADMK)	1991
Tripura	24	26	(CPM)	1988
Uttar Pradesh	50	230	(BJP)	1991
West Bengal	43	188	(CPM)	1991

TD:	Telugu Desam
JD:	Janata Dal
AGP:	Asom Gana Parishad
MG:	Maharashtrawadi Gomantak
SJP:	Samajwadi Janata Party
BJP:	Bharatiya Janata Party
NC-F:	National Conference (F)
JP:	Janata Party
CPM:	Communist Party of India (Marxist)
SHS:	Shiv Sena
MPP:	Manipur People's Party

Table 3.4 (cont.)

HPU: Hill People's Union
MNF: Mizo National Front
NPC: Nagaland People's Council
AIADMK: All India Anna Dravida Munnetra Kazhagam
AD[K]:   Akali Dal (K)
SKSP: Sikkim Sangram Parishad

*Congress (I) ally
*The Punjab elections were boycotted by the most important Akali parties and by most Sikh voters; turnout was extremely low.

Sources: David Butler et al., India Decides: Elections, 1952–1992 (New Delhi: LM Books, 1991); M. L. Ahuja and Sharda Paul, 1989–1992 General Elections in India (Including November 1991 By-Elections) (New Delhi: Associated Publishing 1992), p. 116; India Today, March 31, 1990, July 15, 1991, and March 15, 1992.

and Non-Brahman movements of the twentieth century stand primarily for the promotion of Tamil regional cultural identity and the Tamil language and against the intrusion of the Hindi language into Tamil Nadu. After the death in 1969 of its leader, C. N. Annadurai, the DMK split in 1972 into its present two offshoots, of which the AIADMK, led by the film star, M. G. Ramachandran (MGR), emerged dominant in the 1977 elections and became the ruling party in Tamil Nadu, with MGR as its chief minister until his death in December, 1987. A struggle for succession followed between MGR's wife and his mistress in the course of which the latter, Jayalalitha, emerged as the leader of the AIADMK. In the interim, the DMK prevailed in the 1989 legislative assembly elections only to be dismissed by the President of India before the 1991 General Elections. In the state legislative assembly elections which followed, the AIADMK won an overwhelming victory and became the governing party once again in Tamil Nadu.

The Telugu Desam in Andhra is a much more recent formation than the DMK, having been founded only in 1982. Although it does not have the long history and the deep roots in regional culture and social structure that the DMK and AIADMK have in Tamil Nadu, it appeals to similar political and social forces of regional nationalism and non-Brahmanism. It is also led, like the AIADMK under MGR, by a film star, N. T. Rao (NTR). Under NTR's leadership, the Telugu Desam swept into power in Andhra in 1983 and, in the aftermath of some crude efforts by the Governor of the state to topple the government before the 1984 parliamentary elections, roundly defeated the Congress in the state in those elections and won a two-thirds majority in the legislative assembly elections in March, 1985. However, in the next round of state legislative assembly elections, the Telugu Desam was in turn trounced by the Congress, which took power in the state once again. Although the 1989 election results gave the appearance that Andhra might be settling into a two-party system, most observers of Andhra politics doubt that the Telugu Desam itself will survive the death of its aging leader.

A third major regional party is the Akali Dal in the Punjab, which arose as an offshoot of the Sikh Gurdwara Reform Movement of the 1920s and has since been the principal political arm of Sikhs in the Punjab who have sought a special political status for their community in a state within the Indian Union where the Sikh religion and the Punjabi language would be especially protected and promoted. In 1966, the Akali Dal succeeded in wresting from the central government after prolonged struggle a separate, Sikh-majority province called Punjabi Suba. However, since Sikhs constitute only a bare majority of the population of the Punjab and many Sikhs have always supported the Congress, the Akali Dal was never able to achieve the kind of dominance in Punjab gained by the AIADMK in Tamil Nadu. The Akali Dal instead became involved in a dualistic competition with the Congress for power in the Punjab in which it sometimes succeeded in forming the government, often in coalition with other non-Congress parties.

However, during the 1980s, the political process in this state deteriorated into an extensive pattern of extreme violence in which several explicitly secessionist groups emerged. In 1985, as part of an effort by Rajiv Gandhi to restore peace to the Punjab, elections were held which were won by the Akali Dal. Nevertheless, violence continued in the state. The central government imposed President's Rule in 1987 and intensified police and military efforts to destroy the militant groups. Then again, in 1992, elections were held which were boycotted by most Sikh voters. The Congress, therefore, won the elections easily and formed a government of its own.

Jammu & Kashmir is another state in which there had been an

entrenched political party stronger than the Congress itself. The National Conference of Dr. Farooq Abdullah won the 1987 elections to become the ruling party in that state, governing in 1988 with the support of the Congress, with which it developed a pre-electoral alliance. The National Conference is the descendant of the original All Jammu & Kashmir Muslim Conference founded in 1932, in which Dr. Farooq's father, Sheikh Abdullah, was the dominant force until his death in 1982 when the leadership of the party was taken over by his son. Although the loyalty of Sheikh Abdullah and his party to India was sometimes questioned, it is more accurate to see the Abdullah family and the parties they led as supporters of Kashmiri Muslim identity and regional political autonomy within India, but not as proponents of merger with Pakistan. However, as in Punjab, party politics in Kashmir gave way at the end of the 1980s to extreme civil strife between several armed secessionist groups and government security forces. The precipitant of this disintegration of the political process was the electoral alliance between the National Conference and the Congress and the general belief that the elections were rigged (see chapter 6 below).

In Assam, the principal driving force behind the rise of the regional Asom Gana Parishad (AGP) in the state was the issue of legal and illegal migrations of outsiders into Assam, particularly from West Bengal and Bangladesh and their entry on to the electoral rolls, usually as Congress supporters. After a prolonged and often violent agitation on the part of Assamese students and politicians demanding the removal of illegal migrants from the electoral rolls and from the state and country as well, an accord was reached with the central government on these issues in August, 1985, which was followed by parliamentary and legislative assembly elections in December. In those elections, the AGP won seven of fourteen Lok Sabha seats to the Congress' four and also won a majority in the Assam legislative assembly and formed a government in the state thereafter. However, the AGP government proved to be ineffective, the central government failed to take expeditious steps to implement the accord, and a secessionist movement arose in this state also during the AGP's tenure in office. In the midst of the violence in this state, legislative assembly elections were held in which the Congress defeated the AGP and formed a new government.

In Maharashtra, the last state bastion of the old one-party dominant system, still another regional party, the Shiv Sena, became in the 1990 legislative assembly elections the second largest party in the state. Founded in the 1960s as an anti-migrant movement centered in Bombay and demanding that Maharashtrians be given preference in job recruitment in both the public and private sectors, it expanded its influence in several urban areas in the 1970s and 1980s. During the past decade, it has taken on more the color of an extreme anti-minority Hindu nationalist movement. In 1990, it fought the state legislative assembly elections in alliance with the BJP, winning fifty-two seats against 141 for Congress.

The state units of the CPM too have become, in effect, regional parties at least insofar as their popular support is concerned. The CPM polled 79 percent of its total vote in the 1989 Lok Sabha elections in the two states of Kerala and West Bengal, 82 percent in those two states plus Tripura. The CPM remained in 1992 the ruling party in West Bengal and the principal opposition to the Congress in Kerala.

When one considers also that in several other states, non-Congress parties are either dominant or equal rivals to the Congress in the state legislative assemblies and sometimes control their state's delegation of MPs to the Lok Sabha as well, the position of the Congress as the dominant party in the country seems clearly to have weakened markedly since its peak in 1984. The Congress, in fact, was the largest party in 1992 only in seven of the fifteen states: Andhra, Assam, Haryana, Karnataka, Kerala, Maharashtra, and quite dubiously in Punjab. In the major Hindi-speaking states except Haryana, in Gujarat, and in Tamil Nadu, non-Congress parties were in power.

ELECTORAL POLITICS

The electoral process

As in the British parliamentary system, elections to the Lok Sabha (Lower House) of Parliament must be held within five years of the election of the previous parliament, but they may be called by the President upon the advice of the Prime Minister at any time before the expiration of the normal five-year term of the House. The actual mechanics of the election, including the delimitation of constituency boundaries, the setting of specific dates for the polling in different parts of the country, the establishment and manning of polling booths, the allocation of party symbols, the acceptance or rejection of nominations according to the electoral laws and rules, the counting of votes, the publication of the results, and the like are all supervised by the Election Commission, a semi-autonomous body whose functions are defined in the Constitution of the country.

Until 1971, when Prime Minister Gandhi called the first mid-term election for the Lok Sabha, the general practice was that a general election included the simultaneous scheduling of polling for both the Lok Sabha and the state legislative assemblies. The call by Mrs. Gandhi for a mid-term election in 1971 and the consequent "delinking" of parliamentary and legislative assembly elections at that time included the clear design to separate the national from the state elections and thereby to capitalize upon the national appeal of Mrs. Gandhi against her rivals in the Congress organization and in state politics generally. Since 1971, the general practice has been to hold parliamentary and state legislative assembly elections separately, although they do sometimes coincide in particular states.

At present, the electoral unit, as in Britain, is a single-member constituency, in which the winning candidate is the person who succeeds in gaining a plurality of votes on the first ballot. The only distinction among constituencies concerns whether they are reserved for Scheduled Castes or Scheduled Tribes or not. In a reserved constituency, only persons from designated low caste or tribal groups may contest, but all adults are eligible to vote. The number of reserved constituencies is proportionate to the total population of Scheduled Castes or Tribes within a state. In the country as a whole, approximately 22 percent of the total Lok Sabha and state legislative assembly seats are reserved.

Most Indian constituencies are overwhelmingly rural, containing only a few small towns, in which each polling booth covers a single village or several adjacent villages. In the urban areas, there will naturally be a large number of polling booths set up in ways familiar in industrialized societies within public buildings such as schools.

Most Indians are still unable to read. Therefore, each party and independent candidate is allocated a distinctive symbol (figure 2).

INDIAN NATIONAL CONGRESS (I)

JANATA PARTY

BHARATIYA JANATA PARTY

COMMUNIST PARTY OF INDIA

COMMUNIST PARTY OF INDIA (M)

INDIAN NATIONAL CONGRESS (S)

LOK DAL

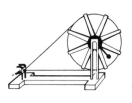

JANATA DAL

BAHUJAN SAMAJ PARTY

Figure 2   Election symbols of recognized national political parties

96

Election campaigns

A campaign in a rural constituency requires a candidate who aspires to success to visit as many as possible of the 100 or so villages in an assembly constituency and at least a sample of the 500 or 600 villages of a parliamentary constituency. Such campaigning, concentrated within the statutory three-week period, is an extraordinarily grueling experience, carried out by jeep, by foot, and by bullock cart, with each candidate scheduling perhaps as many as six village visits a day. In the cities, election campaigning involves neighborhood street corner rallies, house-to-house canvassing by the candidates' workers, and parades through the city with the candidate himself riding in a jeep saluting the crowds as he drives through the town.

There are three principal means of communicating the message of a party or of independent candidates during a campaign. Each well-organized party will issue a printed manifesto in both English and the vernacular language, stating the distinctive positions of the party on the major issues of the day. The second means of communication is through public speeches by candidates and their supporters in the villages and city street corners. The third type of approach to the voters is through private and implicit appeals. Canvassers will, in this respect, depart from the printed manifestoes and public statements of their candidates and will stress ties of caste between the candidate and his brethren, his accomplishments or promises to do things for particular villages and localities, the candidate's probity and his rivals' venality, with emphasis especially on any evidence that can be found or concocted that the candidate's principal rival has had some criminal record or has had some criminal charges filed against him.

Indian voting behavior

A multiplicity of factors affect voter decisions at election time, including appeals to class, community, caste, and faction loyalty as well as the personal attractions of popular and charismatic leaders. In some areas in some elections, especially recently, criminal violence and intimidation of voters also occurs. At the local level, in the countryside, by far the most important factor in voting behavior remains caste solidarity. Large and important castes in a constituency tend to back

97

either a respected member of their caste or a political party with whom their caste members identify. However, local factions and local-state factional alignments, which involve inter-caste coalitions also are important factors in influencing voting behavior.

Issues also matter in India and may sometimes sway many groups of voters in the same direction and create a "wave" or landslide across large parts of the country. One wave developed in 1967 against the Congress on issues of rising prices, scarcity, and the discontent of government employees and students in north India. A second occurred in 1971–72 – first in the parliamentary then the legislative assembly elections – in favor of Mrs. Gandhi in the aftermath of her struggles with the old Congress party bosses and her leadership of the country in the Third Indo-Pakistan War which brought about the independence of Bangladesh. A third swept the Janata coalition into power in 1977 as a consequence of widespread discontent with alleged excesses committed by government during the Emergency regime. In 1984, a fourth wave arose in sympathy with Rajiv Gandhi after the assassination of his mother and in response to his appeals for national unity against forces said to threaten the unity and integrity of the country.

As in most other aspects of Indian political life, there is considerable discontinuity between local practices and the everyday concerns of the voters, particularly in rural areas, and the needs, goals, and fears of politicians striving to build power in the vast political units of the larger states of India and the country as a whole. The national political leaders especially tend to see the great issues facing India in abstract economic terms, articulated in goals of increased aggregate industrial and agricultural production, or in terms of defense of the country against hostile foreign powers and neighbors, or preservation of the country's unity in the face of alleged divisive threats from secessionist forces and from interreligious conflicts. These kinds of issues serve a dual purpose for the national elites: they have a broad mobilizing capacity at election time, especially in the cities, and they draw attention away from their failures to improve the everyday lot of the vast mass of the ordinary people of the country.

Whenever voters in India, especially in the countryside, are asked about *their* problems, rather than about the abstract goals and ideals articulated for them by political elites, their focus is upon economic problems and solutions to the problems of everyday life.[16] For the poorest, the concerns are for food, water, shelter, clothing, and employment. For those living beyond poverty, the issues are prices for their farm produce, irrigation facilities and a regular supply of electricity to keep them functioning, roads and bridges to get to market during the monsoon rains, schools and public sector jobs for their children. All local politicians know very well the salience of such priorities for their constituents and most strive to satisfy some of their needs through channeling of state funds and patronage to their supporters. However, at election time, the campaign issues are often defined quite differently as the politicians strive to persuade the voters that the threat from Pakistan or from secessionists in Punjab and Kashmir or the construction of a temple to Ram in Ayodhya are what really should matter to them.

Parties and elections

Parties do not dominate electoral politics in India to the same extent as in Western parliamentary systems. There are many localities in India where local notables, often descendants of great landlord or princely families, and other persons with independent bases of local power and support within a caste group, for example, have sufficient independent resources either to contest elections successfully on their own or to bargain for the support of established political parties. Moreover, in contrast with Western parliamentary regimes, the notion of party loyalty is extremely weak in India. Persons from factional groups defeated in struggles to gain the party nominations for themselves or their allies and supporters in a general election rarely hesitate either to switch their loyalties to another party which offers them a nomination or to contest the election as independents.

Finally, few parties in India persist and become institutionalized. Although the Indian National Congress is one of the oldest political parties in the world and the Communist parties trace their origins to the 1920s, most other parties in India have had relatively brief existences, in some cases only for a single election, in others for two or three.

It remains possible, nevertheless, to identify in any election broad

[16] See Pradeep K. Chibber *et al.*, "Order and the Indian Electorate: For Whom Does Shiva Dance?" *Asian Survey*, xxxii, No. 7 (July, 1992), 606–616 for a 1991 voter survey.

categories of voters who vote similarly in large parts of the country and to isolate general factors that influence broad groups of people. One can say, for example, that urban working classes in some of India's major cities tend to vote Communist, that the commercial classes in north Indian cities have tended to vote either for the Congress or the Jan Sangh/BJP, that the Congress gains strong support from the richer farmers and former landlords, and that the Lok Dal's strength was concentrated among the middle and rich peasantry. There is also evidence of partisan voting by segments of the electorate across several elections.[17] On the other hand, neither the candidates nor those who wish to interpret the results of Indian elections can afford to ignore the particularities of Indian voting behavior, which contribute to its volatility.[18]

Election results, 1951 to 1992

The vote for the Congress

The Congress organization clearly has been the leading political institution in post-Independence India. Since Independence, there has always been one predominant Congress organization in the country, which has always been either in power or has been the largest opposition party in Parliament and which has also always had broader support in most states of the Indian Union than any other party, even though it has never won a clear majority of the popular votes in the country (table 3.3 above).

The vote for the non-Congress parties

With the exception of the 1977 and 1991 elections, no single non-Congress party has ever polled even as much as half the Congress vote

[17] For example, in West Bengal for the Communists and in Punjab for several political parties. For West Bengal, see John O. Field and Marcus F. Franda, *The Communist Parties of West Bengal*, Vol. 1 in the series of Myron Weiner and John O. Field (eds.), *Studies in Electoral Politics in the Indian States* (Delhi: Manohar Book Service, 1974), and, for Punjab, Paul R. Brass, "Ethnic Cleavages and the Punjab Party System, 1952–1972," in Vol. IV of the same series, *Party Systems and Electoral Cleavages* (Delhi: Manohar Book Service, 1975), pp. 7–69.

[18] Apparent stability in voting behavior over time is often illusory, moreover, as in the case of the Congress. William Vanderbok and Richard Sisson have remarked that "while there is relative consistency of Congress support in terms of votes aggregated on the national level ... there have been pronounced fluctuations of Congress support in the states"; see "The Spatial Distribution of Congress Electoral Support: Trends from Four Decades of

Table 3.5. *Vote shares for the Congress, "national" opposition parties, and others in parliamentary elections, 1952–91 (percent)*

Year	Congress	"National" opposition	All national parties	Other parties and independents	Total
1952	45.0	22.8	67.8	32.3	100.0
1957	47.8	25.2	73.0	27.0	100.0
1962	44.7	33.7	78.4	21.5	100.0
1967	40.8	35.5	76.3	23.8	100.0
1971	43.7	34.1	77.8	22.2	100.0
1977	34.5	50.1	84.6	15.3	100.0
1980	42.7	42.4	85.1	14.9	100.0
1984	48.1	29.7	77.8	22.2	100.0
1989	39.5	39.8	79.3	20.7	100.0
1991	36.4	40.7	77.1	22.8	100.0

Source: As for tables 3.1 and 3.2; also *Lok Sabha Poll*, p. 186.

in the country as a whole. The Election Commission has always made a distinction in publishing the figures for parliamentary elections between "national" parties and other parties. For a time, there appeared to be a trend toward "nationalization" of the party system, with the vote for the "national" non-Congress parties having gone up from the 20–30 percent range in the 1950s to the 30–40 percent range between 1962 and 1971 to the 40–50 percent range in 1977 and 1980, with a corresponding decline in the relative vote shares of the category of "other parties and independents" (table 3.5). The trend, however, was partly illusory and appeared especially chimerical in the face of the 1984 election results, when the collective vote share of the "national" opposition parties was reduced to 29.7 percent, a figure lower than any in the previous five elections. In the last two elections, in 1989 and 1991, the balance between the combined vote for all national parties (Congress and opposition), on the one hand, and other parties and independents, on the other hand, has reverted to the pre-1977 range. Except for the Congress, the Communist parties, and the BJP, none of

Parliamentary elections," in Paul R. Brass and Francis Robinson, *The Indian National Congress and Indian Society: Ideology, Social Structure and Political Dominance* (Delhi: Chanakya Publications, 1987), p. 395. Similar results will be found in comparisons of votes aggregated to the state level with district voting and of district with constituency voting.

Table 3.6. *Congress and its closest competitor, by state,[a]*
parliamentary elections, 1991 (percent vote shares)

State	Congress (I)	Closest competitor
Andhra Pradesh	44.6	32.6 (Telugu Desam)
Assam	28.5	17.6 (AGP)
Bihar	23.9	32.4 (Janata)
Gujarat	28.2	50.6 (BJP)
Haryana	37.2	25.4 (SJP)
Himachal Pradesh	46.2	42.8 (BJP)
Karnataka	42.0	28.7 (BJP)
Kerala	38.8	20.7 (CPM)
Madhya Pradesh	45.3	41.9 (BJP)
Maharashtra	48.3	20.6 (BJP)
Orissa	43.7	34.2 (Janata)
Rajasthan	44.0	40.9 (BJP)
Tamil Nadu	42.6	22.7 (DMK)
Uttar Pradesh	18.3	32.9 (BJP)
West Bengal	36.2	35.1 (CPM)

[a]Only the larger states of the Indian Union have been included. Excluded are Goa, Manipur, Meghalaya, Nagaland, Sikkim, and Tripura, which elect only one or two seats each to the Lok Sabha. Elections were not held in Jammu & Kashmir because of disturbed conditions prevailing there at the time of the 1991 General Elections. Elections in Punjab were postponed for the same reasons until March, 1992, but percent vote shares were not available at the time of writing.
Sources: Lok Sabha Poll, pp. 17–42.

the other "national" parties had endured. Moreover, the second-place party has changed in every election since 1952, when the Socialist party came in second with 10.6 percent of the vote (see table 3.1). It is also important to note that in any single parliamentary election the second-place party is likely to be different in different states (table 3.6). Finally, many of the so-called national parties did not have a genuine national spread at all. In general, therefore, despite the considerable evidence of Congress institutional and electoral decline, it remained the case after the 1991 elections that the Congress was "the only party with a base all over the country" and that no national alternative to the Congress existed.[19]

[19] Pratap Bhanu Mehta, "India's Disordered Democracy: Review Article," *Pacific Affairs*, LXIV, No. 4 (Winter, 1991–92), 538.

Regional parties and state party systems

The most important reason for doubting the existence in India of anything that can be called a national party system is the fact that all the Indian states have distinctive party systems. The extent of variation in patterns of party competition and of regional variations in party strength can be seen by comparing the relative strength of the two leading parties in each state in the 1989 parliamentary and the most recent legislative assembly elections (tables 3.4 and 3.6). In 15 states, the 1989 Lok Sabha elections produced 7 different configurations of first and second-place parties. Moreover, it needs also to be kept in mind that, in the state legislative assembly elections, the leading non-Congress parties do much better in the smaller constituencies and in many states, as a result, they emerge as formidable opposition parties or even as the ruling parties, relegating the Congress to the opposition (table 3.4).

In short, both the attempt to nationalize parliamentary elections by delinking them from state legislative assembly elections and the long-term preeminence of Congress in Parliament have failed to erode significantly the distinctiveness of regional political patterns in India or to establish a truly national party system in the country.

Elections and political mobilization

Turnout increased by 16 to 18 percentage points from 45.7 percent in 1952 to 64.1 percent in 1984 and 62.0 percent in 1989 (see table 3.7). Increasing turnout has also involved political mobilization of new groups of voters. In the legislative assembly elections especially, there has been a process of caste succession in the elections in which candidates both from elite caste groups which were less well repre-sented before and from the larger backward caste groups have entered the electoral arena. Although the processes of political mobilization have affected the lower backward and the lowest castes (Scheduled Castes) as well, there is no firm evidence concerning their actual turnout rates.

The more widespread and politically significant process of political mobilization which has been occurring in many parts of the country has been the increasing mobilization of the middle status backward agricultural castes and the lower backward artisan, service, and

Table 3.7. *Election data, Indian parliamentary elections, 1952–91*

Year	Electorate (in millions)	Polling stations	Votes polled (in millions)	Turnout (percent)
1952	173.2	132,560	80.7	45.7
1957	193.7	220,478	91.3	47.7
1962	217.7	238,355	119.9	55.4
1967	250.1	267,555	152.7	61.3
1971	274.1	342,944	151.5	55.3
1977	321.2	373,908	194.3	60.5
1980	355.6	434,442	202.3	56.9
1984	375.8	479,214	238.4	64.1
1989[a]	498.9	579,810	309.1	62.0
1991[b]	488.4	594,811	276.8	56.7

[a]Elections were not held in Assam in 1989.
[b]Elections were not held in Jammu & Kashmir and in Punjab at the time of the Tenth General Elections.
Sources: Compiled from Robert L. Hardgrave, Jr. and Stanley A. Kochanek, *India: Government and Politics in a Developing Nation,* 4th edn (San Diego: Harcourt Brace Jovanovich, 1986), p. 302; Butler *et al., India Decides,* pp. 10 and 15; Government of India, Election Commission, *Report on the Ninth General Elections to the House of the People in India, 1989* (New Delhi: Government of India Press, 1990), table 5; M. L. Ahuja and Sharda Paul, *1989–1991 General Elections in India (Including November 1991 By-Elections)* (New Delhi: Associated Publishing, 1992), p. 81; *Lok Sabha Poll,* p. 213.

smallholding castes. In some states, the backward castes (and some lower backward castes as well) have successfully displaced the previously dominant elite castes in leadership positions in the Congress. In other states, Tamil Nadu being the leading example, the backward castes have dominated the principal opposition to the Congress – the DMK and the AIADMK in Tamil Nadu – and have succeeded in displacing the Congress from power. In still other states, most notably the north Indian states of U. P. and Bihar, the old elite castes of Brahmans, Rajputs and Bhumihars have remained dominant in the Congress, and in the BJP, while the middle and lower backward castes have been mobilized by other parties: first by the Socialists in the 1950s and 1960s, by the Lok Dal in the 1960s and 1970s, and by the Janata Dal and the SJP in 1989 and 1991. Finally, in two other states, Kerala and

West Bengal, the lower backward and even the Scheduled Castes have been mobilized by the CPM. However, electoral politics and political mobilization in most of India remain dominated by the leading land-controlling castes of elite or middle status.

INTEREST GROUPS AND INTERMEDIARIES

Interest groups

In addition to the array of political parties and revolutionary movements which have existed in India since Independence, there have also been a great number of interest groups. Like the parties, some existed before Independence, some have come into being only since Independence, some are institutionalized, others ephemeral. For analytical purposes, they can be broadly divided into the following types: organized interest groups comparable to similar formations which exist in Western industrial societies, such as trade unions, professional associations, associations of government employees, and the like; "demand groups," defined as broad categories of people who have been mobilized from time to time in movements of one sort or another, such as "students" or "peasants";[20] and influence groups, which operate in non-public arenas such as Parliament or the state legislatures or come into being at critical moments such as a succession.

In the first category of organized interest groups, most of which have apex associations and central offices, are the trade unions, business associations, professional associations, and associations of government employees of various types. In addition to these nationally organized interest associations, which organize groups and have names which are similar to those which exist in Western industrial societies, there are myriad national, state, and local associations of merchants and tradesmen whose existence is noted by journalists or scholars only when a major policy issue affects their interests and precipitates a public agitation. They include associations of food-grain traders, cloth merchants, goldsmiths, and the like.

Such organized interests operate within only a small segment of Indian society, namely, in the sectors dominated by large-scale,

[20] This term comes from Lloyd I. Rudolph and Susanne H. Rudolph, *In Pursuit of Lakshmi: The Political Economy of the Indian State* (Chicago: University of Chicago Press, 1987), pp. 247ff.

bureaucratic organizations: factories, urban trade associations, professional groups, and civil servants whose constituencies comprise no more than 10 percent of the population of the country.[21] These organized groups, moreover, have much less influence than their Western counterparts in the formulation of broad policies and legislation, which has been dominated since Independence by the Prime Minister, the Prime Minister's Secretariat, the Cabinet at times, and the Planning Commission. It is largely after the passage of legislation and after the formulation of rules and regulations that interest representation – as opposed to outright blockage of government legislation – matters in India and it then becomes highly individualized or localized rather than a matter of general policy formulation and implementation. It is the application of general rules to particular cases which matters most for business, for example, and the mediation of labor tribunals in local labor–management conflicts that matters for labor on a day-to-day basis, for another example.[22]

A further feature of the large apex organizations in India is that they are often paper organizations which cannot mobilize their memberships or they cancel each other out in such a way as to leave only the organization recognized by the state with influence or to leave none with influence at the highest levels of government. Finally, there is a general tendency at all levels within even the "organized" sectors of Indian society toward multiplication and fragmentation of organizations: in the case of labor, for example, from the national to the state to the factory level so that, at base, what one has in the factories themselves is often no effective organization at all.[23]

The second broad type of interest formation in India has been given the name "demand group" by the Rudolphs to describe the movements which arise from time to time in India to make demands on behalf of persons in the relatively less organized and bureaucratized sectors of society, such as "students" or "peasants" or whole religious or language or regional groups rather than specific functional groups.[24]

[21] Rudolph and Rudolph, *In Pursuit of Lakshmi*, p. 22.
[22] Rudolph and Rudolph, *In Pursuit of Lakshmi*, p. 277.
[23] Rudolph and Rudolph, *In Pursuit of Lakshmi*, p. 280.
[24] Rudolph and Rudolph, *In Pursuit of Lakshmi*, pp. 252–254.

The third general type of interest association in India is the influence group with informal leaders or elites at its head who are presumed to be able to mobilize larger numbers of people for specific purposes. Examples of this type are caucuses of Muslim or Scheduled Caste MPs in Parliament, who may seek specific concessions from government or generally influence government policies on matters of concern to their constituencies simply by their evident presence or may intervene through their leaders at crisis points such as a succession.[25]

Operating across all three types of representation are two types of interest associations which are either unique to India or at least more prevalent in non-Western societies such as India than in Western industrial societies. These are revivalist movements and caste associations. Revivalist movements are formed either to protect or promote aspects of indigenous culture or practice which allegedly were destroyed or suffered severe disadvantages during the long periods of alien and colonial rule or to eliminate practices which were allegedly introduced and which were not in conformity with traditional practice. Examples of this type of movement would include such very important religious organizations as the Arya Samaj, which arose in western India in the late nineteenth century and became especially prominent in the Punjab where it continues to be a major force today. This movement flourished amid the religious controversies in the Punjab among Christian missionaries, Hindus, Muslims, and Sikhs and took as its main goals the purification of Hindu faith by going back to the original teachings in the Vedas, eliminating accretions since those days such as practices of caste discrimination and untouchability, and defending Hinduism against missionary activities of Christians or Muslims or Sikhs.[26]

A leading non-religious example has been the movement to revive, reform, and promote the teaching and practice of the Ayurvedic system of medicine throughout India. This movement, which can be traced back to the later nineteenth century, has taken modern organizational forms through various formally organized associations,

[25] See, for example, Michael Brecher, *Succession in India: A Study in Decision-Making* (London: Oxford University Press, 1966), pp. 55-56, 72-73, and S. C. Gangal, *Prime Minister and the Cabinet in India* (New Delhi: Navachetna Prakashan, 1972), pp. 37-38.

[26] See esp. Kenneth W. Jones, *Arya Dharm: Hindu-Consciousness in 19th-Century Punjab* (Berkeley: University of California Press, 1976).

publication of journals, and lobbying of prominent political leaders and the central and state governments for support.[27]

Although many revivalist movements have taken the explicit organizational form of modern, bureaucratic interest associations and are indistinguishable in these respects from their non-revivalist counterparts, revivalist movements in general are distinguished by their greater capacity to act as demand groups and to speak or claim to speak on behalf of a much wider group. So, for example, there are permanent interest associations and societies for the protection of the cow in India, which regularly publish journals and lobby state and central legislatures to prevent cow slaughter and to provide *gosthalas* or rest farms for old and non-productive cows. However, these societies, which have existed since at least the late nineteenth century, can also sometimes launch mass movements with the participation of other organizations such as, for example, the Arya Samaj.

The second type of specialized interest association in India is the caste association. Caste associations operate both as formal interest groups in the organized sector of Indian society and as formal and informal interest groups in the small towns and rural areas of the country. The local, informal organization of a *jati* (local caste group) may be mobilized at any time for specific, local, or broader political purposes such as an election campaign or a confrontation with caste rivals or with the local police.

There are also various types of more-than-local organizations of castes into caste associations or informal influence groups. Formal caste associations exist for many caste categories, that is, for castes which are not necessarily interconnected by kinship and other local ties, but which have the same name and a similar status over a broad area. Politicians from large and important castes often also act as leaders of influence groups in the state legislatures, where they may caucus across party lines or within a single dominant party, especially the Congress, to achieve ministerial office for themselves and special favors for their constituents.

With the exception of the Scheduled Castes, there are no significant caste associations at the national, all-India level. Scheduled Castes,

---

[27] Paul R. Brass, "The Politics of Ayurvedic Education: A Case Study of Revivalism and Modernization in India," in Susanne H. and Lloyd I. Rudolph (eds.), *Education and Politics in India* (Cambridge, MA: Harvard University Press, 1972).

however, constitute an officially recognized category, a grouping of the so-called untouchable castes, with a fixed number of seats reserved for their representatives in the Lok Sabha. For virtually the entire post-Independence period, Jagjivan Ram, a member of the government from Independence until his death in 1986, was treated as if he were the spokesman for this grouping of castes.[28]

Intermediaries

In discussing revivalist movements and caste associations as specifically non-Western and Indian types of interest formations, we are stretching the very meaning of the term "interest group" as it is used for Western representative political systems. There are yet two other forms of political "representation" in India which stretch still further the concept associated with the term "interest group" and with reference to which it is preferable to use another term, "intermediaries." The term "intermediaries" will be used here to refer to informal structures and individuals who act as links between the formal institutions of the Indian political order, parties and bureaucratic agencies, and the social institutions of Indian society, caste, family, and village. Two important examples of "intermediaries" are factions and brokers.

Factions

The importance of factions as dynamic components of Indian political parties has already been discussed above, but it is necessary to specify further their linkage role in the Indian political system and their centrality to its functioning.

Although aspects of factions and factional politics found in India exist elsewhere, the combination of features which describe Indian factions are unique and consist of the following elements especially. First are personalized, leader–follower relationships modeled in part on the master–disciple relationship so that some of the followers of faction leaders are, in effect, tied to the leader in a form of political apprenticeship. Secondly, however, it is also the leader's duty to care for the material interests of his followers, failing which all but the most

[28] See, for example, Brecher, *Succession in India*, pp. 49 and 73, W. H. Morris-Jones, "India Elects for Change – and Stability," *Asian Survey*, xi, No. 8 (August, 1971), 725, and Gangal, *Prime Minister and the Cabinet*, p. 48.

intensely loyal will go elsewhere. The factional relationship between leaders and followers and between different factional leaders in broader factional coalitions is, therefore, markedly transactional in character, based on an exchange of favors for support. There is, consequently, a curious and specifically Indian combination of devotion and materialism in the factional tie.

Thirdly, the central concerns of faction leaders and followers in the provinces and districts of India are different from those of the ideologically oriented party leaders in Delhi and in some of the state capitals and center around three sets of issues and interests in particular: land control, inter-caste and inter-communal relations, and access to local resources in general. The ways in which these sets of issues and interests affect state and local politics and the relationships between local and national politics will be discussed in the next chapter. Here, however, it is important to note that these differences in orientation of national party and government leaders, on the one hand, and faction leaders, on the other hand, point to the existence of several sets of discontinuities in the functioning of the Indian political system as a whole: between ideology and practice, policy and implementation, national issues and state and local issues. Factions provide at once an indispensable set of linkages in a subcontinental federal political system in an agrarian society which remains socially fragmented and heterogeneous and a dissolvent which renders impractical most of the proclaimed goals of the national leaders of the country.

In short, factions and personal leader–follower ties have been the principal structural components of the "parties" in the Indian party or, better, the Indian factional system. Aside from the Congress, only the Communist parties in West Bengal and Kerala, perhaps the DMK in Tamil Nadu, and the Akali Dal in the Punjab, which themselves are by no means free of factions, can claim an organizational existence separate from their founding leaders.

Brokers

If factions and faction leaders act as intermediaries between political parties and the people, there is another whole class of intermediaries who act as "brokers" between the people and the administration. They are also called "middlemen" and "fixers" in English, "*dalals*" in north

India and *"pyraveekars"* (persons who follow through on matters and get things done) in Andhra.[29]

It is certain that this kind of specialized brokerage has been going on in India at least since British times, especially with the introduction of the complex revenue administration.[30] However, there is little doubt that a major change and a dramatic increase in the need for brokers occurred after Independence with the extension of rural development activities and benefits to the cultivators. Moreover, the potential profitability of the broker's activities also increased substantially as government began to include cash loans and subsidies in its programs for the rural cultivators.[31] A still further boost in the opportunities for money-making came with the introduction of the poverty programs in the 1970s, which have involved the direct disbursement of cash, subsidies, animals, bullock carts, and other material benefits for designated categories of the rural poor.

The extension of rural development activities has also involved a proliferation of departments, agencies, and special programs to implement them, which are invariably poorly coordinated and often in conflict with each other. The brokers are the only persons in the local scene, aside from the seniormost district authorities, who are in a position to link the disparate activities of numerous development agencies and who have the incentive to do so.[32]

Both Bailey and Ram Reddy have noted that, while the work of the brokers and *pyraveekars* often facilitates communication and program implementation, it also leads to the distortion of information, the diversion of development funds to persons and groups other than those for whom they are intended, and to the spread of corruption throughout the administrative system.[33] The flourishing of the brokerage system, therefore, must be seen as a reflection on the general failure of the administrative system of post-Independence India to function effectively, popularly, and honestly.

[29] F. G. Bailey, *Politics and Social Change: Orissa in 1959* (Berkeley: University of California Press, 1963), and G. Ram Reddy and G. Haragopal, "The Pyraveekar: 'The Fixer' in Rural India," *Asian Survey*, xxv, No. 11 (November 1985), 1148–1162; see also Philip Oldenburg, "Middlemen in Third-World Corruption: Implications of an Indian Case," *World Politics*, xxxix, No. 4 (July, 1987), 508–535.

[30] Ram Reddy and Haragopal, "The Pyraveekar," p. 1151.

[31] Ram Reddy and Haragopal, "The Pyraveekar," p. 1152.

[32] Ram Reddy and Haragopal, "The Pyraveekar," pp. 1157–1158.

[33] Ram Reddy and Haragopal, "The Pyraveekar," pp. 1159–1162 and Bailey, *Politics and Social Change*, pp. 60, 66, 101–102.

MASS MOVEMENTS, VIOLENT AND
NON-VIOLENT

Ever since the early days of mass participation in politics in India, especially since the launching of Tilak's several protest movements, campaigns, and politico-religious festivals[34] and the first all-India non-cooperation movement launched by Gandhi in 1920–21, extra-party, extra-parliamentary movements have been integral, if sporadic elements in Indian politics. Some of these movements have functioned alongside party organization as their mass mobilization wings. Others have sprung up from time to time wholly independent of existing party organizations and eschewing any relationship with them. Still others have formed as violent splinters of existing organizations whose peaceful parliamentary tactics they have come to reject as ineffective.[35]

The long-dominant Congress largely abandoned its agitational heritage after Independence for more than two decades except for occasional tactical purposes when it was temporarily out of power in particular states. However, most non-Congress parties launched mass movements in those days with some frequency or had leaders or associated organizations whose specialized functions involved mass mobilization. The less well-organized parties such as the several Socialist parties used mass agitations as a substitute for formal party organization, launching frequent campaigns large and small to protest against local administrative and police injustices or price rises, to demand implementation of land reform laws, and the like. The better-organized Communist parties have had specialized auxiliaries, particularly the trade unions under their control as well as peasant organizations, whose members could be called upon easily for similar purposes. Charan Singh maintained a separate Kisan Sammelan (Peasant Association) even while he merged his Lok Dal into the Janata party in 1977, which was used to bring hundreds of thousands of peasants to Delhi to demonstrate their support for him and his policies during his quarrels with Prime Minister Morarji Desai.

[34] Richard I. Cashman, *The Myth of the Lokmanya: Tilak and Mass Politics in Maharashtra* (Berkeley: University of California Press, 1975).

[35] For an ominous assessment of some contemporary examples and their relationships to the formal political parties, see Mahendra Prasad Singh, "The Dilemma of the New Indian Party System: To Govern or Not to Govern?" *Asian Survey*, xxxii, No. 4 (April, 1992), 303–317.

During the Emergency, the Youth Congress wing of the Indian National Congress acquired importance as a mobilizational and agitational wing of the party under the leadership of Sanjay Gandhi. Sanjay brought into the Congress large numbers of students and youths, many of them young toughs, hooligans, ruffians, and criminals of all sorts upon whom the Congress has since relied in many local agitations, engagements, riots, and other battles in urban streets with non-Congress parties, many of whom have also resorted to similar tactics during the past two decades.[36]

The Akali Dal in Punjab in the days before the disintegration of the political process there always had a dual leadership: one, a civilian politician who headed the parliamentary party, and a second, a *sant*, who could mobilize the Sikh faithful in the countryside for mass movements when the party was out of power. The BJP, which normally has had available to it the many hundreds of thousands of RSS workers interested in politics, also worked increasingly closely in the late 1980s and early 1990s with two other organizations in the RSS "family": the Vishwa Hindu Parishad and the Bajrang Dal. The former has kept the momentum going for several years around the movement to remove the Babri Masjid and build on its site a temple to Ram in Ayodhya, while the latter has acted as an armed adjunct to "defend" Hindus during processions and the communal riots precipitated by the tensions created as a consequence of this movement.

In the second category of independent mass movements are numerous local peasant movements which have sprung up from time to time in different parts of India. Some, like those of Sharad Joshi in Maharashtra and Tikait in western U. P., have been based on the middle peasantry and have demanded higher prices for their produce, an equitable price structure in general as between farm products and the industrial products and supplies produced in the cities and towns upon which they depend, and increased governmental funding of inputs such as improved seed varieties, fertilizers, irrigation, and power. Other movements, based on the poorer peasants and landless laborers, have demanded access to land through ownership or protected tenancy and sharecropping rights.

[36] Kohli provides several examples of such engagements in the districts, state capitals, and larger towns of India in his *Democracy and Discontent*, e.g., pp. 131ff and *passim*. He has also coined a general term for this process initiated by the Congress, namely, "belligerent mass mobilization"; p. 340.

In the third category, increasingly prominent in recent years, are militant, violent, and terrorist groups, some of which have been offshoots of existing party organizations, others of which have developed independently of them. The most famous of the groups of this type in the late 1960s and 1970s were various revolutionary and terrorist organizations proclaiming radical Communist goals and lumped together under the heading of "Naxalites." In the 1980s and 1990s, the more prominent militant and violent organizations have been associated with separatist, secessionist, and particularist movements. They include a host of groups and gangs in Punjab, the Jammu and Kashmir Liberation Front in Kashmir, the United Liberation Front in Assam, and the Liberation Tigers of Tamil Eelam (LTTE) in Tamil Nadu, among others. The LTTE, though a Sri Lankan organization, became a force in Tamil Nadu under the patronage of the DMK in the late 1980s and intruded massively in Indian politics in May, 1991 by carrying out the assassination of Rajiv Gandhi. In the states of Punjab, Kashmir, and in Assam until recently, these violent movements have completely overshadowed or displaced the formal political process.

Increasingly prominent in contemporary mass movements leading to violence are students and criminals. Many of the universities in India, especially in the north, suffer from dismal facilities, poor teaching, out-dated curricula, and in general an absence of incentives or an environment conducive to study or learning. They are places coveted by upwardly mobile persons from all segments of society whose primary goal is to obtain a government job or training to enter a well-paying profession. Lacking also few avenues for extra-curricular enjoyment beyond the local cinema houses, the universities are centers for political activism where students are easily mobilized for both internal, student union elections and for outside agitations, especially around any movements that focus on employment issues and opportunities relating to their post-graduation life chances. The latter include movements to demand or protest against job reservations for members of a particular caste, language, or other ethnic group. They also include movements, the end result of which would be to increase the life chances of particular groups, such as anti-migrant or secessionist movements. Students have always provided a considerable proportion of mass participants in movements in India, going back to the days of

Gandhi's Non-cooperation Movement to anti-Hindi agitations in Madras in the mid 1960s[37] to the protests against the Mandal Commission recommendations for job reservations for backward castes in the 1990s. They now provide a very large share as well of the militants in violent and secessionist movements.

A second great recruitment pool for contemporary violent movements in India comprises those with no education and no respectable life chances, namely, that large underclass which inhabits all urban areas of the country: *goondas* (thugs, hooligans), criminals, lower caste people living in filthy slums whose participation can be purchased with money and whiskey. These elements are increasingly being organized in the large towns and cities of the country into so-called *mafia* organizations headed by known, named persons who themselves may be partly educated and even of high caste status. They participate in urban movements and help to turn them in violent directions at times to serve their own interests in looting and plundering, at times at the behest of local politicians with whom they have ties.

Formally organized groups with explicit goals such as secessionism, which can be achieved only through violence, remain confined to particular states and regions of the country, mostly in peripheral and relatively small states such as Punjab, Kashmir, and Assam. However, the spread of such organizations to the larger states of the country is one of the most ominous possibilities in India's future. Even now, the ready availability of militant youth and students, as well as criminal specialists in violence, for participation in mass movements of many types has already increased greatly the spread and the incidence of violent conflicts widely across the country.

[37] Kohli, *Democracy and Discontent*, pp. 178–179.

CHAPTER 4

STATE AND LOCAL POLITICS

Parallel trends and counter-tendencies have been at work especially in the post-Nehru period both in center–state relations and in the relations between state governments and district institutions. With regard to center–state relations, the offices and institutions of state government have increasingly been turned into instruments for implementing the will of the central government leadership. The counter-tendencies, partly arising out of India's regional/cultural heterogeneity but also in response to the imposition of Delhi's direct and indirect rule over the states, have been the regionalization of state politics and party systems, the increasing assertion of demands for revision of center–state relations, for regional autonomy, and even for outright secession.

Insofar as district and local politics are concerned, similar processes have been at work. On the one hand, ruling parties in the state governments, particularly the Congress, have allowed district and local institutions of self-government to decline or have limited their powers or have even frequently superseded them altogether in order to maintain tighter control over local systems of patronage and to establish stable bases of local support. The counter-tendency has been the persistence, even the reassertion, of structures of local power which exist independently of government and party organizations and the revival of interest, especially among the non-Congress parties, in the restoration of local institutions of self-government.

STATE POLITICS

Roles of the state governor

The constitutional role provided for the state governors and the practices which have evolved in relation to the office of governor since Independence have provided the focal point of contestation over the relative balance between autonomy and central control in center–state relations. The national leadership in the Constituent Assembly was concerned to maintain the strength of the Center in relation to the states and to have the recourse to intervene in cases of serious instability and political and communal unrest. At the same time, they wished to establish full parliamentary government at the state as well as the central levels, in which a governor with executive power would be inconsistent. The Constitution partly reflects this ambiguity in its specification of the appointment and powers of the state governors.

The Constitution provides that the governors are to be appointed by the President, that is, in effect by the Prime Minister.[1] By far the most difficult and controversial aspects of the governor's roles have centered around the questions of appointment and dismissal of chief ministers and the power to dissolve the legislature and recommend the imposition of President's Rule (PR) on a state.

From Independence to 1967

The major issues in this period of relative state autonomy concerned the relations between the governor and the elected state government and the functions which the governor could rightfully exercise. Former state governor Sri Prakasa, who had been governor both of Madras and U. P. at different times, complained that the governors were not being made use of nor even kept properly informed or consulted by their chief ministers.[2]

Even before 1967, however, there were occasions when the governors were in a position to exercise discretion in the appointment or dismissal of state governments and when they sometimes acted relatively impartially and independently of either the state or central government. Sri Prakasa himself refers to such a situation in his description of his actions in Madras in 1952 when it was not evident whether the Congress or the United Front of non-Congress parties was in the stronger position to form a stable government and when there was also no clear choice within the Congress of a leader with majority support in his own party. Although it does not appear that he was acting on the direction of the Congress, it is clear that his actions were helpful to the Congress in forming a stable government in the state.[3]

---

[1] Granville Austin, *The Indian Constitution: Cornerstone of a Nation* (Oxford: Clarendon Press, 1966), p. 117.

[2] Sri Prakasa, *State Governors in India* (Meerut: Meenakshi Prakashan, 1966), pp. 11–13.

[3] Sri Prakasa, *State Governors in India*, pp. 34–44.

The most famous case involving the imposition of PR in this period was the dismissal of the Communist ministry in Kerala in 1959 after popular demonstrations engineered and exploited by the Congress under the direction of Mrs. Gandhi, then Congress President. Although the state government retained a majority in the legislature, the governor justified his dismissal of it by referring to "a tremendous shift in the minds and in the feelings of the people," that is, in "public opinion,"[4] though no election or public opinion poll was held to support his assessment of this "shift."

The position of the governor in the pre-1967 period can be summed up as follows. In normal times, when there were stable governments and strong chief ministers in the states, the governors were reduced to figureheads and were even ignored. At times of instability, which were then less common than they later became, the governors had to exercise discretion in the appointment and dismissal of government and in making recommendations for the imposition of PR. The Madras case in 1952 involved the installation of a Congress government, the Kerala case in 1959 the dismissal of a non-Congress government. In both instances and in most others during this period, the results were consistent with the interests of the Congress, which were identified with the interests of the country and defined in terms of order, stability, and Congress rule.

From 1967 to 1980

In this period, which begins with the 1967 elections and the Congress loss of power mostly to unstable non-Congress coalitions in half the Indian states, the role of the governor becomes pivotal in state politics. The tone for the whole period was set in 1967 by the actions of the governor of Rajasthan, Dr. Sampurnanand, the former Congress chief minister of U. P., who "did not invite" the leader of the non-Congress Samyukta Vidhayak Dal (United Legislature Party) to form the government, though it claimed a majority in the legislature.[5] Although a case can be made for the governor's refusal to invite the leader of the non-Congress coalition to form the government and instead to recom-

[4] M. V. Pylee, *Constitutional Government in India* (New York: Asia Publishing House, 1965), pp. 646–647.
[5] B. B. Misra, *Government and Bureaucracy in India, 1947–1976* (Delhi: Oxford University Press, 1986), p. 49.

mend the imposition of PR and the suspension of the state legislature, the significance of the Rajasthan incident is not this specific refusal but the beginning of a broader process of the use of the governor's office to further the interests of the ruling party at the Center in installing a government of its choice in a state.

The use of the governor's office to install governments of the Center's choice was not, however, routine or consistent. The Congress government at the Center might decide not to act in a situation of instability where the Congress party itself in a state legislature was not in a strong enough position to form a stable government. Another situation which often confused matters in this period was that the Congress succession crisis occurred at this time, with the consequence that the central government under Mrs. Gandhi might prefer to have a non-Congress government in power in a state than a Congress government dominated by a faction opposed to her leadership.

What is critical about this period insofar as the role of the governor is concerned, however, is that the office was used by the central government to install state governments of its choice when it did decide to act. In a choice between two uncertain alternatives, a potentially unstable non-Congress coalition and a factionalized minority Congress government, the choice would be either the latter or the imposition of PR. In the former case, the designated leader would be given ample time and the support of the central government to promote defections from the non-Congress side in order to form a "stable" government. The governors in these situations did what they were told by the Center, but did not usually play an active role in helping new chief ministers to stabilize their positions or in bringing down chief ministers opposed by the central government.

Although this period includes the years of Janata rule from 1977 to 1979, in which the Janata party directed the governors for their own purposes, its practices were defined primarily by the Congress. If the period begins symbolically with Dr. Sampurnanand's imposition of PR to prevent the installation of a non-Congress government and to facilitate the selection of a Congress chief minister, it ends symbolically during the Emergency in 1976 with the dismissal of the government of DMK chief minister Karunanidhi in Tamil Nadu. The DMK government was dismissed on the grounds of corruption and with the charge that the state government "held out 'veiled threats' of secession" in Tamil Nadu.[6]

After 1980

A further watershed was reached near the end of Mrs. Gandhi's life in 1984 when the governors of two states, Jammu & Kashmir and Andhra, dismissed their respective non-Congress chief ministers on the alleged basis of information which they had that the chief ministers had lost their majorities in their legislative assemblies. Minority governments were installed and the newly installed Congress chief ministers were given a month to prove their majorities. Although this manoeuver succeeded in Jammu & Kashmir, it failed in Andhra where a mass movement was launched, with participation by opposition leaders from the rest of the country, and where the press covered the events fully and in detail. As a consequence of the agitation, the governor of the state was dismissed – though it is generally believed he was acting on the instructions of the central government. When the newly appointed chief minister failed to prove his majority in the House at the conclusion of one month, requesting a postponement instead, he was dismissed by the new governor and the previous chief minister, N. T. Rama Rao, leader of the Telugu Desam, succeeded in demonstrating his majority in the Andhra Legislative Assembly.[7]

In Kashmir and Andhra, the governors were not simply following orders, but were playing direct political roles and usurping the powers of the state legislatures "in the making and unmaking of chief ministers."[8] The misuse of the governor's office in Andhra, however, precipitated a double backlash. Popular protest was so intense both in the state and in other parts of the country that the central government was compelled to resile from its actions, while denying them, and to replace the governor. Second, the governor's and the central government's actions in displacing the leader of a regional party in a southern state precipitated a predictable regional counter-response. In June, 1985, the Andhra government submitted a statement to the Sarkaria

[6] S. R. Maheshwari, *President's Rule in India* (New Delhi: Mainstream, 1977), p. 174.

[7] P. M. Kamath, "Politics of Defection in India in the 1980s," *Asian Survey*, xxv, No. 10 (October, 1985), 1049; Krishna K. Tummala, "Democracy Triumphant in India: The Case of Andhra Pradesh," *Asian Survey*, xxvi, No. 3 (March, 1986), 379–381, 389.

[8] Bhagwan D. Dua, "Federalism or Patrimonialism: The Making and Unmaking of Chief Ministers in India," *Asian Survey*, xxv, No. 8 (August, 1985), 803.

Commission on center–state relations calling for "the abolition of the position of governor and demanding constitutional equality between the states and the Center."[9]

Under Rajiv Gandhi On the first occasion when the central government under Rajiv Gandhi's leadership had an opportunity to continue its previous practices of using the governor's office to install a Congress government, in Karnataka in 1984, it declined to do so.[10] However, after this initial act of restraint, the central government reverted to former practices in its use of the governor's office and, in some respects, took a further step in turning the office into an instrument of central control and surveillance of state governments.[11]

The reversion to past practices was most evident in the politically critical state of Tamil Nadu after the death of MGR in 1987 and the succession struggle which began immediately thereafter. The first act of the governor was to deny the request of the interim chief minister, Nedunchezhian, for a week's time to demonstrate his support in the Assembly and to recognize instead Janaki Ramachandran, the wife of former Congress ally MGR, as "the leader of the majority faction of the AIADMK" and to give "her three weeks to prepare for a vote of confidence in the Assembly."[12] However, the Congress soon became disaffected with Janaki Ramachandran because of reports that Congress (I) MLAs "were being purchased" by her group.[13] Consequently, the Home Minister of the Government of India, Buta Singh, Rajiv Gandhi's leading "troubleshooter" in the mid 1980s, personally went to Madras to persuade the governor to dismiss the Janaki Ramachandran government.

Under V. P. Singh. Upon the accession to power of the National Front government led by V. P. Singh, the President, in January, 1990 called for the resignation of eighteen governors who had been appointed during Rajiv Gandhi's tenure as Prime Minister. This action reflected the belief of the non-Congress leaders that the governor's office had been so politicized during the previous decade of Congress rule that the

---

9 Tummala, "Democracy Triumphant in India," p. 394.

10 Kamath, "Politics of Defection in India in the 1980s," p. 1039.

11 E.g., see *India Today*, February 29, 1988, p. 27 and March 15, 1988, pp. 23–24, on the situation in Meghalaya.

12 *India Today*, January 31, 1988, p. 30.   13 *India Today*, March 15, 1988, p. 37.

impartiality of the governors could not be trusted. At the same time, it further emphasized the transformation of the governor into an agent of the Center and "in effect made the office of governor a spoils position."[14] It also confirmed the predominance of two political practices which have become increasingly entrenched in Indian politics: the assertion of centralized political control over state politics and its corollary, the insistence upon the right of higher levels to interfere in the functioning of lower levels of government.

Under Chandrashekhar. Tamil Nadu once again became the venue for an extraordinary subordination of the governor's office by the central government during the brief prime ministership of Chandrashekhar, who depended upon the support of the Congress and Rajiv Gandhi for his majority in Parliament. In the 1989 state legislative assembly elections, the DMK under Karunanidhi had captured power in the state. The Congress, allied with the AIADMK under the leadership of Jayalalitha, demanded that Chandrashekhar remove the Karunanidhi government on the grounds that the activities of the Sri Lankan Tamil militants supported by the Tamil Nadu government were causing a threat to law and order. However, the Janata-appointed governor refused to make the necessary recommendation required under the Constitution for the dismissal of a state government. Nevertheless, the President dismissed the Karunanidhi government on January 30, 1991.[15]

Conclusions

During the first two decades after Independence the exercise of discretion by governors and their use as instruments of the Center's will were relatively rare, although the Kerala case provided a precedent for the decisive interventions by the Center in the later periods. The Kerala precedent included a decision taken by the central Cabinet to impose PR even before the receipt of the report of the governor.[16]

[14] Krishna K. Tummala, "India's Federalism Under Stress," *Asian Survey*, xxxii, No. 6 (June, 1992), 540.

[15] Tummala, "India's Federalism," pp. 541–544.

[16] Even the highly biased report in favor of the central government's action prepared by the Indian Commission of Jurists, *Report of the Kerala Enquiry Committee* (New Delhi, 1960), admits as much when it says in its chronology of the events for July 29, 1959: "The Central Cabinet discussed the Kerala affairs for more than two hours. Reports from New Delhi indicated that the Central intervention in Kerala was imminent within one or two

Since the succession struggle and the simultaneous period of unstable coalition politics in many states between 1965 and 1971, not only have the governors become entangled in state party and factional politics and intrigues at times, but they have become, as in Kerala in 1959, instruments of the central leadership's desires to control state politics.

The wide discretionary powers of the governor are, in effect, powers exercised by the central government by proxy through the governor. The more frequent use of the governor's office in these ways reflects a significant departure from the "cooperative federalism" of the Nehru era toward incessant intervention in state politics for the purpose of maintaining the ruling party, usually the Congress, in power in Delhi by controlling most of the states. It has also been demonstrated on several occasions during the past decades that the Center may dismiss state governments for political reasons even *against* the recommendation of a governor.

The role of the legislative assemblies

The state legislative assemblies played limited roles in the formulation and enactment of legislation, as venues of serious debate, or as watchdogs over the functioning of the government even in the Nehru period. They did, however, possess one significant power, namely, the power of selecting and replacing the government of the day.

During the non-Congress period of coalition politics, which overlapped as well with the succession struggle in the Congress and the rise of Mrs. Gandhi, the powers of the legislatures as such in this respect declined, but those of the individual members increased. The loyalties of individual members to particular parties or coalitions were so unstable and vulnerable to purchase by the highest bidder that few chief ministers or heads of rival coalitions would be willing to risk a confidence vote in the legislature because the outcome would be unpredictable. Individual legislators remained free to sell their votes but, since few leaders wished to test the reliability of their supporters in the legislature, the curious ritual practice unique to Indian politics developed, known as the "parade" of one's supporters before the governor of the state to convince him of the majority of one side or the

days. The Centre was waiting only for the Governor's Report, and the Report when it came clinched the issue" (p. 41).

other. The power of choosing the chief minister then devolved upon the governor, rather than the legislative assembly.

The decline in the significance of the state legislatures was precipitous, however, after Mrs. Gandhi's consolidation of power in New Delhi in 1971–72, for the non-Congress parties lost power in most of the states and the Congress legislators lost the power to control the selection of chief ministers, which was now done directly by Mrs. Gandhi and her advisers at the Center. Intrigue and dissidence continued perpetually in every state capital, but governments could not necessarily be brought down even by a majority of state Congress legislators if the Center refused to make a change.

After the landslide victory of the Congress under Rajiv Gandhi's leadership in the 1984 Lok Sabha elections, an anti-defection amendment to the Constitution, the 52nd Amendment, was passed requiring defectors to resign their seats in the legislative assembly and recontest them. This requirement would not apply if one-third or more of party members defected for such a defection would be considered a party split. Independents remain free to offer their support to one side or another in the legislature provided they do not formally join a political party. The amendment also is not a significant deterrent to members of small legislative parties.

In effect, therefore, the ultimate power of the legislative body in a parliamentary system to provide or deny a majority to a government has been largely eroded in the Indian states. The no-confidence power of the legislators has been turned into a political resource for individual MLAs. The right to determine the choice of a new chief minister has been taken away in practice to be exercised by the Prime Minister or by the governor of the state acting at his discretion or at the direction of the central government. Often even chief ministers with a majority in the legislative assemblies are removed by the central leadership of the Congress, thereby reducing even further the sanctioning authority of the legislatures.

The powers of the legislative assemblies declined still further under Rajiv Gandhi. During his prime ministership, chief ministers who retained majorities in the state legislatures were removed and new chief ministers installed without even the formal validation of the Congress legislature party. A chief minister who lost support in New Delhi could be summoned to the capital and advised to resign, after which he was likely to submit his resignation to the governor without much further ado.[17]

State party systems

In the face of the centralizing and nationalizing drives of the Congress under Mrs. Gandhi's leadership, the evolution of Indian state party systems has been marked by increasing regionalization. This regionalization is manifested in two ways: by the declining significance of the Congress as the principal political actor in several states despite its still universal presence and by the increasing divergence of each state's politics both from national trends manifested in parliamentary elections and from trends in other states.

The universal presence of the Congress

Even where the Congress had been reduced to seemingly permanent minority status, its role cannot be ignored. Its new roles can best be seen by considering the effects on state politics of intra-party divisions in the Congress, of the delinking of parliamentary and state legislative assembly elections, and of the actions of the national Congress party in relation to ruling non-Congress regional parties.

Intra-party divisions in the Congress continued to be of great importance during Mrs. Gandhi's period of dominance, but their tenor and significance changed considerably. Nationally induced divisions in state party politics have been of enormous import both for the whole character of center–state relations and for the regionalization of state politics. The consequences of these interventions have sometimes been to produce critical realignments in inter-party relations and in the social bases of party support which have been different in each state and which will be discussed presently below.

The delinking of parliamentary and state legislative assembly elections since 1971 has had some influence on the ability of the Congress to play the role of principal actor in state politics and on the forms its role may take. For a time, it appeared that delinking had not only freed national from state politics, but had imposed national upon state politics through the bandwagon effect. That is, once it was clear which party or party coalition was to be in power in Delhi, there was a rush

[17] As in the case of the dismissal of Harideo Joshi as chief minister of Rajasthan in January, 1988: *India Today*, February 15, 1988, pp. 13–15.

by party activists to defect to the winning side and a tendency for the election campaigns in the succeeding legislative assembly elections to emphasize the desirability of strengthening the hands of the ruling leadership in Delhi by bringing its supporters to power in the state capitals as well.

On the other hand, there has also been a counter-effect at work leading to a firmer separation of national and state politics, which has contributed to the entrenchment of strong regional parties in several states. In some states, particularly Tamil Nadu, the Congress has gone to the extent of forfeiting the legislative assembly context to the dominant regional party in exchange for the latter's concession of most parliamentary seats to the Congress. In other states, however, notably West Bengal, the dominant regional party has succeeded in capturing most Lok Sabha seats as well as a majority of the legislative assembly seats.

Congress has used two principal strategies toward dominant or strong regional parties at different times. One is the strategy of division, of exploiting factional differences within a regional party by offering inducements to one faction to defect to the Congress or by simply providing material support to one side in its struggle with its rivals. The second is the strategy of alliance, of joining with one or more local parties to defeat another strong regional party or coalition of parties.

Regionalization of state party systems

State party systems may be divided into several types according to two criteria: the configuration of principal political parties in the state and the structure of competition among them. In general, elections in the states – both for Parliament and for the state legislative assemblies – were marked by a much higher degree of competitiveness in the years between 1987 and 1992 than ever before. Virtually all the states now have competitive party systems in which alternation in power is a real possibility at each election.

The only remnant of the once nearly universal one-party dominant system is the state of Maharashtra. With one minor exception, there has never been any but a Congress government in this state from its inception in 1956 until 1992. In 1978, Sharad Pawar, then a renegade from the Congress (I), formed a Progressive Democratic Front government, which remained in power only until 1980.

In this state, the distance between the ruling Congress and its closest competitor is greater than in any other of the larger states of the Indian Union. Congress polled 48.3 percent of the 1991 Lok Sabha vote in Maharashtra compared to 20.6 percent for the BJP (table 4.1), an interval of 27.7 percentage points. Although the Congress did not succeed in winning a majority of seats in the legislative assembly elections held in March, 1990, it emerged as the largest party after defeating the BJP–Shiv Sena alliance against it and formed a government under Sharad Pawar. Congress dominance in Maharashtra is a mirror of the state's social structure, which itself is dominated like its politics by a single caste category, the Marathas, who in turn control the Congress organization.

Competitive two-party systems: Congress versus the BJP

Other than Maharashtra, the Indian states may be divided into four major groups. The first comprises the three northern Hindi-speaking states of Himachal Pradesh, Madhya Pradesh, and Rajasthan in which there are two principal parties, Congress and the BJP. The latter came to power in all three states in the March, 1990 legislative assembly elections. In the 1991 Lok Sabha elections, the vote shares of Congress and the BJP were quite close in each state and the combined vote shares of the two parties were between 84.9 and 89.0 percent. These three states, therefore, give the appearance of an emerging two-party system.

Competitive multi-party systems: Congress, the Janata parties, and the BJP

The second group includes the rest of the Hindi-speaking states – Bihar, U. P., and Haryana – plus Gujarat, Karnataka, and Orissa. In these six states, inter-party competition is dominated by three forces: Congress, Janata Dal and its fragments, and the BJP. In the northern Hindi-speaking states within this group, the middle status cultivating castes, of whom many are included in the Mandal Commission list of "backward castes," are economically powerful and tend to support the Janata parties. High caste groups, particularly Brahmans and Thakurs, Scheduled Castes, and Muslims have traditionally supported Congress in these states. However, the BJP drew support among the high castes away from Congress in the last election, while Muslims tended to back

Table 4.1. Popular vote percentages of the three leading parties in 1991 Lok Sabha elections by state[a]

State	Congress vote	Largest non-Congress vote	2nd largest non-Congress vote	Combined two-party vote	Combined three-party vote
Maharashtra	48.3	20.6 (BJP)	10.9 (JD)	68.9	79.8
Himachal Pradesh	46.2	42.8 (BJP)	7.0 (JD)	89.0	96.0
Madhya Pradesh	45.3	41.9 (BJP)	4.2 (JD)	87.2	91.4
Rajasthan	44.0	40.9 (BJP)	6.2 (JD)	84.9	91.1
Bihar	23.9	32.4 (JD)	16.9 (BJP)	56.3	73.2
Uttar Pradesh	18.3	32.9 (BJP)	21.6 (JD)	51.2	72.8
Haryana	37.2	25.4 (SJP)	12.5 (JD)	62.6	75.1
Gujarat	28.2	50.6 (BJP)	12.6 (JDG)	78.8	91.4
Karnataka	42.0	28.7 (BJP)	18.5 (JD)	70.7	89.2
Orissa	43.7	34.2 (JD)	9.9 (BJP)	77.9	87.8
Kerala	38.8	20.7 (CPM)	5.0 (ML)	59.5	64.5
West Bengal	36.2	35.1 (CPM)	11.7 (BJP)	71.3	83.0
Tamil Nadu	42.6	22.7 (DMK)	18.1 (AIADMK)	65.3	83.4
Andhra Pradesh	44.6	32.6 (TDP)	9.5 (BJP)	77.2	86.7
Assam	28.5	17.6 (AGP)	9.6 (BJP)	46.1	55.7

[a]Delhi and the smaller states of the northeast have been excluded. Elections were not held in the disturbed states of Punjab and Jammu & Kashmir during the General Elections in May–June 1991.

BJP:	Bharatiya Janata Party	DMK:	Dravida Munnetra Kazagham
JD:	Janata Dal	TDP:	Telugu Desam
SJP:	Samajwadi Janata Party	AGP:	Asom Gana Parishad
CPM:	Communist Party of India	JDG:	Janata Dal (G)
	(Marxist)	ADMK:	Anna DMK
		ML:	Muslim League

Source: All India Radio, Lok Sabha Poll: An A.I.R. Analysis (New Delhi: Government of India, All India Radio, News Services Division, 1991), pp. 17–42.

Janata and SJP candidates as the best bets to defeat the BJP. As a consequence, Congress support was reduced in the Lok Sabha elections to 23.9 percent in Bihar and to 18.3 percent of the popular vote in U. P. where it came in third after the BJP and the Janata Dal. Despite the victory of the BJP in the state legislative assembly elections, the combined strength of the Janata parties (Janata Dal and the SJP) in this state is greater than that of the BJP.[18]

Until the Congress split in 1969, Gujarat was as much a one-party dominant system as Maharashtra, with the Congress vote share ranging between 45 and 55 percent and only one significant opposition party, Swatantra, with a considerable vote share – nearly 25 percent in 1962 – but not enough to represent a serious alternative to the Congress. As in Maharashtra, the structure of one-party dominance was sustained by the control over both party organization and society exercised by a dominant rural caste, the Patidars, though in Gujarat the rural Patidars were allied also with urban Brahmans and Banias.[19] In contrast to Maharashtra, however, the Congress (O) was a formidable rival to the Congress (R) of Mrs. Gandhi.

During the 1970s, the rival Congress organizations struggled for ascendancy. Congress (O), which merged into the Janata party in 1977, captured the bulk of the old Congress' social support among the elite castes while Congress (R) completely altered its social support base by building the "KHAM" coalition of backward castes and minorities.[20]

Although Congress (R) appeared by this strategy to have reestablished a one-party dominant system in the 1980 and 1985 elections, it lacked the organizational base to maintain it or to deal effectively with sustained violent movements launched against it by elements from among the disaffected social and economic elite groups.[21] In the 1990 legislative assembly elections, Congress emerged in third place after the Janata Dal and the BJP. Then, in the 1991 Lok

[18] See Paul R. Brass, "The Rise of the BJP and the Future of Party Politics in Uttar Pradesh," in Harold A. Gould and Sumit Ganguly (eds.), *India Votes: Alliance Politics and Minority Governments in the Ninth and Tenth General Elections* (Boulder, CO: Westview Press, 1993).
[19] Atul Kohli, *Democracy and Discontent: India's Growing Crisis of Governability* (Cambridge: Cambridge University Press, 1990), pp. 241–242.
[20] John R. Wood, "Congress Restored? The 'KHAM' Strategy and Gujarat," in John R. Wood (ed.), *State Politics in Contemporary India* (Boulder, CO: Westview Press, 1984), ch. 8.
[21] Kohli, *Democracy and Discontent*, pp. 252–266.

Sabha elections, the BJP surged far ahead of both Congress and the principal fragment of the Janata Dal – Janata Dal (G) – polling 50.6 percent of the vote and twenty out of twenty-five seats.

Karnataka too was in the Nehru era one of the purest of the one-party dominant states. This early Congress dominance was based primarily on the support of the dominant landed communities in the state, the Lingayats and Vokkaligas. As in Gujarat, however, the Congress split of 1969 introduced serious inter-party division into Karnataka's politics for the first time and precipitated a realignment of the social support bases of the parties. The Congress in the 1970s under the leadership of Devaraj Urs shifted its appeals to the backward castes, while the Congress (O) joined the Janata coalition in the 1977 elections, after which the party system became for a time a competitive dualistic system with the Congress (I) and Janata constituting genuine single-party alternative governments. The Janata party ruled from 1983 to 1989, but disintegrated in factional conflict, whereupon President's Rule was imposed. Congress won a massive victory in the 1989 legislative assembly elections, reducing the Janata party to a bare eleven seats and placing the latter's continued existence as a viable alternative to Congress in doubt. Janata's viability as the principal alternative to Congress in this state was further threatened by the BJP surge in the 1991 Lok Sabha elections, in which it emerged as the second largest party after the Congress.[22]

In Orissa, the name of the principal opposition to the Congress has changed over the decades from the Ganatantra Parishad to Swatantra and now to Janata, but the former landlords and Congress renegades have continued to provide strong support to the current principal non-Congress party. Here, inter-party competition has been largely dualistic between Congress and lately Janata, with the BJP a poor third. Janata itself, as in most other regions of India, is led by a former Congressman, Biju Patnaik.

Competitive dualist systems: Congress vs. the CPM

The third group includes only the two states of West Bengal and Kerala, where the principal opposition to the Congress has come from

---

[22] However, for an assessment of the party system in Karnataka after the 1991 elections and the organizational weakness of the BJP there, see James Manor, "BJP in South India: 1991 General Election," *EPW*, xxvii, Nos. 24 & 25 (June 13–20, 1992), pp. 1268–1272.

the CPM, and where alternation in power is always a real possibility. In both states, each election is fought by competing alliances of parties in which the Congress is the principal partner in one and the CPM in the other. The balance in Kerala has remained close throughout most of the post-Independence period, with neither the Congress nor the CPM alone being in a position to form a one-party government. Since 1980, the CPM- and Congress-led fronts have alternated in power, the CPM in 1980–81 and 1987–91 and the Congress in 1981–82, 1982–87, and after the 1991 legislative assembly elections. In West Bengal, on the other hand, Congress hegemony lasted until 1967 when a period of party fragmentation and government instability was replaced by the new hegemony of the CPM-led front, which has persisted from 1977 to the present (1993).

Competitive regionally specific party systems

The fourth group of competitive party systems are those in which the principal non-Congress party or parties are regionally specific.

Tamil Nadu. After the Congress split of 1969, Mrs. Gandhi formed an alliance with the DMK in which the latter provided support to the Congress in the Lok Sabha and later conceded an agreed number of Lok Sabha seats in the 1971 elections to the Congress in exchange for the support of the Congress (R) against the Congress (O) in state politics. Since 1971–72, the main dynamic in Tamil Nadu politics has been provided by rivalry between the DMK and the AIADMK, a party founded by the film actor, M. G. Ramachandran (known as "MGR") in 1972 after a struggle for power in the DMK following the death of the latter's former leader, C. N. Annadurai. MGR successfully sought an alliance with the Congress (I) at the Center during the Emergency and the AIADMK emerged thereafter as the ruling party in the state from the elections of 1977 until MGR's death in 1987.

During the succession struggle which followed MGR's death, the Congress decided to contest the 1989 mid-term legislative assembly elections alone. In a four-way split among the Congress, the two contending factions of the AIADMK, and the DMK, the latter emerged victorious in the January 21 elections. However, once the succession struggle in the AIADMK was settled in favor of the leadership of MGR's former mistress, Jayalalitha, the Congress and the AIADMK restored their former alliance. The DMK government was dismissed by the President of India on January 30, 1991 on the advice of Prime Minister Chandrashekhar who, in turn, was acting upon the demand of Rajiv Gandhi and the Congress, upon whose support in the Lok Sabha his own government depended. In the ensuing election of 1991 the AIADMK once again came to power in Tamil Nadu.

Although the Congress often emerges as the second largest party in state legislative assembly elections, it really acts as a third force, tilting the balance between the DMK and the AIADMK. For most of the past fifteen years, the Congress and the AIADMK have been allied against the DMK and have divided the legislative and parliamentary seats in the state in such a way that the AIADMK wins power in Tamil Nadu while the Congress takes the majority of seats for Parliament and the DMK is pushed into third position. However, in 1993, the long-term Congress-AIADMK alliance was under pressure as the AIADMK leader, Jayalalitha was reported to be in the process of shifting her party support in national politics to the BJP.

Jammu & Kashmir. Until the disintegration of the political process in Kashmir, the National Conference was much the stronger of the two main parties in electoral support in Kashmir. From 1987 until the imposition of Governor's Rule (the term used for President's Rule in Kashmir) on January 19, 1990, the National Conference ruled the state with the support of the Congress. The principal differences between Kashmir and Tamil Nadu in relation to the two factors of the Congress presence and regionalization were that the Congress was a greater threat to the predominant regional party and that the Center played here a more active and directly interventionist role such that the National Conference, unlike the AIADMK, could never be sure that its alliance with the Congress would not be terminated and its government brought down. Ultimately, however, it was popular discontent with the alliance between the National Conference and the Congress which not only brought down the government, but put an end for the time being to party and electoral politics in this state (see chapter 6 below).

Punjab. Here, when routine politics rather than civil war prevailed, the basic dynamic of politics was provided by the dualistic competition between the Congress and a specifically Sikh political party, the Akali Dal. In contrast to both Tamil Nadu and Kashmir, however, the Congress was the dominant party in Punjab and the dualism was unbalanced. The Center here also frequently played an interventionist role, especially under Mrs. Gandhi, with disastrous consequences, which will be discussed in further detail as well in chapter 6.

Andhra Pradesh. In 1962, the Congress polled 47 percent of the vote and won 57 percent of the seats in the state legislative assembly. With the rise of the Congress and the decline of the CPI in the late 1950s and early 1960s, politics in Andhra revolved for a decade around the struggles of dominant castes for control of the Congress patronage system and around divisions among them.[23]

Two events occurred in the late 1960s, however, which led to a critical realignment of the Andhra Pradesh party system: the national party split in the Congress and the Telangana movement for preferential treatment for residents of Telangana in government jobs and educational admissions, which burgeoned into a demand for a division of Andhra Pradesh and the creation of a separate state of Telangana.[24] Mrs. Gandhi's adroit handling of the Telangana agitation and the new coalition which arose in association with it realigned the Congress support base in relation to opposition parties, but left the Congress still the dominant party in Andhra.

A second realignment of Andhra politics occurred after the defeat of the Congress in the 1977 Lok Sabha elections, with much less felicitous results for it. The displacement of three chief ministers and five state Congress Presidents between 1978 and 1983 provided to the newly formed Telugu Desam party – led by a Telugu film star, "NTR" – the basis for an electoral appeal to regional sentiment in Andhra, namely, opposition to the "imposition" of chief ministers "from New Delhi."[25]

Having been defeated in the party-electoral arena in 1983 by a

[23] On the evolution of party and electoral politics in Andhra, see F. D. Vakil, "Patterns of Electoral Performance in Andhra Pradesh and Karnataka," in Richard Sisson and Ramashray Roy (eds.), *Diversity and Dominance in Indian Politics*, Vol. 1: *Changing Bases of Congress Support* (New Delhi: Sage, 1990), pp. 249–275.
[24] On the Telangana movement, see esp. Myron Weiner, *Sons of the Soil: Migration and Ethnic Conflict in India* (Princeton, N.J.: Princeton University Press, 1978), ch. v.
[25] Vakil, "Patterns of Electoral Performance," p. 261, and Tummala, "Democracy Triumphant in India," pp. 384–385.

regional party, the central Congress leadership decided to use the powers of the governor directly to displace the Telugu Desam from power in 1984 before the imminent parliamentary elections. This demonstration of the Center's willingness to intervene directly in Andhra politics even through extra-legal means provided a further boost to the Telugu Desam, which proceeded to win twenty-eight of the thirty-two Lok Sabha seats in the 1984 parliamentary elections, in the face of the Rajiv Gandhi landslide victory nearly everywhere else in the country.

The consequence, therefore, of the Congress' interventionist strategy was the strengthening of a regional movement, whose organizational base is otherwise limited and whose life was probably extended by the very heavy-handedness of the interventions from New Delhi.[26] In fact, in 1989, when the Telugu Desam became part of the National Front which defeated the Congress in the Lok Sabha elections, it lost to the Congress in the Andhra Pradesh Legislative Assembly elections.

Assam. Congress dominance in the state remained unchallenged through the 1970s, the Emergency, and even the 1977 Lok Sabha elections. As in Andhra, however, the bandwagon effect had its repercussions in Assam after the massive defeat of the Congress in the north Indian Hindi-speaking states and the Congress loss of power at the Center. The Congress split and the alliance between Assamese Hindus and Bengali Muslims collapsed on the issue of the demand from Assamese Hindus in 1979 for the expulsion of illegal immigrants from Bangladesh, mostly Muslims, whose increased numbers on the electoral rolls caused considerable alarm to many Assamese Hindus. The state came under President's Rule, but Mrs. Gandhi, determined to reestablish her hold throughout the country after her return to power in Delhi in 1980, insisted upon holding legislative assembly elections here in 1983. During those elections, boycotted by the Assamese student movement and accompanied by large-scale massacres of Bengali Muslims, the Congress "won" a Pyrrhic victory, but was unable to govern the state.

[26] James Manor, "Appearance and Reality in Indian Politics: The 1984 General Election in the South," in Paul R. Brass and Francis Robinson (eds.), *The Indian National Congress and Indian Society, 1885–1985: Ideology, Social Structure and Political Dominance* (Delhi: Chanakya Publications, 1987), pp. 413–419.

Fresh elections held in September, 1985 were won handily by the Asom Gana Parishad, a party formed out of the Assamese Hindu student movement. Once again, therefore, it is evident that the desperate rush of the central Congress leadership to regain control of the states after Mrs. Gandhi's return to power in 1980 involved ill-conceived interventionist moves from New Delhi, which produced results contrary to those desired, namely, the powerful assertion of regional forces which succeeded in displacing the Congress from power in a state formerly a bastion of support for the ruling party. However, the AGP proved unable to govern Assam effectively and lost its support base in a few years, paving the way for a return of the Congress to power in the 1991 elections.

The strength of national and regional parties and the conditions for their institutionalization

Forty-five years after Independence, it is evident that few political parties in India have been able to persist through time in the country as a whole or in the several states. The persisting parties are distinguished from the ephemeral formations principally in terms of whether or not they control or have privileged access to a major set of material, human, or symbolic resources.

The persistence of the Congress as the preeminent political organization in India for a century has been based upon its strength in all these respects. In the middle periods of its long history, for several decades before Independence and for some time afterwards, it symbolized the Indian nation itself and the aspiration of Indian elites for greatness in a world of nations. Its human resources included numerous extraordinary national and regional leaders, among whom Mahatma Gandhi stood at the center in the pre-Independence period and the Nehru family for forty-five years after Independence. The Congress also controlled, partially before Independence and overwhelmingly after it, the vast and increasing patronage resources of a new state bent on economic development. As the aura of its identification with Indian nationalism has gone and its great leaders have died or been assassinated and its organizational structure has disintegrated, the Congress has become ever more a party whose strength is based primarily on the control and distribution by legal and illegal means of the economic resources controlled by the state.

Of the non-Congress political parties with national aspirations and a wide regional or cross-regional spread, those which have been able to persist have had control of at least some of these types of resources in some parts of the country. The Jan Sangh/BJP, for example, has been able to make use of the skilled and dedicated cadres of the RSS and an ideology of militant Hindu nationalism, which has had a strong appeal to some elite castes, particularly Brahmans and Rajputs in the rural areas, and to Brahman and Vaisya castes in the cities noted for their religiosity. Its attraction has extended socially to other upper Hindu castes and to some backward castes as well in recent years as a consequence of both the Ayodhya movement and the backward castes reservation issue. Because of its focus on building a grand new temple to Ram in Ayodhya, it and its allied organizations have been able to recruit religious leaders, priests, and holy men, to evoke the faith of ordinary Hindus behind its movement and to translate their faith into political support for the BJP. In a country where religious symbols continue to have enormous mobilizing potential, the BJP has succeeded in capturing and monopolizing the political use of some of the most powerful of such symbols, notably the figure of Ram and the image of Ram Rajya (Ram's Kingdom) brought to life under its banner. Moreover, by gaining power in several states in recent years, the BJP gained control over the distribution of the material resources of their governments.

Where they have succeeded in institutionalizing themselves, as in Kerala and West Bengal, the Communist parties have been staffed and led principally by non-charismatic, but skilled and dedicated full-time workers. The CPM in West Bengal, of course, has controlled the resources of the state government since 1977 and has used that control to extend its support throughout the countryside by gaining control of village *panchayats* (councils) and by implementing legislation for the protection of the rights of tenants, sharecroppers, and the landless.

The principal resources available to the Lok Dal were the popular, though not quite charismatic, leadership of Chaudhuri Charan Singh, who developed an image throughout north India as a man dedicated to the small and middle peasantry and to the cause of the backward castes. However, the Lok Dal has not been able to survive his death. Several north Indian leaders, including his son, have contested against each other to inherit his political mantle and his support base.

The preeminent material and symbolic resource of the Akali Dal has been its control over the SGPC, the managing committee which controls all the Sikh *gurdwaras* (temples) and shrines in Punjab and the considerable financial and patronage resources available through it. The Akali Dal also has developed a strong and stable basis of rural support among the dominant Jat Sikh peasantry, which it has reinforced while in power by promoting the interests of this agricultural class in gaining access to the new inputs and the irrigation water necessary to sustain the green revolution in the Punjab and by avoiding the passage of legislation to reduce the size of land holdings. However, fratricidal conflict among Sikhs and confrontations between militant non-Akali Sikh groups against the police and state security forces have led to the fractionalization of the Akali Dal into a multiplicity of groups with no ability to function effectively in the political disorder, criminalized anarchy, and state repression which has prevailed in the Punjab for a decade.

The DMK and the AIADMK in Tamil Nadu have been the inheritors of two persisting dominant ideological and social elements in the history of the Tamil-speaking people from the late nineteenth century, namely, the ideology of Tamil regional nationalism and the social base of the non-Brahman movement. Second, the original DMK and the AIADMK have both been led by charismatic leaders, Annadurai of the DMK, and MGR, a film star, the leader of the AIADMK. The latter was created in a party split after the death of Annadurai in 1969. Third, the DMK and AIADMK have had a rich symbolic and material base in the huge Tamil film industry, which their leaders dominate, and which has provided these parties with a propaganda system for the spread of Tamil nationalism, ample sources of funds, and skilled leaders and workers with a natural ability to appeal to the people. Finally, first the DMK, then the AIADMK succeeded in establishing themselves as the natural governing party of the state of Tamil Nadu, which one or the other of these two parties has governed continuously – except for a break during the Emergency – since 1967.

DISTRICT AND LOCAL POLITICS

District government and administration

Gandhian desires for the dismantling of the colonial bureaucratic structure, the transformation of the Indian National Congress into an organization for constructive work in the countryside, and the creation of a decentralized form of government based on the revival and reorganization of traditional forms of local self-government (the *panchayats*) down to the village level were not taken seriously by the Constituent Assembly of India. Moreover, the entire system of British district administration, which both concentrated authority at the district level and provided for very little participation by representatives of the people, was retained virtually intact, particularly the central importance of the District Magistrate and the district courts and the police.

Community development

Although the old structure of district administration was not only retained but in some ways had its importance enhanced, new administrative hierarchies were also introduced. The Community Development program introduced a new type of administrative system based on the community development block comprising approximately 100 villages each and a network of village level workers (VLWs). Planning was from the top down, with targets sent down the hierarchy from the Planning Commission to the state governments to be implemented at the local level.

The 1957 Balwantray Mehta committee report recommended democratic decentralization of power to the sub-district level to encourage popular participation in decision making at the local level and to "put the bureaucracy under local popular control."[27] In effect, it proposed a system of popular participation parallel to the block administrative system and, in principle, having powers of supervision and control over it.[28]

Panchayati raj (rule of village councils and other rural local bodies)

[27] Shriram Maheshwari, *Rural Development in India: A Public Policy Approach* (New Delhi: Sage, 1985), pp. 52–53.
[28] Stanley J. Heginbotham, *Cultures in Conflict: The Four Faces of Indian Bureaucracy* (New York: Columbia University Press, 1975), pp. 68–69.

was promoted by the central government as a matter of national policy from 1957 to 1963 when the state governments were pressured to adopt some form of democratic decentralization and to involve the people down to the village level directly in the planning process.[29] However, by the mid 1960s, support for *panchayati raj* had declined, even in its strongholds of Maharashtra and Gujarat. Most of the state political leaderships were reluctant to devolve much power to the district level and below for they feared that if such local institutions acquired real powers they would become alternative sources of political influence and patronage, which would threaten their own abilities to exercise influence in the districts and to use such influence as bases of their own power at the state level.

In practice, the introduction and withdrawal of *panchayati raj* institutions in particular states had more to do with calculations concerning the maintenance of power at the state level than with devolution of power to the district levels and below. For example, one of the reasons for the early adoption of *panchayati raj* institutions in Andhra Pradesh was the belief that they could be used "to counter the Communists in the rural areas" of the state where they then still had significant popular support.[30] On the other hand, *panchayati raj* institutions were suppressed or superseded by the ruling party whenever and wherever it felt threatened by a potential loss of power to other parties or when a new faction or party in power at the state level wanted to displace rival local leadership.

In 1977, twenty years after the report of the Balwantray Mehta committee, the Janata government appointed a new committee on *Panchayati Raj* Institutions, chaired by Asoka Mehta, to assess the problems faced by these institutions and to make proposals to remedy them. In the Asoka Mehta scheme, the *zila parishads* (district boards) were to be given control over all the development activities in the district, although the law and order functions would remain under the control of the existing district administrative apparatus.[31] The *panchayati raj* bodies were to have two tiers (mandal and district) and, unlike most of the previously established ones, would have considerable powers of taxation.

[29] Maheshwari, *Rural Development*, p. 53.
[30] Vakil, "Patterns of Electoral Performance," p. 253.
[31] Maheshwari, *Rural Development*, pp. 64–65.

The Janata government did not remain in power in Delhi long enough to begin a national policy process of promoting the adoption of the new scheme of *panchayati raj*. However, *panchayati raj* institutions have been revived or recast along the lines of the Asoka Mehta committee recommendations primarily in non-Congress states where they have been used as instruments for establishing alternative rural power bases for non-Congress parties. The Janata government of Karnataka, for example, adopted most of the recommendations of the Asoka Mehta committee and introduced a new system of democratic decentralization in 1983. A similar structure of *panchayati raj* was established in Andhra as well. Elections to the *zila parishads* and *mandal panchayats* were held in both states in 1987 and won by the Janata party and the Telugu Desam in their respective states.[32]

West Bengal has retained the original three-tiered system of *panchayati raj* institutions in conformity with the recommendations of the Balwantray Mehta committee report, but they were revived and politicized by the CPM government in that state in the late 1970s. Because of the penetration of the village *panchayats* by CPM cadres and party sympathizers and the displacement of the dominant landed classes by smaller landholders, teachers, and social workers, it has been possible to use the village *panchayats* for the implementation of agrarian reforms, notably registration of sharecroppers for purposes of tenancy reform and provision of loans and identification of beneficiaries for anti-poverty programs.[33]

The situation in West Bengal contrasts most sharply with that in Maharashtra, where the traditional three-tiered system also has been retained, but where *panchayati raj* functions as an instrument of Maratha economic dominance and Congress political control in the countryside.[34] These institutions from top to bottom are used primarily as instruments for the differential distribution of patronage to the rural land-controlling castes, which include primarily rural development inputs and jobs, notably the appointment and transfer of

[32] Vakil, "Patterns of Electoral Performance," p. 271 and Amal Ray and Jayalakshmi Kumpatla, "Zilla Parishad Presidents in Karnataka: Their Social Background and Implications for Development," *EPW*, xxii, Nos. 42 & 43 (October 17–24, 1987), 1825.

[33] Atul Kohli, "Parliamentary Communism and Agrarian Reform: The Evidence from India's Bengal," *Asian Survey*, xxiii, No. 7 (July, 1983), 801–802.

[34] Jayant Lele, *Elite Pluralism and Class Rule: Political Development in Maharashtra* (Bombay: Popular Prakashan, 1982), pp. 124–126.

teachers in schools throughout the districts, which are under the control of the *zila parishads*.

In April–May, 1989, the government of Rajiv Gandhi introduced a controversial bill in Parliament to transform the entire system of rural government in the country. The Constitution (Sixty-Fourth Amendment) Bill, 1989 proposed to establish *panchayats* as bodies legally sanctioned under the Constitution of the country, like the central and state governments themselves, with adequate financial resources and with elections supervised by the Election Commission. Although several of the non-Congress parties have been strong advocates of decentralization, their leaders saw this proposal not as a genuine effort to establish village democracy on a firm basis, but as a further attempt by the Congress government at the Center to bypass and undermine the state governments, most of which were then under the control of non-Congress governments. Consequently, since the Rajiv Gandhi government lacked a two-thirds majority in the Rajya Sabha, the amendment could not be passed.[35]

Local government, therefore, like federal–state relations, remained a terrain upon which battles between forces favoring centralization and decentralization appear to be contesting against each other. In fact, however, these struggles are subordinated to the drives of the leaders of all the main parties to control the country from New Delhi. The latter goal makes even ostensible efforts to decentralize power appear rather as further efforts by the leadership of higher governments to interfere in and control lower governmental bodies, to centralize power and control while appearing to do the opposite.

Levels and arenas of district politics

For two decades after Independence, the District Congress Committees (DCCs) were the most influential and important institutions in the district. Since the Congress split, however, the DCCs have declined in importance. Where they have persisted or been revived and have been granted extensive powers, the *zila parishads* have constituted a second or an alternative arena of power and influence at the district level. Other important institutions at the district level which local faction leaders strive to control include especially the district

---

[35] Tummala, "India's Federalism," pp. 548–552.

cooperative and land development banks.[36] The banks are a source of loans which are often distributed nepotistically and corruptly.

In addition to the *zila parishads*, the district banks, and the cooperative institutions, educational institutions constitute valuable political resources for local politicians. Many politicians have founded educational institutions either from their own resources or from resources granted by the state government. Once founded and functioning, these schools and colleges can then be used as patronage resources to hire teachers and to admit students on a preferential basis. Teachers and students so favored then become available for political work during elections. In some states, such as U. P., where grants of land to educational institutions are exempt from land ceilings legislation, ex-*zamindars* (landlords and tax farmers) and ex-*talukdars* (landlords and tax farmers from the former Oudh province, with the title of *raja*) find the establishment of secondary schools and colleges doubly useful as a device to avoid land ceilings legislation by establishing an endowment of land for an educational institution, which then replaces the land as a source of political influence, patronage, and profit.

One of the most impressive sources of local power and patronage anywhere in India is the network of eighty-one cooperative sugar factories in Maharashtra. These sugar factories have become "centres of power, prestige, and patronage" such that the politics of the district "revolve around cooperative sugar factories and other cooperatives."[37]

The existence of a multiplicity of local institutions with resources to distribute provides also potential bases of power for a multiplicity of local factions. However, since the ability to exercise power and influence at higher levels in Indian politics depends upon maintaining solid control of most influence resources within a district, faction leaders struggle with each other to gain control of as many local institutions within the district as possible. Influence at the district level is most important because it provides "control over all the lower levels in a given hierarchy."[38]

[36] Lele, *Elite Pluralism and Class Rule*, pp. 116–117.
[37] B. S. Baviskar, "Factional Conflict and the Congress Dilemma in Rural Maharashtra (1952–1975)," in Sisson and Roy (eds.), *Diversity and Dominance*, Vol. 1, pp. 39–40.
[38] Lele, *Elite Pluralism and Class Rule*, pp. 132–134.

Other structures and sources of local power: caste and land

Two other structures of local power exist independently of all the others and at the same time provide the underlying social bases for building institutional and political power within a district. These are caste and land control, which are often connected.

Throughout India, even where the state governments have come under the control of backward and low caste groups, local power in the countryside rests with representatives of the dominant landed castes, which are differentially distributed in regions, districts, and localities. Very often, outside of Maharashtra, there are two or more important land-controlling castes in a district, each with different sub-district regional support bases, from among whom faction leaders arise who contest for power in the various district arenas, including the factional and party political.

In general, power at the local level, including the ability to contest as a serious candidate in legislative assembly elections, depends upon the existence of a base of caste support in clusters of villages in a constituency, a *panchayat samiti* zone, or a sugar cooperative area, and is enhanced to the extent that there are many such villages in several constituences, *samitis* (councils of representatives from rural areas often comprising approximately 100 villages), or cooperative zones in a district from which a faction leader may draw strong support.

The second great independent source of local power in the countryside is, of course, land control. The very dominance of the so-called dominant castes is based on their control of the bulk of the land in the villages. Land controllers need resources which are available only or principally through cooperatives and state government agencies: access to irrigation water, to credit, seeds, fertilizers, diesel oil for pumpsets, and the like. The bigger landholders seek influence at "the higher levels in the [district] hierarchy" of institutions in order "to gain as much of a privileged access to resources as possible."[39] Despite the abolition of the zamindari system, many of the former landlords and tax farmers retain considerable illegal holdings and resources which can be used to build a base of support in a district independent of caste community, that cuts across various caste groups.

[39] Lele, *Elite Pluralism and Class Rule*, pp. 123–124.

The factional bases of district politics

The characteristic form of politics in the districts of India is factional politics, especially where the Congress has been traditionally dominant or the strongest force in a district. It involves pervasive struggle to gain and retain control of the multiple political resources in a district, as discussed above: the *panchayats*, cooperatives, banks, sugar factories, and party organizations.[40]

Among the various explanations, suggestions, and hints offered over the years to explain this persistent, pervasive factionalism, four interconnected factors now seem most relevant. One must begin first with the overwhelming heterogeneity of Indian society and the distinctiveness, social separateness, and corporate character of some at least of its most important social units, particularly caste, clan, and lineage groups. On the one hand, most political leaders who come up from the localities and districts must have roots in these little societies which they cannot afford to neglect or betray, but, on the other hand, they must ally with other similarly situated persons with different roots in order to build a political coalition broad enough to capture power in the significant political arenas, which are usually more extensive than the areas in which one's own group is dominant.

The second factor is the persistence of the peasant family farm, which is often even today an extended family farm in the sense that several brothers may share land and other resources and may market their produce together. Moreover, even these peasant family farms are not entirely separate entities, for they are part of broader peasant cultivating communities of caste or clan or tribal groups whose members exchange labor, credit, resources, and marriage partners. Sons of such local peasant communities who enter politics expect the support of their communities and are expected to take care of their needs when they achieve local power and influence.

Another force favoring the persistence of local factional conflicts is

[40] See esp. Paul R. Brass, *Factional Politics in an Indian State: The Congress Party in Uttar Pradesh* (Berkeley: University of California Press, 1964); Lele, *Elite Pluralism and Class Rule*; Baviskar, "Factional Conflict and the Congress Dilemma"; Donald B. Rosenthal, *The Expansive Elite: District Politics and State Policy-Making in India* (Berkeley: University of California Press, 1977); and Dharmana Suran Naidu, Congress Party Building in Srikakulam District, Andhra Pradesh, unpublished Ph.D. dissertation, Andhra University, Waltair, 1987.

the existence of large illegal land holdings on the remnants of great landed estates. To retain such a base requires political influence. To acquire political influence outside one's local area, the scion of the local estate must behave like a little raja of times past, acting as the benevolent patron and protector of his former subjects. If he does so, he will be rewarded by the loyal support of his clients, which can then provide a base for faction building, even for gaining virtually total control of a district's political resources.

The third factor which sustains pervasive factionalism in state and district politics – but not the Center – is the importance of inter-level linkages from the top to the bottom of India's federal parliamentary system. The efforts of faction leaders at the state level to gain local control destabilize local politics still further. If a factional group in the ruling party, usually the Congress, succeeds in gaining control over a state government, it will attempt to consolidate its control through applying state influence and pressure upon local leaders and local institutions, placing its own men in power everywhere. Should a non-Congress party or coalition succeed in a general election in gaining power at the state level, one of its first goals will be to gain control of local institutions in the districts.

It is evident that these three factors taken together – the social fragmentation of a heterogeneous society, the persistence of local structures of power independent of government, and the importance of inter-level linkages in Indian politics – are powerful forces for promoting instability and pervasive factionalism at both the district and state levels. How then can one explain the fact that, during the Nehru period, there were some states in which power was successfully aggregated and maintained for a decade or more by a single faction leader?

National power and local politics

Very little research has been done on the linkages between national power and local politics. During the Nehru period, it was generally assumed – probably correctly – that direct political linkages between the center and the localities were uncommon. Rather, the linkages were indirect, mediated by and through the state Congress organizations and governments. District disputes over the selection of Congress candidates to contest elections for the legislative assemblies and parliament were, it is true, ultimately decided by the Central Parliamentary Board in Delhi, especially where agreement was lacking at the local and state levels. However, the local disputes were first filtered through the State Parliamentary Boards and only then passed upward to Delhi. Where a state government and Congress organization were under the united control of a single faction leader, the effective decisions would be taken at the state and district levels.

Wherever a strong faction leader emerged in the states, whose principles were not opposed to those of the central party leadership on matters of economic development planning or secularism, he was likely to be supported wholeheartedly by the central Congress leadership. Such situations existed in West Bengal during the chief ministership of Dr. B. C. Roy, in Punjab under Pratap Singh Kairon, in Tamil Nadu under Kamraj Nadar, in Rajasthan under Mohan Lal Sukhadia, in Assam under B. P. Chaliha, and in several other states for fairly long periods. The existence of such stability at the state level would not eliminate district-level factionalism because social heterogeneity and local structures of power independent of government remained and the dominant faction leader might from time to time find it necessary to move against rivals or to switch allies in particular districts, but the intensity and pervasiveness of district factionalism was reduced. The central leadership of the Congress, however, sought to stabilize the state governments by backing strong and effective leaders where possible and to mediate factional conflicts which threatened the Congress' hold on power in a state government and its electoral fortunes.

The whole pattern of linkages between national and state politics and national and local politics, however, changed as a consequence of the post-Nehru succession struggle, the emergence of Mrs. Gandhi as the dominant leader in the country, and the disintegration of the local Congress organizations which followed. The heads of state and district Congress organizations were appointed from above and were often not drawn from persons with much local prestige or influence. They were there to propagate the slogans of the national leadership at election time, not to build and maintain stable structures of local power. On the one hand, direct populist appeals by the national leader to the local populations have replaced the old mediating linkages of state and district factional and caste networks. On the other hand, it has been shown in U. P. that where local structures of power independent of government and party organization have persisted, the central leadership has been compelled to become involved directly in relationships with influential local leaders without the mediation of the state leaders or state and local party organization.[41] Where such local structures of power are no longer effective and where the Congress and its opposition lack permanent organizations or reliable support bases, criminal gangs have in many places filled the political space.

It appears, therefore, that in the face of the vast changes in leadership, party organization, and political mobilization, which political leaders have brought about in their unceasing efforts to aggregate power to the national level and maintain it, they continue to confront the necessity for mediation between themselves and the little communities and petty potentates of rural India. Neither party organization nor charismatic leadership has been able to completely bypass these persisting structures of local power nor to prevent the rise of new ones based on criminal activities.

[41] Paul R. Brass, "National Power and Local Politics in India: A Twenty-Year Perspective," in Paul R. Brass, *Caste, Faction & Party in Indian Politics*, Vol. 1: *Faction & Party* (Delhi: Chanakya Publications, 1983), ch. 6 (reprinted from *Modern Asian Studies*, XVIII, No. 1 [February, 1984], 89–118).

PART II

PLURALISM AND NATIONAL INTEGRATION

INTRODUCTION

India's linguistic, religious, ethnic, and cultural diversities are prover-bial. So are the political mobilizations and the violent conflicts and antagonisms which have arisen from time to time among and between persons from its distinctive cultural groups. However, it is important to note that neither political mobilization nor ethnic and cultural antagonisms flow naturally out of India's diversities. The 1971 *Census of India* enumerated thirty-three languages with speakers of more than one million, but only fifteen of them have achieved any form of significant political recognition.

The 1981 census enumerates a tribal population of more than fifty million persons divided into hundreds of distinct groups. Many poli-tical mobilizations have occurred among several of the tribal groups from the nineteenth century up to the present, of which a few have developed into bitter, violent, and secessionist movements directed against non-tribals, against particular state governments, or against the Government of India itself. On the other hand, many tribal groups have not mobilized and have not rebelled. Moreover, the forms which tribal mobilizations have taken have been diverse. Some have focused on economic grievances, have appeared to be class-based, and have drawn support from Marxist political organizations. Others have focused on political demands and have been organized and led by tribal leaders and exclusively tribal political organizations.

The whole modern history of India has been deeply affected and badly scarred by conflict between separatist Muslim political leaders and organizations and the Indian National Congress and by con-tinuing Hindu–Muslim riots and pogroms against Muslim minorities in some cities and towns. Even with respect to these conflicts and the associated violence, however, they must be contrasted against periods of Hindu–Muslim cooperation. Moreover, it must be noted and needs to be explained why such conflicts have occurred more intensely in some parts of the country and have been less intense or non-existent in others where Hindus and Muslims also live side by side.

In the 1980s and 1990s India has faced an extremely violent movement among militant Sikhs, some of whom have become secessionist. The Punjab, where most Sikhs live, has become an embattled ground in which a violent guerrilla war is being waged between Sikh militants and the Indian police. Yet, Sikhs and Hindus have cooperated politically in the past and were never before considered to be hostile communal groups.

India has also been generally characterized as a society divided by caste and caste antagonisms. Various Indian censuses before the 1930s enumerated thousands of local castes and dozens of large caste clusters within each linguistic region. Caste mobilization and inter-caste conflict have occurred in India since the late nineteenth century among many such groups. Moreover, in the 1970s and 1980s, inter-caste conflicts between so-called backward and upper caste groups became intense in several states. Once again, however, it needs to be stressed that such mobilizations and conflicts have occurred among specific groups in specific regions at particular times and not others.

Migration of persons from one linguistic region to another, particularly to the relatively less densely populated tribal regions of the country and to the northeastern state of Assam and to the major metropolitan centers such as Bombay and Delhi have also produced situations which have sometimes, but not always, led to migrant-nativist political conflicts.

Part II of this book deals with the major linguistic, tribal, religious, caste, and migrant–non-migrant mobilizations and conflicts which have occurred in India since Independence. In the discussions which follow in the specific chapters dealing with these issues, the following themes and arguments concerning the sources of ethnic and cultural political mobilizations and conflicts are stressed.

First, state recognition in both the pre- and post-Independence periods itself has been a critical factor in explaining the rise of some ethnic and cultural movements rather than others. The British gave official preference to the Bengali language in the east rather than to Assamese and Oriya and to Urdu in the north rather than Hindi. They provided separate electorates and other political concessions to Muslims and Sikhs. They allowed migration of plains people into tribal areas in central India but forbade it in some parts of the northeast. They patronized the non-Brahman movement in south

India when Brahmans were leading the Indian National Congress there.

In the post-Independence period, the government of India and the state governments sought to change the balance of recognition among some groups. Hindi was adopted as the official language of the country and of the north Indian states, definitively displacing Urdu from its remaining bastions in Punjab and U. P. Assamese was adopted as the sole official language of Assam against the wishes of the large Bengali-speaking minority and many tribal groups. Separate electorates for Muslims and Sikhs were done away with, but reservations of legislative seats and administrative and educational places for Scheduled Castes and Tribes were retained or introduced.

State recognition sometimes worked in contrary ways. On the one hand, it strengthened some of the groups so recognized and weakened others. On the other hand, in some cases, it contributed to the development of counter-movements by non-recognized groups. The best examples of this type are the numerous movements among unrecognized "backward castes" who have sought systems of reservations equivalent to those granted to Scheduled Castes and Tribes.

A second factor emphasized here, also a political one, concerns the specific policies and political strategies pursued by the central and state governments in relation to regional and sub-regional cultural entities. One general argument stressed below is that Indian state policy toward minorities has differed in the Nehru and post-Nehru periods. Under Nehru, the central government pursued pluralist policies in relation to major language and cultural movements, recognizing especially most of the large language groups among whom major mobilizations developed for the creation of separate linguistic states. At the same time, however, the Center sought to avoid direct involvement in regional conflicts among different ethnic and linguistic groups. The Center also turned a blind eye or took no action in relation to the discriminatory policies followed by dominant regional groups within the several states of the Union.

In the post-Nehru period, however, the central government has played a more directly interventionist role in regional conflicts between opposed ethnic, communal, and caste groups. It tolerated the disruptive and allegedly murderous and terrorist activities of Sant Jarnail Singh Bhindranwale in the Punjab in order to embarrass its main political rival in that state, the Akali Dal. It followed inconsistent policies in Kashmir, at times seeking to mobilize Hindu support in Jammu, at others seeking to ally with the dominant Muslim political party in the Kashmir valley, the National Conference. During the succession struggles after 1965 between Mrs. Gandhi and her rivals, the central Congress leadership in several states moved to displace upper caste leaders from state Congress organizations and replace them with backward caste persons and to mobilize the votes of the latter castes to defeat its rivals in the state Congress and in the opposition. The consequences of these interventions, some of which may justly be perceived as socially progressive, have nevertheless often had the consequence of intensifying inter-ethnic regional conflicts and of focusing some of them upon the central government itself.

A third factor influencing the mobilization of some groups and not others has been unevenness in rates of social change among different social groups leading in turn to imbalances in their relative access to jobs, educational advantages, and political power. Each region of India has a dominant language group and particular castes, usually of elite status, who have long held disproportionate shares of public employment, educational, and political opportunities. Challenges to the preponderant shares of dominant groups in various life opportunities do not usually come from those most oppressed but from persons from groups who have some resources but not others or from groups among whom processes of social change have begun such as to make elites among them acutely conscious of the disparities between the life chances of persons from their own group and persons from the dominant groups.

A related factor is the extent to which persons from different ethnic and cultural groups actually find themselves in competition for the same niches in the division of labor in society. Migrant laborers who go to areas of the country where the demand for farm or plantation labor is high may not come into conflict with local competitors, whose numbers may be much smaller than those of the migrants themselves. However, it is often the case that educated persons from different religious, language, caste, and other categories compete for the most prestigious and secure jobs in public service and for the educational opportunities to gain access to them. It is not surprising, therefore, that conflict between competing educated classes in search of scarce jobs has been among the most prevalent sources of ethnic conflict not only in India but throughout the developing world.

Another factor influencing the types of conflict which occur in India concerns levels of political action and levels of ethnic loyalties. India is a society which contains both multiple levels of political arenas and hierarchies of loyalties to cultural categories. At the level of the village and its surroundings, *jati*, the local aspect of caste, may provide a basis for economic action, political organization, and social conflict. In a unit as large as a district, however, correspondingly larger units of political action or political coalitions across *jati* boundaries become necessary for effective political action. The unit of loyalty and political action may then become the caste category or caste cluster or a coalition of related castes. At the state level, only the largest caste categories with wide representation throughout large parts of a state may be able to act in solidary and politically effective ways. In many cases, such actions at the state level become impossible and other kinds of loyalties to faction and party become predominant. At the national level, caste becomes virtually ineffective as a basis for sustained political mobilization for the available caste categories at this level lack appropriate social or economic content.

Alternatives to caste as an organizing principle for political conflict also exist at every level in Indian politics, particularly from the district upwards. At those levels, categories such as Hindu and Muslim become more prominent, language loyalties become critical, one's status as a migrant or a "son of the soil" may be decisive, or factional, party, and ideological bases for political division may prevail.

The three following chapters in part II deal with the major types of conflicts which have occurred in post-Independence politics in which different ethnic and cultural categorizations have been used as bases for political mobilization. Chapter 5 focuses on language conflicts, chapter 6 on crises of national unity including secessionist movements in Punjab, Kashmir, and the northeastern region, and chapter 7 on Hindu–Muslim relations, caste mobilization, and caste conflict. The central argument which links the treatment which follows of these different sets of conflicts is that India's cultural diversities do not themselves provide inherent obstacles to national unity or inevitable sources of conflict. Conflicts between language, religious, and ethnic groups tend to center around issues of jobs, educational opportunities, and local political power. The roots of these conflicts have often been quite similar in the pre- and post-Nehru periods. However, a combination of increasingly assertive centralizing drives by the Indian state and its national leadership with an intensified struggle for power in center, state, and locality have contributed to the intensification of conflicts based on such categories in the post-Nehru era.

CHAPTER 5

LANGUAGE PROBLEMS

India's national leaders had to confront several language problems in the first two decades of Independence and what appeared to some of them in the aftermath of Partition to be a real threat of the "Balkanization" of the country. These problems included the official language issue, demands for the linguistic reorganization of the provinces of India whose boundaries during British rule did not conform to linguistic divisions, and the status of minority languages within reorganized states. Most of the language conflicts in the Nehru period, some of which became at times bitter and violent, were ultimately resolved through pluralistic solutions. The central government and the national leadership of the Congress sought to avoid direct confrontations with the language movements and their leaders and adopted instead arbitrating and mediating roles wherever possible. In the case of the movements for linguistic reorganization of states, until mutual agreements were reached among contending language groups and their leaders, the Center attempted to ensure that the state governments were under the control of strong leaders whom it supported in efforts to maintain civil order.

In the post-Nehru period, however, several linguistic, ethnic, and regional movements have escalated to levels of bitterness and violence never experienced in the Nehru period except in the tribal regions of the northeast. It will be argued in the following chapter that the centralizing drives of the Indian state under Mrs. Gandhi's leadership and the manipulative and interventionist strategies pursued by the central government and its leaders in state politics have contributed to the intensity of such conflicts during the past two decades. Most of the problems discussed in this chapter, however, were resolved during the Nehru period and will provide a base for comparison with the unresolved problems which have persisted into the 1980s and 1990s.

THE OFFICIAL LANGUAGE PROBLEM

Before independence, the most salient language issue in Indian politics concerned the relative positions of Hindi and Urdu and of the Devanagari and Persian–Arabic scripts. The intensity of the communal polarization between Hindus and Muslims, especially during the decade preceding Independence, the position of Muslims as the single largest minority category in the population of the country as a whole, and the linking of the Hindu–Urdu issue with the communal question caused this aspect of the numerous language divisions in India to overshadow all others. The Constituent Assembly having begun its deliberations before the Partition of the subcontinent, the early debates on the language issue in the Assembly focused on this controversy. The principal questions at that stage were whether Hindi in the Devanagari script, drawing its vocabulary – especially for coining of new scientific, technological, and administrative terms – from Sanskrit should displace English as the sole official language of the country or whether Hindustani, the common spoken language of north India, written in both the Devanagari and Persian–Arabic scripts, and drawing its vocabulary from English and Urdu more than from Sanskrit, should replace English.[1]

After Partition, however, there was no question any longer of making significant concessions to Muslims on the language issue and the status of Urdu and the Persian–Arabic script became quite incidental to two other matters concerning the official language or languages of the country. The first concerned the question of whether or not and for how long English should be retained as an official language. The second concerned the relationships among the major regional languages of the country and the numerous minor languages and how their speakers would communicate across linguistic boundaries. Although the first issue involved the question of India maintaining a "window to the world" in which English was the dominant international language and the second issue involved the question of Indians communicating with each other in a country with fourteen or fifteen major languages and approximately thirty languages with a million speakers or more (see table 5.1), the two became interrelated.

[1] Granville Austin, *The Indian Constitution: Cornerstone of a Nation* (Oxford: Clarendon Press, 1966), p. 269.

Table 5.1. *Declared mother tongues – 1971 census (provisional figures): showing numerically important mother tongues at country level as of 1971 with strength of 1,000,000 and above arranged in descending order of population*

No.	Mother tongue	Persons	Status
1	Hindi	153,729,062*	Official language of India and of several north Indian states
2	Telugu	44,707,607	Official language of Andhra Pradesh
3	Bengali	44,521,533	Official language of West Bengal
4	Marathi	41,723,893	Official language of Maharashtra
5	Tamil	37,592,794	Official language of Tamil Nadu
6	Urdu	28,600,428	Listed in Eighth Schedule; official language of Jammu & Kashmir
7	Gujarati	25,656,274	Official language of Gujarat
8	Malayalam	21,917,430	Official language of Kerala
9	Kannada	21,575,019	Official language of Karnataka
10	Oriya	19,726,745	Official language of Orissa
11	Bhojpuri	14,340,564*	Minority mother tongue of Bihar and U.P.
12	Punjabi	13,900,202	Official language of Punjab
13	Assamese	8,958,977	Official language of Assam
14	Chattisgarhi	6,693,445*	Minority mother tongue of M.P.
15	Magahi/Magadhi	6,638,495*	Minority mother tongue of Bihar
16	Maithili	6,121,922*	Minority mother tongue of Bihar

Table 5.1. (cont.)

No.	Mother tongue	Persons	Status
17	Marwari	4,714,094*	Minority mother tongue of Rajasthan
18	Santali	3,693,558	Minority (tribal) mother tongue of Bihar and West Bengal
19	Kashmiri	3,421,760	Dominant language of Jammu & Kashmir
20	Rajasthani	2,093,557*	Name used in Rajasthan for several mother tongues
21	Gondi	1,548,070	Minority mother tongue of M.P., Maharashtra, and Orissa
22	Konkani	1,552,684	Official language of Goa, Daman and Diu
23	Dogri	1,298,855	Minority mother tongue of Jammu & Kashmir
24	Gorkhali/Nepali	1,286,824	Minority mother tongue of West Bengal & Assam
25	Garhwali	1,277,151*	Minority mother tongue of U.P.
26	Pahari	1,269,651*	Minority mother tongue of H.P., U.P., and Jammu & Kashmir
27	Bhili/Bhilodi	1,250,312	Minority mother tongue (tribal) of M.P., Maharashtra, Rajasthan, and Gujarat
28	Kurukh/Oraon	1,240,395	Minority mother tongue of Bihar, Orissa, and West Bengal

Table 5.1. (cont.)

No.	Mother tongue	Persons	Status
29	Kumauni	1,234,939*	Minority mother tongue of U.P.
30	Sindhi	1,204,678	Listed in Eighth Schedule; minority mother tongue of Maharashtra, Punjab, and M.P.
31	Lamani/Lambadi	1,203,338*	Minority mother tongue (tribal) of Andhra Pradesh and Maharashtra
32	Tulu	1,156,950	Minority mother tongue of Karnataka and Kerala
33	Bagri	1,055,607	Minority mother tongue of Rajasthan

* In the Reports of the Commissioner for Linguistic Minorities, the 1971 returns for 46 mother tongues including these listed in the table have been grouped with Hindi, giving an "official" figure for Hindi speakers in 1971 of 208,514,005; Government of India, Ministry of Home Affairs, *The Twenty-third Report by the Deputy Commissioner for Linguistic Minorities in India for the Period July, 1982, to June, 1983* (Delhi: Controller of Publications, 1985), pp. 292–298.
Source: R. C. Nigam, *Language Handbook on Mother Tongues in Census of India, 1971* (New Delhi: Government of India Press, 1972).

The status of English and its possible retention in India for official and other purposes raised both practical questions and an emotional question. The practical questions concerned international communication and the transmission through the educational system of modern science and technology for which none of the Indian languages were fully prepared either in vocabulary or in the availability of translated texts. Against this practical question which argued for the retention of English at least for a transition period was the emotional argument that an independent country could not be truly free until its people gave up the use of a foreign language and adopted its own at least within the borders of its own state.

If the latter argument were accepted, however, even with a transition period, the second major issue then arose concerning which one or more of the major languages of India should be adopted as the official language of the country. Only Hindi could make a claim, by virtue of its large number of speakers and extensive spread in the northern part of the country (figure 3), to recognition as the official language of India, but even Hindi fell far short of encompassing a majority of the speakers of vernacular languages and the claims by its proponents to be a link language beyond its own regions of concentration in the north could not be effectively sustained. The second great issue in the Constituent Assembly then became the status of Hindi in relation to the regional languages. Proponents of Hindi called for its recognition as the "national" language of the country, but the representatives of the non-Hindi-speaking areas insisted that their languages were equally "national" and that if Hindi were to be recognized, it could be only as the *official* language of the Union. For internal communication within their own regions, non-Hindi speakers expected to retain the use of their own languages and the right to use English for inter-provincial communication and communication with the central government.[2] This aspect of the language controversy also had an important material component since the language recognized for official purposes would be the language in which those who aspired for employment in the public services would have to be proficient.

It is here that the two issues of English versus the vernacular or national languages and Hindi versus the other national or regional languages of the country merged as the non-Hindi-speaking representatives demanded the retention of English as the only way of blocking the elevation of Hindi, which would give a clear advantage to persons proficient in that language in the competition for scarce employment in the public sector jobs controlled by the Union government. The Constituent Assembly resolved this demand for retention of English for a transitional period by granting to Hindi the status of official language of the country, but postponing the final implementation of it for fifteen years. In the meantime, English would continue to be the official language of the Union and of inter-provincial com-

---

[2] Austin, *The Indian Constitution*, pp. 266–267.

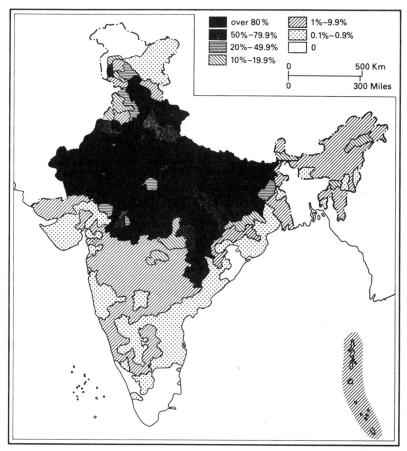

Figure 3   Percent distribution of Hindi speakers by district

Based on Ashok K. Dutt and M. Margaret Geib, *Atlas of South Asia*
(Boulder, CO: Westview Press, 1987).

munication, the major regional languages would continue to be used permanently in their own provinces and would also be recognized as "national" languages through their incorporation into the Eighth Schedule of the Constitution. The latter provision meant in effect that speakers of the major regional languages could continue to use their own languages in the examinations for entry into the Union public services and that they were entitled to other legal and material recognitions and benefits as well. The Constitutional compromise also provided for the establishment of language commissions in 1955 and 1960 "to survey the progress of Hindi," but these commissions were to maintain a "due regard" for the interests of people from the non-Hindi-speaking regions with regard to employment in the public services, implying that Hindi should not become the exclusive language of the entrance examinations if it would go against the interests of non-Hindi-speakers.[3]

The final vote on the compromise amendment providing a solution to the language controversy in the Constituent Assembly revealed the basic lines of division in the country on the matter. On one side were ranged most of the dominant leaders in the Congress organization and the government, with Nehru himself taking the lead in arguing strongly for a pluralist compromise solution, and the representatives from the southern states and from other non-Hindi-speaking states, including Gujarat, Bengal, and Assam. The bulk of the vote against the compromise amendment, reflecting the sentiment in the Assembly for a quick transition to Hindi and the displacement of English, came from the Hindi-speaking states, including members from the Haryana region of Punjab and from Rajasthan.[4] Despite the heat generated during the debate, the ultimate compromise, which was carried by a large majority, was for a multi-lingual solution, including the retention of English for a fifteen-year interim period, after which Parliament would again take up the issue.

Efforts to prepare for the transition to Hindi as the sole official language of the country in 1965, however, made little progress. The emotional identification of speakers of regional languages with their own languages became stronger rather than weaker. Efforts to promote the spread of Hindi in the schools outside the Hindi-speaking

---

[3] Austin, *The Indian Constitution*, p. 296
[4] Austin, *The Indian Constitution*, p. 299.

region had little success in states such as Maharashtra and Gujarat. An attempt to promote national integration and inter-state communication through a Three-Language Formula in the schools also failed. The idea behind this proposal was to promote emotional integration between different language speakers and also to equalize the burdens of language learning in the north and south by requiring the schools throughout the country to teach their own regional language, a foreign language (almost always English), and either Hindi in the non-Hindi-speaking areas or a language other than Hindi in the Hindi-speaking areas. The formula failed for lack of genuine desire to implement it in most states, lack of teachers competent in the various languages willing to move outside their home states, and the recognition in north India of Sanskrit, Urdu, and the regional languages and dialects of the north as alternative third languages in the formula rather than languages of the non-Hindi-speaking regions.[5]

The Lok Sabha took up the question of India's official language once again in 1963, two years before the date designated by the Constituent Assembly for the transition to Hindi. As in the Constituent Assembly, the debates in the Lok Sabha in 1963 were heated, with Hindi proponents demanding immediate implementation of the Constitutional provision on official language and MPs from the South and from Bengal arguing strongly for the retention of English. In the event, a compromise was reached in the passage of the Official Languages Act, 1963, which came close to satisfying most representatives of the Hindi and non-Hindi-speaking regions. Under the terms of the Act, Hindi was indeed to become the sole official language of the country in 1965, but English was to be continued as an "associate additional official language." The Act also provided for a parliamentary review committee to reconsider the situation in ten years with the power to extend the retention of English if Hindi had not made sufficient progress among the non-Hindi-speaking peoples. The remaining controversial point in the Act concerned the power of the parliamentary review committee and the extent of its discretion in recommending the retention or displacement of English. Prime Minister Nehru gave his personal assurances in Parliament that there would be no attempt to impose Hindi on the non-Hindi-speaking states, but

[5] Paul R. Brass, *Language, Religion, and Politics in North India* (London: Cambridge University Press, 1974), pp. 213–215.

the ambiguity remaining in the Act of 1963 left an unresolved tension that soon exploded in the state of Tamil Nadu after the death of Nehru in 1964.

In 1964, during the tenure of Gulzarilal Nanda as Home Minister, a man known for his strong support for Hindi as the official language of the country, a directive was issued from his ministry to all other Union Ministries, in conformity with the constitutional provisions on official language and the Official Languages Act of 1963, to report on the progress made in promoting "the use of Hindi for official purposes and to indicate what steps they proposed to take to use Hindi" after the designated day of transition on January 26, 1965.[6] When news of this directive reached Tamil Nadu, there were massive student demonstrations, riots, and self-immolations, which continued for several months in late 1964 and early 1965, as a consequence of which a grand convocation of the Congress party leadership, Union ministers, and the chief ministers of all the states met in Delhi in June, 1965. At that meeting, a consensus was reached on removing the remaining ambiguities in the Official Languages Act. Under the terms of this compromise, the non-Hindi-speaking states were assured that Hindi would never be imposed upon them, that English would be retained as an associate additional official language as long as even a single non-Hindi-speaking state desired it. In addition, on the material issue of entry into the Union public services, it was agreed that all the languages listed in the Eighth Schedule of the Constitution of India, that is, all the major regional languages as well as Hindi and English, could be used as media of examination.[7]

The compromise of 1965 was introduced formally into the Official Languages Act through the Official Languages (Amendment) Act, 1967. The nature of the resolution of this longstanding controversial issue was a basically bilingual one. The act provided for joint use of Hindi and English in Parliament, for the use of Hindi as the language of communication between the Center and the Hindi-speaking states and the use of English for communication between the Center and non-Hindi-speaking states. However, the Act and the overall compromise also contained multilingual elements, particularly on the matter

---

[6] Michael Brecher, *Succession in India: A Study in Decision-Making* (London: Oxford University Press, 1966), p. 155.

[7] Brecher, *Succession in India*, pp. 165, 171.

Table 5.2. *Number of newspapers by language*

Language	1987 No.	%	1980 No.	%	1970 No.	%	1960 No.	%
English	4,322	17.55	3,440	18.96	2,247	20.36	1,647	20.52
Hindi	7,783	31.60	4,946	27.27	2,694	24.41	1,532	19.09
Urdu	1,676	6.80	1,234	6.80	898	8.14	680	8.47
Regional languages	8,335	33.84	6,493	35.79	3,974	36.01	2,718	33.86
Others[a]	2,513	10.20	2,027	11.17	1,223	11.08	1,449	18.05
Total	24,629	99.99	18,140	99.99	11,036	100.00	8,026	99.99

[a] Mostly bilingual and multilingual publications for which the languages are not given.
Source: Compiled from Government of India, Ministry of Information and Broadcasting, *Press in India, 1988* (Delhi: Controller of Publications, 1988), 19; *Press in India, 1981*, 1 (Delhi: Controller of Publications, 1978), 27; *Press in India, 1971*, 1 (Delhi: Manager of Publications, 1971), 19; *Annual Report of the Registrar of Newspapers for India 1961*, 1 (Delhi: Manager of Publications, 1961), 19.

of the languages of examination for entry into the Indian Administrative Service and other Union services.

In practice, English has remained the dominant language of elite communication in the country as a whole. Within the linguistically reorganized states, the regional languages have become dominant in government, the courts, the schools, and the media. However, English is still an important language even within the various linguistic regions of the country. It is still accepted as a medium of examination for admission into the state services, alongside the official state languages, in every state and union territory in the country.[8] Hindi has not succeeded in displacing English as a lingua franca for the country. It has gained ground against English in the Hindi-speaking regions of the country but not in relation to the regional languages in the non-Hindi-speaking regions. It has remained primarily a lingua franca of north

[8] Government of India, Ministry of Home Affairs, *The Twenty-third Report by the Deputy Commissioner for Linguistic Minorities in India for the Period July, 1982, to June, 1983* (Delhi: Controller of Publications, 1985), pp. 377–378 (hereafter referred to as *CLM*, XXIII).

Table 5.3. *Circulation of newspapers by language (× 1,000)*

Language	1987 No.	%	1980 No.	%	1970 No.	%	1960 No.	%
English	9,727	17.12	10,532	20.68	7,173	24.48	4,147	22.76
Hindi	17,157	30.19	13,709	26.92	5,852	19.97	3,583	19.67
Urdu	2,806	4.94	2,076	4.08	1,455	4.97	1,055	5.79
Regional languages	26,222	46.14	22,911	44.99	13,639	46.54	8,297	45.54
Others[a]	918	1.62	1,693	3.32	1,184	4.04	1,137	6.24
Total	56,830	100.01	50,921	99.99	29,303	100.00	18,219	100.00

[a] Mostly bilingual and multilingual publications for which the languages are not given.
Source: As for table 5.2: *Press in India, 1988*, p. 35; *Press in India, 1981*, I p. 44; *Press in India, 1971*, I, p. 44; *Annual Report of the Registrar of Newspapers for India 1961*, I, p. 43.

India and a regional language of the northern and central states of the Union.

Some of these relationships among the major languages of India are illustrated by the relative standing of English, Hindi, and the regional languages in newspaper concentration and circulation, shown in tables 5.2 and 5.3. It is evident from these tables that English readers continue to constitute a substantial proportion of the literate, newspaper-reading public. However, in the period from 1960–1987, the proportion of English-language newspapers in the country has gone down from nearly 21 percent of the total to less than 18 percent while the share of Hindi-language newspapers has increased from less than 20 percent to above 30 percent. Since the relative share of regional language newspapers has not changed much in the same period, it is evident that the increased concentration of Hindi newspapers is at the expense primarily of the bilingual and multilingual newspapers included in "other languages" and of the English and Urdu language papers, but not at the expense of the regional languages of the country. More than half the newspaper-reading public of India reads newspapers published in the predominant regional languages of the country and in other minority languages, including Urdu (table 5.3). However, if English and "other" language newspapers are excluded from the total, 63 per cent of the total newspaper circulation in the county in 1987 was in vernacular languages other than Hindi.

LINGUISTIC REORGANIZATION OF STATES

The process of linguistic reorganization of states in India was far more prolonged and divisive than the controversy over the official language of India and raised more fundamental questions of center–state relations. The first step in the process occurred in the aftermath of a major movement in the Andhra region of the old Madras province. This led to the appointment of the States Reorganization Commission which published its *Report* in 1955.[9] Following the States Reorganization Act of 1956, the boundaries of the southern states were reorganized in closer conformity with traditional linguistic regions (cf. frontispiece and figure 4). The bifurcation of Bombay province into the present states of Gujarat and Maharashtra followed in 1960. In 1966, Punjab was reorganized and its several parts distributed among three units: the core Punjabi Suba, the new state of Haryana, and Himachal Pradesh. Several new states also have been carved out in response to tribal demands in the northeastern region of the country from time to time. The most recent addition to the states of the Indian Union occurred in May, 1987 with the transformation of Goa's status from that of a union territory to India's 25th state.[10] All the reorganizations except those in the Punjab and in the northeastern region of the country have satisfied the grievances of the principal large language communities of India.

Moreover, in this prolonged process, the "practice" of the Indian state developed a coherent and consistent form somewhat different from the ideology proclaimed by its leaders. Many Indian leaders proclaimed their goals after Independence to be the establishment of a strong state, to which all the diverse peoples of India would transfer their primary loyalties and submerge their cultural differences in a

[9] Government of India, Home Department, *Report of the States Reorganisation Commission*, 1955 (New Delhi: Government of India Press), 1955.

[10] See Arthur G. Rubinoff, "Goa's Attainment of Statehood," *Asian Survey*, xxxii, No. 5 (May, 1992), 471–487.

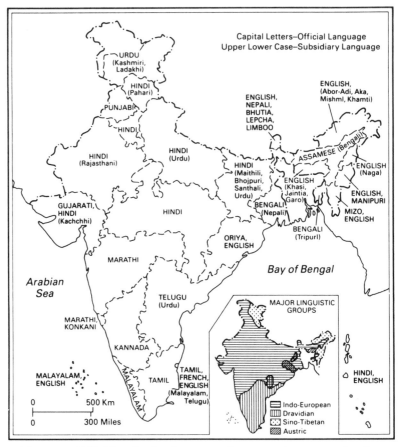

Figure 4   Official and other important languages by state and union
territory

Based on Ashok K. Dutt and M. Margaret Geib, *Atlas of South Asia*
(Boulder, CO: Westview Press, 1987), p. 111, with adjustments based on
Government of India, Ministry of Home Affairs, *The Twenty-fifth Report
by the Deputy Commissioner for Linguistic Minorities in India, for the
Period July 1984 to June 1985* (Delhi: Controller of Publications, 1986),
pp. 402–403.

homogeneous nationalism. Others, somewhat more attuned to the realities of India's diverse cultural differences, thought a "composite" nationalism would emerge combining aspects from the cultures of the various major religious, regional, linguistic, and tribal peoples. Virtually all, however, were fearful of accommodating too readily the demands which emerged so soon after the catastrophic partition of the country and the major struggle which occurred simultaneously with it over the integration of the princely states.

Out of the conflicts which developed between the central government leaders, with their ideology of a strong state and a homogeneous or composite nationalism to support it, and the successive demands of leaders of language movements for reorganization of the internal boundaries of the provinces, a set of rules and an overall state strategy emerged which were more pluralist in practice than the ideology, which appeared integrationist and assimilationist. In effect, the Indian state during the Nehru period took on the form of a culturally pluralist state, in which a multiplicity of major peoples, defined primarily in terms of language, were recognized as corporate groups within the Indian Union with rights equal to all other such groups. As with any pluralist state, of course, recognition on the basis of equality did not extend to all the culturally distinctive groups or even to all the large language groups in India, but only to those language groups which were able to vindicate a claim to dominance within a particular region of the country. Such validation, for the most part, could be made good only by those groups whose languages had already received some official recognition under British rule and had undergone some grammatical standardization and literary development, often involving the absorption of local dialects, and had become entrenched in the government schools in their regions.

The leaders of such language groups were well placed to launch the various movements which occurred, especially during the 1950s and 1960s, for linguistic reorganization of the Indian states. It is important to recognize, however, that not all such movements succeeded but only those which were both well placed to begin with and which were able to prevail against rival groups within the former provinces of British India and against the reluctance of central government leaders to begin and continue a process to which they saw no certain end. In the course of these struggles, the central government developed a set of four formal and informal rules, whose application led to the recognition of the dominance of some language groups and not others in major regions of the country.[11]

The first rule was that the central government would not recognize groups which made secessionist demands, but would suppress them by all means necessary, including armed force. That rule has been applied to various tribal groups in the northeastern part of the country since Independence, where the Indian Army has been engaged in more-or-less continual warfare with and suppression of the secessionist demands of Nagas, Mizos, and others. It has also been applied to the Punjab since 1984 where the police have been engaged, implementing Government of India policy, in a systematic attempt to kill all alleged terrorists who are suspected to be working for the creation of a sovereign state of Khalistan. The armed forces of the Government of India have also been engaged very heavily since 1989 in the violent suppression of a secessionist movement in Kashmir. Between 1990 and 1992, Indian armed forces also sought to root out a secessionist force among the Assamese Hindu population in the state of Assam (see chapter 6 below). Where a linguistic group has dropped its secessionist demands, as the DMK did in Tamil Nadu in the 1960s and as several tribal leaders have done in the northeast, the government of India has been willing to make concessions and even to grant statehood to leaders of groups previously considered secessionist.

The second rule is that the government will not accommodate regional demands based upon religious differences. This rule, heritage of the bitter feelings which remain from the partition of India, was applied especially to the Punjab, the last large Indian state to be reorganized in 1966. The government of India resisted the linguistic reorganization of the Punjab more strongly than it did the reorganization of the former Madras and Bombay provinces for several reasons, but one important one was the initial perception that the demand from the Sikhs for a Punjabi-speaking state was merely a cover for a demand for a Sikh-majority state. Only when a leadership change occurred in the Punjabi Suba movement in the early 1960s to Sant Fateh Singh, in whose sincerity the central government leaders

[11] This formulation of Government of India policies toward regional demands comes from Brass, *Language, Religion, and Politics in North India*, pp. 17–19.

professed to believe, was the decision made to reorganize the Punjab province and create a separate Punjabi-speaking state.

The third rule was that demands for the creation of separate linguistic states would not be conceded capriciously nor on the merely "objective" grounds that a distinctive language was the predominant spoken language in a particular region. This rule developed out of the general reluctance of the central leadership to divide the existing provinces rather than out of any clear principle. In practice, it meant that politicians who set out to demand the reorganization of a province had to mobilize large numbers of people from the concerned region in sustained agitations to persuade the central government that the demand had popular support and was not merely a device for the politicians themselves to acquire power in a new and smaller political unit. Thus, a demand from politicians from western Uttar Pradesh in 1954, supported by ninety-seven members out of 100 in the Legislative Assembly of that province, for the creation of a new province out of western Uttar Pradesh and the then Haryana region of Punjab, but which had no significant popular basis, was never taken seriously by the central government. That "objective" language differences also would not suffice for a demand for reorganization to succeed was also demonstrated in the northern part of Bihar province, where a cultural and literary elite demanded the creation of a separate province for speakers of Maithili, a language distinct from both its neighboring communities of Hindi and Bengali speakers. This demand, which in any case never succeeded in establishing a strong base of popular support, also has been ignored.

The fourth rule was that the central government would not agree to reorganization of a province if the demand was made by only one of the important language groups concerned. The reorganization of the southern province of Madras was taken up first in the process of linguistic reorganization partly because it had strong support from both the Telugu- and Tamil-speaking peoples. However, the reorganization of the former Bombay province was postponed for several years because the demand came primarily from the Marathi-speaking region and was opposed in Gujarat, where for a time it was felt that the loss of Bombay City was too high a price to pay for a separate Gujarati-speaking state. In Punjab also, the reorganization was delayed even longer and has not yet been completed because of the opposition of both Hindi-speaking Hindus from the Haryana region and Punjabi-speaking Hindus within the Punjab region.

During the Nehru period, the reorganization of the southern states and of the Bombay province was carried out successfully through the application of these rules. The way the process was carried out also led to a particular kind of balance in center–state relations, in which the Center avoided placing itself in a position of confrontation with powerful regional groups but instead adopted a posture of mediation and arbitration between contending linguistic-cultural forces. Although the central leadership often played very strong background roles in these disputes, Prime Minister Nehru himself and his Cabinet members always avoided the appearance of being opposed to any popular movement which did not violate the four rules. The Center would emerge forcefully and publicly through either a decision to reorganize or the appointment of a commission to decide the matter only when all conditions for a reorganization had been satisfied.

The completion of the prolonged process of linguistic reorganization of states has left unresolved problems in two regions of the country and within the reorganized states themselves. The two regions where reorganization has not satisfied the demands of all groups are the Punjab and the northeast. Within the reorganized states themselves, there have also been recurring problems concerning the status of minority languages. Insofar as the Punjab and the northeast are concerned, it is important to consider whether the prolongation of inter-ethnic conflicts in these regions arises out of inherent differences in the nature of the issues in comparison with those handled successfully in the south and in the former Bombay province or out of differences in the ways these issues have been treated in the post-Nehru era, in which Indira Gandhi was the dominant leader. The special problems of these two regions will be taken up in the next chapter. The problems of linguistic minorities in the reorganized states have been less explosive than the unresolved problems in Punjab and the northeast, but they too must be considered for a more complete understanding of the process of political integration in post-Independence India.

PERSISTING LINGUISTIC MINORITIES IN THE
STATES

The third important linguistic problem in post-Independence India has concerned the status of minority languages within the reorganized states, each of which contains smaller or larger numbers of speakers of languages other than the predominant regional language (see table 5.4). In contrast to the pluralist policies pursued by the government of India, many of the states have pursued discriminatory policies toward their linguistic (and other) minorities within their boundaries. Moreover, the Center has been unable to protect such minorities effectively against the opposition of the state governments concerned. Among the casualties, for example, have been Urdu in the north Indian states and the various so-called "mother tongues" or "dialects" of Hindi and other larger languages, which have not been granted official recognition by either the central or state governments. Some of these "dialects" – for example, the Maithili language of north Bihar state – are, in fact, separate languages in all but official recognition. To avoid the controversial issue of distinguishing between "languages" and "dialects," however, it is best to follow the practice of the Indian census authorities and use the term mother tongue to encompass both terms.

The languages and mother tongues of India are, in effect, arranged in a hierarchy of official status. At the top are the two languages, Hindi and English, recognized as official languages of the Union. At the next level are the regional languages recognized as official languages in the linguistically reorganized states, all of which are also listed in the Eighth Schedule (table 5.5). At a third level are those languages listed in the Eighth Schedule which have no official status in any province, namely, Sanskrit and Sindhi, the language of the province of Sindh now in Pakistan.

A listing on the Eighth Schedule carries symbolic and material advantages: a presumptive right to recognition as a minority language in states where other languages are dominant, including a presumptive right to recognition as medium of instruction in both primary and secondary school classes in such states, a right to the protection of the President of India (i.e. the central government) on the advice of the Commissioner for Linguistic Minorities against discrimination in use

Table 5.4. *Official and dominant state languages (1971)*

State	Official language(s) (dominant languages)[a]	Percent speaking dominant language[b]
Kerala	(Malayalam) & English	96.01
Gujarat	(Gujarati) & Hindi	90.00
Rajasthan	(Hindi)	91.40
Himachal Pradesh	(Hindi)	88.87
Uttar Pradesh[c]	(Hindi)	88.50
Haryana	(Hindi)	88.00
West Bengal[c]	(Bengali)	86.00
Andhra[c]	(Telugu)	85.40
Tamil Nadu	(Tamil)	84.50
Orissa	(Oriya) & English	84.12
Madhya Pradesh	(Hindi)	83.00
Bihar[c]	(Hindi)	79.70[b]
Punjab	(Punjabi)	79.60
Meghalaya	English (Khasi & Garo)	77.65
Maharashtra	(Marathi)	76.70
Mizoram	(Mizo) & English	75.00
Tripura	(Bengali)	69.00
Karnataka	(Kannada)	66.00
Manipur	English (Manipuri)	63.24
Assam[c]	(Assamese)	60.80
Jammu & Kashmir	Urdu (Kashmiri)	55.50
Sikkim	Bhutia, Lepcha, Limboo (Nepali) & English	64.00
Arunachal Pradesh	English (Nissi/Dafla, Adi, Nepali, Wancho)	58.10
Nagaland	English (Ao, Konyak, Angami, Sema)	53.90

[a] In some cases, the official and dominant regional languages do not coincide. Languages shown in parentheses are both dominant and official languages in their respective states.

[b] The figures for the dominant languages often include regional languages, dialects, and mother tongues some of which are quite distinct. The figures for M. P. and Bihar are especially inflated by such inclusions. The 1961 figures for Hindi in M. P. were 67.00 and for Bihar 44.30 percent. See Myron Weiner, *Sons of the Soil: Migration and Ethnic Conflict in India* (Princeton, N.J.: Princeton University Press, 1978), p. 50 and, for Bihar, Paul R. Brass, *Language, Religion, and Politics in North India* (New York: Cambridge University Press, 1974), p. 65.

[c] Bengali in Assam, Nepali in West Bengal, and Urdu in Andhra, Bihar, and U.P. have the status of additional official languages in selected districts.

Source: Government of India, Ministry of Home Affairs, *The Twenty-Fifth Report by the Deputy Commissioner for Linguistic Minorities in India for the Period July, 1984, to June 1985* (Delhi: Controller of Publications, 1986), pp. 8–9.

Table 5.5. *Number and percentage of speakers of languages listed on the Eighth Schedule of the Constitution of India (inclusive of "variants" grouped with each language by the census commissioner), enumerated according to the language mainly spoken in the household, in descending order of speaker strength, 1981 census*

Language	Number of speakers	% of total population
1 Hindi	264,188,858	39.94
2 Telugu	54,226,227	8.20
3 Bengali	51,503,085	7.79
4 Marathi	49,624,847	7.50
5 Tamil	44,730,389	6.76
6 Urdu	35,323,481	5.34
7 Gujarati	33,189,039	5.02
8 Kannada	26,887,837	4.05
9 Malayalam	25,952,966	3.92
10 Oriya	22,881,053	3.46
11 Punjabi	18,588,400	2.81
12 Kashmiri	3,174,684	0.48
13 Sindhi	1,946,278	0.29
14 Assamese	No census was taken	
15 Sanskrit	2,946	—
TOTAL	632,220,090	95.56

[a] Differences in the bases of enumeration between the figures in this table and table 5.1 need to be noted. The figures in table 5.1 are individual mother tongue figures, those in this table are for the language ordinarily spoken in the household as told to the enumerator by the head of household. Most important, many of the mother tongues listed separately in the mother tongue census are grouped here under the Eighth Schedule languages. This method inflates significantly the number and percentage of Hindi speakers, a matter of very considerable political importance. The percentage of Hindi speakers according to the strict mother tongue criteria of the 1971 census is only 28.09 compared to 39.94 shown in the 1981 census with 48 "variants" grouped under Hindi, including languages so distinct from Hindi as Maithili.

Source: *Census of India, 1981,* Series 1: INDIA, *Paper 1 of 1987: Households and Household Population by Language Mainly Spoken in the Household,* by P. Padmanabha (Delhi: Controller of Publications, 1987), p. 3.

of the language, and representation on language development committees appointed by the central government. Spokesmen for languages such as Maithili, which have not been able to develop strong enough movements to achieve a separate linguistic state, strive to gain recognition in the Eighth Schedule. Since, however, all languages listed in that schedule except Sanskrit and Sindhi have also been recognized as the official language of one or more states, the government of India has opposed such demands, partly because such recogniton to a geographically compact language group would provide a basis for making a further claim thereafter for the creation of a new linguistic state.[12] Moreover, the Government of India also anticipates that listing of further languages in the Eighth Schedule would "lead to an unending demand for addition of more and more languages therein" from among the "more than 3,000 mother tongues ... recorded during the 1971 Census."[13]

At the lowest level are those mother tongues of the people which are not recognized either as official languages of India or of any state and are not listed in the Eighth Schedule. Such mother tongues (along with the officially recognized languages) were recorded fully for the first time in the 1961 census of India, where some 1,652 were listed, many of them spurious in the sense that they are names declared by census respondents who do not know the "proper" name of the mother tongue they speak. Among these mother tongues in 1971, however, were thirty-three (including the fourteen modern languages listed in the Eighth Schedule) with recorded speakers of more than a million (see table 5.1).

There are four Articles in the Constitution of India which protect the rights of linguistic minorities, only one of which, however, specifically refers to mother tongues. Article 350A obliges every state and local authority "to provide adequate facilities for instruction in the mother-tongue at the primary stage of education to children belonging to linguistic minority groups." Articles 20, 30, and 350, which refer to

---

[12] Brass, *Language, Religion, and Politics in North India*, pp. 105–106, 198, 214.

[13] The Government of India and the CLM have also resisted demands for inclusion of other languages on the Eighth Schedule on the grounds that there is no legal-constitutional difference between listed and unlisted languages, a specious argument which ignores practical realities. The CLM himself notes, for example, in the case of Bihar that "languages other than those included in the Eighth Schedule of the Constitution are not being used as media of instruction" at the secondary stage. *CLM*, xxiii, p. 49.

"languages," confer broader rights upon linguistic minorities to preserve their "distinct language, script or culture" (Article 20), "to
establish and administer educational institutions of their choice"
(Article 30), and to submit representations for redress of grievances to
any central or state authority in any language (Article 350). The
struggles of spokesmen for the rights of mother tongues, therefore,
have taken two forms: demands for enforcement of Article 350A and
demands to be recognized, as for example in the Eighth Schedule, as a
"language," not just a mother tongue. In both respects, such spokesmen have faced strong resistance from state governments which wish
to avoid the administrative costs of implementing mother tongue
instruction for a multiplicity of minority languages and, even more
important, from those in and out of government who wish to secure
the dominance of the major regional languages in their states and seek
to assimilate the speakers of such mother tongues to the dominant
language.[14]

The status of the Urdu language

The largest minority mother tongue is Urdu, which claimed sixth place
in the country as a whole in the 1981 census, with more than thirty-
five million speakers, most of whom are concentrated in the north
Indian states. At the spoken level, Urdu is but the name used by
Muslims for the Hindi language, but the script preferred by Muslims is
the Persian–Arabic, whereas that used by nearly all Hindus is the
Devanagari. The literary forms of the two languages also diverge, with
Hindi writers drawing from Sanskrit and Urdu writers drawing from
Persian–Arabic sources in vocabulary and style.

It has been noted above how the case for recognition of Urdu as an
official language of the Union was disregarded in the Constituent
Assembly after the partition of the country in 1947. Urdu, which had
been recognized up to Independence as an official language along with
Hindi in U.P., also lost its place in that state in the Uttar Pradesh
Official Language Act, 1951 in which Hindi was declared the sole
official language of the state.[15] Although Urdu is listed in the Eighth
Schedule of the Constitution, it is an official state language only in the
small state of Jammu & Kashmir. However, it is the single largest

---

[14] *CLM*, xxiii, p. 201.   [15] *CLM*, xxiii, p. 198.

minority language in U. P., where 11.6 million speakers were recorded in the 1971 census comprising 10.5 per cent of the total population of the state. Those figures were reduced to 10.8 million and 9.7 percent in the 1981 census, providing *prima facie* and retrospective support for the charge that census enumerators were deliberately listing declared Urdu speakers as Hindi speakers in north India in contradiction of instructions to the contrary.[16] Nearly seven million speakers (or 8.8 percent of the total population) were recorded in Bihar in 1971. It is a significant minority language in several other states as well, notably Andhra (7.8 percent), Karnataka (9.5 percent), and Maharashtra (6.9 percent).[17]

Despite the large number of declared Urdu speakers in the country as a whole and in north India in particular, the demands of Muslim spokesmen, made through various organizations and movements launched in the 1960s and 1970s for recognition of Urdu as the second official language of the states of U. P. and Bihar, were resisted in both states. Only in the 1980s was Urdu granted the status of a second language – by ordinance rather than formal legislation – for official purposes in fifteen districts of Bihar and in the western districts of U. P., but the U. P. ordinance later lapsed.[18] Moreover, in practice the state governments of both U. P. and Bihar have followed discriminatory policies toward Urdu, which have limited its use as a medium of instruction in the schools and contributed to a severe decline in its use as a medium of communication in north India.

For example, in U. P., with a 1981 Muslim population percentage of 15.93 percent and a recorded population of 9.7 percent Urdu-speakers, only 3.68 percent of students enrolled at the primary stage were receiving instruction in Urdu and only 3.79 percent at the secondary stage in 1979–80. The absolute number of students receiving instruction in Urdu at the primary stage was 352,022. By contrast, the figures for Karnataka were 360,009 and for Maharashtra 438,353, both states

---

[16] Figures on Urdu in U. P. from *Census of India*, 1981, Series 1: INDIA, *Paper 1 of 1987: Households and Household Population by Language Mainly Spoken in the Household*, by P. Padmanabha (Delhi: Controller of Publications, 1987), pp. 7 and 42. On the charge of misreporting, see the statement of Syed Hamid, president of the Anjuman Taraqqi Urdu in *Times of India*, April 9, 1991, cited in *Muslim India*, 101 (May, 1991), p. 220. Whatever may have happened in 1992, the figures for Bihar in 1981 – in contrast to those for U. P. – do not suggest misreporting for the former state in the earlier census.

[17] *CLM*, xxiii, pp. 156, 170, 213.

[18] *Muslim India*, 54 (June, 1987), and *CLM*, xxiii, pp. 55, 372–373.

with much smaller Muslim and Urdu-speaking populations than U. P.[19] Bihar has supplied no figures to the Commissioner for Linguistic Minorities on educational facilities provided for speakers of minority languages since 1972–73. At that time the situation was more favourable than in U. P. for Urdu-speakers at the primary stage where Urdu enrollment was 6.62 percent, but it was only 2.14 percent at the secondary stage in a state where 14.13 percent of the population is Muslim and 8.8 percent are declared Urdu speakers.[20] The consequences of such discrimination could only be a decline in the use of Urdu, reflected for example in the publication of Urdu newspapers and periodicals, which declined from 268 in U. P. before Independence to only 114 in 1970. The number of Urdu newspapers had risen once again to 328 in 1987, but kept far behind the rise in the number and circulation of Hindi newspapers.[21]

Attempts to persuade the central government to intervene decisively on behalf of Urdu with the relevant state governments also have had limited success. A Committee on Promotion of Urdu (Gujral Committee), appointed by the central government in 1972, presented its report to the government in 1975 during the Emergency. The committee recommended, among other measures, the establishment of Urdu medium primary schools wherever the population of Urdu speakers, in a single village or urban ward, exceeded 10 percent, the enforcement in the Hindi-speaking states of a three-language formula for the schools, which would include Urdu compulsorily along with Hindi and English, and the arrangement of facilities for the use of Urdu by the public for communication with officials at the local level.[22]

However, because of opposition from within the cabinet by its

[19] *CLM*, xxii, pp. 442–351. More recent figures for Urdu in U. P. are not available because of the non-responsiveness of the state government to repeated requests from the CLM for such figures; see *CLM*, xxv, pp. 41, 44–45.

[20] *CLM*, xxii, pp. 237, 253.

[21] Brass, *Language, Religion, and Politics in North India*, p. 159, and Government of India, Ministry of Information and Broadcasting, *Press in India*, 1988 (Delhi: Controller of Publications, 1987), pp. 268–270. The number of Hindi newspapers at the end of 1987 was 2,598. Comparative circulation figures for the same year were 372,000 for Urdu and five million for Hindi. Total newspaper circulation in the state was 5.9 million. Therefore, the percentage of Hindi newspaper readers (approximately 85 percent) was close to the percentage of Hindi-speakers in the census whereas the percentage of Urdu newspaper readers (approximately 6 percent) was significantly less than the recorded population of Urdu speakers and very much less than the Muslim proportion in the population.

[22] *Muslim India*, 54 (June, 1987), 257–258.

seniormost member, Jagjivan Ram, no action was taken on the report. The Janata government, with its former Jan Sangh component as well as others opposed to concessions to Muslims and Urdu speakers, also sought to ignore the report. It was, however, released by the Janata party President, Chandrashekhar, on his own authority, which compelled the government to present it to Parliament. Nevertheless, no action was taken on the report during the Janata regime. In 1984, the central government once again took up the Gujral Committee report, but merely appointed a new committee "to review the report and make recommendations for implementation to the Union and State governments." Little effective action has since been taken in the north Indian states.[23] Only in the southern states, such as Andhra and especially Karnataka, where Hindu–Muslim relations have historically been much less hostile than in the north, have effective measures been taken to implement the recommendations of the Gujral Committee concerning the provision of facilities for instruction through the medium of Urdu at the elementary stage and for provision of instruction in the Urdu language at more advanced stages.[24]

The long-standing demand for the declaration of Urdu as the second official language of those states where Urdu speakers constitute a substantial minority of the population, especially in U. P. and Bihar, however, remains unfulfilled. Urdu is recognized only as an additional official language in specified districts of Andhra and Bihar and for "specified purposes" in U. P.[25] Moreover, this type of official declaration has acquired such symbolic significance among militant Hindu political spokesmen that the Gujral Committee itself and most organizations for the promotion of the Urdu language have downplayed this demand and have sought instead the implementation of specific recommendations for the use of the Urdu language for administrative and educational purposes.[26]

Hindi and the mother tongues of North India

The struggle for dominance between Hindi and Urdu in north India, which goes back to the late nineteenth century, is part of a broader process which has an equally long history by which spokesmen for the

---

[23] *Muslim India*, 54 (June, 1987), 257.
[24] *Muslim India*, 57 (September, 1987), 417.
[25] *CLM*, xxv, pp. 402–403.   [26] *Muslim India*, 54 (June, 1987), 257.

Hindi language have attempted to establish Hindi as the regional standard language for the entire region from Punjab to Bengal and Assam in north India, including as well the present states of Rajasthan and Madhya Pradesh. As a practical matter, the struggle has taken the form of achieving official recognition for Hindi as the language of each of the states in this region and excluding other rivals. In the great struggle between Hindi and Urdu, the claims of other north Indian vernaculars were ignored until after Independence. Even after Independence, few sustained demands for formal recognition have been made on behalf of mother tongues other than Hindi and even fewer have been made effectively.

Leaving aside the question of tribal languages for the moment, Grierson's massive *Linguistic Survey of India* identified two great branches of the Hindi language area, which he labeled Western and Eastern Hindi,[27] in each of which were included numerous mother tongues, some of which also had experienced considerable literary development. On the borders of the Hindi language areas, Grierson also identified three groupings of mother tongues so distinctive from Hindi that he gave them separate classifications, to wit, Rajasthani, Bihari, and Pahari, in each of which also were included numerous mother tongues. The ambitions of the promoters of Hindi as the regional standard language of north India have included the absorption of all these mother tongues and of others as well, including Punjabi. With the sole exception of Punjabi, those ambitions have been largely successful so far.

The first great success for the spread of Hindi occurred in Bihar in 1881 when Hindi displaced Urdu as the sole official language of that province. In this struggle between the two competing regional standards, the potential claims of the three large mother tongues which Grierson included in the "Bihari" group – Maithili, Magahi, and Bhojpuri – were ignored. After Independence, Hindi was again given the status of sole official language of the state in the Bihar Official Language Act, 1950. Yet, in the mother tongue census of 1961, only 44.30 percent of the population of the state declared Hindi to be their

---

[27] G. A. Grierson, Linguistic Survey of India, Vol. i, pt. i: Introductory; Vol. v, *Indo-Aryan Family, Eastern Group*, pt. ii: *Specimens of the Bihari and Oriya Languages*; Vol. ix, *Indo-Aryan Family, Central Group*, pt. i: *Specimens of Western Hindi and Punjabi* (Delhi: Motilal Banarsidass, 1967–68).

mother tongue while 35.39 percent declared the several mother tongues included under the designation "Bihari." Within this group, the largest category was Bhojpuri, with nearly eight million declared speakers, followed by Maithili with nearly five million, and Magahi with nearly three million.[28] For the most part, however, the educated speakers of Bhojpuri and Magahi and their political representatives have accepted the inclusion of these two mother tongues as "dialects" of Hindi. Spokesmen for Maithili, however, have always insisted that Maithili is an entirely distinct language from Hindi and went so far as to make a claim for a separate linguistic state in the 1950s and 1960s. Even among Maithili speakers, however, this claim has been largely restricted to an upper caste elite, while many, if not most, middle and lower caste groups in the Maithili-speaking districts of north Bihar have accepted Hindi as their language.

Although the claims of Maithili speakers have not been ignored entirely, success in gaining recognition for the language in Bihar has been limited. Maithili was recognized by the Bihar government officially as a mother tongue in 1949, which meant that Maithili-speaking parents had the right to have their children educated through the medium of Maithili, but the Bihar government never provided enough teachers or textbooks in the language and has refused since 1961 to provide figures showing the numbers of children actually receiving instruction through the medium of Maithili. Other demands, for the teaching of Maithili at the secondary stage and for recognition of Maithili as an official language of administration in districts in the Maithili-speaking region, have been resisted.

In contrast to Bihar, the struggle between Hindus and Muslims over the status of Hindi and Urdu as the dominant regional language of U. P. was so prolonged and divisive that the overwhelming majority of the people of this state declared their mother tongue as either Hindi or Urdu in the 1961 mother tongue census. For example, although there are probably as many or more native speakers of Bhojpuri on the U. P. side as on the Bihar side of the Bhojpuri-speaking region, only 120,119 Bhojpuri speakers were recorded in U. P. in 1961 compared to nearly eight million in Bihar. However, in the northwestern hill districts of U. P., whose languages Grierson included in "Pahari,"

---

[28] Brass, *Language, Religion, and Politics in North India*, p. 65.

nearly 796,880 speakers of Garhwali were recorded in the 1961 census as well as 248,089 speakers of "Pahari-unspecified." In the 1971 mother tongue census, Garhwali and Pahari were ranked twenty-fifth and twenty-sixth in the country as a whole (see table 5.1), each with more than a million speakers, though neither mother tongue has achieved more than token recognition as a medium of instruction in the primary schools.

Several other large mother tongues of north India have received no more than nominal recognition at the primary stage in two other states of north India where the sole official language is Hindi, namely, Madhya Pradesh and Rajasthan. These mother tongues include Chattisgarhi, with nearly seven million speakers (1971 census) in Madhya Pradesh and Rajasthani with more than two million speakers (1971) in Rajasthan. Even speakers of tribal languages which have no connection whatsoever to the Hindi language or even to the Indo-Aryan language family have received little formal recognition in the north Indian states. For example, the 1971 census recorded 3.6 million speakers of Santali, a tribal language in the Munda language family of whom more than half live in the Santal Parganas district of Bihar, most of the rest across the border in Bengal. However, the Deputy CLM reported in 1982–83 that "facilities for instruction through the Santhali language are almost non-existent due to lack of an agreed script for Santhali."[29] Even where tribal languages have had for some time or have recently accepted agreed scripts, the situation is no better outside of the northeastern region of the country.[30]

Moreover, recognition of a mother tongue by a state government is no guarantee that facilities will actually be provided for students in government schools to receive instruction through the medium of their mother tongue. State government rules and regulations generally require that the parents of the children who wish such instruction formally request it and that a certain number of children in each school and classroom must do so in order to receive such instruction.[31] Even

[29] CLM, xxiii, p. 253.   [30] CLM, xxiii, p. 249.

[31] In 1990, the Government of India appointed a committee, known as the Jafri Committee, to consider the extent to which the recommendations of the Gujral Committee had been implemented. The Jafri Committee recommended the substitution of these restrictive rules and regulations by a general requirement that the state governments provide the necessary teachers, classrooms, and schools wherever the percentage of speakers of Urdu – or other minority languages – in an area exceeded 10 percent; *Muslim India*, 100 (April, 1991), pp. 173–174.

then, competent teachers and textbooks in the language may not be available.

Spokesmen for several other tribal languages both in the predominantly Hindi-speaking states and in other states with large tribal minorities have demanded instruction for their children in their mother tongue, but the Scheduled Areas and Scheduled Tribes Commission appointed by the Government of India in 1960 reported that, "in actual fact some of the states have taken this matter very casually."[32] Moreover, the state governments in general have tended to ignore the requests of the Commissioners for Linguistic Minorities and for Scheduled Castes and Tribes even for information on the extent to which speakers of tribal minority mother tongues have actually been provided with facilities for instruction in their mother tongues. For example, the government of Bihar claims to have provided facilities for instruction through the medium of Oraon, Ho, Santali, and Mundari but has not provided any figures to support its claims since 1975–76.[33]

The only language in north India which has succeeded in establishing its separateness from Hindi to the extent of official recognition both in the Eighth Schedule and as the official language of a state is Punjabi. This success, however, was achieved only after prolonged struggle. In Punjab, in contrast to the rest of north India before Independence, promoters of Hindi failed to gain official recognition for the language in that province where English and Urdu remained the official languages until Independence. During the late nineteenth and twentieth centuries, however, there was extensive promotion of the two main vernacular languages of the province, Hindi and Punjabi, by private efforts, particularly of the Hindu reform movement, the Arya Samaj, and by the Singh Sabhas among the Punjabi-speaking Sikhs. In this period, the principal political struggle over language recognition was between Hindus and Muslims over the status of Hindi and Urdu. In this competition, Hindus whose mother tongue was Punjabi began the practice of declaring Hindi as their mother tongue

---

[32] *Report of the Scheduled Areas and Scheduled Tribes Commission*, Vol. I, 1960–61 (New Delhi: Government of India Press), p. 226, cited in P. K. Bose, "Congress and the Tribal Communities in India," in Ramashray Roy and Richard Sisson (eds.), *Diversity and Dominance in Indian Politics*, Vol. II: *Division, Deprivation and the Congress* (New Delhi: Sage, 1990), p. 62.

[33] *CLM*, xxv, p. 51.

in the censuses in order to gain a numerical advantage over Muslims and Urdu. Most Muslims, for their part, actually spoke the various Punjabi dialects, though their political leaders fought to maintain official standing for Urdu.

After Independence, which involved the partition of the Punjab, the emigration of the entire Muslim population to Pakistan, and the immigration of the entire Sikh population from west Punjab to the Indian Punjab, the struggle for recognition now became one between Hindi and Punjabi. In the Haryana region of the Indian Punjab, Hindus were the predominant population and Hindi their language. In the rest of the Indian Punjab, Sikhs were in a small majority compared with Hindus, but both were primarily Punjabi-speaking. The issue of language recognition, however, became tied to the simultaneous demand of the Sikh political party, the Akali Dal, for the creation of a separate province of Punjab, excluding Haryana, in which the Sikhs would be a majority and Punjabi would be the sole official language of the province. The Punjabi-speaking Hindus, however, did not wish to see such a Sikh-majority province created. So, in an effort to defeat the Punjabi Suba movement, Punjabi-speaking Hindus continued to follow the advice of Arya Samaj leaders and declare their language as Hindi. This device enraged Sikh political leaders in the Akali Dal and contributed rather to an intensification of the Punjabi Suba demand, which was ultimately conceded in 1966.

The Punjabi Suba movement and the development of the Punjab crisis of the 1980s will be discussed in further detail in the next chapter. It is relevant to the discussion here concerning minority languages in reorganized states and the related question of the absorption by Hindi in north India of numerous mother tongues from the following points of view. First, it brings out sharply the intensity of the effort of north Indian Hindu organizations such as the Arya Samaj to promote the Hindi language even to the extent of advocating shifts in mother tongue identifications. Second, it also demonstrates that only language groups which derive their support from other-than-linguistic issues can achieve success against the assimilationist drive of the Hindi movement. In the case of Punjabi, as in the case of Urdu, the underlying support for linguistic differentiation from Hindi came from separate religious groups. Third, it also suggests the importance of a distinctive script in achieving separate status for a language in the north Indian context, for both Urdu and Punjabi have scripts of their own, Persian–Arabic and Gurmukhi, respectively.

The status of minority languages in the non-Hindi-speaking states

It is not, however, only the Hindi-speaking areas where processes of linguistic assimilation and differentiation have been occurring. For example, Bengali speakers and the Bengali language in the course of its modern development and standardization during British rule in the late nineteenth and early twentieth centuries came into conflict with Oriya speakers and the Oriya language in Orissa, with Assamese in Assam, and with speakers of tribal languages in Tripura. Even today, in Assam, conflicts persist between Bengalis (18.0 percent of the population of the state) and Assamese and between the Bengali-speaking population and the tribals in Tripura.

Assam provides an example of a region outside the Hindi-speaking area where a struggle between spokesmen for two languages has occurred, in which the speakers of one, Bengali, have attempted to deny the separateness of the other, Assamese. When the struggle for self-assertion was won by the Assamese, however, they then sought to establish the dominance of their own language and to displace Bengali as an official language and a medium of instruction in the schools. Before 1874, when it became "a separate chief commissioner's province," Assam was part of the province of Bengal, in which English and Bengali were the official languages. Assamese was recognized as a separate language and a medium of instruction in the primary and secondary schools and as a court language only in 1871. Assam was reincorporated for a brief period into west Bengal during the Partition, between 1905 and 1912, after which it reverted to its former status as a chief commissioner's province, but with the inclusion in it of two Bengali-speaking districts, Cachar and Sylhet. Even after the separation of Assam from Bengal, the educated classes came primarily from Bengal and from Bengali speakers in the Assam region, who dominated the administrative services and the modern professions, including the teaching profession. The predominance of Bengali speakers in Assam continued even until after Independence. According to the

188

1971 census, Bengali speakers still outnumbered Assamese speakers in the urban areas of the state.[34]

After Independence, however, when the Assamese took control of the state government, they wished to provide greater employment opportunities for Assamese by giving them "preference in appointments to the state administrative services"[35] and by establishing Assamese as the sole official language of the state and the medium of instruction in the schools, which would serve the same purpose of giving an advantage in public employment opportunities to Assamese. Bengali speakers, of course, argued for the retention of both Bengali and Assamese as official state languages. Ultimately, amid rioting and violence between Bengali and Assamese speakers, Assamese was adopted in 1960 as the sole official language of the state.[36] Bitter conflicts between Assamese and Bengali speakers in the state continued, however, and became violent at times, as in 1972 when a struggle developed over the medium of instruction and the language of examination in the colleges of Gauhati University to which the colleges of the predominantly Bengali-speaking district of Cachar were affiliated. In that clash, the proponents of Assamese succeeded in completely displacing Bengali from all the affiliated colleges of Gauhati University.[37]

Within the state of West Bengal itself, a militant movement developed in the 1980s among the Gorkhas in the hills of Darjeeling district, whose mother tongue is Gorkhali (Nepali), the official language of the bordering sovereign state of Nepal. Nepali, which is part of the Pahari language group, including also Garhwali, was the declared mother tongue of 1.3 million people in the 1971 census, most of them living in Darjeeling district.[38] The demands of the movement included citizen-

---

[34] The figures were 516,320 (40.0 percent) Bengali speakers and 499,066 (38.7 percent) Assamese speakers. An additional 15.6 percent of the urban population was recorded as Hindi speakers; *Census of India, 1971, Assam*, Series 3, Pt. I-A: *General Population*, by K. S. Dey (Delhi: Controller of Publications, 1979) and Pt. II–C(ii): *Social and Cultural Tables* (Delhi: Controller of Publications, 1981).

[35] Myron Weiner, *Sons of the Soil: Migration and Ethnic Conflict in India* (Princeton, N.J.: Princeton University Press, 1978), p. 111.

[36] Weiner, *Sons of the Soil*, p. 117. Bengali was given the status of "additional official language" in Cachar district; *CLM*, XXIII, p. 131.

[37] Myron Weiner and Mary F. Katzenstein, *India's Preferential Policies: Migrants, the Middle Classes, and Ethnic Equality* (Chicago: University of Chicago Press, 1981), p. 98.

[38] The percentage of Nepali speakers in West Bengal in 1971 was given as 1.38. Based on the 1981 population figures, the total number of Nepali-speakers in the state, of which the vast majority live in Darjeeling district, is approximately 750,000; *CLM*, XXIII, p. 68.

ship status for all Nepali-speaking immigrants from Nepal, the inclusion of Nepali in the Eighth Schedule of the Constitution, and the creation of a separate state of Gorkhaland within the Indian Union.[39] The latter demand was resisted vigorously by the CPM-led government of West Bengal. In a pattern which has become increasingly common in South Asia in the past decade, this movement engendered considerable violence amounting in early 1988 to a virtual state of civil war in the district between Gorkha activist insurgents and the civil authorities and the police.[40] For a time, it appeared that a lack of coordination between the central government and the state government in responding to the Gorkha National Liberation Front (GNLF) demands was encouraging the latter's militant tactics, as in other similar movements in the Punjab and in the northeast. However, the central and state government leaders ultimately resisted the temptation to take advantage of the situation to further their separate political interests and worked together to reach an accord with the GNLF in August, 1988, whose principal element was the creation of a Gorkha Hill Council within the state of West Bengal. None of the other major demands of the GNLF were conceded in the accord.[41]

The unexpected rise of the Gorkhaland movement suggests that there remains considerable potential in the array of diverse ethnolinguistic groups in India for the development of political movements among at least some of them from time to time. It is not to be expected, however, that each and every one of even the largest unrecognized mother tongues will provide the source for political movements. On the contrary, Hindi and the other regional languages listed in the Eighth Schedule of the Constitution continue to extend their dominance within their own regions and to assimilate to the prevailing regional standard speakers of a multiplicity of local languages, dialects, and mother tongues. Linguistic minorities which have the best chance of maintaining their languages and gaining recognition for them as mother tongues entitled to be used as media of instruction in the primary schools are those listed in the Eighth Schedule living in other states, for example Bengali speakers in Assam or Telugu speakers in

---

[39] *Asian Recorder*, February 27–March 4, 1987, p. 19338.
[40] *India Today*, January 15, 1988.
[41] *Asian Recorder*, September 30–October 6, 1988, pp. 20227–20230.

Tamil Nadu.[42] Even speakers of these and other Eighth Schedule languages, however, confront difficulties outside their home regions. The governments of Punjab and Haryana, for example, insist that there are no linguistic minorities and accord no facilities to minority language speakers in their states, though it is apparent that there are substantial minorities whose mother tongues are Punjabi in Haryana and Hindi in the Punjab.[43]

It is, at the same time, also to be expected that where there are other factors reinforcing linguistic differences, such as religion or job competition for specific places in the economic division of labor in a region or other economic grievances which affect especially the speakers of a distinct language, ethnolinguistic movements will develop, both among Eighth Schedule language speakers living outside their home regions and among speakers of unrecognized mother tongues within their home regions. The importance in the development of these movements of the presence of such other factors is well illustrated by the history of ethnic conflict in the Punjab and Assam. The Punjab and Assam problems are discussed in detail in the next chapter.

[42] Consider the situation in Madhya Pradesh in 1981–82, as reported by the CLM. The largest mother tongue, Chattisgarhi, with a 1971 census population of 6.7 million, is not recognized for any purpose, being considered a dialect of Hindi. The main acknowledged minority languages are the two tribal mother tongues, Bhilli (3.1 percent) and Gondi (2.8 percent), Marathi (2.4 percent), and Urdu (2.3 percent). However, no facilities for instruction through the medium of the tribal languages are provided in the state, while such facilities are provided not only for Marathi and Urdu, but for Bengali, Gujarati, Oriya, Sindhi, and Telugu, all Eighth Schedule languages. *CLM*, xxiii, pp. 29–31.

[43] *CLM*, xxiii, pp. 261–262. According to the 1971 census, the percentage of Punjabi speakers in Haryana was 8.4 and of Hindi speakers in Punjab was 19.9; *CLM*, xxiii, pp. 78, 91.

CHAPTER 6

CRISES OF NATIONAL UNITY: PUNJAB, THE NORTHEAST, AND KASHMIR

Linguistic federalism has proven to be a satisfactory means of maintaining the unity of India and the loyalty of the citizens of its principal language regions. No territorial solution to ethnic problems, however, can by itself satisfy the claims of all minority groups. We have seen that many minority language speakers have remained within the linguistically reorganized states and that several political movements have arisen among them claiming discrimination against their language by the speakers of the dominant regional language in a state.

Moreover, the political leaders of India have not been able to resolve as satisfactorily as in the case of the major language groups the political demands and the political status of non-Hindu and tribal minority groups. States reorganization has either failed or been a far more prolonged and violent process before satisfying the political aspirations of the Sikhs in the Punjab and the tribal peoples in the northeastern region. Outright secessionist movements accompanied by bitter, prolonged, and bloody confrontations between insurrectionary groups and government security forces marked the politics of Punjab, Assam, and the Muslim-majority state of Kashmir as well in the late 1980s and early 1990s. Finally, forty-five years after partition, Indian state leaders had failed to resolve satisfactorily the persistence of Hindu–Muslim communal division, which continued to find expression in vicious killing in cities and towns in many parts of the country.

The question naturally arises, therefore, whether India has departed from its proclaimed secularism and become a state based implicitly on a Hindu definition of nationality. It will be argued here and in the following chapter, on the contrary, that it is the secular ideology itself together with the persistent centralizing drives of Indian state leaders and the unending struggle for power in New Delhi, intensified during Mrs. Gandhi's leadership of the country, which have been more responsible for the failures to resolve the political problems of non-

Hindu minorities. Those very failures in turn have provided the conditions for the rise of a militant Hindu nationalist movement led by the RSS and the multiple organizations within its "family."[1]

FAILURES AND PROBLEMS IN STATES REORGANIZATION: THE PUNJAB AND THE NORTHEAST

The Punjab Crisis and the unity of India[2]

In contrast to the south and Bombay, where language differences were more important than religious differences, religious differences and communal organizations on religious lines were more important in the Punjab in the nineteenth century and up to the partition of the country in 1947, in which Punjab and the Sikhs were at the center of the storm. The Gurdwara Reform Movement of the 1920s brought a critical change in the institutional vitality and political organization of the Sikhs as a community, for it brought into being two organizations which became the central religious and political institutions of the Sikhs. These are the Shiromani Gurdwara Prabhandak Committee (SGPC), a central managing committee for the Punjab *gurdwaras*, which controls the Sikh shrines and its vast resources, and the Akali Dal, the political movement which led the Gurdwara Reform Movement and became the principal political organization of Sikhs in the Punjab before and after Independence.

Another special feature of the Punjab situation was the effect of partition itself, which was a great crisis for the Sikh community. Not only was the Sikh community not granted a special status in post-Independence India, but the demands of the Akali Dal leaders for the inclusion of the Sikhs in the general process of reorganization of states in the 1950s and early 1960s were denied. Only in March, 1966 after a change in the leadership of the Akali Dal and after the Indo-Pakistan War of 1965, in which Sikh soldiers and the Sikh population of Punjab

[1] On the RSS "family" of interrelated organizations, see Walter K. Andersen and Shridhar D. Damle, *The Brotherhood in Saffron: The Rashtriya Swayamsevak Sangh and Hindu Revivalism* (New Delhi: Vistaar, 1987), ch. iv.

[2] The first part of this section draws heavily on a more extended analysis by Paul R. Brass, "The Punjab Crisis and the Unity of India," in Atul Kohli (ed.), *India's Democracy: An Analysis of Changing State–Society Relations* (Princeton, N.J.: Princeton University Press, 1988), pp. 169–213.

played critical roles, was the demand for a Punjabi Suba finally conceded by Prime Minister Indira Gandhi. In this Punjabi Suba, however, Sikhs have a bare political majority without the political dominance sought by the Akali Dal.

A further feature of the Punjab situation which distinguishes it from earlier linguistic reorganizations is that it has never been completed. In particular, there have been three outstanding issues which have not been resolved in the two-and-a-half decades since the reorganization: the status of the capital city of Chandigarh, which remains still the joint capital of Punjab and Haryana; the status of some mixed Hindi- and Punjabi-speaking territories in which Hindus are the predominant population; and the division, for irrigation purposes, of river waters which run through the territories of both states.

Some observers, particularly on the Marxist Left in India, have also laid great emphasis on economic factors in seeking an explanation for the current crisis.[3] As profits declined in agriculture and increasing numbers of young Sikhs sought non-agricultural employment in Punjab, in the Indian armed forces, and abroad in the Persian Gulf and the United Kingdom, such opportunities either declined or failed to keep pace with the increased demand. While such factors have most probably contributed to disaffection and discontent among Sikhs and the absence of satisfying economic opportunities has made many Sikh youths available for mobilization by militants, they do not explain either the origins of the current turmoil in the Punjab or the main factors which have led to its intensification and deterioration into internal war.

The first factor, arising out of the historic drive within the Sikh community to maintain internal cohesion and orthodoxy and the separateness of the Sikhs from Hindus, was the development of a bitter and extremely violent confrontation between militant orthodox Sikh groups and a heterodox Hindu-Sikh sect, the Nirankaris. Out of this conflict emerged the figure of Sant Jarnail Singh Bhindranwale, an important Sikh preacher who saw as his mission the consolidation of the Sikh community, the purification of its practices through enforce-ment of the elements of the traditional Sikh discipline, and the recla-mation of apostate Sikhs.

[3] I have discussed the economic explanations for the Punjab crisis in "Socio-Economic Aspects of the Punjab Crisis," in S. W. R. de A. Samarasinghe and Reed Coughlan (eds.), *Economic Dimensions of Ethnic Conflict* (London: Pinter Publishers, 1991), pp. 224–239.

The second development was a fundamental transformation in the context of center–state relations under Mrs. Gandhi's leadership and the consequent adoption by the central government of an entirely different role in Punjab politics – and in the politics of other states as well – from that adopted by the central government under Prime Minister Nehru in the 1960s. Most important, state politics themselves no longer mattered in their own right as the issue everywhere became the effects of state politics on power in Delhi.

During the Punjabi Suba movement in the 1960s, Prime Minister Nehru was secure in his power in New Delhi and gave his full support in the Punjab to Chief Minister Pratap Singh Kairon, who was the dominant figure in that state's politics for a decade until his assassination in 1964. A united Congress leadership then followed a strategy of dividing the Akali Dal through a variety of methods designed to displace the more extremist Akali leaders and aid more moderate leaders to come to power. In the 1980s, in contrast, Mrs. Gandhi and the central Congress leadership were never willing to repose confidence in a single leader in the Punjab Congress and followed instead a strategy of balancing between opposing groups. The unity of action between the central and state governments, therefore, so important in the 1960s, was absent in the 1980s.

Moreover, in contrast again to the 1960s, when the Congress successfully exploited divisions in the Akali Dal to displace Master Tara Singh and aid the rise to power of the more moderate Sant Fateh Singh, in the 1980s the Congress supported the extremist Sant Bhindranwale to undermine the moderate leadership of the Akali Dal. The central government not only was unwilling to make significant concessions to the moderate Akalis, which would reinforce their credibility in relation to more extremist groups, but its leaders refused to take action against Bhindranwale and terrorist groups whose members had begun to assassinate Hindu opponents and even innocent Hindus as well.

Ultimately, in June, 1984, the central government felt compelled, after a series of assassinations of innocent Hindus in the Punjab and with a general election due by the end of the year, to launch an assault on the Golden Temple in Amritsar, in whose precincts Sant Bhindranwale and his followers had taken sanctuary. Mrs. Gandhi was herself assassinated by two Sikh bodyguards on October 31, 1984. A massacre of thousands of innocent, mostly poor Sikhs, in Delhi, Kanpur, and

Begusarai followed with the complicity or malign neglect of the authorities, the police, and the Congress leaders.

The new Prime Minister, Rajiv Gandhi, reached an Accord with the Akali Dal leadership in September, 1985 to resolve all the outstanding issues. Under its terms, Chandigarh was to be transferred to Punjab within a year, the other substantive issues in dispute were to be submitted to commissions and courts for adjudication, Sikh army deserters were to be rehabilitated, and judicial inquiries into the massacres of Sikhs in places outside Delhi were to be conducted. Aside from the reference of outstanding issues to courts and commissions, which have not been able to arrive at solutions, none of the important substantive provisions of the accord have to this date (1993) been implemented.

In elections held in the Punjab in September, 1985 in the aftermath of the Accord, the Akali Dal won a majority of seats in the Punjab legislature and formed a government under Surjit Singh Barnala. However, neither a restoration of the political process under an Akali government nor the application to the state of severe new measures to detain suspected terrorists under the Terrorist and Disruptive Activities Act (TADA), 1985 brought an end to terrorist actions and the killing of innocent Hindus in the Punjab. The central government again placed the Punjab under President's Rule in May, 1987. The police and other armed forces now attempted a massive crackdown on militants and presumed terrorists.[4]

Although Rajiv Gandhi's policies seemed at first to involve a silent rejection of his mother's and a return to the pluralist policies of his grandfather, the failure to implement most of the provisions of the Accord with the Akali Dal stood in the way of a settlement of the conflict in the Punjab and the return of civil order. Nevertheless, while the police and armed forces continued their relentless operations in Punjab, Rajiv Gandhi made some efforts to find among the militants persons with whom his government could negotiate a settlement. In this process, forty people imprisoned on sedition charges in the Jodhpur jail (referred to in the press as "the Jodhpur detainees") since the assault on the Golden Temple were released, but no progress was made on negotiations with militant leaders during Rajiv's tenure.

[4] Bharat Wariavwalla, "India in 1988: Drift, Disarray, or Pattern," *Asian Survey*, xxix, No. 2 (February, 1989), 194.

In the November, 1989 Lok Sabha elections, polling was allowed in Punjab in which a faction of the Akali Dal led by one of the released militants, Simranjit Singh Mann, won six of the thirteen Punjab seats, leaving only two for the Congress and the rest for other parties and independent candidates, of whom four were supported by militant groups. After the election, the new prime minister, V. P. Singh, sought through the dramatic gesture of personally visiting the Golden Temple to change the atmosphere before making a number of efforts to involve all parties and Akali leaders and groups in a dialogue which might lead to negotiations for a solution to the impasse. However, once again, nothing came of these efforts, President's Rule was extended in the state, and the pace of violent confrontations between terrorist groups and state security forces and the numbers killed reached new highs.[5]

After the fall of V. P. Singh's government, his successor, Chandrashekhar, made further fruitless efforts during his brief tenure as Prime Minister to open negotiations with militants. He also sought to restore the democratic process by calling for the holding of Lok Sabha and Vidhan Sabha elections in Punjab just after the Tenth General Elections in May–June, 1991. Several Akali Dal groups set up candidates for these elections, but the Congress (I), anticipating defeat, boycotted them and several militant organizations opposed them.[6] The latter set out on a systematic effort to kill at least one candidate from as many constituencies as possible, a tactic which ensured the postponement of elections in those constituencies. By the eve of the scheduled elections, one Lok Sabha and twenty-three Vidhan Sabha candidates had been killed. Then, two days before the elections scheduled for June 20, the Election Commissioner, Mr. Seshan, postponed them until a later date.

The postponement was believed by most political observers and journalists to have been either taken after consultation with Congress (I) leaders or done in anticipation by Seshan, a Congress appointee, of the needs of the Congress under the new government of P. V.

---

[5] *India Today*, December 31, 1990, reported 3,560 killed in 1990 up to November 12 (1,896 civilians, 1,199 militants, and 465 state security forces), but the U. S. State Department gave an even higher figure of 4,987 deaths (3,261 civilians, 1,194 militants, 467 state security forces, and sixty-five persons engaged in illegal border crossings to Pakistan); *U. S. Department of State, Country Reports on Human Rights Practices for 1990*, cited in Asia Watch Report, *Punjab in Crisis*, p. 3 fn.

[6] *India Today*, June 30, 1991.

Narasimha Rao.[7] Since the latter had come to office at the head of a minority government, the holding of elections in the Punjab in which twelve additional non-Congress members were certain to be elected, would have weakened, if not undermined, the already tenuous hold of the Congress on power. No other persuasive explanation for this decision, taken after so many lives had been lost, has been offered. It therefore stands as one of the strongest examples in the post-Independence period of the disregard of limits in the struggle for power at the Center in contemporary Indian politics.

Congress, having settled in office after the May–June, 1991 elections, Prime Minister Narasimha Rao turned his attention to the question of elections for Punjab in December, 1991. His government reappointed K. P. S. Gill as head of the Punjab police, a man who had a previous record of successful action against militant, terrorist and criminal groups and gangs in Punjab under the National Front government. While Congress leaders made clear their intention to contest these elections, Akali Dal leaders protested Gill's appointment and the principal Akali factions decided to boycott them.[8]

Elections were held on schedule in March, 1992 in which the Congress won twelve of the thirteen Lok Sabha seats and eighty-seven out of 117 Vidhan Sabha seats. However, despite the presence in the state of 750 companies of paramilitary forces and nine army divisions to maintain order, these forces were not able to bring Sikh voters to the polls, the overwhelming majority of whom refrained from voting. The election results in no way reflected the will of the people of Punjab. Rather, they provided a clear demonstration of the continued strength of the Sikh militants and the disaffection of the Sikh population, including evidence provided by the turnout figures themselves that both militancy and disaffection had spread more widely in the state than ever.[9]

The new Congress chief minister pledged his adherence to the terms of the Rajiv–Longowal Accord.[10] So did Prime Minister P. V. Narasimha Rao.[11] Nevertheless, shortly after the election, representatives of the four Akali factions which had boycotted the polls met in Anandpur Sahib with representatives of two Sikh student organi-

[7] *India Today*, July 15, 1991.   [8] *India Today*, February 15 and 29, 1991.
[9] *India Today*, March 15, 1992.   [10] *India Today*, March 31, 1992.
[11] *Spokesman*, August 3, 1992.

zations and the leaders of various militant groups as well.[12] The leaders and representatives of all groups gathered at the site declared that their goal was now the creation of a separate sovereign state of Khalistan.

How far this decision reflected the actual wishes of the top leaders of the Akali parties was not clear since they were all in jail at the time of this gathering. Moreover, the Khalistan demand has either not been promoted in fact or has been disowned since by several of the principal Akali leaders who have instead reasserted the traditional adherence of all the moderate Akali groups to a 1973 Anandpur Sahib resolution calling for regional autonomy for all the Indian states.[13] What is clear is that the two main institutions of the Sikh community, the Akali Dal and the SGPC, have either themselves been captured by militants[14] or have been factionalized, neutralized, and displaced from playing any effective moderate role in Punjab politics.

Nevertheless, it became evident in September when municipal elections were held, which were not opposed by the militants, that the moderate politicans were eager for some solution which would allow them to return to their political vocations. Eight Akali Dal factions were reported to have sponsored candidates in these elections.[15] Around the same time, it was reported that Akali leaders were planning to unite to launch a peaceful movement to demand implementation of the Rajiv–Longowal Accord.[16]

Still, whether under President's Rule or an elected government, Punjab as a whole has been in effect in a state of internal war and anarchy for some time. Total war which did not spare the family members of combatants was being waged in the late 1980s and early 1990s between numerous militant groups, on the one hand, and the Punjab police and security forces, on the other, in which the death toll continued each year to range in the thousands.

After the reappointment of K. P. S. Gill as Director General of Police and the simultaneous launching of a major army operation known as Operation Rakshak II, the government claimed a significant reduction in civilian deaths at the hands of terrorists, the decimation in police killings of militant leadership, and a decline in recruitment of

---

[12] *India Today*, April 15, 1992. [13] *Spokesman*, August 3 and September 7, 1992.
[14] The SGPC leadership was taken over in November, 1990 by a "militant supporter Baldev Singh Sibia," *India Today*, April 30, 1992.
[15] *Spokesman*, September 14, 1992. [16] *Spokesman*, September 7, 1992.

new members to militant groups.[17] These successes were, however, accompanied by increasing and well-documented reports of police illegalities, excesses, and brutalities including summary executions of alleged captured militants and extreme forms of torture in unacknowledged police custody in special buildings reserved for interrogation purposes.[18]

The militants for their part hardly have a better record. Many so-called militant groups are outright criminal gangs engaged in smuggling, extortion, and kidnapping for personal profit.[19] Most others have engaged in deliberate massacres and other killings of civilians, particularly Hindus,[20] for the sole purpose of demonstrating their power and the inability of the police to prevent them from doing what they wish or for the purpose of frightening the Hindu population in general in order to encourage their flight from Punjab.

Many people believe that the Punjab crisis has gone beyond the stage where it can be settled by means of negotiations over the original issues in dispute and that the opportunity for a settlement in terms of the Rajiv–Longowal Accord has now passed.[21] In the minds of many Sikhs, the 1984 massacres in Delhi and the fact that no one has yet been convicted and punished for participation in them looms larger than the status of Chandigarh or other disputed matters. Moreover, since 1984, the numbers killed in Punjab have passed 16,000, of whom a considerable proportion were Sikh youths killed by the police.

Yet, the achievement of a sovereign status for Punjab under the name of Khalistan is an illusion, which no Indian government will ever allow. The government security forces have the power and the will to continue to smash every source of militant opposition in Punjab for as long as necessary. In the process, however, the commitment of the Indian state to democratic procedures, civil liberties, and secular nationalism has been eroding along with its international credibility as

[17] *India Today*, September 15, 1992. The truth of these claims was acknowledged also in the Sikh newspaper, the *Spokesman*, September 14, 1992. At the same time, the state government did not feel sufficiently secure to agree to the withdrawal from its territory of the army, which has played an indispensable supportive role in the police drive to crush and kill militants. *Spokesman*, September 7, 1992.

[18] *India Today*, October 15, 1992 and Asia Watch Report, *Punjab in Crisis: Human Rights in India* (New York: Human Rights Watch, 1991), esp. ch. iv.

[19] *India Today*, October 31, 1992.

[20] Asia Watch Report, *Punjab in Crisis*, ch. v.

[21] *Cf. India Today*, March 31, 1992, p. 28 on this point.

a great democracy as the bloodbath continues, immigrants from Punjab seek asylum in increasing numbers abroad, and human rights organizations condemn India's treatment of its minorities.

The present impasse was reached neither because the Sikhs are an intractable minority who must inevitably have a state of their own nor because of falling farm prices or lack of employment opportunities for Sikh youth. It was reached because the struggle for power at the Center of the Indian Union passed the limits required for the functioning of a balanced federal parliamentary system. The crisis in Punjab is a crisis for the federal system and for the Indian state.

In the midst of this crisis, two stark alternatives have been proposed. On the one side stands the BJP, whose spokesmen continue to insist that Sikhs are Hindus, members of one nation,[22] that the Punjab crisis can be brought under control by sealing the borders with Pakistan, and that no fundamental changes in center–state relations are required. On the other side are those in the Janata Dal, the CPM, several regional parties, some even in the Congress, and many journalists and Indian academics who argue that events in the Punjab demonstrate that India can no longer "be run on an unitary basis"[23] and that the federal system must be transformed to "give greater autonomy to the states."[24]

The reorganization of Assam

In Assam and the northeast, special problems arose immediately after Independence which made states reorganization a far more difficult and violent process than elsewhere at the time for here the central government faced explicit, unequivocal secessionist demands from non-Hindu tribal groups.

Several sets of ethnic confrontations intersect in Assam: between Hindus and Muslims, linguistic groups (particularly Assamese and Bengali speakers), plains peoples and tribal hill peoples, plains tribals and non-tribals, and the indigenous population and a large migrant population. Here, the specific problems of states reorganization

[22] See the remarks of Govindacharya, then BJP General Secretary, in *India Today*, August 15, 1991, p. 57.

[23] Remarks of Prem Bhatia, former chief editor of the Punjab newspaper, *The Tribune*, in *India Today*, August 15, 1991, p. 61.

[24] Remarks of Vasant Sathe, former minister for Information and Broadcasting in Mrs. Gandhi's government, in *India Today*, August 15, 1991, p. 67.

centered around the demands of the tribal peoples, though the several sets of ethnic issues at times overlapped and influenced each other. Moreover, in the 1990s, new insurrectionary and secessionist movements have arisen in Assam both among the plains tribal peoples and among the dominant Assamese Hindu population as well.

At Independence, there were a multiplicity of tribal groups in Assam, speaking a wide variety of mother tongues. Although the languages of the tribal peoples are entirely distinct from Assamese and although Christianity spread to many of them, language and religion were secondary issues in the demands of the spokesmen of the tribal peoples for separation from the province of Assam and secession from India. The main argument for separation and secession was that tribal peoples were simply not Indians at all.

The reorganization of Assam and the border region, formerly called the Northeast Frontier Agency (NEFA), took place in stages and led to the formation of four new predominantly tribal states: Nagaland, granted statehood in 1963; Meghalaya formed as a separate state in 1972 for the Garo, Khasi, and Jaintia tribes; Arunachal Pradesh, the name given to NEFA, created as a Union Territory then converted to full statehood in 1972; and Mizoram, formed into a Union Territory in 1971 and granted the status of a separate state in 1987.[25] Of several tribal movements, the two which have attracted the most attention because of their widespread popular support, explicitly secessionist goals, and prolonged insurrectionary activities were those of the Nagas and the Mizos.

The Naga and Mizo insurrections

The Naga demand for secession was made by the famous Naga leader, Angami Zapu Phizo, at the time of Independence when the Assam government violated an agreement with the Naga National Council to recognize it as "the principal political and administrative force in the Naga Hill district" and proceeded to extend "its administration to the Naga area."[26] When the Naga movement turned into a violent insur-

---

[25] Myron Weiner and Mary F. Katzenstein, *India's Preferential Policies: Migrants, the Middle Classes, and Ethnic Equality* (Chicago: University of Chicago Press, 1981), p. 115.

[26] Dua, "India: Federal Leadership and Secessionist Movements on the Periphery," in Ramashray Roy and Richard Sisson (eds.), *Diversity and Dominance in Indian Politics*, Vol. II: *Division, Deprivation and the Congress* (New Delhi: Sage, 1990), p. 198.

rection, the central government adopted a policy of suppression by military means, which at times involved an entire Indian Army division and various other paramilitary and police forces, the complete suspension of civil liberties in the hills, and other drastic measures such as the regrouping of villages to separate them from the guerrillas.[27]

At the same time, as in the Punjab, the central government demonstrated its willingness to negotiate with moderate non-secessionist leaders. "After prolonged negotiations," the central government agreed to the formation of Nagaland as the sixteenth state of the Indian Union in March, 1960.[28] In the meantime, the Indian army continued its military operations against the Naga rebels, which persisted until 1978, despite the arrangement of cease-fire agreements in 1964 and 1975.[29]

Throughout the Nehru period, the central government refused to have anything to do with secessionists, but encouraged the formation of non-secessionist groups among the Nagas, negotiated with their leaders, and even granted a separate Naga state to them. Under Mrs. Gandhi, however, the methods changed considerably. In 1966–67, she negotiated directly in New Delhi with secessionist leaders, thereby undermining the position of the non-secessionist, Naga Nationalist Organization chief minister of the newly formed state of Nagaland.[30] In fact, during both her tenures as Prime Minister, in Nagaland as in all other states in the Indian Union, Mrs. Gandhi and the central government played a direct interventionist role in the politics of the state, in which the interests of maintaining a Congress government under a chief minister personally loyal to the Prime Minister overrode the previous policy of supporting non-secessionist Naga political organizations and refusing to deal with secessionists.

The Mizo insurrection began later than that of the Nagas, in 1959, after a famine during which the Assam government allegedly failed to provide adequate relief to the people. The Mizo National Front (MNF), led by L. C. Laldenga, was a political outgrowth from this

---

[27] Pradip Kumar Bose, "Congress and the Tribal Communities in India," in Roy and Sisson, *Diversity and Dominance in Indian Politics*, vol. II, pp. 74–77.

[28] Dua, "India: Federal Leadership," p. 200.

[29] Dua, "India: Federal Leadership," p. 201 and Bose, "Congress and the Tribal Communities in India," pp. 77–78.

[30] These negotiations ended without an agreed solution; Dua, "India: Federal Leadership," pp. 201–202.

time.[31] In March, 1966, "the MNF declared Independence for Mizoram"[32] and Mizo forces launched an insurrection. The central government suppressed the revolt, then took the conciliatory step of detaching the Mizo Hills district from Assam, which was converted into a Union Territory called Mizoram. However, some insurgent activities persisted.[33]

After the 1972 elections, the Congress succeeded in forming a government which, though it managed to remain in power until 1977, faced strong opposition from the People's Conference led by T. Sailo. Following the same pattern as in Nagaland, Mrs. Gandhi sought to find a more effective counterforce to the Congress opposition by making a deal with the leader of the insurgency, Laldenga, who was allowed to fly to New Delhi to negotiate directly with her in 1982. The Congress won the 1984 elections to the Mizoram Legislative Assembly by emphasizing its new relationship with Laldenga, whose own interest also lay in defeating the more moderate opposition to the Congress, which had been in power between 1977 and 1982.[34] In 1986, Rajiv Gandhi and Laldenga signed an accord granting full statehood to Mizoram, after which the incumbent Congress chief minister was removed and replaced by Laldenga.[35]

Once again, therefore, in Mizoram as in Nagaland and in the Punjab, both Mrs. Gandhi and her son departed from the consistent policies of the Nehru period of refusing to have any dealings with secessionist leaders and preferred instead to make alliances with any local and regional forces that would secure or regain power for the Congress itself.[36] The dangers in such a policy, however, include not only the distortion of the old balance in center–state relations, but the weakening of the independent bases of local moderate leaders, which places the Center, particularly the Congress, in the position either of permanent involvement in regional politics or of dependence upon local militant leaders in order to maintain its own base in a region. Moreover, in November, 1992, despite the Congress' political predominance in most of the northeastern states, major incidents of

---

[31] Dua, "India: Federal Leadership," p. 203.
[32] Dua, "India: Federal Leadership," p. 203.
[33] Dua, "India: Federal Leadership," p. 204.
[34] Dua, "India: Federal Leadership," p. 206.
[35] Dua, "India: Federal Leadership," p. 211.
[36] Dua, "India: Federal Leadership," pp. 207ff.

violence, killings, and demonstrations against state authority or other tribal groups were reported not only from Nagaland and Mizoram, but from the other predominantly tribal states of Manipur and Tripura and from tribal groups in Assam itself.[37]

Conflicts between migrants and non-migrants in Assam

History of migration. Since the beginning of the present century, some "six and a half million migrants and their descendants have settled in Assam."[38] These new migrants in their different ways monopolized or dominated virtually all new opportunities for resource exploitation or for jobs in the modern sectors of the economy and in government service.[39] The migrations have been so large as to threaten to transform the indigenous Assamese Hindu population into a minority.[40] If one looks at language figures alone, which give a highly simplified but nevertheless important view of a major aspect of ethnic diversity in Assam, Assamese speakers constitute a majority in the countryside, but a minority of 39 percent in the total urban population, where they are outnumbered by Bengali speakers (40 percent) and where Hindi speakers constitute another 16 percent of the total.[41]

Assamese and Bengali speakers in Assam: job competition and the language issue. Under the British, Assam was initially integrated into the Bengal presidency and the Assamese nobility were displaced by Bengalis in the new administrative services.[42] The use of Bengali as the principal medium of instruction in the schools further enhanced the advantage of Bengali speakers in obtaining employment in the state, with the result that Bengalis came to dominate up through the post-Independence period to the present in high-paying public and private sector jobs and "in middle-class occupations" generally.[43] It was in this context that the language issue emerged as the focus of conflict

[37] *India Today,* November 30, 1992.
[38] Myron Weiner, *Sons of the Soil: Migration and Ethnic Conflict in India* (Princeton, N.J.: Princeton University Press, 1978), pp. 80–81.
[39] Weiner, *Sons of the Soil,* pp. 96, 103–104; B. P. Singh, "North-East India: Demography, Culture and Identity Crisis," *Modern Asian Studies,* xxi, No. 2 (1987), 265.
[40] Sanjib Baruah, "Immigration, Ethnic Conflict, and Political Turmoil – Assam, 1979–1987," *Asian Survey,* xxvi, No. 11 (November, 1986), 1188.
[41] *Census of India, 1971, Assam,* Series 3, pt. I–A: *General Population* by K. S. Dey (Delhi: Controller of Publications, 1979) and pt. II–C (ii), *Social and Cultural Tables* (Delhi: Controller of Publications, 1981).
[42] Weiner, *Sons of the Soil,* pp. 91–92.   [43] Weiner, *Sons of the Soil,* pp. 94–95.

between Assamese and Bengali Hindus in the post-Independence period, with the former pushing for Assamese as the sole official language of state administration and as the medium of education in the schools and the Bengalis demanding a dual language policy. The passage of an act making Assamese the sole official language of the state led to riots in 1960.[44]

Assamese Hindus, Bengali Muslims, and migrants from Bangladesh. The second great controversy between migrants and non-migrants in Assam in the post-Independence period took the form of a directly political conflict between the indigenous Assamese Hindu and tribal populations, on the one side, and the mostly rural Bengali Muslims, on the other side. In contrast to the situation in Punjab after Partition, millions of Muslims remained in eastern India, including Assam, where many had no legal status. In order to protect themselves from expulsion, therefore, Bengali Muslims allied with the Assamese within the dominant Congress.[45]

The factors which led to the break-up of this alliance were political and were connected as much with national as with local political realignments. The split in the Congress after the Emergency and the 1977 elections had a profound impact in Assam where the party divided "into pro- and anti-Indira Gandhi factions" and where the two Congress parties combined could win only thirty-four seats out of 126 in the legislative assembly elections of March, 1978. The split in the Congress also "ended the postindependence coalition of Assamese Hindus and Bengali Muslims."[46] In the meantime, the demographic context had dramatically changed during the Pakistan civil war from March, 1971 onwards, when there was a considerable "influx" of both Hindu and Muslim Bengalis into the state.

In this context, therefore, of the break-up of old political and ethnic coalitions and the absence of stable government in Assam, the Assamese movement was launched demanding the expulsion of illegal migrants,[47] most of whom were Bengali Muslims. The issue first arose in 1979 in a by-election in a constituency containing a large number of

[44] Weiner, *Sons of the Soil*, p. 117.
[45] Weiner, *Sons of the Soil*, p. 124; Weiner and Katzenstein, *India's Preferential Policies*, pp. 102 and 115–116.
[46] Weiner and Katzenstein, *India's Preferential Policies*, pp. 116–117.
[47] Weiner and Katzenstein, *India's Preferential Policies*, p. 119.

East Bengali immigrants, which "drew public attention to a rapid expansion of the number of voters since the previous elections two [years] earlier."[48] At this point, Assamese Hindus, who had seen themselves before primarily in competition with Bengali Hindus for middle-class jobs now also articulated the broader fear of being overwhelmed "numerically, politically, and culturally" by a "massive migration influx."[49] In the absence of agreement between the leaders of the protest movement and the government, governmental stability in the state was weakened and routine electoral politics could not be carried on. Although state assembly elections were held in 1983, they provided an occasion for mass murder.[50]

The next phase in the political and ethnic realignment of Assam politics occurred with the accession to power of Rajiv Gandhi as Prime Minister and the signing of an accord between the central government and the Assam movement leaders providing for the identification, detection, and deletion of alleged illegal migrants from the electoral rolls and ultimately their expulsion from the state. The 1985 elections which followed brought the Asom Gana Parishad (AGP) to power, a party based on the Assamese movement, dominated by Assamese Hindus in coalition with plains tribals, tea plantation workers, and Assamese Muslims.[51]

The AGP government was an utter failure and ultimately fell apart amidst the multiple strains brought about by the unenforceability of the Assam Accord, internal factionalism, and the rise of two new insurrectionary movements in the state. Despite a lack of major accomplishments and early and repeated accusations of incompetence and corruption against his government and several of his ministers during his tenure,[52] AGP chief minister, Prafulla Mahanta, the leading figure in the AASU movement, remained unchallenged within his party for the first four years after his installation. However, as the failures and inadequacies of Mahanta's chief ministership became apparent and his position consequently weakened, dissent against his leadership broke into the open in August, 1989 when he, his wife, and

---

[48] Baruah, "Immigration, Ethnic Conflict, and Political Turmoil," pp. 1191–1192.
[49] Weiner and Katzenstein, *India's Preferential Policies*, p. 90.
[50] Baruah, "Immigration, Ethnic Conflict, and Political Turmoil," pp. 1192–1193.
[51] Baruah, "Immigration, Ethnic Conflict, and Political Turmoil," pp. 1204–1205 and Singh, "North-East India," p. 281.
[52] *India Today*, November 15, 1988.

other members of his cabinet were accused of involvement in several scandals and moves were made to displace him from power.[53] Although these moves did not succeed, they contributed to the general discrediting of the AGP government.

Moreover, leaders of the AGP's progenitor, the AASU, also declared their dissatisfaction with the AGP government. The principal issue concerned the inability of the latter to make significant progress in implementing the main features of the Assam Accord, for which the AASU had fought so long and hard.[54] The AASU had expressed its dissatisfaction with the progress made in implementing the Accord in October, 1987,[55] which it then emphasized by staging an agitation reminiscent of the movement days, a blockade on the shipment of oil out of Assam to the rest of India.[56] Six months later, it was reported that only 164 foreigners had been deported out of three million which the AGP had estimated were illegal migrants and subject to expulsion under the terms of the Accord.[57]

Under the terms of the Accord, migrants who had come to Assam between 1966 and 1971 were to be disfranchised and those who had come after 1971 from Bangladesh were to be deported. Despite the Accord, all other parties in the state, including the Congress, whose leader, Rajiv Gandhi, had signed the Accord with the AASU, wanted the electoral roll to be prepared according to the existing population in the state in 1985.[58] However, because of the insistence of the AASU that substantial revisions in the rolls should be made before any further elections were held in Assam, the 1989 Lok Sabha elections could not be held in the state.[59]

Under pressure from the AASU, the AGP obtained a signed commitment from the central government on January 27, 1990 that the Accord and the revision of the rolls would be carried out according to a fixed schedule.[60] As a consequence of this agreement, a new electoral roll was prepared and released on October 1, 1990, which was acceptable to all political parties.[61] The central government then dissolved

[53] *India Today*, August 15, 1989.   [54] *India Today*, February 15, 1987.
[55] *India Today*, October 31, 1987.   [56] *India Today*, March 31, 1987.
[57] *India Today*, September 15, 1988.
[58] *India Today*, August 15, 1989.
[59] *EPW*, xxiv, Nos. 51 & 52 (December 23–30, 1989), 2800.
[60] *India Today*, March 15, 1990.
[61] *EPW*, xxv, No. 44 (November 3, 1990).

the legislative assembly and imposed President's Rule in preparation for legislative assembly elections.[62]

The Congress leadership at the center responded slowly to AGP requests for more rapid implementation of the Accord and clearly found the developing differences between the AGP and the AASU a matter for satisfaction and potential political benefit.[63] In fact, as the AGP government declined in popularity, former chief minister Hiteswar Saikia, a bitter opponent of the AGP from his days as chief minister during the AASU agitation and eager to humble the AGP government, which had indicted him on corruption charges in November, 1987,[64] sensed the AGP's new vulnerability and began to rally opposition to it before the anticipated 1989 Lok Sabha elections.[65]

Consequently, the AGP joined the National Front of non-Congress parties which defeated the Congress in the 1989 Lok Sabha elections.[66] However, as just noted, the Election Commission decided not to hold elections in Assam (as well as Punjab) in November, 1989 along with the rest of the country. Nevertheless, the AGP was included in the National Front government formed after the election.[67]

Tribal unrest. The several reorganizations of Assam in response to the demands of tribal groups left behind within the boundaries of the state two further areas with sizable tribal populations. One group of tribes, concentrated in the remaining hill areas of the state in the Karbi Anglong and North Cachar Hill districts, demanded the creation of an autonomous unit within Assam.[68] The second, a much larger group of tribes within which the largest are known as Bodos, are plains tribals living in the heartland of Assam mostly on the northern bank of the Brahmaputra river, but with some on the southern bank as well.[69]

Like other tribal peoples elsewhere in the northeast and in other parts of India, Bodo leaders complained that they had lost lands to

[62] *EPW*, xxvi, No. 19 (May 11, 1991), 1189.   [63] *India Today*, March 31, 1988.
[64] *India Today*, November 30, 1987.   [65] *India Today*, August 15, 1989.
[66] *EPW*, xxiii, No. 32 (August 6, 1988), 1600–1601 and xxiv, No. 24 (June 17, 1989), 1308.
[67] *EPW*, xxv, No. 29 (July 21, 1990), 1566.
[68] *India Today*, February 15 and September 15, 1987.
[69] Monirul Hussain, "Tribal Question in Assam," *EPW*, xxvii, Nos. 20 & 21 (May 16–23, 1992), 1047–1050; the Bodos, also called Bodo-Kacharis, comprise nearly 40 percent of the total remaining tribal population in Assam and a larger percentage, closer to half, of the plains tribal peoples.

non-tribal peoples, that they were educationally backward, and that their language was not taught in schools to their own children. The last two grievances make the Bodo movement of a piece with so many others of its type in modern Indian history, for the language issues are inseparably connected to the question of jobs. The fact is that nearly all Bodos know and use Assamese in their daily lives, but the few Bodos who do receive secondary or higher education face stiff competition for public sector jobs from the dominant Assamese Hindu castes,[70] who have also benefited in their competition with Bengalis by the establishment of Assamese as the sole official language of the state. The natural step for the Bodos in this situation, therefore, is to demand recognition for their language and the creation of a separate state in which their language and culture would be recognized and Bodo-speakers would *ipso facto* get most of the public sector jobs.

Since the Bodos are plains tribals, they suffered also from the impact of legal and illegal migrations and encroachments on lands in the Brahmaputra valley by Bengali Hindu refugees and Muslim illegal migrants from East Pakistan/Bangladesh and consequently participated actively in the anti-migrants' movement led by the AASU.[71] However, the Plains Tribal Council, a Bodo-dominated organization, participated in the 1983 elections boycotted by the latter.[72] Moreover, once the AGP government was in power and failed either to reward Bodo leaders for their participation in the AASU agitations or to do anything substantial about the removal of migrants or the betterment of the Bodos, an All-Bodo Students' Union (ABSU) was created to demand the establishment of a separate state of Bodoland.[73]

On January 1, 1987, ABSU presented a memorandum containing a long list of demands, which it followed with an agitation in March, 1987. The primary demands were for the establishment of a separate Bodo state on the north bank of the Brahmaputra river, comprising nearly half the remaining area of the state of Assam, the creation of autonomous district councils for the Bodos who would be left behind

[70] Hiren Gohain, "Bodo Stir in Perspective," *EPW*, xxiv, No. 25 (June 24, 1989), 1377.

[71] Gohain, "Bodo Stir in Perspective," p. 1378 and Hiren Gohain, "Bodo Agitation and Ideological Blinkers," *EPW*, xxiv, No. 40, 2272.

[72] *EPW*, xxiii, No. 3 (July 23, 1988), 1500.

[73] The Bodo demand for a political unit of their own was made as early as 1927 before the Simon Commission appointed by the British authorities. After Independence, demands for a separate state were first made by the All-Bodo Students Union (ABSU) and an organization called the Plains Tribes Council of Assam (PTCA) in 1967. *India Today*, April 30, 1989.

on the south bank, and the addition of Bodo-Kacharis and other tribes living in the hill district of Karbi Anglong to the list of tribes in the Sixth Schedule of the Constitution, entitling them to certain privileges and safeguards.[74] They also demanded increased job reservations for Bodos and the inclusion of their language in the Eighth Schedule of the Constitution of India.[75]

After the failure of a long series of agitations on behalf of their demands, the Bodo movement turned more and more to deliberate violence in 1988 and 1989. In the now standard pattern of escalating violence in insurrectionary movements in India, the police reacted to Bodo violence with undisciplined violence and massacres of their own.[76]

That the migrant issue was of considerable importance for the Bodos was made evident in violent attacks committed during the movement against Muslim settlers in areas inhabited mostly by Bodos. However, Bodos have felt displaced as well by "non-tribal Assamese" in the area, by Hindu settlers from outside the area, and by Nepalis.[77]

Violence reached a peak in August, 1989 when Bodo activists attacked and burned the villages of non-Bodos and Assamese Hindu and non-tribal groups massed and responded with similar attacks against Bodo villages.[78] In the aftermath of the carnage, an agreement was reached among the ABSU leader, the AGP chief minister, and a minister from the central government on August 28, 1989 in New Delhi under which the Bodo militants would cease the violence while the state government would withdraw emergency legislation previously introduced giving it special powers to deal with the insurgency, but the agreements did not hold.[79]

Effective measures to suppress the insurgency and arrive at a lasting political solution were handicapped by the fact that the parties in control of the state and central governments, the AGP and the Congress, respectively, were hostile.[80] The continuance of the Bodo agitation served Congress purposes to the extent that it discredited and weakened the AGP government in the state. Thus, the safety and

[74] *EPW*, xxiv, No. 13 (April 1, 1989), 645; *India Today*, April 30, 1989.
[75] *India Today*, March 15, 1989.
[76] *India Today*, April 30, 1989.
[77] Udayon Misra, "Bodo Stir: Complex Issues, Unattainable Demands," *EPW*, xxiv, No. 21, May 27, 1989, 1146–1147.
[78] *India Today*, September 15, 1989.   [79] *India Today*, September 30, 1989.
[80] *India Today*, September 15, 1988 and March 15, 1989.

security of the population from violent death – the minimal requirement which Hobbes conceded the state must provide to retain its
legitimacy – becomes as much a matter of political calculation as any
other valued right or good.

Just as the AASU spawned the AGP, so the ABSU gave birth to its
own political party, the Bodo People's Action Committee (BPAC),
which won all eight seats to the Assam Legislative Assembly and the
one Lok Sabha seat as well in the 1991 elections from the areas
inhabited principally by Bodos.[81]

A major obstacle to the achievement of the Bodo demand for a
separate state is that the Bodos are not in fact in a majority in the area
which they claim for their own.[82] They share the area not only with
migrants, but with other non-Bodo tribal peoples. Ultimately, in
negotiations with the state and central governments, Bodo leaders
agreed to accept the award of a Bodo Autonomous Council within the
state of Assam comprising all "the Bodo dominated areas of lower
Assam," "including approximately 2,000 villages having more than 50
percent tribal population."[83]

With the Bodos as with the other small tribes of the northeast, the
ultimate futility of the logic of creating homogeneous linguistic-
cultural units is laid bare. Such movements ultimately seek political
chimeras in societies unable to forge and implement policies for
economic growth or social justice, namely, salvation through a state of
one's own in which all the public sector jobs in economies without
adequate resources to justify large public sectors will go to those who
claim to be the indigenous inhabitants of the soil. The futility of this
search for economic satisfaction in a culturally homogeneous state of
one's own is especially evident in the northeast because of the porosity
of the international borders as a consequence of which settlers come in
search of land and job opportunities not only from other parts of India
but from Bangladesh and Nepal as well.

The United Liberation Front of Assam (ULFA). The most serious
problem faced by the AGP government in Assam was a militant and
violent movement which challenged its own base among the predomi-

---

[81] Hussain, "Tribal Question in Assam," p. 1049.
[82] Hiren Gohain, "Bodo Stir in Perspective," *EPW*, xxiv, No. 25 (June 24, 1989), 1379.
[83] *India News*, February 16–28, 1993; see also *India Today*, March 15, 1993.

nant Assamese Hindu population. ULFA, formed originally by dissidents from the AASU and the All Assam Sangram Parishad in 1980,[84] became a serious problem for the Assam government within a year of the latter's formation,[85] but came into the forefront only in 1990 after the failure of the AGP government to achieve any of its goals.

While the AGP attempted to work out with the central government detailed plans for implementing the Assam Accord and revising the electoral rolls, ULFA expressed its loss of faith in both the AGP and the central government by demanding secession from India and launching a violent movement to achieve its aim, including bank robberies and killings.[86] Although both the AGP and AASU declared their opposition to secession,[87] their ability to deal effectively with the ULFA movement was hampered by the fact that ULFA was itself a bastard child of their own previous movements challenging them in their own strongholds with a similar appeal to Assamese Hindu resentments against the alleged loss of their territory to foreigners and their exploitation by the central government.

The AGP chief minister also revealed the heart of the problem and the bedrock support of all the Assamese Hindu movements of the past decade by stating in an interview that ULFA was able to build its strength by appealing to the more than a million educated unemployed young people in the state. He blamed the central government for not providing sufficient projects to provide employment to them.[88] Nevertheless, the state and central governments responded by making use of TADA to meet ULFA force with state counterforce and began killing and arresting the organization's leaders and activists.

In November, 1990, the Government of India imposed President's Rule on Assam and began military action under Operation Bajrang to suppress the insurrection and arrest and imprison ULFA activists. ULFA members fought back and killed ninety-seven people, including twenty-five Congress (I) members.[89] The central government, now under Prime Minister Chandrashekhar and dependent on the support of the Congress, removed the governor of the state, an appointee of

---

[84] *India Today*, March 31 and May 15, 1990.   [85] *India Today*, February 15, 1987.
[86] *India Today*, February 15 and October 15, 1987; Kamarupee, "AGP Facing Multiple Challenges," *EPW*, xxiv, No. 46 (November 18, 1989), 2533; *EPW*, xxv, No. 5 (February 3, 1990), 232–233; *EPW*, xxv, No. 20 (May 19, 1990), 1060–1061.
[87] *India Today*, September 15, 1990.   [88] *India Today*, May 15, 1990.
[89] *India Today*, March 31, 1991.

the previous National Front government, on the demand of Rajiv Gandhi and extended President's Rule, which was due to expire on May 27.[90] By April 20, 1991, the authorities felt the operation had been sufficiently successful to bring it to an end.[91]

ULFA now called upon its members and supporters to avoid participation in the May–June, 1991 legislative assembly and parliamentary elections in Assam, which opened the way for a Congress victory and its return to power in the state after a lapse of five years. ULFA leaders were apparently surprised by the victory of the Congress (I) in these elections[92] and the installation as chief minister of Hiteswar Saikia, an inveterate opponent of ULFA,[93] who had been chief minister earlier during the AASU anti-migrants' agitation and had taken a hard line against that movement as well.[94]

ULFA greeted the formation of the new Congress government on July 1, 1991 with a dramatic capture of fourteen hostages from different parts of the state, including a Soviet technician posted at Coal India, who was killed. Negotiations followed[95] after which five hostages were returned in exchange for twenty-six ULFA militants.[96] However, negotiations broke down thereafter, ULFA militants killed two of the hostages, and the Saikia government called the army back to the state to launch on September 15, 1991 a major new attempt to break the militants, given the name, "Operation Rhino."[97]

By January, 1992, the ULFA movement appeared to have been broken and divided internally. While Operation Rhino was in progress, Saikia had been carrying on negotiations with ULFA leaders and succeeded in splitting the organization, bringing over the least diehard elements.[98] Representatives of the latter agreed to "accept the Indian Constitution, seek a solution to [their] grievances within the constitutional framework" of the country, and renounce violence. As a consequence, the chief minister consulted with the Prime Minister and

---

[90] *India Today*, April 15, 1991.

[91] *EPW*, xxvi, No. 37 (September 14, 1991), 2124; *India Today*, October 15, 1991.

[92] However, Kamarupee claimed that Congress (I) "struck a deal" with ULFA before the election, which seems unlikely considering what followed after the elections; "Congress Returns to Brahmaputra Valley," in *EPW*, xxvi, No. 25 (June 22, 1991), 1510.

[93] *India Today*, September 30, 1991.   [94] *India Today*, January 15, 1992.

[95] Kamaroopi [sic], "Enigma of ULFA," *EPW*, xxvi, No. 30 (July 27, 1991), 1786–1787.

[96] *India Today*, January 15, 1992.   [97] *India Today*, October 15, 1991.

[98] *India Today*, January 15, 1992.

the defence and home ministers of the Government of India, who agreed to suspend Operation Rhino.[99]

The government's negotiations with the moderates were sweetened with the offer of Rs. 110 crore in the form of "rehabilitation" grants for defecting ULFA members, which were to be used to help them reintegrate into civilian life and employment. These inducements helped in securing the defection of an estimated 3,000 activists.[100]

It is noteworthy that the Congress (I) government of Assam succeeded in confronting the ULFA insurrection and dividing it by following the methods used in similar situations in the 1960s during Nehru's time, notably in the Punjab. First, the government made absolutely clear that the secessionist goals of ULFA would not be considered and applied massive force to break it. Second, the government simultaneously carried on negotiations with the aim of splitting off the moderates and isolating the extremists. Third, the state and central governments, both under Congress (I) leadership, consulted regularly and acted in unison, even though significant disagreements were reported to have existed particularly between the chief minister and the home minister of the Government of India. It should be noted also that the methods adopted were different from those practiced under Mrs. Gandhi and Rajiv as well in Punjab and Assam, both of whom either used for their own purposes or negotiated with the extremist rather than the most moderate elements.

JAMMU & KASHMIR[101]

The Kashmir problem has occupied a prominence in Indian and South Asian domestic and international politics far beyond what would appear warranted by its size, its small population, and its limited resources. Three wars between India and Pakistan have been fought on and over its territory, the issue of its status has been before the United Nations since 1948, and it became an issue as well in superpower

---

[99] *India Today*, March 31, 1992.   [100] *India Today*, August 31, 1992.

[101] Recent new writings on the Kashmir problem consulted in preparing this section include especially the following: Sumit Ganguly, "Avoiding War in Kashmir," *Foreign Affairs*, LXIX, No. 5 (Winter 1990–91), 57–73; *Human Rights in India: Kashmir Under Siege*, May 1991, An Asia Watch Report (New York: Human Rights Watch, 1991); Jagmohan, *My Frozen Turbulence in Kashmir* (New Delhi: Allied Publishers, 1991); and Ashutosh Varshney, "India, Pakistan, and Kashmir: Antinomies of Nationalism," *Asian Survey*, XXXI, No. 11 (November, 1991).

politics for many years and a factor in the triangular conflicts among India, Pakistan, and China. The concern here will be with explaining two of its features: its persistent importance in Indian politics and the rise in the late 1980s of a violent and explicitly secessionist movement involving a brutal confrontation between militant guerrilla movements and the Indian armed forces which has surpassed in intensity even the internal war in Punjab.

As is well known, Kashmir was one of the princely states of India which, under British rule, had a semi-autonomous status. At Independence, though these states all theoretically reverted to sovereignty, their real choices were confined to merger with either India or Pakistan. In practice, all other states were merged by choice, coercive persuasion, or force into Pakistan if their population was predominantly Muslim and into India if their population was predominantly Hindu.

The conflict between India and Pakistan over Kashmir arose because, though the state's population was predominantly Muslim, its ruler was Hindu, and it abutted both India and Pakistan, making its merger into either a real possibility and the option for full independence a possible goal as well. In the event, Pakistan forced the issue by allowing irregular and Pakistan army elements to advance toward the state capital of Srinagar, which precipitated the formal – though reluctant and originally limited and conditional – accession of the state into the Indian Union, followed by the first Indo-Pakistan War and its conclusion in an informal partition of the state into two parts, of which the largest and most populous remained with India.

Kashmir's importance in Indian politics arises from several interrelated features of its history and status in the Indian Union. The first is its symbolic connection with the very ideological basis of the Indian state. It has been frequently reiterated by everyone who has written on the subject that the integration of Kashmir into Pakistan after its accession to India could not be accepted because it would appear to validate Jinnah's argument that there were two nations in South Asia, one Hindu and one Muslim, whose members could not live together in peace within the same political unit. Validation of the two-nation theory would also *ipso facto* deny the legitimacy of its opposite, the Indian nationalist ideology which proclaimed that India was a secular state which could accommodate religious diversity in a pluralist democracy.

Further, because of the peculiar constitutional circumstances under which Kashmir was integrated into the Indian Union, with an exemption from the full application of the Indian Constitution to its territory, its special status also has come to be seen as a potential threat to the integrity of the Indian Union. Under Article 370 of the Constitution of India, the Indian Parliament cannot legislate on items listed on either the Union or concurrent list of powers without the approval of the Kashmir Legislative Assembly which, along with other special features, appears to give to the state of Jammu & Kashmir a kind of regional autonomy. Militant Hindu nationalists have always objected to the special status of Kashmir as unwarranted and have demanded the abrogation of Article 370 and the full integration of the state into the Indian Union on the same basis as every other state.

Thus, the integration of Kashmir into the Indian Union was never completed to the satisfaction of all important ideological and political forces either in Kashmir or in India as whole. Since 1948, the politics of Kashmir and arguments about its status have been influenced by internal regional differences, by changes in center–state political alliances, and by shifting political tendencies and the development of new political forces within the state.

Regional aspects of Kashmir politics

Although Kashmir at Independence was a Muslim-majority state, it was divided then – and continues to be – into three distinct culture regions: the Kashmir valley, Jammu, and Ladakh. The population of the Kashmir valley, which was wholly absorbed into India, has been nearly 95 percent Muslim and predominantly Kashmiri speaking.

Jammu, with a population before Independence somewhat less than that of the valley, but one-and-a-half times larger in area, was 61 percent Muslim in 1941. Its inhabitants were primarily speakers of Dogri, a Punjabi language. The loss of a substantial portion of Jammu to Pakistan in the first Indo-Pakistan War reversed the religious population proportion in the part remaining in India, which now had a Hindu majority of about 64 percent.

Ladakh is bigger than Jammu and Kashmir combined, but contains a tiny population of less than 150,000 people, mostly Tibetan Buddhists.

The three regions of the state of Jammu & Kashmir have had different political orientations and have spawned as well regional separatist movements within the state. Many Hindus in Jammu have supported militant Hindu parties which have demanded the full integration of the entire state in the Indian Union through the abrogation of Article 370, although there has also been at times a demand for separation of Jammu from Kashmir.

Center–state alliances and politics in Jammu & Kashmir

Despite its special status and its particular form of regional autonomy, the central government and political leaders have intervened as much or more in Kashmir since Independence than in any other state of the Union. Consequently, the history of its politics from Independence until the outbreak of the recent internal war cannot be understood without knowledge of center–state political relations and alliances.

As in other princely states in pre-Independence India, the Indian National Congress was unable to establish political roots in Jammu & Kashmir. The most important popular political force in the state was the All Jammu and Kashmir Muslim Conference, formed in 1932, which split into two factional offshoots in 1940. The leading faction was the National Conference of Sheikh Mohammad Abdullah, strongest among Muslims in the Kashmir Valley, and allied with the Indian National Congress. The second was the Muslim Conference, strongest among Muslims in Jammu and allied with the Muslim League in its drive for Pakistan.[102]

From Independence until the outbreak of internal war in 1989, the main issues in Kashmir have revolved around its status, regional conflicts within the state, and the relationships between the state and central governments, all of which are inseparably interconnected. The history of these interrelated issues can, with some considerable reduction in complexity, be collapsed into three principal phases.

The first phase, from 1947 until 1953, is one of close alliance between the central government under Nehru's leadership and Sheikh Abdullah, who became Prime Minister of the state. However, Sheikh Abdullah was placed between two extreme forces in the politics of the state: those who were pro-Pakistan and those who favored full merger with India. The latter were represented in Jammu by the Praja Parishad, which called for abrogation of Article 370, supported by the militant Hindu nationalist party, the Bharatiya Jana Sangh. Despite –

---

[102] Jagmohan, *Frozen Turbulence in Kashmir*, pp. 78 and 81.

or perhaps because of – his alliance with the Center, which under-mined his credibility with pro-Pakistan elements, Sheikh Abdullah began indirectly to assert his own distinct position on the status of Kashmir, which implied something beyond regional autonomy, which some central leaders read as covert support for independence for Kashmir from both India and Pakistan.[103] Consequently, Sheikh Abdullah was dismissed by the central government in August, 1953, arrested, and jailed.

The second period in Kashmir's post-Independence political history is the longest and most complex. It is characterized by the estab-lishment of a close relationship between the leaders of the National Conference in the state and of the Indian National Congress at the center, approaching a virtual merger between the two parties. It is in effect a period of dependence of Kashmir political elites upon the Center during which the state became a kind of fiefdom for politicians who declared their full loyalty to India and their adherence to the finality of Kashmir's accession to India, in exchange for which they received enormous funds for "development" of the state, which became an inexhaustible supply of patronage and a vast source of corrupt income as well.

However, the alliance between the state and central governments was not able to contain completely alternative political forces or to resolve underlying political issues. Severe rioting broke out in 1963 in Srinagar upon news of the theft of the hair of the Prophet Mohammed from the reliquary of the city's principle mosque, which, though no Hindus were implicated in the theft, had repercussions for Hindu–Muslim relations in large parts of the country.

Sheikh Abdullah remained a popular leader even in jail and was released by Nehru shortly before his death in 1964 in an effort to reach an overall and definitive settlement of the Kashmir issue with Pakistan. The effort collapsed after Nehru's death and the Sheikh, who was criticized for having met several foreign leaders on a trip abroad, including Chou En-lai, was put in jail again upon his return to India in 1965.

In the meantime, as the National Conference and the Indian National Congress became virtually indistinguishable and ultimately

[103] On this point, see Varshney, "India, Pakistan, and Kashmir," p. 1005 and Jagmohan, *Frozen Turbulence in Kashmir*, pp. 95ff.

merged formally, old political forces reemerged on opposite sides: a Plebiscite Front, supported by Sheikh Abdullah, along with other groups supporting a popular vote to determine the ultimate future of Kashmir, on the one side, and the Jan Sangh calling for abrogation of Article 370 and full merger with India on the other. In addition, there were also some outright pro-Pakistan Muslim groups and others in Jammu calling for autonomy for that region either within or outside of Jammu & Kashmir.

Once Mrs. Gandhi had established her supremacy in national politics, she extended her interventionist strategy to Kashmir politics, absorbing all the important anti-Abdullah former National Conference leaders into the Congress, which won fifty-seven of seventy-five seats to the Kashmir Assembly in the elections of 1972. Then, in 1974, Mrs. Gandhi released Sheikh Abdullah from jail and reached an Accord with him in 1975 under which he accepted the finality of Kashmir's accession to India, while the Center agreed to retain Article 370. He was permitted to reestablish his National Conference party and was appointed chief minister of the state, a position he occupied until his death in 1982 despite increasing tensions between his party and the Congress in the state.[104]

The political succession to Sheikh Abdullah unsettled further both the internal politics of the National Conference in Kashmir and the Accord between that party and the Indian National Congress, between the state and the Center. Sheikh Abdullah's son, Dr. Farooq Abdullah, was elected leader of the National Conference and succeeded his father as chief minister, much to the dissatisfaction of his sister and brother-in-law, G. M. Shah, who coveted the position of leadership for himself. Dr. Farooq Abdullah also soon lost credibility with the central leadership who considered him an erratic, politically immature, and unreliable person whose inconsistency and lack of leadership qualities were threatening the peace and stability of the state.

The Congress, therefore, supported and encouraged G. M. Shah's faction in its attempts to win over defectors from Farooq to the former's side. Outside, the Congress successfully displaced the BJP from the Jammu region as the party of Hindu sentiment with attacks on Farooq as an "anti-national" leader. The *coup de grâce* was

---

[104] Jagmohan, *Frozen Turbulence in Kashmir*, pp. 105–108.

delivered to Farooq in July, 1984 when Jagmohan, an authoritarian and narcissistic bureaucrat so loyal to Mrs. Gandhi that he could be counted upon to anticipate her desires without explicit instructions which would embarrass her, was appointed Governor of the state. He proceeded immediately after his arrival to manage the conflicts between the Shah and Farooq factions within the National Conference in such a way as to provide justification for the dismissal of Farooq as chief minister and his replacement by G. M. Shah.[105]

The third and fateful phase in Kashmir politics began with Farooq's dismissal. The new chief minister proved unable to govern effectively. Both the National Conference and the Congress in Kashmir had been discredited among the increasingly politically conscious population of the state, especially among the new generation of youths who had come to recognize how little the relationship between the state and the center, the National Conference and the Congress, had done for the betterment of the state and their own life chances despite the vast amounts of money which had been poured into the state's treasury from the Center. Governor's Rule was imposed upon the state in March, 1986, which was followed six months later by the imposition of President's Rule.

In the meantime, Rajiv Gandhi, who had come to power at the Center after his mother's assassination, sought to restore the previous Congress–National Conference relationship by reaching an Accord with Farooq under which the two parties agreed to fight the 1987 legislative assembly elections jointly and to form a coalition government thereafter, if successful.[106] However, opposition to both parties had grown considerably and had intensified so much as a consequence of this alliance between two discredited forces that the elections had to be rigged to prevent a full demonstration of the strength of parties opposed to the coalition, especially that of an alternative coalition of parties known as the Muslim United Front.[107]

---

[105] However, see Jagmohan's own account and defence of his actions in *Frozen Turbulence in Kashmir*, ch. vii, which should be compared with that of Farooq Abdullah (as told to Sati Sahni) in *My Dismissal* (New Delhi: Vikas, 1985).

[106] Varshney, "India, Pakistan, and Kashmir," p. 1015.

[107] Varshney, "India, Pakistan, and Kashmir," p. 1016 and Ganguly, "Avoiding War in Kashmir," p. 63. In an interview in *India Today*, August 31, 1992, Farooq Abdullah virtually admitted that these elections were rigged, though he denies that he rigged them or that the Congress–Conference coalition would have lost had they not been rigged. He did

In the 1987 elections, the two alliance partners, the National Conference and the Congress won sixty-six of the seventy-six seats to the Legislative Assembly, but the routine political process soon became irrelevant as disaffected Kashmir youth in the Valley turned increasingly to armed militant revolt against the Indian state.[108] As in Punjab, there has been a proliferation of fighting groups divided roughly into two camps: those whose focus, "fundamentalist" or otherwise, is on their identity and/or religiosity as Muslims favoring merger with Pakistan and those whose primary identity is with the distinctive culture, region, and language of Kashmir, favoring independence from both India and Pakistan. It is generally believed that the Jammu & Kashmir Liberation Front, which advocates Independence for a secular Kashmir state, containing both Muslim and Hindu populations, is the most popular fighting force in the Valley.[109]

By the time of the change of government at the Center to the National Front led by V. P. Singh, the situation in Kashmir had gone out of control. V. P. Singh was unable to regain control of the situation in Kashmir, indeed compounded its difficulties by simultaneously pursing a soft and a hard line, sending sympathetic negotiators such as George Fernandez to negotiate with the militants while at the same time reappointing Jagmohan as governor on January 18, 1990.

Farooq Abdullah could not countenance a second term with the Governor who had before so unceremoniously dismissed him and resigned, whereupon Governor's Rule was declared the day after Jagmohan's arrival. The latter, despite considerable bluster, exuding of self-confidence, and application of massive force, failed also to make any headway in containing the rising strength of the militant groups and was himself dismissed in May, 1990 after the police fired upon a group of mourners in a funeral procession for the slain religious-political leader, Mirwaiz Maulvi Farooq. He was replaced by Girish Chander Saxena, previous head of India's intelligence bureau known as RAW (Research and Analysis Wing), under whose

concede that the Muslim United Front might have won twenty seats instead of ten if the elections had been held more fairly.

108 The Muslim United Front leader, Maulana Abbas Ansari, is not alone in believing that, "But for the '87 elections, which were rigged, the youth would not have picked up guns nor even known that Nehru had promised a plebiscite"; *India Today*, April 30, 1992.

109 Varshney, "India, Pakistan, and Kashmir," p. 1017.

governorship a full-scale internal war was launched against the militant groups operating in the state.

This internal warfare has become more intense, more brutal, and more violent than the situation in Punjab.[110] For a time, despite the increasing brutality and intensity of the struggle, it remained largely one between militants and state security forces. However, the small population of mostly Brahman Hindus in the Valley, numbering approximately 125,000, ultimately felt or were made to feel insecure and all but a few thousand have left for Jammu or other parts of India.[111]

The central government under Prime Minister P. V. Narasimha Rao declared that its objective for Kashmir was the restoration of normalcy and the holding of elections to restore the political process.[112] However, elections held in Kashmir in the foreseeable future would provide nothing but an occasion for even more severe violence and, if held, would be even more of a farce than those held in Punjab in 1992. The moderate, non-violent politicians utterly lack credibility in Kashmir and cannot even appear in public for fear of their lives. The National Conference is in an even weaker position than the Akali Dal, its counterpart in Punjab.

Three political choices are open to the central government in Kashmir. One is to continue the relentless drive to suppress secessionism and all demands that smack of it, such as a plebiscite, and to hold out always the promise of the restoration of normal political processes once violent insurrectionary activities have come under control. It has been sufficiently demonstrated above that suppression of threats to India's national unity wherever they occur by the application of massive force has been one of the most consistent policies pursued by the central government since Independence. An alternative policy is to take seriously the demands of moderate politicians in Kashmir for a reenforcement of the regional autonomy provisions which have given it a special status in the Indian Union[113] and to seek a

---

[110] It has also involved extensive, "gross and systematic human rights abuses" by the state security forces, documented in the Human Rights Watch Asia Watch Report, *Kashmir Under Siege*, p. 3 and *passim* and in extremely shocking pictures published from time to time in *India Today*. Human rights violations have also been committed by the militant organizations; see ch. v of *Kashmir Under Siege*.

[111] *India Today*, July 15, 1992.   [112] *India Today*, August 31, 1992.

[113] This is essentially the position of Farooq Abdullah; *India Today*, August, 31, 1992.

political settlement on that basis. However, with the exception of Farooq Abdullah, all other moderate and militant leaders are united on a single demand for a plebiscite, for self-determination for the people of Kashmir to decide their own future in accordance with United Nations resolutions to which in international law the government of India remains subject.

It is not only the long-standing policy of the Government of India in dealing with explicit and implicit secessionist movements which now stands in the way of any compromise settlement in Kashmir, but the rise and spread of militant Hindu nationalism in north India during the past decade. The BJP, whose success in the 1991 elections was aided significantly by its exploitation of the Ayodhya issue through the *rath yatra* of its then leader, L. K. Advani, sought in 1992 to continue its surge with the help of another motorized journey, called an *ekta yatra* (unity journey) from the south of India to Kashmir. The *yatra* was designed to demonstrate the BJP's commitment to the unshakable unity of India and the full and irrevocable incorporation of Kashmir into it. The BJP caravan was attacked en route through Punjab and the office of the Director General of Police in Srinagar was bombed and the senior police officers of the state severely injured two days before the flag-planting ceremony. The *yatra* ended in farce in Srinagar where only the state security forces witnessed the planting of the Indian flag by the BJP leaders.[114] The BJP efforts thus demonstrated the opposite of its ostensible goal, that the government of India and its security forces still lacked the ability to control militancy, violence, and challenges to India's national unity in both Punjab and Kashmir.

Explanations

There are three prevailing explanations for the rise of an insurrectionary movement amongst Kashmiri Muslims against the Indian state in Kashmir. One is an argument which always presents itself in movements such as these, that it reflects the primordial desires of the Kashmiri Muslims. In fact, however, the course of modern Kashmiri history demonstrates the opposite: the absence of any clear universally accepted ultimate goal for Kashmiri Muslims, let alone the rest of the non-Muslim population of the state. Since Independence Kashmiri

[114] *India Today*, February 15, 1992.

Muslims have been divided on whether they prefer independence, merger with Pakistan, regional autonomy, or closer union with India.

The second explanation is that the Indian state has taken a "too soft and permissive attitude" with political forces who have set out to exploit the special status of Kashmir and to manipulate religious and separatist sentiments for their own political advantage.[115] Funds meant for the development of Kashmir have been misused for corrupt purposes, failing to provide employment opportunities for the state's poor people. Consequently, in this atmosphere, "terrorists," "pro-Pakistan elements," "fanatics," and "fundamentalists" aided and abetted by Pakistan came to hold sway over the minds of the innocent people of Kashmir.[116] The solution in this view is suppression of militancy by brute force while providing the people roads, clean water, environmental preservation, schools, and other benefits of development.[117]

A third explanation, the point of view adopted here, is rather that the central government has been not "soft and permissive," but manipulative and interventionist and that it has not kept its promise to respect in practice the limited autonomy granted to Jammu & Kashmir under the terms of accession. The Indian state has also failed in Kashmir as elsewhere in India to provide an economic environment in which a new generation of Kashmiris could see realized the expressed hopes, ideals, and promises of the national leadership for a better life, for jobs, for the amenities of modern life or even a decent life for most people. Lacking satisfying life chances and the political opportunities to express their dissatisfactions and seeing the corrupt behavior of the state's politicians and the violation by the Indian government of its promises, the unemployed, underemployed, newly educated youth of Kashmir have taken to arms under the belief or the illusion that an independent Kashmir or a Kashmir merged with Pakistan will somehow be able to provide both a true expression of the political will or the religious sentiments of the Kashmiri people while at the same time improving their life chances.

Unfortunately for all concerned, these hopes are an illusion.

[115] This is the position of Jagmohan, argued in great detail in *Frozen Turbulence in Kashmir*; the citation is from p. x. His views, especially concerning the "soft and permissive" attitude of India's political leaders are shared by the BJP.

[116] Jagmohan, *My Frozen Turbulence in Kashmir*, pp. 13 and 112ff.

[117] Jagmohan, *My Frozen Turbulence in Kashmir*, p. 14.

Pakistan, whose role in these events has been marginal, nevertheless remains a party to them and cannot be ignored. Its own instabilities and internal conflicts contribute to the general pattern of increasing instability and deterioration of politics and center–state relations throughout the subcontinent. No responsible leadership in South Asia seems willing to move in a direction which might prevent India and Pakistan from following the path of the Soviet Union and Yugoslavia, namely, a restructuring of the relations both between these two states and between their centers and their constituent units through the establishment of truly federal or confederal systems.[118]

CONCLUSION

Many alternative explanations for the resurgence of regional and communal conflicts in the past fifteen years have been offered, including the persistence of immutable primordial cleavages in Indian society, their underlying bases in economic or class differences, and specific policies and political tactics pursued by the central and state governments. The analysis here has given primacy to the latter. However, it is also true that the problems in the Punjab, in the northeastern region, and in Kashmir have been complicated by the presence of other factors which were not present in the linguistic reorganizations of states which took place during the Nehru period.

In the Punjab case, the most important difference is the fact that the Sikhs are a separate religious as well as linguistic group. In the northeast, the issues have been tangled by the presence there of several tribal minorities, whose demands have been secessionist, by the migration of large numbers of people from other provinces of India, particularly West Bengal, to the northeastern states of Assam and Tripura especially, by illegal migrations from Bangladesh as well, and by the presence of large numbers of both Hindus and Muslims among the migrant and local populations. In Kashmir, the issues have been complicated by the internationalization of the dispute, the special status which Kashmir has had since its integration into the Indian Union, and its perceived integral connection with the opposed founding ideologies of the two principal successor states to the British Raj.

[118] Cf. *GPD*, "Indo-Pak Relations: Getting to the Roots," *EPW*, xxvii, No. 36 (September 5, 1992), 1889–1890.

Nevertheless, the argument here is that the policies pursued by the Government of India after Nehru's death have played a major role in the intensification of conflicts in these three regions and have in the process highlighted a major structural problem in the Indian political system. That problem arises from the tensions created by the centralizing drives of the Indian state in a society where the predominant long-term social, economic, and political tendencies are toward pluralism, regionalism, and decentralization. Although the same tensions existed in the Nehru years, central government policies then favored pluralist solutions, non-intervention in state politics except in a conciliatory role or as a last resort, and preservation of a separation between central and state politics, allowing considerable autonomy for the latter. From the early 1970s, however, during Mrs. Gandhi's political dominance, the central leaders have intervened incessantly in state politics to preserve their dominance at the Center, the boundaries between central and state politics have disappeared in the critical north Indian states and in the states under discussion in this chapter especially and have been challenged elsewhere as well, and pluralist policies, though not discarded, have been often subordinated to short-range calculations of political benefit.

CHAPTER 7

COMMUNAL AND CASTE CONFLICT: SECULARISM, HINDU NATIONALISM, AND THE INDIAN STATE

Hindu nationalism, Muslim separatism, and secularism, the official ideology of the Indian National Congress during the nationalist movement and of the Indian state since Independence, have existed side by side in Indian politics since the late nineteenth century. Although the three ideologies and the political organizations and movements they have spawned from time to time have always been perceived as mutually antagonistic, they have shared common goals. Before Independence, they all sought to unite either the entire population of the country or one of the two largest segments of it into united wholes to contest for power at the center of the Indian political system. Moreover, these are the only possible bases for uniting the vast heterogeneous populations of the Indian subcontinent, divided amongst language, caste, tribal, religious sectarian, and many other groupings.

Hindu nationalism has offered the prospect of uniting the country around the idea that all those who consider themselves "Hindus," whatever their sect, language, or caste are joined in fact by systems of beliefs, philosophical principles, and rituals going back to the Vedas, that they share a common history preceding both the British and the Muslim invasions, and that, as the "majority" population of the country, their beliefs and history ought to provide the ideological basis for an Indian state properly conceived as a Hindu state. Muslim separatists took the position that all the Muslims of South Asia constituted one nation different from the Hindus and that the two nations could only live together as equals, sharing power in a single state, or they would have to part and live in separate states. Secular nationalists argued that these very differences emphasized the need to remove religion and sense of community from the center of Indian politics and to establish the independent Indian state as a neutral force standing above these two antagonistic forces, preventing them from

tearing each other and the Indian state apart, and recognizing all citizens of India, Hindus, Muslims, and others, as entitled to equal rights
as individuals without reference to their religion or communal
affiliation.

The violent partition of the country and the Hindu–Muslim killings
which preceded and accompanied it, followed by the assassination of
Mahatma Gandhi by a person considered to be a Hindu fanatic associated with the RSS, discredited for several decades the ideologies of
both Hindu nationalism and Muslim separatism and made secularism
appear the only possible basis for the modern Indian state. Nevertheless, forty-five years after partition, Hindu–Muslim communal division has once again become a central feature of Indian politics and
vicious communal killings have been increasing in numbers and frequency and spreading geographically in recent years. At the same time,
Hindu nationalism represented in the RSS and its "family" of organizations – the BJP, Vishwa Hindu Parishad (VHP), and Bajrang Dal[1] –
has reached a new peak of popular support and political importance.
Muslim separatism as a counterforce in the pre-Independence sense is
no longer a viable possibility, but Muslim solidarity has increased in
recent years as well, as a consequence especially of the struggle over
the Babari Masjid (Babur's mosque) in the Hindu city of Ayodhya.

As Hindu nationalism and Muslim consciousness have intensified,
the secular ideology has come under attack from several quarters.
Hindu nationalists declare it false, a "pseudo-secularism," which has
actually favored Muslims and other minorities. Muslims find that the
secular state has not been able to protect their lives, property, and even
their mosques against Hindu attacks. Many intellectuals who are
neither Hindu nationalist nor Muslim separatist also now argue that
India needs a new state ideology that recognizes religious pluralism
and the importance of faith in people's lives, and stresses the message
of tolerance said to be present in all Indian faiths rather than secular
neutrality.[2]

[1] On the RSS "family" of interrelated organizations, see Walter K. Andersen and Shridhar D. Damle, *The Brotherhood in Saffron: The Rashtriya Swayamsewak Sangh and Hindu
Revivalism* (New Delhi: Vistaar, 1987), ch. iv. The Bajrang Dal (literally "Party of Steel"), a
relatively new addition to the family, is a kind of primitive force of storm troopers.
[2] See esp. Ashis Nandy, "The Politics of Secularism and the Recovery of Religious
Tolerance," *Alternatives*, XIII (1988), 177–194 and T. N. Madan, "Secularism in Its Place,"
Journal of Asian Studies, XLVI, No. 4 (November, 1987), 747–760.

The ascendance of Hindu nationalism has been taking place in the face of a completely contradictory force: increased inter-caste conflict within the Hindu fold itself. Caste conflicts between elite and middle caste groups, which have had a long history in the several states of the Indian Union, exploded on the national scene in August, 1990 under the prime ministership of V. P. Singh with the announcement for the first time since Independence of the commitment of the central government to a policy of reservations of public sector jobs for the intermediate or backward castes in Hindu society. This very policy announcement itself contributed to an intensification of the Hindu nationalist drive, for the leaders of the BJP saw this as undermining their goals of achieving Hindu unity by dividing Hindu castes in a competition for jobs.

Thus, in the late 1980s and 1900s, the Indian state faced challenges to its unity not only from regional forces in Punjab, Kashmir, and Assam, but from forces contesting its very identity and definition. In fact, the persistence of the former threats to Indian unity have been a major factor in the rise of Hindu nationalism. The outcome of the struggle for control of the Indian state will also profoundly affect the contest between central and regional forces. A state captured by Hindu nationalism will be a state devoted to the ruthless suppression of all perceived minority threats to the integrity of the Indian state.

This chapter focuses on communal and caste conflict and their history in the post-Independence period, on Hindus united and Hindus divided in the political senses. The BJP and the RSS seek to unite Hindus against Muslims, while preventing internal caste, sectarian, and regional differences from dividing them and preventing their rise to power. The future of the Indian state, its very viability depends upon the outcome of these contradictory struggles.

THE PERSISTENCE OF HINDU–MUSLIM
COMMUNAL DIVISION

According to the 1981 census, Muslims constitute 11.4 percent of the total population of the country. More than half of the Muslim population lives in the three states of U. P., Bihar, and West Bengal (see table 7.1 and figure 5).

Table 7.1. *Number and percentage of Muslims to the total population of the major Indian states, 1981 census*

State[a]	Number	Percent
1 Jammu & Kashmir	3,843,451	64.19
2 West Bengal	11,743,259	21.51
3 Kerala	5,409,687	21.25
4 Uttar Pradesh	17,657,735	15.93
5 Bihar	9,874,993	14.13
6 Karnataka	4,104,616	11.05
7 Maharashtra	5,805,785	9.25
8 Gujarat	2,907,744	8.53
9 Andhra Pradesh	4,533,700	8.47
10 Rajasthan	2,492,145	7.28
11 Tamil Nadu	2,519,947	5.21
12 Madhya Pradesh	2,501,919	4.80
13 Orissa	422,266	1.60
14 Punjab	168,094	1.00
TOTAL[b]	75,512,439	11.35

[a]Assam, excluded from the 1981 census of religion, had a population of 3,590,000 Muslims according to the 1971 census, comprising 24.0 percent of the total.
[b]Figures do not add to total, which includes all states and union territories.
Source: Census of India, 1981, Series-1: *India*, Paper 3 of 1984: *Household Population by Religion of Head of Household*, by V. S. Verma (Delhi: Controller of Publications, 1985).

Congress policy toward Muslims

The Congress, since before Independence, has had a political alliance with orthodox Muslims, and specifically with those associated with the Jamiyyat-ul-Ulama, an organization of Muslim clerics associated with the famous orthodox Islamic university at Deoband in western U. P. The Jamiyyat's cooperation with the Congress has involved a political bargain in which the *ulama* have given their support on the assumption that the Muslim Personal Law would be maintained, as would endowments, mosques, and other institutions and aspects of Muslim culture.[3]

[3] Yohannan Friedmann, "The Attitude of the *JAM'IYYAT-'ULAMA'-HIND* to the Indian National Movement and the Establishment of Pakistan," *Asian and African Studies*, VII (1971), 173–174.

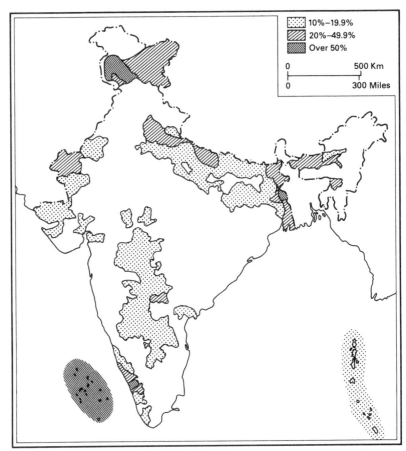

Figure 5   Distribution of Muslims, 1971, to total population by district
Based on Ashok K. Dutt and M. Margaret Geib, *Atlas of South Asia*
(Boulder, CO: Westview Press, 1987).

The apparent liberality and secular approach of the Congress leadership toward the Muslims under Nehru and later under Mrs. Gandhi drew to the Congress the most secular, liberal, and often Marxist Muslim politicians as well.

Muslim grievances in north India

In addition to the issue of the status of Urdu discussed in chapter 6, in the years since Independence, Muslim political spokesmen have raised several other issues concerning the protection of the Muslim minority, its culture and institutions.

The status of the Muslim Personal Law

The absence of a uniform civil code for all Indians and the status of the Muslim Personal Law were dramatized most recently in the Shah Bano case of 1987 in which the civil courts awarded alimony to a divorced Muslim woman contrary to the provisions of the *shariat*. When agitation against the Shah Bano case decision among orthodox and conservative Muslims developed, intensified, and appeared to gain mass support, Prime Minister Rajiv Gandhi capitulated to conservative Muslim opinion to the extent of passing the Muslim Women (Protection of Rights on Divorce) Bill. The latter, passed on May 6, 1987, literally adopted the provisions of the *shariat* into secular law.

The question of the status of the Aligarh Muslim University

A third issue has concerned the status of the Aligarh Muslim University (AMU), which has had central symbolic importance as the pre-eminent educational institution for Muslims in India for nearly a century. The AMU functioned until 1951 under a special charter, which contained three controversial features: a provision for compulsory religious education of the students, its residential character, and its administration by Muslims.

The 1951 amendment to the Aligarh Muslim University Act, 1920 modified the original charter in all three respects. A further amendment in 1965, which threatened the autonomy of the University, precipitated an agitation to restore the act of 1920. Despite promises made by Mrs. Gandhi thereafter, the Aligarh Muslim University (Amendment) Act, 1972 failed to respond to the most important Muslim demands, causing on the contrary further resentments. Only after the Janata government reopened the issue in 1978, and the Congress responded with new promises to Muslims in the 1979 election campaign, was a new Amendment Act passed in 1981 which satisfied most Muslim opinion by recognizing explicitly the minority character of AMU.[4]

Muslims in the political parties and in government service

Muslims have generally been underrepresented in the national and state legislatures,[5] and, with some exceptions,[6] in the central and state government services. Among the recent demands, therefore, of Muslim political organizations such as the Muslim Majlis-e-Mushawarat (MMM), is the extension of "reservations for the Muslim community as a Backward Class in public services and higher education."[7]

Contemporary Muslim politics and political organization

Muslim political parties, interest associations and leadership

Kashmir is the only state in India where Muslims are in a majority and where the once-dominant party, the National Conference, was led by Muslims.

In Kerala, because of the concentration of Muslim numbers in Malabar, the Muslim League has been able to play a balancing role between the Congress- and Communist-led coalitions which have alternated in power there for the past two decades.[8] As a result, the League was a member of every government in the 1960s and 1970s,

---

[4] Paul R. Brass, *Language, Religion, and Politics in North India* (London: Cambridge University Press, 1974), pp. 223–227, and Violette Graff, "The Muslim Vote in the Indian General Election of December, 1984," in Paul R. Brass and Francis Robinson (eds.), *The Indian National Congress and Indian Society, 1885–1985: Ideology, Social Structure and Political Dominance* (Delhi: Chanakya Publications, 1987), p. 465.

[5] Paul R. Brass, *Language, Religion, and Politics in North India*, pp. 228–230; Ghanshyam Shah, "Strategies of Social Engineering: Reservation and Mobility of Backward Communities in Gujarat," in Ramashray Roy and Richard Sisson (eds.), *Diversity and Dominance in Indian Politics*, Vol. II: *Division, Deprivation and the Congress* (New Delhi: Sage, 1990), p. 136; G. Thimmaiah and Abdul Aziz, "The Political Economy of Land Reforms in Karnataka, a South Indian State," *Asian Survey*, XXIII, No. 7 (July, 1983), 816; Graff, "The Muslim Vote," p. 458.

[6] Such as Mysore/Karnataka; Thimmaiah and Aziz, "The Political Economy of Land Reforms," p. 823.

[7] *Muslim India*, No. 55 (July, 1987), p. 297.

[8] Graff, "The Muslim Vote," p. 437.

was able to protect Muslim interests effectively, and succeeded to the extent of compelling the state government to create a Muslim-majority administrative district.

In the 1987 legislative assembly elections in Kerala, the League was once again a partner in the Congress-led United Democratic Front (UDF), to which it contributed fifteen of the sixty seats won by the coalition. However, the UDF lost the election to the CPM-led Left Democratic Front (LDF), which formed the government thereafter. The UDF returned to power after winning the 1991 elections. In the government of chief minister Karunakaran, the Muslim League was given four important cabinet positions.[9]

The dominance of the Muslim League among Muslims in Kerala has been challenged by the rise of a new, more militant Muslim organization, the Islamic Sevak Sangh (ISS), formed in 1988 in response to the Ayodhya dispute. Like the RSS, it seeks to organize and consolidate the Muslim community in Kerala, to intensify its commitment to Islam, and to "defend" Muslims against the perceived militant Hindu threat. The ISS has rapidly acquired mass support among Muslims in Kerala. Violent clashes have occurred between the ISS and RSS threatening a communalization and polarization of politics between Hindus and Muslims in this state, which has been largely free of communal conflict and riots for many years.[10]

In north India, no Muslim political organization can hope to succeed in having a significant effect as an exclusively Muslim political party. Consequently, the strategies pursued have alternated between loyalty to the dominant party, the Congress, during the first fifteen years after Independence, on the one hand, and attempts to use the Muslim vote as a balance in inter-party conflicts in the hope of persuading some parties and candidates of various secular political parties to be more sympathetic to Muslim causes, on the other hand.

The latter strategy was tried notably by the MMM, formed in August, 1964 during a meeting of Muslim leaders in Lucknow.[11] In 1967, it published a *People's Manifesto* and bargained with political parties and candidates to support it. The non-Congress coalitions which came to power in the two north Indian states after 1967,

---

[9] *India Today,* July 31, 1991, p. 32.   [10] *India Today,* September 15, 1992.
[11] Brass, *Language, Religions, and Politics in North India,* p. 248.

however, failed to satisfy Muslim demands. The MMM declined in significance thereafter.

In recent years, the MMM has come under the control of the controversial Syed Shahabuddin. However, as the Babari Masjid issue came to overshadow other matters of concern to Muslims in the late 1980s and early 1990s, organizations formed specifically around that issue became more prominent. The Babari Masjid Movement Coordination Committee (BMMCC) also has been led by Syed Shahabuddin. Differences on the strategy and tactics pursued by the BMMCC and Syed Shahabuddin led to the formation of another organization focused on the mosque called the Babari Masjid Action Committee (BMAC).

Other parties, associations, and leaders

Outside of Kashmir, north India, and the deep south, there are a few other Muslim political organizations and leaders who have played continuous roles in local and national politics. These include the Majlis-i-Ittehad-i-Muslimeen of Hyderabad city, a communal party which has been in existence for several decades,[12] as well as interest groups of several types. Such organizations include, among others, the Jamiyyat-ul-Ulama-e-Hind, whose primary political purpose has been to defend the Muslim Personal Law and oppose "any attempts by the state to change or interfere with it through either specific laws or through the enactment of a uniform civil code"[13] and the Jamiyyat-e-Islami (JUI), fundamentalist, revivalist, and missionary in orientation, rather than orthodox, though it shares with the Jamiyyat-ul-Ulama the goal of preserving the *shariat* for Muslims in India.[14]

Syed Abdullah Bukhari, the Imam of the Jama Masjid in Delhi, has played a personal role in national politics since 1977 when he spoke out against Mrs. Gandhi and the Emergency and campaigned against the Congress for the Janata in the Lok Sabha elections. In 1980, the Imam, disaffected with the Janata regime, supported the Congress, but

[12] Graff, "The Muslim Vote," p. 439. The Majlis won the largest number of seats in the 1988 municipal elections in Hyderabad, thirty-eight out of 100 compared to twenty-four each for the Congress (I) and the Telugu Desam and was thereby able to elect its candidate as mayor; Jaya Kamalakar, "Ethnic Politics in Municipal Corporations," *EPW*, xxiii, No. 19 (May 7, 1988), 945–946.

[13] Brass, *Language, Religion, and Politics in North India*, p. 238.

[14] Violette Graff, "*La Jamaat-i-Islami en Inde*," in Olivier Carré and Paul Dumont (eds.), *Radicalismes Islamiques*, Vol. ii (Paris: L'Harmnattan, 1986), pp. 62–63.

he again moved to oppose the Congress in 1984. He and his son, the Naib Imam Ahmad Bukhari, have increasingly opposed the Congress and adopted militant postures with regard to the Babari Masjid issue.[15]

Syed Shahabuddin, a former Indian Foreign Service officer,[16] has become a prominent spokesman for Muslim causes, particularly with regard to the Babari Masji issue. He also publishes a monthly journal, *Muslim India*, in English and Urdu, which keeps track of the status of all issues and controversies of concern to Muslims. Although he was for a time a member and office bearer of the Janata Dal, his general political position has been that Muslims should support secular parties, including the Congress, to confront and isolate the BJP in Indian politics, and to call for combined action, even coalition, by the secular and Left parties for that purpose.[17]

Muslim voting behavior

General pattern of Muslim voting behavior since Independence

All observers agree that Muslims voted predominantly for the Congress until 1962, but that there was a withdrawal of Muslim support from that party in the 1967 General Elections in the aftermath of rising Muslim discontent over the issues of Urdu, the status of the Aligarh Muslim University, and the increased level of communal violence (see below) especially in the north.

In 1971, Muslims not only returned to the Congress but were said to have "voted to an unprecedented degree" solidly for Mrs. Gandhi, who presented a strong secular image.[18] There is widespread – though not universal – agreement that the Muslims, especially in north India, shifted their voting behavior once again in 1977 away from the Congress to the Janata coalition.[19] Hostility among Muslims to the

---

[15] *India Today*, October, 31, 1992.

[16] Graff, "The Muslim Vote," pp. 433 and 435.

[17] See, for example, *Muslim India*, No. 95 (November, 1990), pp. 482–483 and No. 101 (May, 1991), pp. 194–195.

[18] W. H. Morris-Jones, "India Elects for Change – and Stability," *Asian Survey*, XI, No. 8 (August, 1971), 722–723, 728.

[19] Myron Weiner, *India at the Polls, 1980: A Study of the Parliamentary Elections* (Washington, D.C.: American Enterprise Institute, 1983), p. 121; Barnett R. Rubin, "The Civil Liberties Movement in India: New Approaches to the State and Social Change," *Asian Survey*, XXVII, No. 3 (March 1987), 375; Graff, "The Muslim Vote," p. 430; but, see also Harry W. Blair, "Electoral Support and Party Institutionalization in Bihar: Congress and the Opposition, 1977–1985," in Richard Sisson and Ramashray Roy, *Diversity and Domi-*

demolition scheme to remove squatter settlements and shops from congested urban areas was said to have especially influenced Muslims.[20]

Internal division within the Janata coalition in which the Lok Dal leaders themselves charged that the Jan Sangh and the RSS were responsible for an increase in incidents of communal violence led Muslims "who had supported Janata in 1977" to shift away from its remnants in the 1980 election and to return to voting for the Congress in larger numbers.[21]

In the 1984 election, minority demands receded into the background while the Hindu majority was mobilized in an atmosphere of hostility to minority demands and behavior. The Congress itself appealed to Hindu nationalism and communalism in this election. The upshot was that Muslim voting behavior was similar to 1980. The general consensus is that approximately half the Muslim electorate voted for the Congress, as did the rest of the country, and that there were considerable regional variations in the Muslim vote.[22] The natural diversity of Muslims in India appeared to be now reflected in the diversification – regionalization and localization – of Muslim voting behavior.

However, the Babari Masjid/Ram Janmabhumi dispute and the communal rioting which occurred in the course of it affected significantly the Muslim vote in the 1989 elections and even more profoundly in the 1991 elections, especially in the north. In the 1991 elections, many Muslim voters appear to have followed a strategy recommended by Muslim political leaders, particularly Shahabuddin,[23] to vote in each constituency for whichever secular party was in a position to defeat the BJP. In the last two elections, the long-term tendency toward the political integration of Muslims in the electoral process has been

nance in Indian Politics, Vol. 1: Changing Bases of Congress Support (New Delhi: Sage, 1990), pp. 143–144.

[20] Myron Weiner, India at the Polls: The Parliamentary Elections of 1977 (Washington, D.C.: American Enterprise Institute, 1978), p. 40. Among the shops and stalls demolished at the time were those surrounding the Jama Masjid, which were owned by the Imam himself, Syed Abdullah Bukhari.

[21] Weiner, India at the Polls, 1977, pp. 19–20.

[22] Graff, "The Muslim Vote," pp. 443, 460; also Lloyd I. and Susanne H. Rudolph, In Pursuit of Lakshmi: The Political Economy of the Indian State (Chicago: University of Chicago Press, 1987), p. 194; and Robert L. Hardgrave, Jr., "India in 1984: Confrontation, Assassination, and Succession," Asian Survey, xxv, No. 2 (February, 1985), 142–143.

[23] Muslim India, No. 101 (May, 1991), pp. 194–195.

reversed. Muslims have felt it increasingly imperative to vote as Muslims for their own protection.

Hindu–Muslim communal violence

The numbers of communal incidents and of persons killed in them increased significantly between the mid 1960s and 1982 – the last year for which official figures are available – as indicated in table 7.2. It is evident from the figures that, with rare exceptions, the numbers of Muslims killed were usually much higher than the numbers of Hindus. Moreover, in most major riots police firings are directed disproportionately at Muslim mobs and many of the Muslims killed in these riots are killed in the police firings themselves, rather than by Hindu rioters.[24]

A new and extensive wave of severe communal rioting occurred in north India in 1990–91 in the aftermath of the *rath yatra* of L. K. Advani and the *kar seva* movement (see below), and before and during the May–June, 1991 elections. During the 1991 election, much violence was deliberately fomented by particular candidates or parties either to win votes or to ward off defeat by arousing communal sympathies and animosities. Propaganda by the BJP and its allied organizations, particularly the VHP, played a significant part in this process of provoking communal violence.[25] Yet another wave extending to other parts of the country occurred in December, 1992 in the aftermath of the destruction of the Babari Masjid at Ayodhya.

Hindu–Muslim polarization: The Babari Masjid/Ram Janmabhumi (Ram's birthplace) dispute

The symbolic focus of the communal resurgence in the 1980s and 1990s has been the controversy surrounding the Babari Masjid in the Hindu pilgrimage city of Ayodhya. The controversy has acquired a broad significance for the two religious communities in India, leading to attempts on the part of both Muslim and Hindu politicians to redefine the status and boundaries of the two communities and their relationship to each other. It has involved the self-conscious and

---

[24] Communal Riots and Minorities, unpublished official Government of India paper, no further publication details.
[25] See Paul R. Brass, "The Rise of the BJP and the Future of Party Politics in Uttar Pradesh," in Harold A. Gould and Sumit Ganguly (eds.), *India Votes: Alliance Politics and Minority Governments in the Ninth and Tenth General Elections* (Boulder, CO: Westview Press, 1993).

Table 7.2. *Incidents of communal violence and numbers of persons killed by community, 1954–82*

Year	Incidents		Hindus	Muslims	Others/ police	Total	
					Killed		
1954	83		N.A.	N.A.	N.A.	N.A.	
1955	72		N.A.	N.A.	N.A.	N.A.	
1956	74		N.A.	N.A.	N.A.	N.A.	
1957	55		N.A.	N.A.	N.A.	N.A.	
1958	41		N.A.	N.A.	N.A.	N.A.	
1959	42		N.A.	N.A.	N.A.	N.A.	
1960	26		N.A.	N.A.	N.A.	N.A.	
1961	92		N.A.	N.A.	N.A.	N.A.	
1962	60		N.A.	N.A.	N.A.	N.A.	
1963	61		N.A.	N.A.	N.A.	N.A.	
1964	1070		N.A.	N.A.	N.A.	N.A.	
1965	173	(676)[a]	N.A.	N.A.	N.A.	N.A.	
1966	133	(132)[a]	N.A.	N.A.	N.A.	N.A.	
1967	209	(220)[a]	N.A.	N.A.	N.A.	N.A.	
1968	346		24	99	10	133	
1969	519		66	558	49	674[c]	
1970	521		68	176	54	298	
1971	321		38	65	0	103	
1972	240		21	45	3	70[c]	
1973	242		26	45	1	72	
1974	248		26	61	0	87	
1975	205		11	22	0	33	
1976	169		20	19	0	39	
1977	188		12	24	0	36	
1978	219	(230)[b]	51	56	1	108	(110)[b]
1979	304		80	50	31	261	
1980	427		87	278	10	375	
1981	319		N.A.	N.A.	N.A.	196	
1982	474		N.A.	N.A.	N.A.	238	
TOTAL	6933		530	1498	159	2723	

[a] Source (1).
[b] Sources (1) and (4).
[c] Row totals do not add up because of an irresolvable error in the source figures.

Sources: (1) 1954–1968: Centre for Research in Rural and Industrial Development, Communal Violence and its Impact on Development and National Integration (no publication details), citing Ministry of Home Affairs, *Bulletin for the National Integration Council*, May 16, 1969, p. 8 and Ratna Naidu, *The Communal Edge to Plural Societies: India and Malaysia* (Ghaziabad: Vikas, 1980). (2) 1965–1967: Government of India, Ministry of Home Affairs, *Report, 1966–67*, p. 51 and *Report, 1967–68*, p. 40. (3) 1968–1980: Communal Riots and Minorities, unpublished, undated, mimeo report, p. 1. (4) 1981–1982: Government of India, Ministry of Home Affairs, *Report, 1982–83* (New Delhi: Government of India Press, 1983), p. 3.

deliberate resurrection by national political leaders of a long dormant local dispute and its transformation into a vital issue affecting the faiths and requiring the solidarity of the two communities.

The mosque known as Babari Masjid was allegedly constructed by one of Babur's generals in the sixteenth century on top of a temple of the god Ram, which was allegedly destroyed for this very purpose, a common practice of the Muslim invaders in north India. However, a platform sacred to Hindus as the birthplace of Ram remained beside the mosque. In the mid nineteenth century, these two adjacent sites provided occasions for religious, political, and legal confrontations between Hindus and Muslims concerning the appropriate uses of the site. In 1885, the dispute reached the district courts where a Hindu sub-judge and an English district judge both denied a Hindu application for permission to build a temple on the *chabutra* (platform) site and instead ordered the installation of a railing to separate the *chabutra* and the mosque to forestall communal confrontations.

After Independence, some local Hindus thought the time had come to restore the entire site to its original purposes for the worship of Ram and it was taken over surreptitiously by a group of fifty to sixty persons in the night, who installed Hindu idols on the mosque premises. On December 29, 1949, however, in response to Muslim demands for removal of the idols and restoration of the mosque, the district court attached the buildings, locked them, and placed them in the hands of a receiver. A title suit was instituted by Muslims in 1950, which has been pending ever since.

After a lapse of thirty-six years, in January, 1986, an agitation was begun by a Hindu organization, the Vishwa Hindu Parishad (VHP), with the support of the RSS and the BJP, for the restoration of the site as a place of Hindu worship. The VHP was founded in 1964. Its goals were not confined to Ayodhya. Its leaders prepared a list also of numerous mosques in India allegedly built upon former Hindu temples, of which the most prominent were, in addition to the one in Ayodhya, the mosque in Mathura alleged to be built upon Krishna's birthplace and Kashi Vishwanath in Banaras. This movement clearly sought to build Hindu unity by emphasizing "the antagonism between Hindus and Muslims."[26]

[26] Peter van der Veer, "'God must be Liberated!' A Hindu Liberation Movement in Ayodhya," *Modern Asian Studies*, xxi, No. 2 (1987), 292.

A writ petition was instituted simultaneously with the beginning of the agitation at Ayodhya. In contrast to the delay of thirty-six years in response to the Muslim-instituted title suit, the Hindu petition was heard by a Hindu district judge in Faizabad within a week and the petition to unlock the site for Hindu worship was granted. A writ petition was filed against the order thereafter by Muslims in February, 1986. Again in contrast to the expeditious handling of the Hindu petition, this writ petition has been pending ever since.[27]

After February, 1986, the issue was transformed into a national controversy. On the Muslim side, a national Babari Masjid Movement Coordination Committee (BMMCC) was established and other Muslim organizations were also mobilized to agitate for a speedy solution of the controversy in favor of the restoration of the site as a mosque. On the Hindu side, the Vishwa Hindu Parishad, the RSS, the BJP, and leading Hindu religious figures have continued to campaign for the restoration of the entire site to Hindus for the reconstruction of a grand temple to Ram. The Hindu organizations, however, far surpassed Muslim groups in mobilizing public action on this issue through a movement to rebuild the temple with consecrated bricks brought to the site by Hindu faithful.[28]

While the courts remained supine, the U. P. government immobile, and Hindu–Muslim confrontations on the increase, appeals were made to then Prime Minister Rajiv Gandhi, who at first sought to avoid a decision on the issue. However, the situation changed completely with the call for general elections to be held in November, 1989. The Congress leadership had for a decade been moving away from its longstanding alliance with the Muslim minority leadership in India in an attempt to build stronger support among the Hindu majority voters in areas of the country where the party had either lost power or needed to expand its social base in order to ward off loss of power. Many Muslims blamed the Congress for allowing the opening of the site to Hindu worship and for permitting a foundation-laying ceremony to take place in connection with the Shilan march (march to bring bricks to the site for construction of the temple), which contributed to the defeat of the Congress in the 1989 elections. In those elections, the BJP vote and representation in Parliament increased, although the National

[27] *Muslim India*, No. 99 (March, 1991), p. 109.
[28] *India Today*, October 31, 1989.

Front formed the government under Prime Minister V. P. Singh while the BJP supported it from outside.

However, V. P. Singh's "Mandal" decision on a reservations policy for public sector jobs for backward castes (see below) appeared to undermine the BJP drive to consolidate the Hindu vote in the country under its own banner and instead to divide it and make use of Hindu divisions and Muslim support to isolate it. The Mandal decision forced the party leadership to prepare for a new election and to seek to strengthen its base in U. P. and Bihar with its only strong weapon, the demand to build a new temple to Ram on the existing site of the Babari Masjid in Ayodhya.

It was obviously with these considerations in mind that L. K. Advani, leader of the BJP, announced his decision to launch his *rath yatra* (journey by [motor] chariot) from the Somnath temple in Gujarat on September 25, 1990 to Ayodhya on October 30, following a long and circuitous route through the Hindi-speaking heartland, with the circuit concluding in the states of Bihar and U. P. The BJP–Vishwa Hindu Parishad–Bajrang Dal–RSS combine of militant Hindu organizations left a bitter trail of communal antagonisms, riots, and deaths in the wake of the *rath yatra*.

On October 23, 1990, the chief minister of Bihar, Laloo Yadav put a stop to the *rath yatra* by arresting L. K. Advani in Samastipur. After L. K. Advani's arrest in Bihar, the BJP withdrew its support from the government of V. P. Singh, which thereby lost its majority in Parliament. A four-month interregnum followed under the prime ministership of Chandrashekhar while the BJP and all other parties prepared for new elections, which were held in May–June, 1991.

The BJP made the greatest electoral effort in its history during this election, in which it exploited fully the Ayodhya issue, anti-Muslim hostilities which its leaders and workers had themselves done so much to inculcate in the upper caste Hindu population of the country, particularly in north India, and the Hindu–Muslim riots which occurred before and during the election campaign. Although the BJP failed to achieve its goals of winning 140 to 150 seats in Parliament[29] and lost ground in the three states in which it held power (Rajasthan, Madhya Pradesh, and Himachal Pradesh), it emerged as the second largest

[29] Walter K. Andersen, "India's 1991 Elections: The Uncertain Verdict," *Asian Survey*, xxxi, No. 10 (October, 1991), 985.

party in Parliament with 119 seats and as the ruling party in the state of U. P. The Congress, for its part, came to power with a weak minority government at the Center and was reduced to third position in the state of U. P.

Congress, under a weak leader heading a minority government, had to seek to isolate the BJP to prevent any combination of its large delegation of MPs from combining with others to obstruct its functioning or bring it down. For its part, the BJP had to be watchful to avoid giving cause or pretext for the central government to dismiss the U. P. government which now formed the jewel in its hoped-for crown.

Nevertheless, the centrality of the Ayodhya issue for the new leadership of the BJP under Murli Manohar Joshi at the Center and Kalyan Singh in U. P. was made clear as soon as the latter took office. Their first act after the installation of the U. P. government was to take the entire state cabinet and all MLAs and MPs from U. P. to Ayodhya where the chief minister was quoted as promising unequivocally that the new temple would be constructed on the site then occupied by the mosque building.[30] In the following months, a series of administrative and legal steps were taken by the U. P. government to facilitate Hindu access to the site and to gain control of all lands surrounding it.

While the U. P. government took legal steps to acquire or make it possible for the VHP to acquire all land and structures surrounding the mosque, the latter proceeded in tandem with plans for a mass *kar seva* (voluntary work) in November–December, 1991.[31] A critical step was taken in November, 1991 when the U. P. government issued a notification for the acquisition of a 2.77-acre disputed site adjacent to one side of the mosque, following which VHP and Bajrang Dal activists moved into the mosque complex and began to clear the land and structures immediately around the mosque in preparation for the construction of the temple. The Muslim leadership of the Babari Masjid Action Committee (BMAC) saw clearly that the government's move would be followed by a transfer of the acquired land to the VHP and challenged the action in the state High Court, which issued an injunction against any such transfer of the land or construction upon it. The High Court orders were reaffirmed by the Supreme Court of India on November 15, 1991.[32]

[30] *India Today*, July, 31, 1991.   [31] *India Today*, September 30, 1991.
[32] *India Today*, August 15, 1992.

Frustrated by the court order restraining it from further action with regard to the 2.77-acre site, the state government, on March 21, 1992, transferred to a VHP organization forty-two acres of state park land near the mosque upon which VHP workers immediately began construction activity.[33] In April, the national executive committee of the VHP, meeting in Hardwar, announced its intention to resume temple construction at Ayodhya within the month.[34] The *kar seva* was intensified in August when thousands of *kar sevaks* in defiance of court orders engaged in eighteen days of construction activity, laying the foundation of the new temple on one side of the mosque.[35]

As events moved with increasing rapidity and the determination of the militant Hindu leadership to continue construction of the temple even against court orders was reiterated, the Prime Minister initiated a long series of negotiations among the militant Hindu movement leaders and representatives of Muslim political organizations, including the BMAC.[36] However, the negotiations ended without agreement on November 6, 1992.[37]

Shortly after termination of the negotiations, Ashok Singhal, the General Secretary and preeminent leader of the VHP, announced that *kar seva* would recommence on December 6 and would not stop until the construction of the temple was completed.[38] The government of India referred to the Supreme Court the issue of whether the announced *kar seva* would constitute a violation of its injunction against "any construction activity" in the area of the mosque. For its part, the state government pleaded that the court allow "singing of hymns on the disputed site." The Supreme Court accepted the U. P. government's plea, but also sent a special judge to the site to monitor activities there and ensure that no violations of its orders against construction activity took place. The Government of India then moved "160 companies of paramilitary forces" to U. P. in case of a breach of law and order at Ayodhya.[39]

In the meantime, the BJP leadership coordinated its actions in such a way as to allow the entry of thousands of *kar sevaks* openly carrying demolition equipment to Ayodhya while orders were issued from the

[33] *India Today*, April 15, 1992.   [34] *India Today*, April 30, 1992.
[35] *India Today*, August 15, 1992, p. 14.
[36] *India Today*, August 31 and October 15, 1992.
[37] *India Today*, December 15, 1992.
[38] *India Today*, November 30, 1992.   [39] *India Today*, December 15, 1992.

chief minister's office preventing the intervention of any state security forces. In short, thousands of militants, under the banner of Hindu political organizations all joined together in the RSS family, openly defied court orders while the government of the largest state in the Union blocked any effective intervention on the part of the Government of India and its military and paramilitary forces to prevent the demolition of the mosque on December 6, 1992.

On the question of Hindu consciousness and Hindu–Muslim antagonisms

The magnification and intensification of the struggle over the Babari Masjid/Ram Janmabhumi site convey two images which have recurred in the modern history of India, that is, especially for the past 200 years. These images are, first, that there are two well-defined religious communities in India, Hindus and Muslims, and second that they are not only utterly separate but antagonistic to each other. In contrast to the images conveyed, two of the most important facts concerning the Hindus and Muslims of South Asia are their heterogeneity and fragmentation, on the one hand, and the persistence of the intermingling of religious practices and observances among Hindus and Muslims at the local level. Hindus and Muslims throughout India are each divided by language and by caste divisions as well. Moreover, there are differences of religious belief, practice, ritual, and sect within the two communities.

Insofar as Ram and his birthplace are concerned, this is not a matter which excites the Hindus of India equally in all parts of the country. In fact, in south India, under the influence of another political movement, Ram has been rejected by many Hindus and his picture burned as a symbol of the domination of north Indian Brahmans "over the peoples of Tamilnad."[40]

Nor can it be argued that the Hindus of north India or even Ayodhya have been seething for centuries over the alleged destruction of the temple of Ram and its replacement by a mosque. On the whole, in Ayodhya as elsewhere in India, Hindu–Muslim relations have

---

[40] Robert L. Hardgrave, Jr., "Religion, Politics, and the DMK," in Donald E. Smith (ed.), *South Asian Politics and Religion* (Princeton, N.J.: Princeton University Press, 1966), p. 227.

fluctuated depending upon political developments rather than on the deep religious feelings of Hindus and Muslims in the country.[41]

Most important, the history of the movement does not support the view that it arises somehow out of deeply held Hindu feelings and out of hostilities between Hindus and Muslims. Rather, it is a deliberate creation of political elites who have set out to arouse Hindu consciousness and feelings concerning the god Ram and to direct them to a specific, material site on this earth, to promote Hindu–Muslim antagonisms for political purposes, and to define the Hindu community as a political entity.[42]

Muslim political leaders as well contributed to Hindu–Muslim polarization on this issue when they deliberately set out to launch a major counter-movement in the BMMCC and made some atrocious blunders in the process, including a call for a boycott of India's Republic Day ceremonies in 1987. This badly handled counter-movement in turn gave additional strength to the Hindu determination to see the site restored for the proper worship of Ram.

CASTE CONFLICT AND PREFERENTIAL POLICIES

Caste and caste conflict in post-Independence politics

The Nehru period

The leadership of the nationalist movement and of the Indian National Congress in virtually the entire subcontinent was in the hands primarily of men from the elite Hindu castes, especially Brahmans in most regions, Kayasthas in north India, Banias in many regions, and other regional high caste groups in other parts of the country. In between the elite and lowest castes in India are a huge number of both agricultural and artisan castes, of middle status, some of whom are land controlling castes, others or whom are economically nearly as disadvantaged as the low castes. The more disadvantaged castes among this broad spectrum of Indian society are generally called "backward castes" or "backward classes."

Among both the elite and middle status castes, a process of caste succession had begun before Independence and was intensified after it

---

[41] Van der Veer, "'God must be Liberated!'", p. 287.
[42] Van der Veer, "'God must be Liberated!'", p. 299.

with the adoption of adult franchise by which, in election after election, new leaders from previously unrepresented or underrepresented castes began to emerge and the castes themselves to be mobilized. In some states, the newly mobilized castes were integrated into the Congress system, while in others they provided a support base for opposition parties.

Many other, more specific factors have contributed to the rise of inter-caste conflicts in several states and localities in the post-Independence period. The intermediate castes acquired increased voting power through adult suffrage and increased economic power through *zamindari* abolition (abolition of the landlord, tax-farming system). Intermediate castes with economic resources sought not only political power but educational benefits and urban jobs for their children. As they acquired such opportunities, they came increasingly into conflict with persons from upper caste groups represented in far greater proportionate and often absolute numbers in educational and political institutions.

The post-Nehru period

During the grand succession struggle which developed after Nehru's death, especially after the split in the Congress in 1969 and during and after the 1971 elections, the Congress led by Mrs. Gandhi intensified its appeal to the disadvantaged groups in order to counter the power of the state party bosses, which rested mostly on the upper and landed castes. Electoral support from these disadvantaged groups was of critical importance in Mrs. Gandhi's triumph in the 1971 elections.[43] The loss of support from the Scheduled Castes and other disadvantaged groups was a major factor in the heavy defeat of the Congress in the post-Emergency 1977 elections. In the 1980 elections, Congress again drew heavy support from the Scheduled Castes and Scheduled Tribes,[44] who have continued to support the Congress more strongly than upper or backward caste groups ever since.[45]

[43] W. H. Morris-Jones, "India Elects for Change – and Stability," pp. 722–723.

[44] Myron Weiner, "Congress Restored: Continuities and Discontinuities in Indian Politics," *Asian Survey*, XXII, No. 4 (April, 1982), 340 and *India at the Polls, 1980: A Study of the Parliamentary Elections* (Washington, D.C.: American Enterprise Institute, 1983), pp. 19–20.

[45] See, for example, the exit poll by caste and community for the 1991 Lok Sabha elections in *India Today*, July 15, 1991, p. 35.

Reservations and the political roles of disadvantaged and backward castes and classes

The mechanism of reservation of seats in the legislatures ensures the election of a fixed proportion of Scheduled Castes and Scheduled Tribe representatives to Parliament and the state legislatures. Jagjivan Ram, the famous Scheduled Caste leader from Bihar and a minister in the central government throughout most of the Nehru and post-Nehru periods, was always thought to be able to control forty to sixty votes in Parliament and was deferred to in the Congress for that reason. He also played a swing role at several critical points in the post-Nehru period: when he threw his support to Mrs. Gandhi in the second (1966) succession, when he stayed with Mrs. Gandhi during the Congress split in 1969,[46] and when he deserted Mrs. Gandhi and joined forces with the Janata in 1977.

Although the lowest castes and tribes have provided a critical support base for the Congress and a few leaders like Jagjivan Ram have been coopted into positions of power at the national and state levels, for the most part politicians from these groups have remained outside the inner circles of party and government power and have been dependent upon more powerful upper caste leaders. In contrast, however, during the post-Nehru period, a shift in both the leadership and the support bases of the Congress parties to the non-dominant or "lower" backward castes did occur in some states, notably in Karnataka and Gujarat. In other states, particularly in north India, where the elite castes of Brahmans, Rajputs, and Bhumihars have been more numerous and well entrenched both economically and politically, there has been an intensification of conflict between them and several of the backward castes.

Central government policies

Since Independence, the central government has provided a variety of benefits, protections, and programs for the Scheduled Castes and Scheduled Tribes, including reservations of seats in legislatures, places in educational institutions, and posts in government departments. As a consequence of the latter, the representation of Scheduled Castes and

---

[46] S. C. Gangal, *Prime Minister and the Cabinet in India* (New Delhi: Navachetna Prakashan, 1972), p. 38.

Scheduled Tribes in public employment has begun to approach their proportion in the population. However, Scheduled Castes and Scheduled Tribes remained forty years after the adoption of such reservations much less well represented in the higher classes of government service than in the lower ranks.[47]

The central government has not, however, followed the same policies in relation to the backward castes. The Constitution refers vaguely to a third category of persons, besides the Scheduled Castes and Scheduled Tribes, who are entitled to special protections against discrimination and to special benefits for their advancement. The adoption of "preferential treatment for backward class peoples" was specifically sanctioned in Articles 15(4) and 16(4).[48]

However, the issues both of extending special benefits to the backward castes and of designating the specific castes to be included in any measures enacted for their benefit have been far more controversial than the issues surrounding the specification of Scheduled Castes and Scheduled Tribes and the extension of benefits to them. A consensus had already been reached among the national leadership before Independence both on the desirability of extending special benefits to these groups and, for the most part, on the specific castes and tribes to be included. The designated castes were already listed on a schedule by the Government of India (Scheduled Castes) Order, 1936.[49] A similar list of Scheduled Tribes had been prepared in 1935.[50]

No such consensus existed with regard to the backward castes. Although there was some ambiguity concerning the status of many of the Scheduled Castes, there was at least a common referent around the idea of including castes which, as groups, had been subject historically to numerous discriminations at the hands of the caste Hindus summarized by the term "untouchability." With regard to the backward castes, there is no such single criterion which could be easily applied throughout the country, for the status and economic well-being of the

---

[47] Aditya Nigam, "Mandal Commission and the Left," *EPW*, xxv, Nos. 48 & 49 (December 1–8, 1990), 2652–2653.

[48] John R. Wood, "Reservations in Doubt: The Backlash Against Affirmative Action in Gujarat," in Roy and Sisson, *Diversity and Dominance in Indian Politics*, Vol. II, p. 150 and A. Ramaiah, "Identifying Other Backward Classes," *EPW*, xxvii, No. 23 (June 6, 1992), 1203.

[49] Marc Galanter, *Competing Equalities: Law and the Backward Classes in India* (Delhi: Oxford University Press, p. 130).

[50] Galanter, *Competing Equalities*, p. 149.

numerous intermediate castes between the "untouchable" group and the elite (or "twice-born" castes) vary greatly from region to region.[51]

The first Backward Classes Commission was set up by the central government in 1953. It reported in 1955. Although the Commission expressed doubts about adopting "caste as the basis for identifying backward classes,"[52] it nevertheless "identified 2,399 castes as socially and educationally backward"[53] and proposed the adoption of a policy of reservations for backward classes in government services, with a range in the percentage of reserved posts from 25 to 40 percent in different categories.[54] The central government, however, "did not accept the recommendation of the Commission on the ground that it had not applied any objective tests for identifying Backward Classes."[55] Discussion of the report in Parliament did not take place until 1965, at which time the Congress government failed to support its recommendations.[56]

It was not until 1978, after the Janata party displaced the Congress from power at the Center, with considerable support in north India from backward caste groups, that the central government again took up the issue of preferential treatment for the backward castes and appointed the Second Backward Classes Commission on January 1, 1979. The second commission, which submitted its report in December, 1980,[57] unlike the first, explicitly recommended the adoption of "caste as a criterion"[58] and identified "3,248 castes or communities comprising 52.4 percent of the population of India, roughly 350 million people."[59] However, by the time the Commission submitted its report, the Congress had returned to power. The Congress central

---

[51] Galanter, *Competing Equalities*, ch. 6.

[52] Subrata Mitra, "The Perils of Promoting Equality: The Latent Significance of the Anti-Reservation Movement in India," *Journal of Commonwealth and Comparative Politics*, xxv, No. 3 (November, 1987), 296; Wood, "Reservations in Doubt," p. 151.

[53] Ghanshyam Shah, "Strategies of Social Engineering: Reservation and Mobility of Backward Communities of Gujarat," in Roy and Sisson, *Diversity and Dominance in Indian Politics*, Vol. II, p. 120.

[54] S. Guha, "Comprehending Equalities," review of *Competing Equalities: Law and the Backward Classes in India* by Marc Galanter in *EPW*, xxvii, Nos. 31 & 32 (August 1–8, 1992), 1658.

[55] Shah, "Strategies of Social Engineering," p. 120.

[56] Guha, "Comprehending Equalities," p. 1659.

[57] A. Ramaiah, "Identifying Other Backward Classes," *EPW*, xxvii, No. 23 (June 6, 1992), 1204.

[58] Mitra, "The Perils of Promoting Equality," p. 298.

[59] Wood, "Reservations in Doubt," p. 152.

government did not present the report to Parliament until April 1982, and then took no decision on it.[60]

Nearly a decade later, on August 7, 1990, Prime Minister V. P. Singh announced that the Mandal Commission recommendations would be implemented and that consequently 27 percent of all jobs under the direct control or influence of the central government would be reserved for persons from backward castes,[61] raising the total of reserved positions – including those for Scheduled Castes and Tribes – to close to 50 percent. The announcement antagonized the bulk of upper caste opinion, particularly in north India, and precipitated some shocking protest incidents in which upper caste students whose life chances might have been affected by the policy, burned themselves to death or otherwise committed suicide or committed grievous harm to themselves.[62]

Both the number of castes identified in the Mandal Commission Report and their estimated total population as well as the criteria used to identify and enumerate them have been highly controversial matters, discussed widely in both polemical and academic articles.[63] Although the political parties have taken different positions on the question of devising adequate criteria for determining backwardness, none have opposed the idea of a system of reservations for backward groups. The dividing line in contemporary Indian politics and public opinion is between those who argue that no policy other than a

[60] Shah, "Strategies of Social Engineering," p. 120.

[61] However, the Mandal Commission recommendations for similar reservations in educational institutions were not part of the V. P. Singh government's decision and scientific and technological institutes and departments as well as military services were also excluded from it; Ghanshyam Shah, "Social Backwardness and Politics of Reservations," *EPW*, xxvi, Nos. 11 & 12 (Annual Number, March, 1991), 607.

[62] These incidents were in turn played up by the upper caste-dominated press in a way which may have encouraged them, including extremely ugly and provocative front- and inside-page pictures of burning and burned young men and women featured by *India Today*. *India Today* writers apparently did not see any inconsistency in their acknowledgment, in the midst of their grotesque coverage of these incidents, that the self-immolating youth were spurred on by "the overwhelming media publicity that comes in the wake of every immolation attempt." See the issues of October 15 and October 31, 1990, from which the quotation is drawn and the remarks by Ramaiah, "Identifying Other Backward Classes," p. 1205 on this kind of news coverage.

[63] See, e.g., Ramaiah, "Identifying Other Backward Classes," pp. 1203–1207. A recent report of the Anthropology Survey of India, People of India project, cited in *India Today*, November 15, 1992, lists only 1046 backward castes, a figure less than one-third of that given in the Mandal Commission Report and less than one-half that given in the First Backward Classes Commission Report.

caste-based one can quickly and effectively rectify existing imbalances in education and employment, on the one hand, and those who insist that equity requires the adoption of objective and scientific criteria which pinpoint the truly backward in all castes and communities, on the other hand. The Janata Dal continues to favor the first approach, Congress, the BJP, and the CPM the second,[64] while some from the radical Left argue for transcending the caste issues and conflicts and launching a "struggle for greater employment opportunities" for all "the backward-caste poor."[65]

Petitions challenging the V. P. Singh government's decision on the Mandal Commission's recommendations were before the Supreme Court and a stay order was in effect[66] when the new Congress government took office after the May–June, 1991 elections. The Court thereupon demanded to know from the new government its position on the previous government's decision.[67] In response, P. V. Narasimha Rao announced on September 25, 1991 that his government would modify the Mandal plan of reservations by introducing economic criteria in determining backwardness. An additional 10 percent of reservations were to be added for economically deprived persons of any caste.

State government policies and problems

Backward caste movements have arisen in most, but not all, of the Indian states since Independence.[68] The movements in Karnataka, Tamil Nadu, and Maharashtra have a long history before Independence, those in the other southern states, in the north, and in Gujarat became significant only after Independence.

The south

The AIADMK and its principal rival in Tamil Nadu politics, the DMK, both trace their origins to the Dravidian movement of the late

---

[64] For a fine analysis of the opposing points of view, with trenchant comments on the defects in the arguments on both sides and the hypocritical character of several such arguments, see Shah, "Social Backwardness and Politics of Reservations," pp. 601–610.

[65] B. Sivaraman, "This Mandalist Myopia," *EPW*, xxvi, No. 6 (February 9, 1991), 314–315.

[66] *India Today*, October 31, 1990.   [67] *EPW*, xxvi, No. 30 (July 27, 1991), 1773.

[68] There have as yet been no broad-based backward caste movements in the states of Assam, Madhya Pradesh, Orissa, or West Bengal; Shah, "Social Backwardness," p. 603. The reasons, which cannot be gone into here, are different in each case. A decision to increase

nineteenth century and to the Justice Party and the Self-Respect Movement of the 1920s and 1930s, all of which drew heavily upon non-Brahman castes and sought to displace the Brahmans from their preeminent positions of leadership in public life and government service in the province. The Tamil organization, the Dravida Kazagham, forerunner of the DMK, was the first in post-Independence India to begin a major agitation for backward caste reservations in the erstwhile Madras province in 1950. The Madras government issued the first such order in 1951.[69]

However, the appointment of the First Backward Classes Commission had to await the installation of a DMK government.[70] The commission was appointed in 1969 and submitted its report the following year. The DMK accepted the Commission's recommendations to raise the existing reservations from 25 to 33 percent for backward castes and from 16 to 18 percent for Scheduled Castes and Scheduled Tribes. In 1979, the AIADMK government of MGR raised the reservations for backward castes to 50 percent.

As a consequence of challenges in the courts, the Supreme Court ordered the Tamil Nadu government to appoint a Second Backward Classes Commission (Ambasankar Commission) to resolve some of the issues raised in petitions before it. The Ambasankar Commission conducted an extensive survey of the backward classes in the state and submitted its report in 1985. It proposed recognition of 198 backward castes, of whom twenty-four had previously been considered advanced castes. The estimated population proportion of these 198 castes was 67 percent, but the Commission recommended reservations of 32 percent in order to keep the total, including those for Scheduled Castes and Tribes, at 50 percent.

The return to power of the DMK government under chief minister Karunanidhi in 1989 led to a further modification. In response to a demand from one of the larger and best-organized backward caste groups, the Vanniyars, whose spokesmen felt they were not receiving

reservations in Madhya Pradesh led to widespread disorder and withdrawal of the order in 1985 (M. N. Srinivas, "The Mandal Formula," *Times of India* (Ahmedabad), November 17, 1990), but no prolonged movements for reservations followed. Orissa has no reservations for backward castes. Those in West Bengal are for the poor irrespective of caste.

[69] Shah, "Social Backwardness," p. 606.

[70] The account below of the history of reservations policy in Tamil Nadu is derived from P. Radhakrishnan, "Ambasankar and Backward Classes," *EPW*, xxiv, No. 23 (June 10, 1989), 1265–1268.

an adequate share of posts under the existing scheme, the new government instituted "compartmental reservations" under which 20 percent of the 50 percent of reserved places were kept for the most backward castes.

Party competition for the support of the backward castes in Tamil Nadu has, therefore, led to a generous policy of reservations for them. It has also led to a situation in which the reserved list has become an open arena of contestation among the majority of caste groups in the state both for recognition as "backward" and for a special place on the reserved list.

Andhra. A Backward Classes Commission was not appointed in Andhra until after the Congress split, in 1970, when the Congress (I) was seeking to broaden its popular base here and elsewhere among the Scheduled Castes, backward castes, and minorities.[71] Since 1975, the state government has provided reservations for ninety-two categories of "backward" castes and communities.

In 1986, the Telugu Desam government of N. T. Rama Rao (NTR) decided "to raise the quota of reservations for backward classes from 25 percent to 44 percent."[72] When the courts declared that the new reservations policy was unconstitutional, the chief minister withdrew the additional reservations and was then confronted with an agitation by "backward-caste associations," which "launched a statewide protest, setting buses on fire, demonstrating and clashing with the forward castes and with the police."[73]

Karnataka. In Karnataka, the Congress leadership and popular base in the 1950s came predominantly from Lingayats and Vokkaligas.[74] Although these two communities are the dominant land-controlling groups in Karnataka, they both received recognition as backward castes entitled to preferential treatment.

Under the Congress regime of Devaraj Urs in the 1970s, a Backward Classes Commission (the Havnoor Commission) advocated special concessions to the Backward classes and "recommended a

---

[71] Vakil, "Patterns of Electoral Performance," pp. 255–257.
[72] Mitra, "The Perils of Promoting Equality," p. 309, fn. 4.
[73] Myron Weiner, "Rajiv Gandhi: A Mid-Term Assessment," in Marshall M. Bouton (ed.), *India Briefing, 1987* (Boulder: Westview Press, 1987), p. 11.
[74] Vakil, "Patterns of Electoral Performance," p. 251.

reclassification of the backward castes,"[75] under which Lingayats were dropped from the list.[76] Urs accepted the report, but modified it by adding several groups to the reservations list and increasing the overall reservation percentage from the recommended 32 to 40 percent.[77] However, he accepted the de-recognition of the Lingayats as a backward community, while retaining the other principal dominant caste of Vokkaligas on the list.[78]

The Congress continued under Urs' leadership to broaden its base among the backward castes by selecting a large number of candidates from among them to contest the 1978 elections. However, Urs' adoption of the Havnoor Report divided the Congress. Urs was not displaced as leader of the Congress (I), which led to a split in the party.[79] After the split, the Congress reduced its dependence upon the non-dominant backward castes and increased the representation of the dominant Lingayat and Vokkaliga communities.[80]

The Janata party under the leadership of Ramakrishna Hegde succeeded in defeating the Congress in two legislative assembly elections in 1983 and 1985. Its base also was primarily among the two dominant landed castes.[81]

In the meantime, in the wake of court proceedings challenging the government orders issued in pursuit of the Havnoor Commission recommendations, the state government agreed to appoint the Second Backward Classes Commission (Venkataswamy Commission) in April, 1983.[82] The Venkataswamy Commission presented its report in 1986. The Commission reduced significantly the list of backward castes, dropping all the economically, educationally, and politically favored groups previously included in such lists, notably both the Lingayats and Vokkaligas.[83] The exclusion of the Vokkaligas from the list was politically untenable for the Janata government under Hegde.

[75] Vakil, "Patterns of Electoral Performance," p. 259.

[76] Shah, "Social Backwardness," p. 605.

[77] P. Radhakrishnan, "Karnataka Backward Classes," EPW, xxv, No. 32 (August 11, 1990), 1749.

[78] Amal Ray and Jayalaksmi Kumpatla, "Zilla Parishad Presidents in Karnataka: Their Social Background and Implications for Development," EPW, xxii, Nos. 42 & 43 (October 17–24, 1987), 1829.

[79] Vakil, "Patterns of Electoral Performance," p. 259.

[80] Vakil, "Patterns of Electoral Performance," p. 263.

[81] Ray and Kumpatla, "Zilla Parishad Presidents," p. 1826.

[82] Radhakrishnan, "Karnataka Backward Classes," p. 1749.

[83] Radhakrishnan, "Karnataka Backward Classes," p. 1750.

Therefore, instead of accepting and implementing the report, Hegde rejected it and issued an ordinance bringing "almost all the castes in the state within the ambit of the backward classes," but with the "Vokkaligas and Lingayats ... classified under separate groups of backwardness."[84] The consequence of these several efforts to reserve places for designated backward castes without antagonizing important, economically and politically powerful non-Brahman castes was that the list of castes entitled to reservations in Karnataka reached 92 percent of the population, though the places reserved for them were only 50 percent.[85]

Still a third Backward Classes Commission was appointed by the Janata government in March, 1988, headed by Justice Reddy.[86] It adopted caste as the principal criterion for identifying backwardness, which it found to be the best predictor of that condition. It excluded the dominant castes left out by the Havnoor Commission, but modified the list by including sub-groups of Lingayats identified as backward. The report recommended 38 percent reservations for the backward castes identified. By the time the Reddy Commission submitted its report, a Congress (I) government under Veerendra Patil was in power. Patil's government announced its intention to implement the report, but did nothing to do so.[87]

The history of backward caste reservation policies in Karnataka brings out clearly the critical importance of the dominant non-Brahman castes in their effective implementation. No government in Karnataka can survive for long without the political support of at least one of these two groupings of Lingayats or Vokkaligas. Yet, their inclusion, along with other obviously advanced castes, vitiates policies meant for the truly backward castes.

The north

The situation in the northern states has been entirely different. In these states, the elite castes of Brahmans, Rajputs and Bhumihars are important land-controlling castes. However, there are also several large and important middle status peasant castes – notably Jats,

---

84 Vakil, "Patterns of Electoral Performance," p. 270; Mitra, "The Perils of Promoting Equality," p. 309, fn. 4.
85 Radhakrishnan, "Karnataka Backward Classes," p. 1750.
86 Radhakrishnan, "Karnataka Backward Classes," p. 1749.
87 Radhakrishnan, "Karnataka Backward Classes," p. 1754.

Yadavs, and Kurmis – who vie with the elite castes for both economic resources and political power in the countryside. During the 1960s and 1970s, several political parties in the north, particularly the Samyukta Socialist Party (SSP) under the leadership of Dr. Rammanohar Lohia and the BKD/Lok Dal of Chaudhuri Charan Singh developed strength among the middle status peasant and other backward castes and advocated policies of preferential treatment for them.

In Bihar, a Backward Classes Commission was appointed by the Congress government in 1971 and recommended the introduction of reservations for backward classes in government departments and schools and colleges. However, the Congress, dominated by upper castes, ignored the recommendations. Then, in 1978, during the Janata period in Bihar, chief minister Karpuri Thakur, formerly of the SSP and himself from the lower backward caste of Nais (barbers), announced a policy of reserving 26 percent of jobs in state government service for the backward classes.[88] The announcement precipitated widespread upper caste protest agitations in the state, as a consequence of which a compromise formula was devised which introduced economic criteria into the reservations scheme. The "revised formula" was introduced on November 18, 1978.[89]

In Uttar Pradesh, the most important land-controlling groups of castes have been the Brahmans, and the various Rajput castes and clans. The important backward castes are the Ahirs (Yadavs), Kurmis, and, in western U. P., the Jats. During the 1960s in eastern U. P., the SSP built a broad base of support among the backward castes. After Charan Singh, the Jat leader from western U. P., left the Congress in 1967 to become the first non-Congress chief minister of the state, he drew support especially from his own caste of Jats, but also from the more widely distributed Yadav caste category. During this period, "16 percent of state government jobs [were] reserved for the backward classes."[90]

The Mandal Commission recommendations accepted by the V. P. Singh government in August, 1990 were perceived by the dominant

---

[88] Indu Bharti, "The Bihar Formula," *EPW*, xxv, No. 44 (November 3, 1990), 2407; see also Myron Weiner and Mary F. Katzenstein, *India's Preferential Policies: Migrants, the Middle Classes, and Ethnic Equality* (Chicago: University of Chicago Press, 1981), p. 133.

[89] Bharti, "The Bihar Formula," p. 2407; see below also for further discussion of the Karpuri Thakur formula.

[90] Weiner and Katzenstein, *India's Preferential Policies*, p. 133.

upper caste groups in U. P. as profoundly threatening to their interests. Moreover, at the time the decision was taken, the administration of the state was under the control of a Janata Dal chief minister, Mulayam Singh, a Yadav who was considered hostile to upper caste interests. Consequently, upper castes voted heavily for the BJP, which took power in the state in July, 1991. Although a backward caste person was selected as chief minister, upper castes dominate the leadership of the BJP in this state.

Maharashtra

Maharashtra, like Tamil Nadu, experienced an early non-Brahman movement, which led ultimately to the gradual displacement of Brahmans by the predominant rural land-controlling caste of Marathas from the 1930s onwards. Their dominance has been so well established that no reservations policy beyond that for the Scheduled Castes and Tribes has been adopted.

The problem of Gujarat

Political background. Upper caste Brahmans and Banias dominated the Congress organization before Independence and the state government and party organization after Independence through the 1960s.[91] The Patidars and Kunbis, the largest and most prosperous middle peasant castes, were also important in the district organizations since the days of Sardar Patel – himself a Patidar – from the 1920s, but the bigger landowners among them, who resented the continued dominance of the upper castes and opposed Congress land reforms, joined the newly formed Swatantra party during the 1960s. Left out of the Congress or hostile to it throughout the nationalist movement and the early post-Independence years were two important groupings of castes, both taking the label of Kshatriyas: one upper caste grouping of ex-princes and large landlords and the other a heterogeneous collection of backward castes, of which the Kolis were the largest and claimed Kshatriya status.

The 1972 legislative assembly elections mark the beginning of a decisive change in Gujarat politics when the Congress absorbed the bulk of the backward caste leaders and voters. Madhavsinh Solanki, a backward Kshatriya leader, who had been elected to the legislative

[91] Shah, "Strategies of Social Engineering," p. 123.

assembly on the Congress ticket in 1962 and in 1967, emerged as one of the strongest state leaders of the Gujarat Congress.

It was not until 1976, however, during the Emergency, that the first Congress (I) government under the leadership of Madhavsinh Solanki was formed. Solanki distributed the majority of portfolios in his government to persons from backward castes, especially Kshatriyas, and adopted a strategy of alliance among Kshatriyas, Harijans, Adivasis, and Muslims in the 1977 elections. However, the Congress was defeated in the post-Emergency 1977 elections.

Then, in 1980, the Congress (I), now with Solanki as the chief minister designate, pursued the same alliance strategy even more vigorously, which was now also given the name "KHAM," each letter in the acronym standing for a component of the coalition.[92] Of the 140 successful Congress candidates, ninety-six came from one of the groups in the KHAM coalition. Solanki became chief minister, and more than two-thirds of the Cabinet members were drawn from these four disadvantaged groups.[93] Under Solanki's leadership between 1980 and 1985, the Congress base among the KHAM categories, particularly the Kshatriyas, was consolidated. In Solanki's cabinet appointed in March 1985, fourteen of twenty ministers were Kshatriyas.[94]

Backward Classes Commissions in Gujarat. The first Backward Classes Commission (called the Bakshi Commission) was appointed in 1972 and presented its report in 1976. It identified eighty-two castes and communities as backward and recommended reservations of 10 percent of places in government service and educational institutions for them.[95] The Congress took no decision on the report, but its recommendations were later accepted by the Janata government in 1978, which reserved 10 percent "of lower level and 5 percent of

---

[92] Shah, "Strategies of Social Engineering," pp. 133–134; John R. Wood, "Congress Restored? The 'Kham' Strategy and Congress (I) Recruitment in Gujarat," in John R. Wood (ed.), *State Politics in Contemporary India: Crisis or Continuity?* (Boulder: Westview Press, 1984), pp. 210–214.
[93] Wood, "Reservations in Doubt," p. 157.
[94] Atul Kohli, *Democracy and Discontent: India's Growing Crisis of Governability* (Cambridge: Cambridge University Press, 1990), p. 259.
[95] Shah, "Strategies of Social Engineering," p. 120; also Wood, "Reservations in Doubt," p. 157.

higher level government posts" for the designated backward categories.[96]

After the Congress government returned to power in 1980 under Solanki's leadership, it appointed another Backward Classes Commission (the Rane Commission), which submitted its report in October, 1983. This Commission "rejected caste" as the basis for identifying backward categories and adopted instead economic criteria, with an emphasis on occupation, identifying sixty-three such occupations as backward and recommending 28 percent reservations for persons coming from the designated occupational groups.[97]

Background and development of the anti-reservation movement. In Gujarat, the initial introduction of "systematic reservations in postgraduate medical courses" in 1975 precipitated an immediate protest reaction from upper caste students and "student strikes lasting about twenty days."[98] A second, more serious set of incidents occurred between January and March, 1981, leading to extensive rioting in "Ahmedabad and its surrounding villages" in which more than "fifty people, mostly Scheduled Castes, were killed."[99]

These medical course-related incidents, however, pale by comparison with the violence of 1985, which began as a direct reaction to the broader reservation policies of the Congress state governments under the leadership of Chief Minister Solanki. After the Rane Commission report and just before the 1985 elections, on January 10, the Solanki government announced a major increase in the percentage of reservations for "other backward classes" from 10 to 28 percent.[100] However, the reservations were to be allotted on the basis of caste rather than economic criteria.[101]

The anti-reservation agitation began in the medical and engineering colleges, but soon spread to colleges and secondary schools throughout Ahmedabad, leading to their closure by the authorities.[102]

[96] Wood, "Reservations in Doubt," p. 160.
[97] Shah, "Strategies of Social Engineering," p. 120; Wood, "Reservations in Doubt," p. 160; Howard Spodek, From Gandhi to Violence: Ahmedabad's 1985 Riots in Historical Perspective, unpublished paper, 1987, pp. 5–6.
[98] Mitra, "The Perils of Promoting Equality," p. 302.
[99] Wood, "Reservations in Doubt," p. 159.
[100] Mitra, "The Perils of Promoting Equality," p. 303.
[101] Kohli, *Democracy and Discontent*, p. 258.
[102] Spodek, From Gandhi to Violence, p. 5.

It soon turned also into controlled rioting, fusing "caste, class, communal and police-citizen conflict[s]" which had nothing to do with the reservations policy.[103]

The Solanki government, which had just come to power in March after a landslide victory for the Congress with a 55.5 percent vote, was forced to resign in July, 1985 and the new government cancelled "the proposed increase in reservations."[104] By the end of the long months of violence, 275 people had been killed and 12,000 people displaced and put in relief camps.[105]

The new chief minister, Amarsinh Chaudhury, was a tribal and a "pro-reservationist" and the Congress in Gujarat continued to be dominated by backward castes, Scheduled Castes, and Scheduled Tribes. The "politicization" of the disadvantaged groups in Gujarat is a permanent aspect of Gujarat politics which was further "enhanced" by "the events of 1985." On the other hand, the 1985 riots also demonstrated the impossibility of ignoring the opposition and resentments of the upper and middle castes, who remain powerful and numerous, in implementing an expanded reservations policy.[106]

Conflict and consensus in reservations policies

It has been argued that the difficulties in implementing consistent and acceptable preferential policies for other backward castes/classes in the several states have revealed the need for a "national political consensus" comparable to that achieved "on the treatment of the 'untouchables' during the decades immediately preceding Independence."[107] Why then has the central government not undertaken this task?

One reason simply is that the configuration of intermediate castes and their relative social, educational, and economic well-being vary considerably from state to state, much more so than with respect to Scheduled Castes. The relative position of the elite castes and their ability to resist reservations policies also has varied greatly.

In practice, the adoption of preferential treatment for backward castes and the assignment of castes to categories entitling them to such

---

103 Wood, "Reservations in Doubt," p. 147.
104 Mitra, "The Perils of Promoting Equality," pp. 302–303; Spodek, From Gandhi to Violence, pp. 13–15.
105 Wood, "Reservations in Doubt," p. 162; Spodek, From Gandhi to Violence, p. 1.
106 Wood, "Reservations in Doubt," pp. 167.
107 Mitra, "The Perils of Promoting Equality," p. 309.

treatment has arisen out of two processes: 1) demands from particular backward caste groups left out of the system of political distribution of patronage and 2) processes of competitive political mobilization by political parties in elections. Two major factors preventing the adoption of a consistent, "objective" national policy toward the backward castes have been the resistance of the upper castes to further extensions of the reservations system in general and of the dominant middle castes to any system of reservations which would leave them out.[108] It was not clear, therefore, that overall, a national policy could be constructed that would gain more votes for the party or coalition that introduced them than it would lose. Even the Janata Dal, which sought to consolidate its backward caste support base through the Mandal decision probably lost more upper caste votes than it gained from the backward castes in the 1991 election.

Despite the heat generated by the V. P. Singh decision on Mandal and the apparently major differences among the leading political parties on the matter of backward caste reservations, the bases for a compromise and a national consensus on the matter already exist. A formula was devised in 1978 by Karpuri Thaukur, the radical Socialist leader and former chief minister of Bihar, which combined both caste and economic criteria.[109] His plan provided for 20 percent reservations for backward castes, which were to be divided into two groups: "most backward" and "less backward." Twelve percent of the reserved posts would be kept for the former and 8 percent for the latter. In addition, 3–4 percent reservations were to be provided for women and another 3–4 percent for economically disadvantaged persons from any caste or community.

A further advantage of the Karpuri Thakur plan is that the total 20 percent reserved for backward castes is lower than that for Scheduled Castes and Scheduled Tribes, reducing the grounds for resentment from these segments of the population. Finally, the formula keeps the overall reservation percentage just below 50 percent, thereby avoiding

---

[108] While some backward castes are well-positioned to take advantage of job reservations, others are little better off than many Scheduled Castes, having hardly any educated persons to qualify for higher status government jobs; Shah, "Social Backwardness and Politics of Reservations," p. 605.

[109] Indu Bharti, "The Bihar Formular," *EPW*, xxv, No. 44 (November 3, 1990), 2407 and Anil Nauriya, "Reservations in Public Employment: Modified Mandal Scheme," *EPW*, xxvi, No. 43 (October 26, 1991), 2455–2456.

a challenge in the Supreme Court and also reducing the likelihood of further strong reactions from upper castes in north India, who would be able to continue to compete for at least 50 percent of the places, a proportion still far above their population proportion. While the Karpuri Thakur plan as such is only one possibility among several potential compromises, it illustrates well the factors that could effectively be combined to produce a compromise formula and a national consensus. A similar compromise appears to be emerging in practice at the national level, for the Congress government of Narasimha Rao chose not to oppose the Mandal decision of V. P. Singh, but to amend it by introducing additional, economic criteria.

Reaching a definitive and lasting national consensus will depend not on any inherent difficulties in working out a scheme, but on political calculations by party leaders concerning the advantages and disadvantages of further inter-party electoral mobilization of the population on the reservations issue.[110]

CONCLUSIONS

The persistence of Hindu–Muslim conflicts is easily explained by those who believe in the naturalness and inevitability of such tensions between culturally and religiously distinct groups. However, if one does not accept this easy explanation, then there is a paradox to be unravelled. The evidence summarized above concerning Muslim political behavior in post-Independence India, especially voting behavior, suggested a high degree of integration into the Indian political order. On the other hand, this integration has been taking place in the face of increased Hindu hostility and communal violence directed against Muslims.

It is necessary to seek the sources of broader anti-Muslim hostility not only among Hindu communal ideologies and organizations, but in the secular ideology which, since Independence, has exalted the state and its unity as the highest political value and has in the process placed the state at the center of the communal question, assigning it the role of preventing disintegrative communal conflict and protecting "minori-

---

[110] Cf. Shah, "Social Backwardness and Politics of Reservations," p. 607, who argues that the politicians have been moved on this issue primarily by "pressure and political exigency" with no "long-term perspective" on the country's future.

ties." Nehru himself and Mrs. Gandhi more so appealed to Muslims for support by implying that their own safety against Hindu communalists could be ensured only by remaining loyal to the Congress. Toward the end of her life, Mrs. Gandhi's opportunism on this matter was further revealed by the shift of the Congress under her leadership toward appeals to Hindu sentiment, carried further by her son, Rajiv, in the 1984 and 1989 elections.

Most important, however, has been the rise of a new ideology of Hindu nationalism, which has turned the official secular ideology on its head. The militant Hindu argument is that India cannot be a true secular state as long as Muslims are allowed to have separate personal laws, a University of their own in which Muslims predominate, are allegedly given special privileges, and occupy a state, Kashmir, with a special status in India. It is a great mistake to view this ideology as Hindu "fundamentalist." It is, like secularism in India, an ideology of state exaltation, which the BJP wishes to infuse with Hindu symbols in order that a united India may come to occupy a respected place among the great states in the modern world.

A major perceived obstacle to that goal has been the division among Hindus themselves, reflected especially in the last few years in intercaste conflict. Those divisions have been especially pronounced in the north, which is also the center of strength of Hindu nationalism. In the 1991 elections, the multiple divisions in Hindu society actually worked to the advantage of the BJP. Backward castes fragmented politically while the upper castes united behind the BJP, particularly in the state of U. P., but elsewhere as well.[111] However, while the BJP benefited from those divisions, its ultimate goals are to consolidate Hindus and to bring the backward and Scheduled Castes and Tribes as well into the political Hindu fold.

Most of the Indian states have managed to accommodate policies of caste reservations and the conflicts associated with them. They have done so in part by turning the reserved list into a prize in the general arena of party politics in a process by which the ruling party in each state adjusts the list when it comes to power to accommodate its principal supporters. Moreover, it has also been shown that a national

[111] See Paul R. Brass, "The Rise of the BJP and the Future of Party Politics in Uttar Pradesh," in Gould and Ganguly, *India Votes* and James Manor, "BJP in South India: 1991 General Election," *EPW*, xxvii, Nos. 24 & 25 (June 13–20, 1992), 1268–1272.

consensus on this issue is within reach. Were such a consensus to be reached, it would be another vindication of the viability of pluralist policies in the Indian politicial order comparable to the accommodations reached on official language and states reorganization.

Yet, while consensus seems in the realm of possibility on the issues of caste conflict and job reservations, it remains elusive on the matter of Hindu–Muslim relations, as it does on the perceived threats to national unity in Punjab, Kashmir, and Assam. The reasons for the greater intractability of these last two sets of problems are not because Indians cannot accommodate pluralist policies in relation to non-Hindu groups nor because of any fundamentally irreconcilable cultural differences between Hindus and Muslims or Hindus and Sikhs. It is because these two types of issues seem in the minds of most national leaders of the country to strike at the very basis of the Indian state and its future place in a world of states. On these matters, the differences between the secular parties and the Hindu nationalist parties are less significant than they appear for all are in pursuit of national greatness.

National greatness requires eliminating secessionism and preventing Hindu–Muslim conflict from tearing the country apart in violence. All sides believe a strong central state is necessary to achieve both objectives, though they differ on the means insofar as Hindu–Muslim conflict is concerned. Secular leaders have preferred a policy of accommodating Muslim minority demands while Hindu nationalists want an end to such accommodations and the full integration of Muslims in India as politically "Hindu" Indians. As long as the Indian state is seen as the arbiter between Hindus and Muslims and its very definition dependent upon the character of Hindu–Muslim relations, solutions will be difficult to reach on the perennial communal question.

PART III

POLITICAL ECONOMY

INTRODUCTION

Some observers of Indian politics, economic development, and social change since Independence argue that it is not state policies, the complexities of building political power in India, or the centralizing drives of Mrs. Gandhi which are principally responsible for the political disintegration and economic failures of the past twenty years. These are all rather reflections of deeper economic forces and of the dominance of particular social classes over Indian society and economy. One view is that there are structural forces in Indian society, entrenched social classes, whose actions constrain the political elites from implementing policies against the former's interests. State policies increasingly have come to reflect the interests of the dominant classes – the rich farmers who benefit from government price support and input subsidy programs, industrial capitalists who have profited from the import substitution policies and have learned to turn to their advantage the industrial licensing system, and the professional bureaucrats who have gained considerable corrupt income from their administration of programs for the benefit of the farmers and their control over the investment decisions of the industrialists and the business classes.[1]

According to another view, the countryside has come under the increasing political and economic dominance of the landed castes. The commercialization of Indian agriculture in the post-Green Revolution period has let loose forces which have undermined traditional social relations in the countryside and have promoted class polarization and class conflict. The latter are in turn largely responsible for increased political instability and violence in the countryside.[2]

[1] See Pranab Bardhan, *The Political Economy of Development in India* (Oxford: Basil Blackwell, 1984) and the critique by Myron Weiner, "The Political Economy of Industrial Growth in India," *World Politics*, xxxviii, No. 4 (July, 1986), 596–610.

[2] See esp. Francine R. Frankel, *India's Political Economy, 1947–1977: The Gradual Revolution* (Princeton, N.J.: Princeton University Press, 1978) and, for two critiques of it, Atul Kohli, "Democracy, Economic Growth, and Inequality in India's Development," *World Politics*, xxxii, No. 4 (July, 1980), 623–638 and Paul R. Brass, "Class, Ethnic Group, and Party in Indian Politics," *World Politics*, xxxiii, No. 3 (April, 1981), 454–457.

These structural class and economic explanations agree that "accommodative politics"[3] have failed and cannot succeed in the face of growing class antagonisms in the countryside and the increasing dominance of India's "proprietary classes." Their prognosis, in the event of the continuation of the present regime and its policies, is for the intensification of violent class conflict in the countryside. To avert it, they propose the displacement of the dominant rural classes through more thoroughgoing agrarian reform, the strengthening of the Indian state and of its autonomy from the now dominant social classes, and a return to and a more rigorous implementation of policies of state-directed, centralized economic planning and heavy public investment in an economy dominated by the public sector.

The arguments to be developed in part III are rather different. The economic policies associated with Nehru and his principal economic advisor, P. C. Mahalanobis have run their course. They have little economic merit and less political support left for them. They suffered from inherent defects to begin with and have been so manipulated by political and bureaucratic elites in the past thirty years as to become an obstacle to the country's further progress. The central leadership of the country has at length reached the conclusion that the Nehruvian system of state-directed industrial planning has become an obstacle to economic growth and was in the process of implementing plans to jettison large parts of it in 1992–93.

Insofar as the rural areas are concerned, the existence of dominant castes at the local level is recognized and their constraining effects on many types of policies are acknowledged. At the same time, the view taken here is that the policies of heavy industrialization through centralized economic planning have been ill-adapted to India's economic resources, to the basic needs of its peoples, to its social order, and to the political values of its educated classes. Moreover, many of the policies adopted for the agricultural sector have been self-contradictory or have not been implemented. Land reforms were introduced after Independence to promote a system of peasant proprietorship in which inequalities in land ownership would be reduced, all cultivators would own their lands, and their holdings would be economically viable. These reforms, however, were only partly imple-

---

[3] Frankel, *India's Political Economy*, p. 27.

mented while more radical reforms such as cooperative farming were proposed.

Poverty, hunger, and malnutrition have persisted in the rural areas less because of the oppressions and exactions of the landed castes in the countryside than because government policies have not encouraged the development of alternative forms of employment. Meanwhile, as is to be expected, the locally dominant classes and bureaucrats take advantage of the ameliorative anti-poverty programs which have been introduced in the 1970s and 1980s and extract benefits and profits for themselves from them.

In the face of the distortions in resource allocations for economic development in India since Independence and the contradictory policies often pursued, one of the more impressive, though still limited, economic achievements has been the adoption in parts of the country and for some crops, notably wheat, of the package of practices which have promoted the increase in agricultural production that goes by the name of the Green Revolution. The successes of the Green Revolution were in turn criticized for promoting commercialization of agriculture, the creation of a *kulak*[4] class, and the inevitable development of class polarization and class conflict in the countryside. The argument in chapter 9, however, is that the focus on the so-called new *kulak* class distorts the realities of the Indian countryside, in which the vast majority of peasants are small and medium cultivators in need of policies and subsidies that would help to make them viable farmers. Moreover, despite the persistence in contemporary India of local protests by the poor and landless in scattered areas of the Indian subcontinent, there is no evidence of either a general class polarization or an impending class war in the countryside.

---

[4] The term *kulak* in the Leninist literature refers to rich peasants and farmers who employ and exploit farm labor to whom they are also generally antagonistic.

CHAPTER 8

POLITICS, ECONOMIC DEVELOPMENT, AND SOCIAL CHANGE

POLITICS AND POLICIES: MAJOR ISSUES OF ECONOMIC DEVELOPMENT AND SOCIAL CHANGE

Two discontinuities marked the debates on politics and policies concerning major issues of economic development and social change in India after Independence and marred the effective implementation of most of the policies adopted. One was a discontinuity of discourse between adherents of foreign models for economic development and social change, many of them Marxists, and proponents of alternative strategies that are usually called "Gandhian" and derived inspiration and sought legitimacy from Gandhi's writings and speeches. Though the models for economic development were foreign, the motives of the Indian leadership in adopting them were authentically nationalist, arising out of the belief that rapid heavy industrialization was required to ensure India's independence in every sense and to achieve great power status.[1]

The second discontinuity was between levels in the Indian polity, between the goals set at the Planning Commission and in the inner circles of policy making in the central government in Delhi, on the one hand, and the realities of regional and local structures of power and decision making in the provincial capitals and in the districts, on the other hand, which prevented effective implementation of policies formulated at higher levels and, in later years, even penetrated upwards to influence decision making in Delhi itself. The con-

[1] Nayar describes the adherence to the heavy industrialization strategy that came to dominate Indian economic development policy as arising out of a "modernization imperative" which dictated the strategy to be adopted if the above goals were to be achieved. Baldev Raj Nayar, *The Modernisation Imperative and Indian Planning* (Delhi: Vikas, 1972). In a similar vein, John Toye characterizes the nationalism and the economic development strategy associated with it as "mimetic," though no less authentic for that; *Public Expenditure and Indian Development Policy, 1960–1970* (Cambridge: Cambridge University Press, 1981), pp. 21–27.

Table 8.1. Sectoral allocation of expenditure in the Five Year Plans (in percentages)

Sector	First Plan 1951–56	Second Plan 1956–61	Third Plan 1961–66	Annual Plan 1966–69	Fourth Plan 1969–74	Fifth Plan 1974–79	Sixth Plan 1980–85	Seventh Plan 1985–90
Agriculture and allied sectors	14.8	11.7	12.7	16.7	14.7	12.3	12.8	12.6
Irrigation and flood control	22.2	9.2	7.8	7.1	8.6	9.5	12.5	9.4
Power[a]	7.6	9.7	14.6	18.3	18.6	18.8	19.8	19.1
Village and small industries	2.0	4.0	2.8	1.9	1.5	1.3	1.8	1.5
Industry and minerals[a]	2.8	20.0	20.1	22.8	18.2	24.1	21.0	22.4
Transportation and communications	26.5	22.0	24.6	18.5	19.5	17.8	15.9	16.4
Others	24.0	23.4	17.4	14.7	19.0	16.6	16.2	18.6
Total	100.0	100.0	100.0	100.0	100.0	100.0	100.0	100.0
Total plan expenditure (Rs. billion)	19.6	46.7	85.8	66.3	158.8	286.5	975.0	1,800.0

[a]Power alone comprised 16.9 percent of total Sixth Plan expenditures and 19.0 percent of the Seventh. Evidently, items previously included under the heading of "industry and minerals" have been grouped with "power" under the broader category of "energy."

Sources: V. N. Balasubramanyam, The Economy of India (London: Weidenfeld and Nicolson, 1984), p. 80; Sixth and Seventh Plan figures calculated from Government of India, Ministry of Finance (Economic Division), Economic Survey, 1985–86 (Delhi: Controller of Publications, 1986), pp. 137–139.

sequences of these discontinuities for policy making and implementation in India can be demonstrated in relation to the major issues and themes that recurred in the formulation of the goals and evaluation of the results of India's five year plans.

Public sector and private sector

The first issue was the debate over the relative roles of the public and private sectors in economic development planning. The basic outlines and strategy of Indian economic development planning in the post-Independence era were set during the Second Five Year Plan from 1956 to 1961 (see table 8.1), whose principal architect was P. C. Mahalanobis. The central core of that plan was a move toward capital intensive, fast-paced heavy industrialization, led by the public sector, which would build the key industries and control the commanding heights of a new modern industrial economy for India, leaving the private sector "to play a complementary role in the mixed economy."[2] Although the strategy knowingly implied heavy dependence on imports, foreign exchange, and foreign aid in the short term, it was justified in the long term through the import-substitution aspect of the strategy, which promised ultimate self-sufficiency by making it possible for India to produce machines that produce other machines.

The Mahalanobis–Nehru strategy did not draw its principal inspiration from a reasoned analysis and assessment of the political economy of India: of its resources, social structure, and the immediate needs of its people. Instead, it drew upon a model of what a modern industrial society and a big military power looked like in the twentieth century and upon the methods used in the past by the big industrial military powers to achieve their current status, and drew up the requirements for India to achieve a similar status irrespective of its own resources, social structure, and the needs of its people. Although the model was based largely on the achievements of the Soviet Union, leavened by social democratic values, it implied heavy dependence on foreign aid from the capitalist countries for success. It also meant the sacrifice or postponement of virtually all other ideal goals to which Nehru and the planners paid lip service: the development of agriculture, the creation

---

[2] Isher Judge Ahluwalia, *Industrial Growth in India: Stagnation Since the Mid-Sixties* (Delhi: Oxford University Press, 1985), p. 147.

of employment opportunities, balanced regional development, and improvement in the well-being and quality of life of the rural poor.

The heyday of the strategy was the decade between 1955–56 and 1965–66, when India was able to draw vast foreign aid resources from both the capitalist and socialist countries and to build the heavy industrial base in steel, chemicals, machine tools, cement, and the like that the country has today. However, a major crisis for the public sector, capital intensive, heavy industrialization strategy arose during the discussions surrounding the formulation of the Fourth Five Year Plan as a consequence of a decline in foreign aid, problems of internal resource mobilization, and the heavy dependence of India on the U.S. for food aid occasioned by the neglect of agriculture in the plans. During these discussions, which involved a three-year hiatus between the end of the Third and the adoption of the Fourth plan, the coherence of the planning process itself, achieved by focusing on the public sector heavy industrialization strategy, was lost and the planning process became more and more open to the conflicting pulls of competing strategies and competing demands for resources, and to political manipulation. A further consequence of the loss of momentum in the mid 1960s was an increasingly evident deceleration in the rate of growth of the economy, traceable primarily to a decline in the rate of industrial growth. This decline has been attributed to, among other causes, the slowdown in public investment since the end of the Third Plan, the inefficiency of public-sector enterprises, and the restrictions placed on private enterprise by bureaucratically imposed import control procedures designed to ensure priority to the public sector and to import-substituting enterprises.

In the face of the crumbling of the entire structure of public investment and government regulation of private investment, the old ideological debate between public and private sector adherents emerged once again with the rise to power of Rajiv Gandhi and the formulation of the Seventh Five Year Plan. Rajiv Gandhi's government resisted demands for a reinstatement of the pre-Fourth Plan public investment strategy and instead shifted the balance in the planning process in favor of private investment while taking several modest measures to "liberalize" the licensing, import control, and foreign trade regimes which have been criticized for restricting private enterprise and for distorting and corrupting the entire development process.

Industry and agriculture

A second recurring issue in public discussion of the planning process in India, closely related to the first, concerns the relative attention paid to and the resource allocations for industry and agriculture in the plans. The controversy on this broad theme has, over the years, matured into competing, alternative models for economic development and alternative growth strategies. The leading alternative approach to Indian economic development, identified with former Prime Minister Charan Singh and other Gandhian-inspired political leaders, took as its premises that capital and land are in short supply, while labor is abundant and under-employed. India's needs, therefore, are to conserve capital and maximize the use of labor by promoting labor-intensive, employment-generating industries and land-augmenting strategies to increase the product from the land.[3]

Although the momentum of the heavy industrialization strategy was considerably slowed during the Fourth Plan that followed the 1965–67 food crisis, there was no major change in the overall allocations between industry and agriculture. Instead, this time, the fortuitous arrival on the scene in 1965 of Norman Borlaug, with his dwarf wheat seeds, introduced the potential for the "green revolution" in India. The Government of India quickly saw the possibilities of the new seeds and adopted the so-called New Agricultural Strategy for India based on the adoption of the high yielding seed varieties (HYVs). Although the New Agricultural Strategy was in principle a central component of the Fourth Plan, the actual increases in the relative allocations for agriculture were marginal (see table 8.1).

The first and only major challenge to the entire public sector heavy industry strategy came with the Janata government that captured power in 1977 in the midst of the Fifth Plan and during discussions for the Sixth. The Janata government period produced discussion of an entire alternative strategy based on agriculture, rural development, creation of employment opportunities for the rural poor through the establishment of small-scale industries in the countryside, and the diversion of significantly increased resources from the public sector heavy industry projects to the new programs. The Sixth Plan, however,

---

[3] Charan Singh, *Joint-Farming X-Rayed: The Problem and its Solution* (Bombay: Bharatiya Vidya Bhavan, 1959).

though it did take some significant steps in the new directions, did not succeed in displacing completely the old strategy and replacing it with a new one. Moreover, the allocations for agriculture, irrigation, power, and village and small-scale industries all declined in the Seventh Plan.

As with the public sector–private sector controversy, so with the related industry–agriculture debate, there was no resolution, nor firm reestablishment of the old course nor any dramatic setting out upon a new one. Instead, planning became a process of competition and struggle over resources, goals, strategies, and patronage without an overall design, a piece of patchwork rather than a coherent structure. In that process, agricultural investment has continued to lag behind non-agricultural investment.[4]

Agrarian reform

A third issue concerned the place of agrarian reform and reorganization within the overall economic development strategy. Beyond the virtually unanimous sentiment after Independence for abolition of intermediaries and other exploiters of the peasantry, there was division among Congressmen concerning more drastic forms of agrarian reform and reorganization. There was a broad consensus among the central leaders that inequalities in the countryside were inconsistent with the democratic and socialist goals of the Congress and that, therefore, land ceilings should be imposed and that the surplus land made available be distributed amongst the poorer farmers and the landless. However, agriculture being a state subject, the central leadership could only set guidelines and attempt to persuade state leaders to institute land ceilings and implement redistribution. The state leadership of the Congress virtually everywhere had no interest in such proposals, which could only antagonize the party's predominant rural supporters, the principal land-controlling castes in the countryside.

---

[4] A. Ganesh Kumar has argued that, in the decade of the 1980s, agricultural investment declined to a range between 10 and 15 percent of total investment from the levels of 15 to 20 percent in the two previous decades. At the same time, the "annual compound rate of growth of gross irrigated area" also declined significantly. He attributes both declines to falling levels of government investment in agriculture. If these declines continue, the anticipated result is increasing "income inequality in rural areas" and an insufficient rate of growth in foodgrains production, which will require renewed imports; "Falling Agricultural Investment and Its Consequences," *EPW*, xxvii, No. 42 (October 17, 1992), 2307–2312, citations from pp. 2307 and 2312.

Virtually everywhere, therefore, land ceilings legislation was a farce and land redistribution practically non-existent or cruel to those who "benefited" from it by receiving barren, unproductive, or alkaline soil to farm without resources to make use of it.

In fact, contrary to the proclaimed goals of all post-Independence land reform legislation, both the number and proportion of marginal landholdings (less than one hectare) have increased and unrecognized tenancies – the principal target of all land reforms before and since Independence – have increased significantly.[5] Only in West Bengal and Kerala, because of the influence of the Communist (Marxist) parties in those states, have there been moderately effective measures of agrarian reform of benefit to the poor farmers and agricultural laborers. In all other states, either the legislation has been deliberately faulty (Karnataka) or the Green Revolution has led to the establishment of "capitalist farming" and the enlargement of the operational size of holdings through leasing in of lands from small and non-viable cultivators. Nowhere, including even West Bengal and Kerala, have agrarian reforms made possible the transfer of sufficient land to the rural poor to turn measurable numbers of them into "economically viable" cultivators.[6]

Agricultural development policies

The fourth issue concerns the methods to be used to bring about rural change and increased agricultural productivity within the existing allocations for agricultural development. The basic pattern of rural development emphasized in the first two Five Year Plans was extensive and integrated rural development with programs that were to be spread evenly across the country for the benefit of all and that would include overall improvements in the quality of rural life generally, not simply improvements in agricultural techniques. In the 1960s, however, as a consequence of perceived failures in the earlier approach, the emphasis shifted to *intensive* development of favored districts through the Intensive Agricultural District Programme (IADP) and to technical changes in agriculture through the development of an elaborate research and extension system radiating out from

---

[5] V. M. Rao, "Land Reform Experiences: Perspective for Strategy and Programmes," *EPW*, xxvii, No. 26 (June 27, 1992), A-51.

[6] Rao, "Land Reform Experiences," pp. A-52 to A-57.

new agricultural universities modeled on the American land grant system.

The new approach was consistent with the overall design of the planning process instituted by Nehru and Mahalanobis since it did not call for drawing significant resources away from the heavy industry strategy. The New Agricultural Strategy was to follow up and reinforce the change in policy already introduced in favor of intensive agricultural development with the emphasis on new technologies and the adoption of the new high yielding varieties rather than on overall rural development. The High Yielding Varieties Program (HYVP) also, like the IADP before it, could be integrated into the plans without affecting the priority commitments to urban, capital-intensive industrialization.

There have been no major shifts in the basic strategy toward agriculture since the adoption of the HYVP, but there have been two tendencies at work, one to modify, another to reinforce it. The modification came in the form of an attempt to extend the benefits of the new seeds to the small farmers. Then, in the late 1970s, further efforts were made to intensify the agricultural extension system through the World Bank-sponsored Training and Visit System, which reinforced strongly the exclusive emphasis on agricultural technology rather than on Community Development, while seeking to extend that technology to the small farmers as well. In effect, therefore, the currently favored resolution of the issue of extensive versus intensive, community development versus agriculture-oriented rural programs is in favor of agriculture-oriented, but extensive development designed to reach all farmers who can possibly benefit from new seeds and improved methods.

Mobilization of resources and center–state relations

The adoption of the Nehru–Mahalanobis strategy made Indian economic development foreign exchange-dependent and required vastly increased domestic savings and revenue mobilization. In the early 1960s, in conformity with Third Plan resource requirements, pressures were put upon the state governments, which have constitutional authority over land revenue and agricultural taxation, to raise resources from the rural areas through such devices as betterment levies, agricultural income taxes, and surcharges on the existing land revenue.

The efforts to mobilize resources to support an urban-biased, capital-intensive industrialization strategy precipitated a counter-challenge, mostly political, but with some intellectual and ideological support already noted above, in favor of an alternative development strategy that would shift the allocation of resources from industry to agriculture and from the center to the states. The overall political movement in the Indian states generally since the 1960s has been away from centralized planning and urban industrial development to demands for more resources from the center for agriculture and rural development in the states.

Assessing the growth performance of the Indian economy

There are several ways by which the overall growth performance of the Indian economy since Independence have been measured. These include: 1) comparisons with pre-Independence performance; 2) comparisons of economic growth rates with population growth rates; 3) comparisons of achievements in relation to targeted goals; 4) comparisons with other developing countries; 5) overall assessments of India's changing status in the world economy. These five possible ways of assessing India's economic growth performance lead to quite different results, with the first producing the most favorable, the last the least favorable.

The overall growth rate of the Indian economy between 1950 and 1980 is generally taken to be approximately 3.5 percent per year. This figure compares very favorably with most estimates of pre-Independence growth rates of "no more than 1 per cent per annum for the first half of the twentieth century."[7] However, by comparison with population growth rates, that is, in terms of per capita income growth, India's rate of growth for the same period goes down to a very modest 1.3 percent per year, after deducting the 2.2 percent annual rate of population increase.[8] The average annual growth rate per capita for the years between 1965 and 1988 has been estimated by the World Bank at a somewhat higher 1.8 percent.[9]

[7] V. N. Balasubramanyam, *The Economy of India* (London: Weidenfeld and Nicolson, 1984), p. 43.
[8] Balasubramanyam, *The Economy of India*, pp. 30–31.
[9] World Bank, *World Development Report 1990* (Oxford: Oxford University Press, 1990), p. 178.

Moreover, using the 3.5 percent growth rate unadjusted for population growth as a basis for comparison with other countries, India's growth performance compared unfavorably between 1950 and 1980 with the most dynamic economies in the developing world and even with that of China. Its level of performance is roughly comparable to the mediocre- and low-performing developing countries "such as Pakistan, Kenya, Sri Lanka, Egypt and Indonesia."[10] There was no significant change in India's overall growth rate from 1965 to 1988, which averaged 3.6 percent. However, the unadjusted growth rate for 1980–88 showed an increase to 5.2 percent, entirely accounted for by an increased rate of growth in industry, which reached 7.6 percent for the later period while agricultural growth declined from 2.5 to 2.3 percent.[11]

If one attempts to assess India's growth performance in relation to the central goals of the Five Year Plans from the Second Plan forward, which were to establish India as a modern, self-sufficient industrial military power, the results on the face of things appear more favorable. India's achievements in these respects, however, have been questioned by Surendra Patel who argues that India's growth performance was so poor, in fact, that there was an overall decline in India's position in the world economy that bodes ill for its future influence in world affairs. Patel showed that, by virtually every measure of economic achievement, India did worse than nearly all other countries in the world and that, as a result, there had been a "regression" in India's position in the world economy. India's share of world trade declined from 2 percent in 1950 to 0.5 percent in 1980, with the result that India had become "practically a marginal trading partner among the Third World countries."[12] India's share in world industrial output declined from 1.2 to 0.7 percent in the world as a whole, from 12 to 4.6 percent among developing countries.

This "regression," however, needs to be balanced against India's other achievements and assessed in relation to its own goals. Since

[10] Balasubramanyam, *The Economy of India*, p. 43. Comparative figures for growth rate per capita in the 1965–88 period are 5.4 for China, three times the Indian growth rate in the same period. India also remained in the later period behind all the other countries cited for comparison by Balasubramanyam for 1950–80; World Bank, *World Development Report 1990*, p. 178.

[11] World Bank, *World Development Report 1990*, p. 180.

[12] Surendra J. Patel, "India's Regression in the World Economy," *EPW*, xx, No. 39 (September 28, 1985), 1652.

India's early development goals emphasized import substitution rather than export promotion, its relatively poor performance in world trade is understandable. Moreover, the dramatic industrialization of small countries such as Hong Kong, Singapore, Taiwan, and South Korea accounts for much of India's apparent "regression" in manufacturing among the developing countries generally. Finally, India's avoidance of the massive debt burdens of countries such as Mexico and Brazil is certainly a measure of national strength which affects favorably its international standing. Although India's outstanding external debt as a percentage of GNP increased from 13.7 to 18.7 percent between 1970 and 1988, it nevertheless remained the lowest among all developing countries except China.[13]

However, if one accepts that Indian development policy in the 1950s set out deliberately to sacrifice or postpone the achievement of all other goals (such as the welfare of the people, employment, increased agricultural production, removal of poverty, illiteracy, and disease, and the like) in order to establish India as an increasingly self-reliant, modern industrial military power and one judges the growth performance of the Indian economy in that respect alone, it would appear that the regional and world status and image India achieved was not consistent with its economic accomplishments.

The persistence of regional imbalances

It is well known that the consequences of British rule were manifested unevenly in the different regions and provinces of India and that there were considerable differences as well between areas ruled directly by the British and most of the princely states. Most of the amenities of modern life, such as higher education and hospitals, were concentrated in the urban areas, though in many provinces there was a spreading out of such facilities to the district headquarters towns as well.

At Independence, therefore, there were substantial regional differences in India between the provinces that had experienced greater urban, industrial growth and higher educational expansion, such as Bombay, Madras, and West Bengal, and the rest of the country; between urban enclaves such as Kanpur and Ahmedabad within otherwise overwhelmingly rural states; between agriculturally better off

---

[13] World Bank, *World Development Report 1990*, p. 224.

Table 8.2. *Estimates of per capita income (state-wise) for different years (in rupees at current prices), states ranked in descending order on last column (major states only[a])*

State	1960–61	1970–71	1980–81	1986–87
1 Punjab	366	1,070	2,620	4,719
2 Haryana	327	877	2,351	3,925
3 Maharashtra	409	783	2,244	3,793
4 Gujarat	362	829	1,967	3,223
5 West Bengal	390	722	1,643	2,988
6 Tamil Nadu	334	581	1,324	2,732
7 Karnataka	296	641	1,454	2,486
8 Kerala	259	594	1,385	2,371
9 Andhra Pradesh	275	585	1,358	2,333
10 Assam	315	535	1,221	2,204
11 Rajasthan	284	651	1,220	2,150
12 Uttar Pradesh	252	486	1,272	2,146
13 Madhya Pradesh	252	484	1,181	2,020
14 Orissa	217	478	1,173	1,957
15 Bihar	215	402	943	1,802

[a]States with populations above 10 million.
Sources: 1960–61, David Butler *et al.*, *India Decides: Elections 1952–1991* (New Delhi: Living Media India, 1991), p. 112; 1986–87, *Statistical Outline of India, 1989–90* (Bombay: Tata Services, 1989), p. 16.

areas such as the canal-irrigated areas of Punjab and parts of other regions, and the rest of the country.

On the whole, most indexes designed to measure the relative standing of the several states do not show much change since Independence. The more urbanized states and the states that benefited from intensive irrigation development ranked high in per capita income and net domestic product at Independence and they continue to rank high today (see table 8.2).[14] Those states that experienced little of either urban or rural development before Independence ranked low in per

[14] See also Grace Majumdar, "Trends in Inter-State Inequalities in Income and Expenditure in India," in L. S. Bhat *et al. Regional Inequalities in India: An Inter-State and Intra-State Analysis,* Papers presented at an all-India conference on Centre-State Relations and Regional Disparities in India at New Delhi in August, 1980 (New Delhi: Society for the Study of Regional Disparities, 1982), p. 33, and *Asian Recorder,* August 20–26, 1986, p. 19045.

capita income and net domestic product then and continue to do so today.

The fact that the relative position of most states has remained approximately the same since Independence does not at all mean that there have been no significant changes in the poorer states or that most benefits of planned development have accrued to the better-off states and been denied to the more backward ones. Since public and private investment have continued in the better-off regions as well, it is simply that such investments have not altered the relative positions of the various regions of the country.

Balanced regional development has been a repeatedly declared goal of the central government and of its two principal agencies that can influence the process, namely, the Planning Commission and the Finance Commission. It has been the policy of the several Finance Commissions to use the mechanism of resource transfers as a device for inter-state equalization or, in other words, "as a means of redressing regional imbalances."[15] In fact, however, such redistributive transfers have been resisted effectively, for the most part, by the better-off states in the controversies that have surrounded the deliberations of the successive Finance Commissions.

Similar issues have occurred concerning the deliberations of the Planning Commission, which also has repeatedly declared balanced regional development to be one of its major goals in allocating central assistance to the states. However, the equalizing impact of the Planning Commission's distribution of central resources also has been very limited.[16] Insofar as industry is concerned, it has been shown that the four most industrialized states (Maharashtra, Gujarat, West Bengal, and Tamil Nadu) have received between 40 and 59 percent of the total number of industrial licenses issued annually by the central government between 1974 and 1986.[17]

Whatever the reasons, there is virtual unanimity among scholars who have analyzed inter-regional disparities in India on two points:

[15] Government of India, *Report of the Finance Commission, 1973* (Delhi: Controller of Publications, 1973), p. 8.

[16] B. S. Grewal, *Centre–State Financial Relations in India* (Patiala: Punjabi University, 1975), pp. 56–61, and H. K. Paranjpe, "Center–State Relations in Planning," in S. N. Jain *et al.*, *The Union and the States* (Delhi: National, 1972), p. 218.

[17] Sunil Mani, "New Industrial Policy: Barriers to Entry, Foreign Investment and Privatisation," *EPW*, xxvii, No. 35 (August 29, 1992), M-88.

the disparities have increased and central policies on resource transfers and industrial planning have not only been unable to prevent the increasing gap between the rich and poor states, but may have contributed to accentuating the disparities. In consequence, therefore, it can only be concluded with respect to the repeatedly reaffirmed goals of the Five Year Plans to achieve "balanced regional development" and reduction of inter-state disparities that "the results of planned development" have not been "in consonance with this national objective."[18]

THE MOVE TOWARD LIBERALIZATION OF THE INDIAN ECONOMY AND THE DISMANTLING OF NEHRUVIAN STATE-DIRECTED PLANNING

In the late 1950s, C. Rajagopalacharia, a grand old man from the Independence movement, a former chief minister of the erstwhile Madras province, and the founder of the Swatantra party, coined the term "permit-license-quota" Raj to describe the system of state-directed economic development planning instituted under Nehru. By this phrase, Rajaji, as he was called, meant to say that the new Indian state was not a developing Socialist state, but an administrative state dominated by bureaucrats who controlled the distribution of permits, licenses, and quotas required for the establishment and expansion of business enterprises. Over the decades afterwards, the "permit-license-quota" Raj became ever more firmly entrenched, ever more corrupt, and ever more detrimental to the development of efficient, internationally competitive industrial enterprises.[19]

Under Mrs. Gandhi, who lacked ideological faith in the structure created by her father, planning became less systematic, there was some relaxation of price controls, import restrictions, and creation and expansion of industries and industrial capacity,[20] but the system of controls remained firmly in place and a source of enrichment for the

---

[18] M. M. Ansari, "Financing of the States' Plans: A Perspective for Regional Development," *EPW*, xviii, No. 49 (December 3, 1983), 2077.

[19] T. N. Srinavasan has remarked "that the discretionary regulatory system instituted in the name of planning for national development instead became a cancer in the body politic"; "Reform of Industrial and Trade Policies," *EPW*, xxvi, No. 37 (September 14, 1991), 2143.

[20] Atul Kohli, *Democracy and Discontent: India's Growing Crisis of Governability* (Cambridge: Cambridge University Press, 1990), p. 310.

Congress party and many of its top leaders as well as the bureaucrats. Rajiv Gandhi not only lacked his grandfather's socialist beliefs, he seemed much more favorably inclined to free market principles and began a process of liberalization of the system of import controls and "licensing regulations," and limitations on the expansion of existing industrial enterprises.[21] However, after an initial burst of enthusiasm with promises of dramatic changes, liberalization under Rajiv moved in a slow and piecemeal fashion, leaving the basic structure in place.[22]

It was only after the appointment of P. V. Narasimha Rao as Prime Minister in July, 1991 and his selection in turn of Manmohan Singh as finance minister, that a more determined attempt to dismantle Nehru's system began. Several domestic and international factors combined to make this new effort possible. Although most parties continued to pay lip service to the Nehru legacy, there was not much ideological commitment left in favor of it outside of the Communist parties and the intellectual Left. On the contrary, there was a reluctant, but widespread consensus that the system of public sector enterprises had become an increasing burden on the economy and a drain on public resources rather than a spur to development.

Second, the collapse of the Soviet Union, India's principal trading partner, and the disorientation of the Eastern European economies, disrupted long-term patterns of aid and trade with the former Socialist bloc countries. Third, the country's foreign exchange reserves had declined to a point where the Government of India would imminently have been in the position of being unable to honor its international financial obligations, making it necessary to appeal to the IMF for $6 billion in credits. Acceptance of such a large obligation to the IMF meant acceptance of its standard terms: devaluation of the rupee,

[21] Kohli, *Democracy and Discontent*, p. 318.

[22] Kohli attributes the loss of momentum to Rajiv's political ineffectiveness especially with the precipitous decline in his popularity after 1986; *Democracy and Discontent*, pp. 315–324. He stresses also the impact of grass roots opposition and the continuing hold of socialist ideology among the rank and file of the Congress. However, he leaves out entirely a consideration of the obvious benefits to corrupt political and bureaucratic elements in maintaining the old system, well demonstrated by Stanley Kochanek in his "Regulation and Liberalization Theology in India," *Asian Survey*, xxvi, No. 12 (December, 1986), 1284–1308" and "Briefcase Politics in India: The Congress Party and the Business Elite," *Asian Survey*, xxvii, No. 12 (December, 1987), 1278–1301. Strangely, he also completely ignores the ties of the Gandhi family to the likes of Dhirubhai Ambani, the new textile magnate of Reliance Industries, in influencing Rajiv's decision to eliminate restrictions on capacity increases in the textile mill sector, a policy change which violated long-standing commitments to small-scale cloth producers.

elimination of deficit financing, control of inflation, liberalization of the industrial licensing system, and relaxation of the terms for the entry of multinational companies into the Indian market.[23] These changes constituted only the beginnings of a set of moves to dismantle the old structure of state-directed detailed economic development planning and to allow greater freedom for market forces. The proposed changes articulated in the "New Industrial Policy Statement" (NIPS) call for reducing "barriers to entry in the Indian manufacturing sector" through elimination of licensing requirements, reducing restrictions on foreign investment, and deregulation of industrial groups previously reserved for the public sector, opening them to private sector entry.[24] However, even if this dismantling/opening process continues, the Government of India will be faced with several alternative choices for financial decision making and allocation of public investment along the paths to the desired goals of rapid economic growth and poverty alleviation. One set of choices is simply to continue the dismantling process, eliminate most restrictions on private enterprise, sell off the public sector industries, and reduce public investment to concentrate primarily on transportation and communication.

A second alternative is to seek to imitate the export-led, labor-intensive growth paths followed by Japan, Taiwan, Korea, Hong Kong, and Singapore. The third is to reallocate public investment toward agriculture, following the strategy articulated by Charan Singh in the late 1950s and by John Mellor and Michael Lipton in the 1970s.

---

[23] K. Shankar Bajpai, "India in 1991: New Beginnings," *Asian Survey*, xxxii, No. 2 (February, 1992), 210.

[24] These policy changes, the extent of their departure from previous policies, and their likely consequences are analyzed in Sunil Mani, "New Industrial Policy: Barriers to Entry, Foreign Investment and Privatization," *EPW*, xxvii, No. 35 (August 29, 1992), M-86 to M-94; citation from p. M-88. The author argues in general that the NIPS proposals do not constitute as radical a set of departures from previous policies as many observers have imagined and that they do not promise a major reduction in "the discretionary role of the government in industrial planning," p. M-53. K. S. Krishnaswamy has further remarked that, government policy statements notwithstanding, the corrupt bureaucratic mechanisms for "obtaining 'clearances' from government departments" remain in place; "Which Direction and What Atmosphere?" *EPW*, xxvii, No. 28 (July 11, 1992), 1471. For other criticisms of the New Economic Policy, see Arun Gosh, "New Economic Policy: A Review," *EPW*, xxvii, No. 23 (June 6, 1992), 1175–1178 and "Self-Reliance, Recent Economic Policies and Neo-Colonialism," *EPW*, xxvii, No. 17 (April 25, 1992), 865–868. Gosh takes quite the opposite position from the two other authors cited, arguing that the new policies constitute "a total break from the past" (p. 865), detrimental to the well-being of the vast poor population of the country.

This strategy calls for heavy public investment in irrigation, flood control, and drainage; in biological research and agricultural extension; and in the provision of off-farm employment in the rural areas through the encouragement of small-scale industries.

In 1992, proponents of the combined policies of liberalization of the import–export regime, dismantling of state-directed detailed planning, and export-led growth dominated economic policy making at the Center. It is hoped that such policies will lead to expansion and diversification of manufacturing capacities, increased employment, and stimulation of agricultural production. These policies, like the capital-intensive heavy industrialization policies which preceded them, offer no direct benefits to the poor, whose conditions again are expected to improve through the general "trickle down" effects of an expanding economy. In contrast, those who have argued for an agriculture-led, employment–oriented set of policies claim that they will lead to faster growth of the agricultural sector, to earlier attainment of full employment, to simultaneous and more rapid improvements in the living conditions of the poor, and ultimately as well to stimulation of the manufacturing sector as the consumption demands and buying power of the rural population expand.[25] However, not only does the NEP constitute a policy quite opposite to an agriculture-led one, it lacks utterly a strategy for agriculture.[26]

THE PERSISTING PROBLEMS OF POVERTY, HUNGER, AND MALNUTRITION

The persistence of widespread, extreme, and endemic poverty in India forty-five years after Independence raises fundamental issues concerning the appropriateness of the economic development strategy adopted by the Indian state and its ability to provide an environment in which the basic, minimal needs of its population can be satisfied. The commitment in the early 1970s by the Government of India to new approaches to abolish poverty and the failures of most of the programs adopted since then to achieve that goal reveal some of the basic

[25] See Brian M. Trinque, "The New Economics of Growth: An Assessment after 15 Years," *Contemporary South Asia*, I, No. 1 (1992), 67–91.
[26] JM, "Waiting for the Rains," *EPW*, xxvii, Nos. 20 & 21 (May 16–23, 1992), 1043–1046.

limitations of the Indian political system and the constraints imposed by the dominant classes in the Indian state and in the countryside upon successful formulation and implementation of policy innovations on behalf of the poor.

The commitment to abolish poverty was connected with major political changes in the functioning of Indian politics introduced by Mrs. Gandhi in the early 1970s. The recognition at the time of the persistence of widespread poverty implied either a major failure in the previous economic development strategy or at least pointed to its association with consequences that were no longer considered tolerable. The commitment to abolish poverty raised once again very sharply the question of whether or not it was feasible or realistic to envision the elimination of extreme poverty and inequality in India without major structural changes in society to sustain such an ambitious program.

The Indian "war on poverty" provides an example of the problems involved in formulating and implementing policies in India's multi-level political system. The weaknesses of most of the programs adopted arise in large part out of the difficulties involved in formulating policies in New Delhi to be implemented at the state and local levels with the existing bureaucratic apparatus. Many of the problems encountered in the implementation of anti-poverty programs also reveal the extent to which locally dominant classes are able to absorb and even profit from programs meant for the poor.

The pervasiveness of poverty

When scholars and planners talk about poverty and the poor in India, they are not usually referring to a small, disadvantaged segment of the population, but to virtually half the population of the country, with the incidence varying from state to state in a range from less than a quarter of the rural population in Punjab and Haryana to two-thirds of the population in West Bengal.[27] These rural poor, who are mostly of intermediate and low caste status, come from the landless agricultural laborers and the small peasantry with "tiny plots"[28] of land or

---

[27] Montek S. Ahluwalia, "Rural Poverty in India: 1956/57 to 1973/74," in Montek S. Ahluwalia et al., India: Occasional Papers, World Bank Staff Working Paper No. 279 (Washington, D.C.: World Bank, 1978), p. 17.

[28] D. N. Dhanagare, "Agrarian Reforms and Rural Development in India: Some Observations," offprint from Research in Social Movements, Conflict and Change, Vol. vii (JAI Press, 1984), p. 196.

with holdings that are inadequate to provide a subsistence for the household population dependent on their produce.

In most of rural India the bulk of the land, usually above half the cultivated area, is controlled by an elite of peasantry with economic holdings between five and twenty-five acres, comprising usually less than 20 percent of the rural population, and coming primarily from the dominant rural classes and castes of intermediate and upper caste status. Members of this class or group of castes are generally in controlling positions in local political and development institutions and take a keen interest in all rural development activities, including programs for the poor and for poverty alleviation.

The nationalist leaders who took power at Independence were aware both of the pervasiveness and depth of poverty in India, along with associated problems of unemployment and underemployment, and of the inequalities in resources and income among the rural population. However, as has been noted above, that leadership chose not to attack these problems directly. Their first priority was heavy industrialization. The problems of the poor were to be alleviated in the short term by land reforms, community development, food procurement, price control, and rationing in times of scarcity. In the long term, however, the solution to poverty was to come through the "trickling down" to the mass of the poor population of the economic benefits that would arise from a dynamic, industrializing economy.

The incidence of poverty in India and its measurement

Most measures of the incidence of poverty in India establish a "poverty line" based on the amount of income required for a person to purchase a given caloric norm of food per day.[29] In 1971, Dandekar and Rath published in the *Economic and Political Weekly* a landmark study on poverty in India, giving precise estimates of the numbers, consumption expenditures, and calorie intake of the poor in 1960–61 and of the changes that had occurred in all three during the decade of

[29] Ahluwalia, "Rural Poverty in India," p. 7. Another index that is often used side-by-side with others is Sen's poverty index, which measures the intensity of poverty in an index that combines a measure of the distance between the poverty line and "the mean consumption of the poor, as well as the extent of inequality amongst the poor"; Ahluwalia, "Rural Poverty in India," p. 5, and A. K. Sen, "Poverty, Inequality, Unemployment: Some Conceptual Issues in Measurement," *EPW*, VIII, Special Number (August, 1973).

the 1960s.[30] Defining the poor as those persons required to live on less than 50 paise[31] per day in the rural areas and 75 paise per day in the cities, 38 percent of the rural population and nearly 50 percent of the urban lived below this level of virtual destitution, which implied an inadequate calorie intake as well.

During the decade of the 1960s, covering the Third Five Year Plan and the Annual Plan years between it and the Fourth Plan, the main benefits of increased income and expenditure accrued to the upper middle and richer sections of the population. The bottom 40 percent, that is, virtually all the poor, did not benefit at all from the economic changes that occurred during the decade. Moreover, the per capita expenditure of most of the rural and urban poor actually declined, significantly so (15 to 20 percent) in the case of the poorest of the poor, the bottom 10 percent of the population. Dandekar and Rath argued that the results till then had shown that the process of economic development would not improve the position of the poorest in India in the foreseeable future unless specific policies and programs were adopted for their benefit.

The Dandekar and Rath report on poverty in India came at approximately the same time as the beginning of Mrs. Gandhi's *garibi hatao* campaign and the poverty programs that followed it. Their report, therefore, has provided a benchmark since then for assessing the direction of change, if any, in the numbers and condition of the poor, the relative successes and failures of the various poverty programs introduced since 1971, the extent to which there is any correlation between the performance of the economy and the general condition of the poor and whether or not an entirely different overall strategy for solving the problem of poverty in India is required.

Trends and fluctuations in the incidence of poverty

In an important World Bank-sponsored study published in 1978, Ahluwalia established on the basis of the available survey and statistical data that there had been no discernible long-term trend in the incidence of poverty in the country as a whole between 1960–61 and 1973–74. The incidence of poverty had neither increased nor decreased

---

[30] V. M. Dandekar and N. Rath, "Poverty in India: Dimensions and Trends," *EPW*, VI, No. 1 (January 2, 1971), 25–48, and No. 2 (January 9, 1971), 106–46.
[31] There are one hundred paise to the rupee.

during this period, although there had been considerable fluctuations up and down in the interim.[32]

On the whole, the all-India findings did not differ significantly from state to state. For most states, the absence of a long-term trend and "the pattern of fluctuation" was similar to that "for India as a whole."[33] Detailed case studies at the local level have also confirmed a persisting high incidence of poverty.[34]

Poverty and agricultural performance

There is a curious agreement among some scholars and politicians concerning the relationship between poverty and agricultural production and development. Those who favor greater emphasis on agriculture in resource allocation and less on capital-intensive industrialization argue that the best way to eliminate poverty in an agrarian society with abundant labor and limited land per person is to focus on increasing production per acre with available manual and animal power rather than by introducing capital-intensive machinery, thereby increasing employment opportunities on the land and the available supply of food.[35] On the other hand, some who have favored continued emphasis on the heavy industrialization strategy have argued that the new agricultural technology makes it possible to avoid major resource reallocations by increasing agricultural productivity and employment through the adoption of the HYVs. The New Agricultural Strategy was adopted with just that hope in mind, namely, that a small increased allocation of funds for agricultural development would lead to a large increase in production and a reduction in poverty through the "trickle down" effect, making it possible to retain the public sector-led heavy industrialization strategy.

The absence of a trend in the incidence of poverty parallels the absence of any long-term trend in "the growth of agricultural output" from 1956–57 to 1973–74, which "just about kept pace with the growth of the rural population."[36] However, the fluctuations in the

---

[32] Ahluwalia, "Rural Poverty in India."

[33] Ahluwalia, "Rural Poverty in India," p. 16.

[34] Indira Hirway, "Direct Attacks on Rural Poverty," review of *Direct Attack on Rural Poverty: Policy, Programmes and Implementation* by Prabhu Ghate (New Delhi: Concept Publishing Company, 1984), *EPW*, XXI, No. 1 (January 4, 1986), 22.

[35] Charan Singh, *Economic Nightmare of India: Its Cause and Cure* (New Delhi: National, 1981), p. 112.

[36] Ahluwalia, "Rural Poverty in India," p. 25.

incidence of poverty also paralleled fluctuations in agricultural performance in India as a whole and in half the states (Andhra Pradesh, Bihar, Karnataka, Madhya Pradesh, Maharashtra, Tamil Nadu, and Uttar Pradesh). Ahluwalia found a definite association between improved agricultural performance and "reductions in the incidence of poverty,"[37] which supported the view that there had been "some trickling down of benefits from increases in agricultural production."[38] The results suggested that the "trickle down" effects of increased agricultural output were more limited in states where land reforms had been least effective or where other factors such as more rapid population growth were at work as well. These latter associations were, however, less clear than the general association between fluctuations in the incidence of poverty and in agricultural output per head, with the former declining when the latter increased in India as a whole, in half the Indian states, and in most of the other states as well when the influence of other adverse factors was accounted for.

A reanalysis by Prasad of Ahluwalia's figures appears to resolve the doubts about the association between poverty and agricultural growth. After breaking down Ahluwalia's figures into two periods, pre- and post-Green Revolution, he found a clear "trend of decline" in the incidence of rural poverty in all the major states after 1967–68, a negative correlation between "the poverty percentage" and "per capita agricultural production," and an association between the decline in the poverty percentage over time and increased "per capita foodgrain production." Although the decline in the incidence of rural poverty "has been low," Prasad argues, it is because the rate of growth in agriculture also has been slow.[39]

The linkage established by both Ahluwalia and Prasad between poverty reduction and agricultural growth supports the following conclusions. 1) "Trickle down" effects benefiting the poor do occur with increased agricultural output. 2) Since, however, the incidence of rural poverty by all accounts has remained very high and the per capita rate of growth in agriculture slow, there is a need for further, more rapid and more widespread extension of the HYV technology. 3) It is

---

[37] Ahluwalia, "Rural Poverty in India," p. 25.
[38] Ahluwalia, "Rural Poverty in India," p. 28.
[39] Pradhan H. Prasad, "Poverty and Agricultural Development," *EPW*, xx, No. 50 (December 14, 1985), 2221–2224.

unlikely, however, that a suffficiently high, sustained rate of increase in agricultural productivity will occur even with the spread of HYV technology to obviate the need for further measures to help the poor directly. 4) There is indirect evidence that the persistence of "semi-feudal"[40] relations in agriculture and of exploitative tenancy and sharecropping arrangements act to increase poverty and to offset the positive effects of agricultural growth in reducing poverty. 5) There is, therefore, a case on this evidence to reinforce other justifications for at least bringing tenancy and sharecropping arrangements in the states of the eastern region, where such arrangements are most unfavorable to the cultivators and agricultural performance also is below most other states, in line with the basic pattern of peasant self-cultivation in the more prosperous agricultural regions of the country. 6) In the absence of a major structural reorganization of agrarian society and economy, special programs for the poor are required to eliminate or reduce poverty significantly.

Poverty programs: origin and types

The initiation of large-scale anti-poverty programs as increasingly important and integral components of the planning process occurred after the 1971 parliamentary elections in which Mrs. Gandhi's central election slogan was *garibi hatao* (abolish poverty). The adoption of this slogan and of the programs that followed it were part of Mrs. Gandhi's political strategy of building an independent national support base that would free her from political dependence upon the party bosses in the states, whose own support bases were primarily among the dominant rural proprietary castes and the urban commercial classes. Although the 40 to 50 percent rural and urban poor lacked political weight, they represented a potential national vote bank that was far larger than any alternative sources of votes for her rivals.

The programs that followed involved further centralization of the planning process in relation to programs that were to be implemented throughout the country, in the rural areas, and at the local level. Although implementation had to be carried out through the existing bureaucratic apparatus and local political institutions, the development of the schemes and proposals was done primarily in New Delhi. These programs also provided the central political leadership with new

[40] The term is Prasad's, "Poverty and Agricultural Development."

and vast patronage resources to be disbursed to states and districts throughout the country.

The new anti-poverty programs were launched in the early 1970s simultaneously with a centrally sponsored move to institute a second stage in reducing and enforcing more effectively land ceilings that had been adopted earlier in most states. There was, therefore, an overall central design at this time to eliminate poverty, reduce inequalities in the countryside, and erode the traditional dominance of the rural landed castes. The state governments, however, continued to depend upon the dominant rural classes for political support in the countryside.

The anti-poverty programs themselves fell into two broad types. One was designed to actually lift beneficiaries above the poverty line by providing them either "with productive assets" or skills or both "so that they can employ themselves usefully to earn greater incomes."[41] Under this heading of "beneficiary-oriented" programs were the Small Farmer Development Agency (SFDA), the Marginal Farmer and Agricultural Labor (MFAL) program, and most recently the Integrated Rural Development Program (IRDP). The IRDP, introduced in 1978–80 under the Janata regime, consolidated the existing programs such as the SFDA and MFAL, and also introduced the *antayodaya* principle of beginning with the poorest.[42]

The second type of program was designed to be ameliorative only, to provide temporary wage employment for the poor and landless in seasons when employment opportunities are reduced and in areas such as dry and drought prone districts where they are less available than in more favored districts even in the best of times. These programs have had names such as the Crash Scheme for Rural Employment (CSRE), the Drought Prone Areas Program (DPAP), the Pilot Intensive Rural Employment Project (PIREP), the National Rural Employment Programme (NREP), and the like.[43]

The most important of the anti-poverty programs in terms of

[41] Nilakantha Rath, "'Garibi Hatao': Can IRDP Do It?" *EPW*, xx, No. 6 (February 9, 1985), 238.

[42] *Antayodaya* means "uplift of the poorest." Under this principle, the selection of initial beneficiaries is to be done from among the poorest persons and families in each village in a community development block, who are to be provided with productive assets sufficient for them to lift themselves above the poverty line.

[43] John W. Mellor, *The New Economics of Growth: A Strategy for India and the Developing World* (Ithaca: Cornell University Press, 1976), pp. 101–102 and Rath, p. 245.

resource allocations have been the beneficiary-oriented IRD programs. In the Sixth Plan, nearly three times as much funding (Rs. 4,500 crores[44]) was provided for the IRDP, compared to Rs. 1,600 crores for the NREP.[45] In the Seventh Plan, however, somewhat more funds were allocated for employment programs (Rs. 2,487 crores for the NREP and Rs. 1,744 crores for the Rural Landless Employment Guarantee Programme [RLEGS]) than for the IRDP (Rs. 3,474 crores).[46]

Altogether, however, the funds allocated for the three main anti-poverty programs in the Seventh Plan – IRDP, NREP, and RLEGS – constituted only 4 percent of the total plan allocations.[47] In effect, therefore, the anti-poverty programs remain a supplement in a broader economic development strategy, which continues to avoid radical institutional solutions to poverty and inequality and to rely upon the long-run hope that the benefits of growth and development will ultimately "trickle down" to the poor.[48]

Poverty programs: performance and implementation

The principal justification for the beneficiary-oriented programs as opposed to the employment-oriented poverty programs is that the former are designed to solve the problem of poverty by providing income-generating assets to the poor whereas the latter merely provide a subsistence income at state expense and do not offer a solution. While the IRDP idea makes sense in principle and has the added appeal that it threatens no one, in practice evidence has been accumulating that the IRD programs have not had the desired effects. Moreover, it has provided large new sources of patronage and corrupt income for local politicians, bureaucrats, and locally influential persons.

The IRD asset creation programs involve a wide range of persons and institutions in their implementation, thereby making its workings incomprehensible to the poor, requiring intermediaries between the poor and the agencies and persons who are supposed to help them, and

---

[44] One crore is 10 million.   [45] Rath, "'Garibi Hatao': Can IRDP Do It?", p. 245.
[46] Government of India, Planning Commission, *The Seventh Five-Year Plan, 1985–90*, Vol. ii: *Sectoral Programmes of Development* (Delhi: Controller of Publications, 1985), p. 70.
[47] Calculated from Government of India, Planning Commission, *The Seventh Five-Year Plan*, Vol. i: *Perspectives, Objectives, Resources*, p. 28.
[48] B. M., "Policy-Frame for Seventh Plan," *EPW*, xx, No. 28 (July, 1985), 1165.

multiplying the opportunities for the non-poor to make quick and large profits from them. Raj Krishna, Rath, Paul, and other observers have pointed to numerous deficiencies in implementation of the IRDP and have argued that only a small percentage of the total beneficiaries have actually received productive assets of sufficient quality to generate the income to keep them permanently above the poverty line.[49]

The poor performance of the poverty programs notwithstanding, the most recent available estimates of the rural population in poverty, for 1988, indicated a secular decline from 53 percent in 1970 to 44.9 percent in 1983 and to 41.7 percent in 1988.[50] Although the planners have claimed credit for this decline as a consequence of their anti-poverty programs, the more likely explanation is the persistence of a modest upward trend in the growth rate of foodgrains production throughout these years. Hardly any professional economists outside the Planning Commission credit the results to the anti-poverty programs, whose performance generally fell below the standard of other plan programs.[51]

Moreover, these changes in the proportion of rural persons below the poverty line provide little comfort for those who live off slogans for abolition of poverty, for the decline in the proportionate incidence of poverty has been outpaced by the birth rate among the poor. Consequently, the absolute numbers of the rural poor increased from 236.8 million in 1970 to 252.3 million in 1988. As for the Scheduled Castes and Scheduled Tribe populations, their proportions in poverty were 54.2 percent and 62.2 percent, respectively, in 1988. Finally, the more rapid rate of growth in the urban than in the rural population of the country has been accompanied by a larger absolute increase in the urban poor than in the rural poor, from 50.5 million in 1970 to 70.1 million in 1988. When the figures for rural and urban populations in poverty are combined, the grand total comes to 322.3 million, of whom 156.5 million are below the "ultra poverty line," the poorest of the poor, the utterly destitute living without means or dignity.[52]

[49] Raj Krishna, "Growth, Investment and Poverty in Mid-Term Appraisal of Sixth Plan," *EPW*, xvii, No. 47 (November 19, 1983), 1972–1977; Samuel Paul, "Mid-Term Appraisal of the Sixth Plan: Why Poverty Alleviation Lags Behind," *EPW*, xix, No. 18 (May 5, 1984), 760–766; and Rath, "'Garibi Hatao': Can IRDP Do It?"

[50] *India: Poverty, Employment, and Social Services* (Washington, D.C.: World Bank, 1989), p. 175.

[51] Paul, "Mid-Term Appraisal," p. 763.

[52] Figures from World Bank, *India: Poverty, Employment, and Social Services*, pp. 175–176.

DOMINANT CLASSES, ECONOMIC
DEVELOPMENT AND THE INDIAN STATE

How can one explain the persistence for so long of a system that fell so far short of achieving any of its principal economic goals? The predominant leadership at Independence was not the creature of any dominant class. Rather, it was a leadership acting relatively independently, from a powerful state and political base, in the service of deeply felt nationalist and ideological goals. It was able to adopt an economic development strategy that, in the short and intermediate run at least, would clearly not be in the interests of many classes and groups in Indian society not only because of the strength of the state and the party, but because of the weakness of the potential opposition and because some of its policy measures did benefit important classes and groups.

The former *zamindars* and princes who had been collaborators with the British Raj were in no position to contest the power of the state and the Congress organization. Much room was left for the private sector and indigenous industrial entrepreneurs who were now protected from competitive British colonial enterprises as well as from any new threats from modern multinational corporations as a result of the import-substitution policy and measures associated with it that gave protected monopolies to domestic industries.

More important, however, was that the Congress, by 1947, had developed a very strong rural support base among the upper tenantry, the petty landlords, and the owner-cultivators or peasant-proprietors who controlled the Congress organizations in the districts. Although the national Congress leaders talked about agrarian reforms, even including joint cooperative farming (or collectivization), which were not at all in the interests of the locally dominant rural classes, it gradually became evident to most of them that no serious structural reforms and redistribution were planned and that even the moderate land ceilings measures introduced in most states could be frustrated quietly. In effect, therefore, the national Congress leadership was able to pursue an economic strategy that neglected agriculture and favored urban industrial development for three reasons: 1) it eliminated or reduced significantly the power of the former landlord class and empowered the new class of independent rural landowning proprietors; 2) it provided sufficient rural development patronage to its main rural supporters among this new class; 3) it took no really effective measures to threaten the interests of the new class.

The idea of the relative autonomy of Indian state leadership can be applied also to Mrs. Gandhi's long period of dominance to explain both the persistence of the overall strategy and the new emphases in economic policy that were introduced from 1971 onwards. Early in the period of Mrs. Gandhi's dominance, the weaknesses of the Nehru strategy had become increasingly evident in industrial stagnation, in the failure of the agricultural sector to increase productivity, in the persistence of mass poverty, unemployment and underemployment, in urban decay, and in increasing inflation.

In the midst of these considerable economic difficulties, Mrs. Gandhi waged a major political struggle against the party bosses who had dominated state politics in her father's days and emerged victorious and in complete control of the central and state governments. She sought to remedy some of the major economic problems that had become evident by the end of her father's life, most notably through the New Agricultural Strategy and the anti-poverty programs introduced after the 1971 election campaign. With her power consolidated in the country in the mid 1970s, she sought once again, as her father had done, to compel the state leaderships to introduce serious land ceilings legislation and to redistribute surplus land to the poor.

We have seen, however, that none of these measures proved effective. The New Agricultural Strategy helped to promote the Green Revolution which, however, has been a very partial revolution, as will be shown in the next chapter. Anti-poverty programs have followed upon one another in rapid succession, but have not had a major impact upon the incidence of poverty and malnutrition, though both have declined somewhat in recent years. The second round of land ceilings legislation proved to be as much of a farce as the first.

This explanation of policy failures under both Nehru and Mrs. Gandhi focuses on leadership, on political and organizational factors, and on the structure of center–state relations. Questions nevertheless remain concerning the ways in which this system benefited important social classes who helped sustain it. Bardhan has argued that the system satisfied or allayed potential discontent from several important groups through "the proliferation of subsidies and grants to placate ...

them." These subsidies included high support prices for urban consumers and hence lower wage costs for industrialists; and low-priced materials and services as well as protection from competition for the industrialists.[53]

There is no doubt that the top business and industrial leaders since before Independence favored a policy of government-supported rapid industrialization, including encouragement by government for development of new industries and protection for indigenous industries. However, most Indian businessmen would have preferred, and lobbied consistently for, an increased role for the private sector, a liberalized import–export regime, and a general reduction in the role of the public sector and of government controls over the economy. Although businessmen as a class had relatively little influence over the direction of economic policy, individual businessmen and business houses nevertheless prospered in India's "mixed economy" by influencing the implementation of government regulations.[54]

If the business classes accepted a system which they did not like, the professionals and urban intellectuals, and especially the professional bureaucrats, provided stronger support for it. The latter, particularly the upper levels of the administrative service and the "battalions of bureaucrats [who] wield the weapons of monopoly control, foreign exchange regulation, industrial licensing and credit and input rationing to keep the industrialists on the defensive and to increase their own political leverage and corrupt income"[55] provided powerful support for the system. Moreover, through their education and personal relationship with the bureaucratic personnel, the more successful and politically astute among the professional and urban intellectual classes generally could gain preferential access to the privileges of education, housing, foreign travel, scarce consumer goods, and good jobs for themselves and their children.

As for the agricultural classes who appeared to gain little from the system, it became evident as early as the early 1960s, that the class of middle and upper peasantry had become dominant in most state governments, that they were in a position to frustrate all attempts at

[53] Pranab Bardhan, *The Political Economy of Development in India* (Delhi: Oxford University Press, 1984), p. 61.
[54] Stanley A. Kochanek, *Business and Politics in India* (Berkeley: University of California Press, 1974), ch. 15.
[55] Bardhan, *The Political Economy of Development*, p. 58.

serious land ceilings legislation or rural resource mobilization, and that their common interests often cut across party divisions. These groups acted primarily as a constraining, restraining, and frustrating force against the implementation of Government of India policies at the state level. The richer farmers, like big industrialists and businessmen, operated effectively within and gained benefits and privileges from a system they did not like and which did *not* serve their class interests, but which was sufficiently corrupt, incoherent, and flexible that privileged segments in the rural areas could twist it to their advantage.

The ability of the national leadership of the country to neutralize or placate dominant social classes and groups helps to explain also its pursuit of policies of state aggrandizement while neglecting the needs of the bulk of the rural population of the country. State and private investment allocations were channeled principally to the cities in factories, roads, five-star hotels, and sports stadia for such prestige international events as the Asian Games while the rural areas, especially the rural poor, received pitifully small allocations for investment in the land, in cheap agricultural implements, in drinking water, or in agricultural research and extension.[56]

This critique of Indian economic development policy as reflecting an "urban bias" has been widely shared and has led to proposals from foreign economists, Gandhian and other non-Marxist economists and intellectuals in India, and the leaders of agrarian-based parties in India such as Charan Singh for major changes in Indian economic development strategy. The types of changes envisioned by such critics would involve massive shifts of resources for extensive agricultural development for the benefit of *all* the viable peasantry, for vastly increased funds for rural development generally, including provision of basic amenities of life for the villages of India, and for a labor-intensive strategy of promoting local, small-scale industries. Such a policy shift, however, remains remote because the Indian state and its policies continue to be dominated by a political class which adheres ideologically to the drive for industrial and technological modernity, even if state-directed economic development planning is no longer to provide the motor for it.

[56] Michael Lipton, *Why Poor People Stay Poor: A Study of Urban Bias in World Development* (New Delhi: Heritage, 1980), p. 13.

CHAPTER 9

POLITICAL ASPECTS OF AGRICULTURAL CHANGE

AGRARIAN ISSUES IN INDIAN POLITICS

The year 1966 was a major turning point in the history of Indian agricultural development policy. In that year, three significant sets of events occurred that profoundly affected the determination of Government of India policy makers to intensify measures to increase agricultural production as rapidly as possible in order to make India self-sufficient in foodgrains. The first was the great drought/famine of 1966–67 in north India, which followed upon a previous bad year for Indian agriculture and which occurred simultaneously with scarcity conditions in other areas of the country. The second was the initial harvesting of the new HYVs of wheat brought to India in the winter of 1965–66 by Norman Borlaug and his associates and planted in several locations in north India and elsewhere during the *rabi* (winter) season of 1966. The third was a combination of domestic and international factors affecting U.S. government foreign policy making, including the Vietnam war, U.S. balance of payments problems, and the potential use of U.S. food exports for hard currency payments to alleviate those problems.

Although these three sets of events constituted a turning point, the solutions adopted to deal with the crisis events of 1966–67, namely, the drought and shifts in U.S. attitudes toward India, were entirely consistent with previous Indian government policies for economic development, agricultural development, and agrarian reform. Those policies, which focused on the rapid adoption of the HYVs and the associated technology, ignored the long-standing issues of agrarian reform and were designed to be acceptable to the dominant political and economic elites in the provincial capitals and in the Indian countryside. They fed into and reinforced historic regional and social imbalances in economic development in India. They ignored the problems of the small cultivators in vast regions of the country, most notably in the great rainfed paddy-growing areas of India stretching from eastern U. P. to Bengal and including as well large parts of Madhya Pradesh, Orissa, and Assam. They also failed to solve, only postponed facing the hard solutions to, the basic production problems of Indian agriculture in those areas of the country that comprise the bulk of its territory and population and that depend upon the monsoon or lack either adequate irrigation or dependable rainfall.

The new strategy for agriculture

Government of India policy makers, while recognizing the special needs of the "backward" areas of the country, such as eastern U. P. and Bihar, and while calling for policies to rectify existing regional imbalances and disparities in development and in income, adopted a New Strategy for Agriculture that led to the concentration of resources and technology in the already more advanced regions of the country and among the "progressive farmers" who were in a position to adopt them. The new strategy for agriculture was less a strategy than a hope, less a major shift in direction than a modest intensification of resource allocations for agriculture to existing areas and programs, fortified by the promise of the new HYVs to increase production quickly and dramatically. The plan outlay for agriculture was increased somewhat and new programs for particular areas and crops were established. The Intensive Agricultural District Programme (IADP) was maintained and new resources were provided for the districts involved in the program. The main orientation of the HYVs was to the bigger farmers with the knowledge, resources, and local influence to be in a position to adopt the new HYVs and purchase the necessary inputs. These bigger farmers were given the euphemistic label of "progressive farmers" and their "emergence" was heralded as "a notable development in 1966–67"[1] that augured well for the future of the new strategy.

Nor did the new strategy involve any dramatic shifts in the relative share of total resources devoted specifically to programs designed to increase agricultural production. Overall allocations for agriculture, irrigation, and flood control increased only marginally from 20.5 percent of the total Third Plan expenditure to 23.8 and 23.3 percent, respectively, in the Annual Plans from 1966–69 and in the Fourth Plan (see table 8.1). It was hoped that the new HYVs would be so successful that it would not be necessary to alter the broader goals of economic

[1] *Economic Survey of Indian Agriculture, 1966–67*, p. viii.

development for India, which continued to emphasize industrial development and power generation.

Policies toward the agricultural sector

The various drives to increase agricultural production in post-Independence India, of which the new strategy was the most important, were carried out within a broader framework of policies toward agriculture and the agricultural sector of the population. Those policies can conveniently be classified under four headings: land reforms and measures to protect specific categories of the rural population; policies relating to the pricing, procurement and distribution of foodgrains and cash crops; policies concerning the selection of particular areas of the country for intensive agricultural development; and policies relating to technology transfer.

Land reforms and special programs for disadvantaged sectors

The principal land reforms in post-Independence India were the various measures that eliminated the *zamindari* system and other types of intermediary rights to the land and the land revenue. Such measures were passed ultimately in all the Indian states, with varying degrees of effectiveness in design and execution.

The second stage of land reform in all the states of India was the passage of land ceilings laws designed to limit the size of landholdings to a relatively small multiple of an economic holding and to redistribute surplus lands in the hands of former landlords among the poorer peasants and the landless. These laws were much less effectively designed and implemented in all states than the laws eliminating intermediaries, which at least ultimately succeeded in their principal purpose.

It has long been apparent to informed observers of the "progress" of land reforms in most of the Indian states that there has been no serious intention to link the issue of agricultural production with that of agrarian reorganization either through land ceilings and land redistribution or through the establishment of cooperative farms. Rather, the state governments in India have been content to establish in the countryside a system of land ownership or land tenure that eliminates revenue intermediaries between the cultivator and the state, that gives title to the actual operator-manager-cultivator of the land, but that also permits extensive sharecropping. The cumulative result of the legislation to abolish intermediaries and to limit the size of landholdings has been to curtail significantly the political and economic control over the land of the former big *zamindars* and *talukdars*, to perpetuate the local political and economic influence of the major elite proprietary castes such as the Brahmans, Rajputs, Jats, and Bhumihars in north India, and to enhance the independence and economic power of the major cultivating castes of middle status, particularly the Ahirs (Yadavs) and Kurmis in north India, the Jats of western U. P., Haryana, and Punjab, the Marathas in Maharashtra, the Kammas and Reddis in Andhra, and the like.

Price, procurement, and distribution policies

If the Indian government's agricultural production programs were designed to leave the prevailing patterns of rural control and dominance in the countryside intact and to avoid precipitating rural class conflict, its price, procurement, and distribution policies were designed to provide incentives to cultivators to increase agricultural production without diverting significant resources from plans for rapid industrialization of the country and without causing prices of foodgrains to rise in the cities that would precipitate urban political protest and urban–rural conflict. The devices used to further these goals were: 1) price support policies that were meant to provide producers sufficient incentives to increase foodgrain production and production of selected crops but that would not push prices so high as to cause inflation; 2) the establishment of a system of ration and fair price shops for public distribution of foodgrains to the poor and lower middle classes, sometimes at below-market prices; 3) procurement policies to acquire grain at fixed prices from both traders and farmers to ensure an adequate supply of food for both the cities and deficit rural areas; 4) a policy of single-state food zones that prohibited the transport and sale of grain across state boundaries in order to contain food deficits to areas where crop failures actually occurred and to prevent price fluctuations from occurring in non-deficit states through the operations of the free market; and 5) import policies that allowed for the purchase under the U.S. Public Law 480 program of vast quantities of foodgrains that served to keep consumer prices down and to supply foodgrains to deficit areas. The import of U.S. foodgrains under the P.L. 480 program relieved the pressure upon government in India to procure sufficient food by its own efforts to feed the population of the country and made it unnecessary to face up to redistributive pressures that might otherwise have mounted.[2]

These policies were internally self-contradictory and often ineffectively implemented. Procurement targets were rarely achieved except in states like Punjab and Haryana, which produced foodgrains far beyond the needs of their populations. The desire to keep consumer prices low conflicted with the desire to ensure adequate prices for producers. Food imports became a substitute for internal procurement efforts and also depressed producer prices.

The occurrence of the Bihar and east U. P. famines in 1966–67 after a previous year of crop failures in other parts of the country and at a time when the supply of food from the U.S. had become politically conditioned[3] threatened to bring the whole structure down. Had U.S. food imports not again saved the day, the state and national governments would have had to face very starkly issues of "inter-regional and inter-personal equity in distribution"[4] that would have placed the severest strains on center–state relations, urban–rural relations, and relations among class and caste groups in the countryside. In these respects, therefore, as in others, the hopes placed on the new strategy and its HYV Program were very great, for the failure of the program would threaten the political stability of the country and the peace of the countryside.

The intensive area approach

Problems of increasing agricultural production have been viewed by Indian policy makers since Independence primarily in aggregate terms and in terms of consumer needs rather than in terms of the needs and goals of the farmers themselves. The peasantry of India have been often looked upon either as obstacles to progress and increased production because of their alleged backwardness, lethargy, or poverty, or as potential instruments for solving the consumption needs of the

---

[2] For a useful review of these developments, see R. N. Chopra, *Evolution of Food Policy in India* (Delhi: Macmillan, 1981).

[3] See James Bjorkman, "Public Law 480 and the Policies of Self-Help and Short-Tether: Indo-American Relations, 1965–68," in Lloyd I. Rudolph and Susanne H. Rudolph *et al.*, *The Regional Imperative* (Atlantic Highlands, N.J.: Humanities Press, 1980), pp. 201–262.

[4] *Congress Bulletin* (January–March, 1966), p. 490.

country could they only be brought out of their deplorable condition and induced to produce more. A basic distrust of or lack of faith in the capacity of the Indian peasantry as a whole and an orientation toward maximizing production to solve aggregate consumption needs dictated a policy of focusing on those areas of the country where conditions seemed to favor rapid production increases.

The hope that a selective concentration of resources in the agricultural sector would solve India's production–consumption problems was clearly tied into the increased emphasis on allocation of the major new resources for the Second Plan to heavy industry and a consequent reduction in the proportionate allocation of resources for agriculture. The policy was adopted most explicitly in the Third Plan, with its definitive shift toward the goal of rapid industrialization of India and its simultaneous adoption of the Intensive Agricultural District Programme (IADP) "which envisioned concentration of resources and efforts in specially endowed areas to achieve a quick breakthrough in production."[5]

The approach adopted in the Third Plan called for concentration of resources in selected districts, for the identification within those districts of "progressive farmers" best able to adopt intensive methods of agriculture, and for an emphasis on "profitability at the farm level."[6] In other words the thrust of the program was to create in selected districts in India a profitable sector of commercial agriculture. When the new strategy and the HYVs were adopted in 1966–67, they were grafted on to the IADP and IAAP. Although the HYVP was not confined to the latter districts, the IADP districts were assured of the provision of the necessary inputs to sustain the HYVs, whereas other districts were not.

Technology transfer

Technology transfer was an integral and inseparable part of the new strategy, which was based on the beliefs that new technologies were available from the international crop centers for the two major food crops of wheat and rice, that the technologies were transferable to

[5] Government of India, Ministry of Agriculture and Irrigation, *Report of the National Commission of Agriculture, 1976*, Pt. 1: *Review and Progress* (Delhi: Controller of Publications, 1976), p. 149.

[6] *Report of the National Commission on Agriculture, 1976*, Pt. 1: *Review and Progress*, p. 149.

India, and that the institutions and values associated with agricultural development in other parts of the world also were applicable to India. The basic elements in the package of practices, concepts, and institutions that the Government of India eagerly adopted were: 1) the new seeds themselves, which involved the creation of new seed farms around the country, the establishment of a National Seeds Corporation to produce, stock and supply "foundation seeds,"[7] and the founding of the Tarai Seed Development Corporation at the Agricultural University in Pantnagar (U. P.); 2) the acceptance of the necessity for chemicalization of Indian agriculture through the production and use of fertilizers, pesticides, weedkillers, and other plant protection chemicals; 3) a commitment to national and international cooperative research to develop new and improve existing seed varieties by establishing new research institutes and enlarging the links of older research institutes in India with CIMMYT (International Maize and Wheat Improvement Centre), IRRI (International Rice Research Institute), and other international crop research agencies; 4) the acceptance of the American concept of developing modern scientific agriculture through the creation of a network of land grant colleges in every state in the country where teaching, research, and extension would be integrated and through which the latest results of scientific research in agriculture could be spread to the farmers in the country.

THE EXTENT AND LIMITS OF THE GREEN REVOLUTION

Since the inauguration of the New Agricultural Strategy, there have been considerable increases in aggregate foodgrain production in India, from 95 million tons in 1967–68 to a record 170 million tons in 1988–89, which was the best monsoon year in at least a decade.[8] However, trend lines for foodgrain production for India as a whole from 1950 move only gradually upward and do *not* indicate a sharp upward movement since 1967–68.[9] The quality of the monsoon

---

[7] *Report of the National Commission on Agriculture, 1976*, Pt. 1: *Review and Progress*, p. 156.
[8] *India: Poverty, Employment, and Social Services* (Washington, D.C.: World Bank, 1989), p. 3.
[9] World Bank, *World Development Report 1984* (New York: Oxford University Press, 1984), p. 93.

remains the best predictor of annual foodgrain production in India. The average annual growth rate in foodgrains production was 2.7 percent between 1950 and 1985 which compares to an annual average growth rate of 2.1 percent in population in the same period. The growth rate from 1968 to 1989 was even less, 2.5 percent,[10] while the average growth rate in population was 2.3 percent from 1965 to 1980 and 2.2 percent from 1980 to 1988.[11]

Moreover, although the trend line goes gradually upward, it is marked by fluctuations up and down, some of them significantly downward. Cereal yields in India overall remain among the very lowest in the world, averaging 2.0 tons per hectare in 1989 compared to 5.4 in Egypt, 6.0 in Korea, and 5.7 in Japan.[12] In short, therefore, in terms of aggregate production increases, the Green Revolution has not altered the basic, slightly upward trend line, it has not eliminated major downward fluctuations produced primarily by severe regional droughts, and it has not altered India's standing as one of the least productive agricultural countries in the world today.

Nevertheless, it would be a mistake to infer from these aggregate figures and trend lines for India as a whole that the Green Revolution has had no significant effect on agricultural production and productivity in India. Regionally, the greatest effect has occurred in the wheat-growing areas of Punjab, Haryana, and western U. P.,[13] but the new dwarf wheats have also increasingly spread down the Gangetic plain as far as Bengal (figure 6). Although the Green Revolution has to some extent brought about increases in rice production as well as wheat production, these effects also have been concentrated regionally, principally to the three southern states, of Andhra, Tamil Nadu,

[10] *India*, p. 4; however, the growth rate for cereals production reported by the World Bank for 1965 to 1989 was 3.2; *World Development Report, 1992: Development and the Environment* (New York: Oxford University Press, 1992), p. 202.

[11] *World Development Report, 1990*, p. 228.

[12] World Bank, *World Development Report, 1992*, pp. 202–203.

[13] Two-thirds of the wheat production in the country comes from Punjab, Haryana, and U. P. and most of the wheat grown in U. P. comes from the western districts of the state adjacent to Punjab and Haryana; Government of India, Ministry of Agriculture, *Indian Agriculture in Brief* (Delhi: Controller of Publications, 1985), p. 332. Growth rates for foodgrain production in the three northeastern states of Punjab, Haryana, and Himachal Pradesh have consistently been many times higher than for other regions of India and for the country as a whole. For example, the growth rate between 1962–65 and 1980–83 for these states was 6.81 percent compared to 0.74 percent for the eastern region and 2.75 percent for the entire country; Brian M. Trinque, "The New Economics of Growth: An Assessment after 15 years," *Contemporary South Asia*, I, No. 1 (1992), 68.

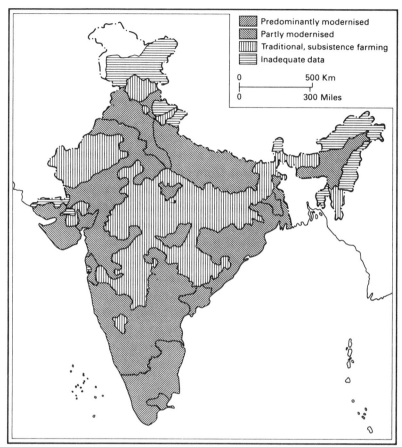

Figure 6   Use of modern techniques to produce rice and wheat under the high-yielding varieties program, 1976

Ashok K. Dutt and M. Margaret Geib, *Atlas of South Asia* (Boulder, CO: Westview Press, 1987).

and Kerala, on the one hand, and to Punjab, Haryana, and western U. P. as a winter crop, on the other hand.

Moreover, it remains true that the Green Revolution's most spectacular effects have occurred with wheat production. A comparison of yields for rice and wheat in the post-Green Revolution period, that is, from 1969–70 to 1988–89, brings out the difference. The average yield of rice went up by 60.1 percent in this period, whereas it went up by 97.1 percent for wheat (table 9.1). Although wheat production has increased enormously in India as a result, both because of increased yields and shifts in sown area from other crops (particularly inferior millets and pulses) to wheat, rice remains the principal food crop in India in area, production, and consumption, constituting 23.3 percent of the gross cropped area in 1980–81 compared to half that for wheat (12.8 percent), 31.4 percent of the total sown area under food crops and 39.4 percent of total foodgrain production in 1983–84 compared to 18.7 and 29.8 percent, respectively, for wheat.[14]

The overall results of the Green Revolution, therefore, can be summarized broadly as follows. There have been only marginal increases in rice production in contrast to a trebling of wheat production. Production of some other inferior grains and pulses, consumed mostly by the poor, has also gone down as wheat production has increased. The overall per capita availability of food in India, therefore, has not increased much and continues to fluctuate very considerably. For example, although the record harvest of 1989 also provided the highest level of per capita grain availability since Independence, the amount of grain available per person in the previous year, 1988, was only 441 grams per person, lower than the 1962 figure of 461 (see table 9.2).

Nevertheless, the Green Revolution, though it does not deserve the name insofar as India as a whole is concerned, "continues to increase productivity and production"[15] in various regions in the subcontinent. Such considerable increases in production, concentrated in particular regions, on particular crops, especially in irrigated areas, and in the winter season have, therefore, perpetuated existing regional

---

[14] Calculated from *Indian Agriculture in Brief*, pp. 44–45, 236. The most recent available figures for the percentage contribution of rice and wheat to total foodgrain production show little change in the relative shares of the two crops, being 41.5 percent for rice and 31.7 percent for wheat in 1988–89; Agrawal, *India*, p. 114 (citing *Economic Survey, 1989–90*).

[15] Farmer, "Perspectives on the 'Green Revolution'," p. 81.

Table 9.1. *Index numbers of agricultural production, area, and yield of principal crops, 1969–70 to 1988–89[a] (post-Green Revolution), base year 1969–70 = 100*

Crop/Year	Production	Area	Yield
All cereals			
1970–71	114.1	102.0	110.4
1975–76	128.8	104.0	118.8
1980–81	143.1	104.5	129.3
1985–86	167.3	103.7	149.6
1988–89	149.6	105.1	166.9
Rice			
1970–71	107.4	101.5	105.8
1975–76	124.7	106.7	116.9
1980–81	137.2	108.6	126.3
1985–86	163.7	111.3	147.1
1988–89	181.2	133.3	160.1
Wheat			
1970–71	132.1	114.9	115.0
1975–76	159.9	128.8	124.1
1980–81	201.1	140.3	143.4
1985–86	260.6	144.8	180.4
1988–89	299.1	151.7	197.1
Coarse cereals			
1970–71	114.7	98.0	117.2
1975–76	111.8	93.1	118.2
1980–81	106.7	88.8	118.8
1984–85	115.1	83.1	137.0
All pulses			
1970–71	104.4	102.5	102.1
1975–76	115.3	111.2	105.0
1980–81	95.8	103.2	95.6
1985–86	120.1	112.2	108.4
1988–89	123.9	106.9	117.2
Gram			
1970–71	99.7	101.7	98.0
1975–76	112.9	108.2	104.3
1980–81	83.2	85.6	97.2
1984–85	87.3	89.2	97.9

[a]For coarse cereals and gram, the latest available figures were for 1984–85.
Source: Government of India, Ministry of Finance, *Economic Survey, 1985–86* (Delhi: Controller of Publications, 1986), pp. 108–110; A. N. Agrawal *et al.*, *India: Economic Information Year Book, 1990–91* (New Delhi: National, 1991), p. 115 (citing *Economic Survey, 1989–90* and *Indian Agriculture in Brief*, 22nd edn, 1989).

Table 9.2. *Per capita net availability of cereals and pulses,*
1951–1989

| Year | Per capita availability per day (in grams) | | |
	Cereals	Pulses	Total
1951	334	61	395
1956	361	70	431
1961	400	69	469
1962	399	62	461
1963	384	60	444
1964	401	51	452
1965	419	62	481
1966	360	48	408
1967	362	40	402
1968	404	56	460
1969	398	47	445
1970	403	52	455
1971	418	51	469
1972	419	47	466
1973	381	41	422
1974	410	41	451
1975	366	40	406
1976	374	51	425
1977	386	43	429
1978	423	46	469
1979	432	45	477
1980	380	31	411
1981	416	38	454
1982	415	39	454
1983	397	39	436
1984	436	42	478
1985	416	38	454
1986	434	42	478
1987	436	36	472
1988	408	33	441
1989	456	41	497

Source: Economic Survey, 1985–86, p. 120 and Agrawal, *India* (citing *Economic Survey, 1989–90*), p. 61.

imbalances, and created new ones, leading overall to "increased inter-regional disparities in agricultural production and so in prosperity."[16] Rates of return to growers are highest in "wheat, paddy, and cash crops."[17] Insofar as paddy is concerned, the rates of return per hectare are highest in Karnataka, Punjab, Haryana, Tamil Nadu, and Andhra Pradesh. The highest rates of return for wheat are in Punjab, Haryana, Rajasthan, and Bihar. Punjab and Haryana, therefore, rank high with regard to both major foodgrains as well as with cash crops such as cotton and mustard. Farmers in other states show high rates of profitability with respect to only one of the two major crops. Gujarat ranks high with regard to cash crops such as cotton and groundnut. Taking all major crops together, the high productivity, high profit states are Punjab, Haryana, Gujarat, and Tamil Nadu, the lowest are Assam, Himachal Pradesh, Maharashtra, and Orissa. All other states have participated in Green Revolution shifts in yields, productivity, and profitability to farmers only to a limited extent, that is, with regard only to particular crops or regions within a state. Moreover, there is a close connection between irrigation and profitability in Indian agriculture, which has "mainly risen in irrigated areas growing high value crops."[18]

In the Punjab, agriculturally the most advanced and best-documented Green Revolution case study, the technological changes associated with the Green Revolution have been consolidated among virtually all farmers in all parts of the state, particularly with regard to wheat, the state's principal crop. At the same time, this very consolidation means that the rates of increase in production, yields, and profitability of farm operations have peaked. Yield gains are expected to continue at a modest rate into the indefinite future, but no further dramatic breakthroughs are anticipated in this state.[19] Thus, the Punjab achievement stands in sharp contrast to agriculture in most of the rest of the country. The contrast, however, can be grounds for either despair or hope, the former arising from the still limited, regional- and crop-specific concentration of Green Revolution advances, the latter arising

---

[16] Farmer, "Perspectives on the 'Green Revolution'," p. 178.
[17] Sarthi Acharya, "Rates of Return in Indian Agriculture," *EPW*, xxvii, No. 3 (January 18, 1992), 112.
[18] Acharya, "Rates of Return in Indian Agriculture," p. 119.
[19] D. S. Sidhu and Derek Byerlee, "Technical Change and Wheat Productivity in Post-Green Revolution Punjab," *EPW*, xxvi, No. 51 (December 28, 1991), A-159 to A-166.

from the vast untapped potential for such advances in much of the rest of the country.

The focus on Green Revolution-associated changes in productivity and profitability should not distract attention from the principal persisting fact concerning Indian agriculture, which is that it remains for the most part, for most cultivators "of subsistence type using extensive manual/animal inputs."[20] Nor should one fail to note that in the less favored areas of the country, scarcity and even famine conditions are recurring phenomena.

The most controversial issues surrounding the Green Revolution concern its social consequences, that is, whether it has increased, reduced, or had no effect on social disparities. One radical Marxist critique of the Green Revolution argues that it has benefited mostly the big farmers, "rich peasants," *kulaks*, or capitalists. Moreover, so the argument goes, it has led to an increasing gap between rich and poor peasants and landless, to "differentiation of the peasantry," class polarization, "growing landlessness," and "agrarian revolts."[21] Most non-Marxist perspectives, however, see greater diffusion of the gains of the Green Revolution, while recognizing its "differential spread"[22] and while also recognizing that it is not a panacea or a substitute solution for other problems of agrarian order, industrial–agrarian relations, and economic development in India.

In general, it is known that HYVs respond most favorably to good water control, require greater capital inputs for seeds, fertilizer, pesticides, weedkillers, are more "labor intensive" also, and do not benefit especially from "economies of scale."[23] Clearly, therefore, bigger farmers are in a better position to take the risks involved in adopting such a technology, especially in the early stages, but it is also accessible to the small and middle peasantry. However, the following qualifications to these general observations need to be made.

The poorest farmers in the least favored rainfed paddy-growing regions simply do not have the resources to purchase and arrange timely supplies of needed inputs. In more favored areas, the small and marginal farmers do benefit from and will adopt technologies that

[20] Acharya, "Rates of Return in Indian Agriculture," p. 119.
[21] Farmer, "Perspectives on the 'Green Revolution'," pp. 187–188.
[22] Farmer, "Perspectives on the 'Green Revolution'," p. 189.
[23] Edison Dayal, "Regional Response to High Yield Varieties of Rice in India," *Singapore Journal of Tropical Geography*, IV, No. 2 (1983), 88, 90.

provide substantial increases in yield and profitability with small risks. However, in the rice-growing areas especially, the new technology often offers only marginal improvements that carry high risks. Only the bigger farmers can afford to experiment with and stand to gain from the adoption of such technological changes. These qualifications, however, do not mean that the technology is particularly limited to the rich.[24] It has spread among and benefited "many small farmers,"[25] but not in such a way as to change dramatically their structures of opportunities in life.

Those who have benefited most from the Green Revolution have also become ever more market-oriented and price conscious and, therefore, more oriented to influencing state policies on product and input prices and grain procurement. In the 1970s, non-party political movements among middle peasants and larger farmers demanding "remunerative prices" for farm products and other adjustments in the terms of trade between agriculture and the non-agricultural sectors acquired strong support in western U. P. and Maharashtra which threatened the local support bases of previously entrenched political parties and caused concern to national policy makers.[26] One consequence of these agitations was the inclusion in the 1980s of farmer representatives on the Commission for Agricultural Costs and Prices, which determines the procurement and support prices for agricultural products.[27] Despite this gesture, the cost–price structure for agricultural products has been such as to reduce significantly "the percentage of profit margin" even in the Punjab. Moreover, a Committee on Agricultural Policies and Programmes found in 1990 that there continued to be a great and widening disparity between "per capita farm and non-farm incomes" in favor of the latter.[28]

The principal rural beneficiaries of the government's price policies have been the "medium and large farmers" who have the "bulk of marketable surplus" while the rest remain squeezed between agricultural prices that barely cover their costs for inputs. This result would seem to support the argument that government policies for

[24] Farmer, "Perspectives on the 'Green Revolution'," pp. 189–190.

[25] M. Lipton, "The Technology, the System, and the Poor: The Case of the New Cereal Varieties," offprint, Hague, Institute of Social Studies, 1977, p. 123.

[26] V. M. Rao, "Fixing Agricultural Prices: Issues and Experiences," review of *Agricultural Price Policy in India* by A. S. Kahlon and D. S. Tyagi, Allied, 1989, in *EPW*, xxvii, No. 13 (March 28, 1992), 639.

[27] Rao, "Fixing Agricultural Prices," p. 641.

[28] Rao, "Fixing Agricultural Prices," p. 643.

agriculture are made to order for the dominant rural classes. However, the price structure is only partially designed to support farmers. It has also – in fact principally – been designed to sustain a public distribution system which continues to provide cheap food to urban consumers, including those who can afford to pay more, while also providing corrupt income to the bureaucracy which administers the procurement and distribution systems.[29] In effect, therefore, cheap food badly needed in the countryside is diverted to the cities while the rural poor continue to lack sufficient food at affordable prices to provide an adequate caloric intake throughout the year.

Why has the Green Revolution not lived up to its hopes? First, the orientation of the New Agricultural Strategy, as of the IADP before it, was toward increasing aggregate production in the country as a whole. That orientation, it has already been noted above, led to favoring the already favored areas and relying on the "progressive" farmers. Alternative orientations to solving rural poverty, making small farms viable, and eliminating landlessness were either rejected outright or included as secondary goals. Secondly, the basic capital-intensive industrialization orientation was retained. Agriculture, and especially rice cultivation, continued to be slighted in resource allocations. Third, it was generally believed that the new technology was exogenous and was adequate for the job. It had only to be imposed somehow upon a backward, illiterate, and resistant peasantry. All these assumptions turned out to be wrong or misinformed.

There have been technological factors as well that have limited the spread of the Green Revolution, particularly insofar as rice is concerned. The technological reasons for the failure of a Green Revolution in rice, emulating the authentic one for wheat, are numerous but they all reflect the greater ecological diversity of the rice-growing areas. Therefore, Farmer argues that the search for a single variety or a small number of varieties adaptable "to a wide range of environments" must give way to a search for varieties that are adaptable to local and seasonal variations.[30]

It is not, however, only more research and improved technology

---

[29] Rao, "Fixing Agricultural Prices," p. 644.
[30] B. H. Farmer, "The 'Green Revolution' in South Asian Ricefields: Environment and Production," *Journal of Development Studies*, xv (1979), 317. See also Barrie M. Morrison, "The Persistent Rural Crisis in Asia: A Shift in Conception," *Pacific Affairs*, lii, No. 4 (Winter, 1979–80), 631–646.

that are required but a new set of underlying assumptions, values, and goals. If the Green Revolution is to spread widely in India, values must shift from developing technology to increase the urban food supply as rapidly as possible while maintaining the lowest prices possible for urban consumers to another set of goals which would be oriented toward the needs of the poor and marginal food-producing peasantry. In the latter case, the goals would have to change toward helping the barely viable or nearly viable peasants to develop technologies suited to their local environments, which would enable them regularly to produce enough food to feed themselves and their families and to enter the market as well with a modest surplus or with a crop which provides them with enough cash to obtain the other basic needs of rural life.

The original emphasis on increasing aggregate production in the country as a whole by concentrating resources in favored areas and providing support to "progressive" farmers was justified by reference to the myth of impending Malthusian catastrophe. Unless food production was increased rapidly and dramatically, starvation loomed for the millions, especially for the poor urban consumers. This myth gained strong support in India especially at the time of the Bihar famine. Like all myths, it contained a partial truth, while ignoring other possibilities and potentials, notably the fact that agricultural production in India did somehow, even without adequate support and resources, manage to keep somewhat ahead of population increases and that a major diversion of resources to agricultural production activities might move the trend line upward more sharply. Like all myths also, it hid some harsh realities from public opinion, such as the greater prevalence of rural than urban poverty and the widespread rural malnutrition that would not be solved by policies that focused on aggregate production increases and channeling food supplies to cities and towns.

Among the most serious impediments to the adoption of an agricultural strategy designed to preserve the small farmers and increase their productivity are the implications of such a shift for overall economic development in India and the lack of dramatic results to be anticipated from such a shift. For, a truly agriculture-oriented economic development strategy would require both a reallocation of resources away from urban, industrial development and a willingness to accept a slow, gradual process of change instead of crash programs with dramatic results. It would require an overall policy to promote extensive, continuous, incremental changes designed to preserve the viability of small farmers and promote the viability of marginal farmers.

There is not much evidence, however, to suggest that Indian policy makers are prepared to initiate and sustain such a major shift in priorities. The pressures and prospects for change from the agricultural sector itself, therefore, need to be explored.

THE ABSENCE OF A REVOLUTIONARY TRADITION OR POTENTIAL IN THE INDIAN COUNTRYSIDE

In his work on *Agrarian Radicalism in South India*, Bouton has noted that there is a sharp division of opinion among scholars on the issue of peasant revolt and revolution in South Asia. At one extreme is Barrington Moore, who has argued that peasant revolts in India have been sporadic, ineffective, and, with rare exceptions such as Telangana in 1948, insubstantial. At the other extreme is Kathleen Gough, who compiled a list of seventy-seven peasant revolts from the end of Moghul rule to the post-Independence period to support her view that there is a vital revolutionary tradition in India and a basis for revolutionary peasant action in the present that has not been properly exploited by contemporary radical parties.[31] Interest in the bases for such action has intensified among both scholars and policy makers in India in recent years out of a concern (or hope) that technological changes in agriculture precipitated by the Green Revolution have intensified social disparities, caused depeasantization/proletarianization and class polarization, and therefore have created a new potential for peasant revolution.

The most significant aspect of Gough's long list is the support it provides for Stokes' argument that the most important peasant revolts

---

[31] Marshall M. Bouton, *Agrarian Radicalism in South Asia* (Princeton, N.J.: Princeton University Press, 1985), p. 6, and Kathleen Gough, "Indian Peasant Uprisings," *Bulletin of Concerned Asian Scholars*, VIII, No. 3 (July–September, 1976), 2–18. See also A. R. Desai (ed.), *Peasant Struggles in India* (Delhi: Oxford University Press, 1979) for a comprehensive survey of the major tribal and peasant revolts of the nineteenth and twentieth centuries.

have occurred among clan and caste communities.[32] It is especially noteworthy that the very largest proportion of revolts in Gough's list, somewhere between a third and a half, were either exclusively tribal in origin or contained a significant tribal element. Another very large proportion occurred among specific caste groups or religious minorities. Thus, most of the peasant revolts under British rule occurred either among tribals, who are a small minority in the subcontinent as a whole, have suffered from especially severe discrimination and oppression, and are often outside the basic structure of Hindu village agrarian organization, or among ethnic and religious groups whose solidarity could not be explained satisfactorily in class terms alone and did not extend beyond members of their own group.

When we come to the post-Independence period, the case for the existence of a tradition of "peasant uprisings which were primarily class struggles" is based upon seven episodes, all directed by one or another of the several Communist parties in India. Of these, the most famous and important are: "the Tebhaga uprising" in north Bengal in 1946; the Telangana insurrection in the former Hyderabad princely state in 1948; "peasant struggles involving land claims and harvest shares in 1966–71" in Andhra; the Naxalbari incidents in a subdivision of Darjeeling district in West Bengal in 1967, and some other "Naxalite" incidents in small areas in Andhra, Bihar, and elsewhere in India in 1969–70, of which the uprising in Srikakulam district of Andhra was the largest.[33]

Tebhaga

The Tebhaga movement was a movement principally of sharecroppers against the *jotedars* or rich peasants in four districts of north Bengal, demanding an increase in their share of the crop from one-half to two-thirds. The Tebhaga movement also drew strong support from tribal groups "who have a long tradition of militant struggle" in this area.[34] Alavi, however, argues that the principal role in this movement was played by middle peasants who also "supplemented their incomes

---

[32] Eric Stokes, *The Peasant and the Raj* (Cambridge: Cambridge University Press, 1978), ch. 12.
[33] Gough, "Indian Peasant Uprisings," p. 12.
[34] Hamza Alavi, "Peasants and Revolution," in Kathleen Gough and Hari P. Sharma (eds.), *Imperialism and Revolution in South Asia* (New York: Monthly Review Press, 1973), pp. 322–323.

by sharecropping."[35] There was, in addition, a communal element in this movement, though it did not dominate it. The non-tribal peasants were mostly Muslims, the *jotedars* both Hindu and Muslim. The Communist cadres were "mostly Hindu." Although the movement as a whole, therefore, cannot be characterized as a primarily communal uprising, it foundered on the communal issues that led to the creation of Pakistan. Since the peasant rising was in districts most of which went to East Pakistan in 1947, the Hindu Communist organizers left for India "and the movement was virtually decapitated."[36]

Telangana

The most widespread, violent, and long-lived peasant action in India since Independence – it actually began in 1946 – was the famous Telangana movement. In origins, the Telangana movement resembles other less extensive and even non-violent peasant actions that occurred during the nationalist movement and centered around eviction of tenants and "oppressive feudal extortions."[37] It swelled into a widespread, violent insurrectionary movement principally for three reasons. First, the response of the government of the princely state of Hyderabad was very harsh and violent. Second, the issue of the peasant movement quickly merged with the broader question of the merger of Hyderabad into the Indian Union and took on both communal and nationalist aspects. Although Muslim peasants also participated in the Telangana movement against the landlords, who in turn were both Hindus and Muslims, the more violent the movement became the more it looked like an action of Muslim armed forces defending the authority of a Muslim ruler and oppressing the rural population, whose vast majority were Hindus. Naturally, therefore, the Telangana movement also drew support from Hindus who favored the destruction of the Hyderabad state and its merger into the Indian Union. A third feature of the Telangana movement was the very fact that the Communists provided the organizational basis for it, which itself was made possible by the abstention of the Indian National Congress from nationalist mobilization in the princely states.

[35] Alavi, "Peasants and Revolution," p. 323.
[36] Alavi, "Peasants and Revolution," p. 325.
[37] Mohan Ram, "The Communist Movement in Andhra," in Paul R. Brass and Marcus Franda (eds.), *Radical Politics in South Asia* (Cambridge, MA: MIT Press, 1973), p. 295.

Naxalbari

The most famous incidents of radical agrarian protest in India since Telangana took place in the Naxalbari subdivision of Darjeeling district in West Bengal in 1967.[38] The ingredients which precipitated these incidents comprised the following: the existence of "a tea-plantation economy" with large tea estates, whose owners also controlled extensive paddy lands which were often allowed to lie fallow; a large population of tribal cultivators working on the tea plantations and covetous of these uncultivated lands; a history of tribal uprisings with indigenous leadership; local resentment in the 1960s over the failure to implement land reform legislation; a strong local Communist party organization, factionalized, but containing dedicated local revolutionary cadres. To these ingredients were added in March, 1967, the installation of the first Communist-led government in the state, placed soon after taking office in the uncomfortable position of having to confront a revolt led by members of a splinter group from the CPM itself.

The incidents which precipitated the violence associated with the name of Naxalbari occurred after a decision taken by one of the local Communist party factions to launch agitations against the landlords in possession of large illegal landholdings. Groups of tribal cultivators went round the area confronting the landlords and taking "possession," usually symbolically, of land which was considered to be illegally held. After the killing of a policeman on May 23, 1967, the movement became increasingly violent as the police began to take stronger counter-measures and the movement participants began to threaten terrorist actions after which a number of murders and incidents of arson occurred. The movement ended only after the Communist-led state government decided in July to take decisive action to suppress the revolt with a large police force and to jail its leaders.

Although the movement itself, therefore, was suppressed quickly and failed to achieve significant results, it spawned a new period of revolutionary romanticism in Indian politics in the 1970s. Numerous "Naxalite" incidents occurred, characterized principally by the tactics of terrorist violence against large landholders, in pockets in several

[38] The account here is largely derived from Marcus F. Franda, *Radical Politics in West Bengal* (Cambridge, MA: MIT Press, 1971), pp. 152–168.

areas of the country, notably in Bihar and Andhra. Some larger revolts also occurred which borrowed consciously from the Naxalite experience and sought the advice of the leaders of the original revolt in Naxalbari.

Srikakulam

A second major Naxalite movement, actually more violent and long-lived than the one in Naxalbari itself,[39] occurred in Srikakulam district of Andhra Pradesh in the late 1960s. The movement was centered in the forest areas of Srikakulam among the tribal population known as *girijans*. During British rule, many persons of the tribal population of Srikakulam had progressively lost land to non-tribals, had become indebted to moneylenders and reduced to debt bondage, had become proletarianized, and had become a largely impoverished population among whom "chronic hunger" was endemic.[40] Although the Andhra government passed new legislation after Independence to prevent alienation of tribal land to non-tribals and to reduce tribal debt and eliminate debt bondage, the laws were not implemented. Moreover, other post-Independence legislation to "protect" and develop forest lands led to "the steady loss of tribal access to forest land" and further "harassment and exploitation" of the tribal population "by private contractors, moneylenders, and government officials."[41]

The CPM had been involved in organizing the *girijans* in Srikakulam and neighbouring districts of Andhra since the late 1950s. Incidents of violence between the Communist-led Girijan Sangam workers and the police began in 1968.[42] In late 1968 and early 1969, the local Communist cadres adopted a "Maoist" line and affiliated with the All India Coordination Committee of Communist Revolutionaries, which "converted itself into the Communist Party of India (Marxist–Leninist) (CPML) on 22 April 1969."[43]

During 1969 and 1970, the revolutionaries pursued a line of "annihilation of the class enemy," which "in practice," according to Mohan Ram, "turned out to be nothing more than the murder of landlords

---

[39] Leslie J. Calman, *Protest in Democratic India: Authority's Response to Challenge* (Boulder, CO: Westview, 1985), p. 19.

[40] Calman, *Protest in Democratic India*, pp. 21–23.

[41] Calman, *Protest in Democratic India*, p. 31.

[42] Ram, "The Communist Movement in Andhra," p. 313.

[43] Ram, "The Communist Movement in Andhra," p. 314.

through conspiratorial squad actions, unrelated to mass movements or mass struggle."[44] The annihilation movement predictably was met with a massive police response from the Andhra government, whose forces succeeded in suppressing the movement and killing or arresting "all of the frontline leaders of the CPML" by mid-1970.[45]

The Andhra movement, 1969–1971

The fourth post-Independence peasant uprising that has found a place in radical lore in India was the movement led by a Maoist formation, the Andhra Pradesh Revolutionary Coordination Committee (APRCC), among tribal people in three districts of Andhra between 1969 and 1971. The movement began in April, 1969, with forcible occupation by tribals of "government wasteland, forest land, and landlords' farms."[46] Repression "by police and paramilitary forces" followed which, however, precipitated a broader movement that ultimately required intervention by the Indian Army in March, 1971.

Summary

The following features of the major post-Independence peasant uprisings are especially noteworthy. First, all involved tribal peoples. Second, the two most impressive movements, Tebhaga and Telangana, occurred at the time of Independence and became enmeshed in broader communal and nationalist trends which initially gave added force to them, but ultimately doomed them. Third, all the movements were localized to parts of districts within a single linguistic region. Fourth, Communist cadres took the lead in organizing these movements. Fifth, all the major movements preceded the Green Revolution. There has been no major movement anywhere in India since the Green Revolution for which even a *prima facie* case can be made that it arose as a consequence of technological changes in agriculture.

Post-Green Revolution incidents

There have, however, been numerous instances of highly localized confrontations, involving considerable violence and repression, which

---

[44] Ram, "The Communist Movement in Andhra," p. 315.
[45] Ram, "The Communist Movement in Andhra," p. 316.
[46] Mohan Ram, "The Communist Movement in India," in Gough, *Imperialism and Revolution in South Asia*, p. 354.

radical observers have attributed to changes brought about by the Green Revolution. Probably the most famous was the Kilvenmani incident in Thanjavur district in December, 1968, when forty-three women and children, families of striking Scheduled Caste farm laborers, were burned alive in their huts. The incident came at the end of "a chain of events" involving strikes for higher wages by local laborers at paddy harvest time, followed by the importation by the local landlords of outside laborers, which in turn precipitated clashes between local and imported laborers and the hiring by the landlords of *goondas* (hooligans) to rough up the laborers and their families. Rather than providing "evidence of a burgeoning revolutionary situation,"[47] the Kilvenmani incident demonstrates the ultimate power of the landlord groups even in a district which has a long history of mass, Communist-led, class action by the rural proletariat. Finally, although it occurred in an IADP district, neither the events that preceded it nor the incident itself can be easily used to demonstrate the precipitation of class warfare produced by Green Revolution technological changes. The incident in fact preceded the Green Revolution proper, which only came to Thanjavur in the years after 1968.

The strongest evidence against the argument that the Green Revolution has had a radicalizing effect is the relative absence of major peasant movements in the one area in India where there is no dispute that a Green Revolution has taken place that has altered significantly the older agrarian structure, namely, Punjab and Haryana. Indeed, in his review of the consequences for peasant and laborer class action in Punjab and Haryana up to 1977, Byres could find only one major incident of class confrontation between rich peasants and laborers in a single village in Ludhiana.[48]

[47] Terrence J. Byres, "The Political Economy of Technological Innovation in Indian Agriculture," in Robert S. Anderson *et al.*, *Science, Politics, and the Agricultural Revolution in Asia* (Boulder, CO: Westview Press, 1982), p. 57.

[48] Byres, "The Political Economy of Technological Innovation," p. 53. There is an argument that the Punjab movement of the 1980s, including the rise of Bhindranwale, is itself to be attributed to the inequalities produced by the Green Revolution, and particularly the dissatisfaction of "the ones left behind by it"; Iqbal Singh, *Punjab under Siege: A Critical Analysis* (New York: Allen, McMillan and Enderson, 1986), p. 130 and ch. 6. See also Sucha Singh Gill and K. C. Singhal, "The Punjab Problem: Its Historical Roots," *EPW*, xix, No. 14 (7 April, 1984), pp. 603–608, and Prakash Tandon, "Another Angle," *Seminar*, 294 (February, 1984), pp. 35–37 for analyses that include aspects of the Green Revolution in broader socio-economic explanations. My own view is that such explanations are at best remote causes for a movement which is better understood in terms of political and sectarian conflicts, as indicated above, ch. 6 and in Paul R. Brass, "The Punjab Crisis and the Unity of

In contrast to the situation in Punjab and Haryana, reports from Bihar, one of the regions in India least affected by the Green Revolution, have indicated a considerable increase in rural class confrontations and repressive violence by landlords and other dominant land controlling castes. Most of the violent incidents that have occurred in Bihar and the non-violent movements as well have special features that do not suggest either the beginnings of a broad revolutionary situation or a close connection with technological changes in agriculture.

In the late 1960s and early 1970s, there was a series of violent actions led by Naxalites as well as some non-violent movements among the peasantry in several places in Bihar. The Naxalite revolutionary activities were limited to a few pockets in scattered areas of the state and to isolated acts of terrorism in a number of places. Nor do the major incidents themselves provide support either for the view that there is a latent revolutionary movement in the Bihar countryside or that the incidents were a response to technological changes in agriculture. Rather, the following features seem more prominent in them: 1) heavy involvement of tribal populations; 2) situations of dispossession or other kinds of exploitation of peasants, sharecroppers, and laborers by large landlords and commercial farmers from outside the local area holding massive illegal farms; 3) location of several incidents in border and forest areas outside the centers of traditional, settled village agriculture; 4) a strong connection with unimplemented land reforms or outright violations of land reform laws.

There is one apparent exception to this pattern in Bihar. Throughout the 1970s up to the present, Bhojpur district, located in the most agriculturally advanced region of Bihar, served since the late nineteenth century by the Son Canal system and by the IADP and HYVP since the Green Revolution, has been a recurrent scene of agrarian violence. There is some evidence that agrarian violence in this district has been connected to attempts by landowners to increase their gains from the Green Revolution through reneging on or reducing traditional payments to attached laborers in the form of land and grain and through labor-displacing tractorization.

Like Thanjavur, Bhojpur has had a long history of agrarian struggles, going back to the Mutiny. A second feature in common with

India," in Atul Kohli (ed.), *India's Democracy: An Analysis of Changing State–Society Relations* (Princeton, N.J.: Princeton University Press, 1988).

Thanjavur district is the simultaneous existence of both a relatively high degree of concentration of landownership among rich peasants and former landlords with a high proportion of landless laborers in the total work force.

Mobilization of the poor and landless was launched after 1967 by outside Naxalite elements working with local Scheduled Caste leaders. As in Thanjavur, landlords and the local police hit back and beat and murdered Scheduled Caste and backward caste laborers in several villages. However, whereas laborers in Thanjavur, despite the Kilvenmani incident, have had powerful support from Communist party organizers and have benefited from ameliorative reforms introduced by the Tamil Nadu state government, it is the landlords who have emerged more powerfully in Bhojpur. With the complicity of the Congress state government and the local police, the local landlords became generally armed, well organized, and ready to let loose their "musclemen" upon landless laborers who caused trouble in any part of the district.

Insofar as the question of the relationship between technological change in agriculture and agrarian unrest is concerned, there are two principal similarities between Bhojpur and Thanjavur. First, Bhojpur district, when it was part of the district of Shahabad, was close to the top in growth rates of agricultural productivity between 1963–64 and 1971–72,[49] that is, in the years just before and just after the Green Revolution, which suggests an association between post-Green Revolution changes in Bhojpur and recent agrarian tensions. Second, however, the current phase of unrest began with the Naxalites in 1967 *before* any significant Green Revolution changes occurred in Bhojpur.

Conclusion

The above review of major peasant movements in India since Independence suggests the following general conclusions concerning their extent, the conditions for their occurrence, and the reasons why they have not been more common, more sustained, and more widespread.

1. There has been no peasant revolt in India since 1948 that has

[49] Calculated from Government of India, Ministry of Agriculture, Directorate of Economics and Statistics, *Bulletin on Rice Statistics in India (District-Wise)* (Delhi: Controller of Publications, 1974).

been as prolonged and widespread as the one in Telangana. The Telangana revolt itself was regionally confined.

2. There have been only two periods of sustained revolutionary activity in India since Independence. The first was the time of Independence itself when there were two major movements in progress in different parts of the country at approximately the same time: Tebhaga in Bengal and Telangana in Andhra.[50] The second was the post-Naxalbari period from 1967 to the early 1970s when a number of separate movements and incidents occurred in different parts of the country, notably in Naxalbari itself, in Srikakulam, in other Andhra districts, and in pockets in Bihar.

3. The existence of an organized Communist movement in a locality has been one of the more important factors in sustaining peasant and tribal uprisings. The uneven distribution of the organizational strength of the Communist and other radical parties in India is, therefore, another factor, along with their internal divisions on strategy and tactics, that have limited the extent of the peasant movements that have been guided by them.

4. However, it is clear that an even more significant limitation on peasant rebellions in India has been the fact that the predominant leaderships of both leading Communist parties in most of the post-Independence period have been reformist, oriented to parliamentary and electoral politics rather than toward revolutionary action.

5. It is evident that the majority of the cases of peasant unrest since Independence – and a very large proportion of all instances of such unrest in modern Indian history – have either been nearly exclusively tribal-based or have "involved a large component of tribal people."[51] It is clear why tribals are so prone to revolt. They are among the most unfairly treated groups in India. They have suffered loss of land, loss of access to forest resources, and increasing indebtedness leading to debt bondage. The miseries they have suffered affect most members of their groups. The tribal groups themselves are in any case more internally cohesive and less internally differentiated than village societies in predominantly Hindu India. Most important, their victimizers

---

[50] A third movement, in part of the former princely state of Travancore, also was in progress at this time, in which urban and rural wage demands were merged with a movement led by the CPI to thwart efforts of the prince to establish Travancore as an independent state; see Sumit Sarkar, *Modern India: 1885–1947* (Madras: Macmillan, 1983), pp. 441–442.

[51] Gough, "Indian Peasant Uprisings,"p. 12.

are invariably aliens, usually Hindus originally from the plains. Finally, the tribals find no recourse from government, which adds to their frustrations by passing laws to aid them that are not implemented. Indeed, government officers at the local level tend rather to be seen and to behave as their oppressors, harassing them, extracting corrupt income from them, and cooperating and socializing with their exploiters, the landlords and moneylenders to whom they are indebted.

6. Aside from predominantly tribal revolts, the other principal source of violent agrarian unrest is the discontent of landless laborers in some areas of India. However, such discontent has led to revolts or violent confrontations only under special circumstances.

7. The power of the Indian state and its armed police forces also needs to be noted. Even if the basis existed for the spread of violent agrarian movements from one district to another in India, it would not be permitted by the authorities, who have never hesitated to meet local violent uprisings with overwhelming force. Alleged "Naxalites" were hunted and killed by the police throughout the 1970s. In West Bengal, between 1974 and 1977, the Congress government with the aid of the armed forces as well as the police, virtually suspended the civil liberties of all suspected Naxalites who were systematically rooted out, imprisoned, and executed arbitrarily in a regime of "state-sponsored terrorism."[52] In several districts of Andhra, where some tribals have become more "assertive" and politically conscious, killings, massacres, and arson perpetrated against tribals by land-owning caste Hindus have been taking place with some frequency in recent years. In contrast, state action against caste Hindus accused of these acts has been minimal, the police are usually absent or ignore their actions, and state police power comes down most heavily against the tribals who participate in protest movements and agitations.[53] There is, therefore, no "vacuum of power"[54] in the Indian countryside such as existed in China in the 1930s and 1940s or in Vietnam with the withdrawal of French colonial administration.

8. It is clear that agrarian unrest in India is very much the excep-

[52] Atul Kohli, *Democracy and Discontent: India's Growing Crisis of Governability* (Cambridge: Cambridge University Press, 1990), p. 283.

[53] K. Balagopal, "Post-Chunder and Other Chunders," *EPW*, xxvi, No. 42 (October 19, 1991), 2399–2405.

[54] Calman, *Protest in Democratic India*, p. 10.

tion rather than the norm and that it is the extraordinary stability of agrarian society in the face of caste divisions, considerable inequalities, and pervasive poverty that requires explanation.

CASTE AND CLASS IN THE INDIAN COUNTRYSIDE

Since Independence, debate has raged, particularly among Marxist economists, concerning whether or not there is now a fairly uniform hegemonic class of rich farmers who are the new "lords of the land" virtually everywhere in India.

The rise of this new class has been associated particularly with three sets of events. The first is the land reforms adopted in nearly all parts of the country, which abolished the tax-farming system, but did not involve effective land ceilings with land redistribution, thus enhancing the position of the groups with land below the big ex-landlords. The second set of events were various government policies adopted by the state governments, which themselves came to be largely controlled by persons from the dominant peasant castes, such as price supports, easy credit, and subsidized inputs of all sorts, which favored the peasantry. The third was the technological changes associated with the Green Revolution which, it is argued, benefited principally the members of this new class and increased substantially the profitability of their farm operations.

This new class of rich farmers is generally characterized not only as capitalist, but as a politically dominant class as well. Its dominance is evidenced and expressed in numerous forms: through its control of local institutions of government and administration, such as the district boards, the *panchayats*, the cane unions or cooperatives, the managing boards of educational institutions, and the like, all of which assure its members of continued preferential access to economic resources and to education; through its organization into caste *senas* or armies which suppress or repress any signs of revolt or even unwillingness on the part of laborers to work at the desired low wages for the *kisans* (peasant cultivators) and *maliks* (owners); through its brutality in such notorious places as Kilvenmani in Tamil Nadu and several places in Bihar, where rebellious or recalcitrant laborers and their families were murdered by irate and vengeful land-owners; and through their continued control of most state governments in India.

This widespread attempt to identify a universal hegemonic rural capitalist, exploiting class in India, which has become virtually an accepted orthodoxy among both Indian and foreign political economists, suffers from several deficiences. These include oversimplification, elevation of the exceptional to the general, and a distorted view of the benefits which the peasants are said to receive from their alleged partial control of the Indian state.

Oversimplification occurs in the identification of the rich farmer or *kulak* class itself. While there are certainly many big peasants in India now who fit the description of capitalist farmer, if not *kulak*, most peasants from the dominant castes are not for the most part either labor-exploiting or capitalist in the sense of treating their land and its produce *primarily* as commodities for exchange and investment. Most continue to depend on family and animal power for the bulk of their labor requirements and operate farms whose produce both satisfies considerable subsistence requirements as well as being sold in the market. Only a minority have sufficient landholdings in relation to the number of dependents who must be fed from the produce of their lands to enable them to orient their production primarily for sale in the market.

Elevation of the exceptional to the general includes extending the range of the Green Revolution and its consequences far beyond the limited regions, crops, and groups in the country who have benefited from it to the country as a whole, which allows one to argue that there is a rural hegemonic capitalist class all over the country which has benefited from it. While the Green Revolution has led to the development of programs, such as input subsidies, which apply throughout the country and benefit the larger farmers everywhere, their impact is much more substantial in the Green Revolution areas proper. Moreover, in those areas where the Green Revolution has had *less* effect, the consequences of the extension of benefits such as input subsidies, are more likely to divide the landed castes in struggles for differential access to these benefits than to create a rural hegemonic class united against the lower classes.

Finally, the benefits which peasants have received from the Indian state are exaggerated. As large-scale irrigation projects and other development benefits in the countryside became available, as the Green Revolution in some parts of the country made agricultural operations more profitable, and as the state extended credit and subsidies to the farmers, planners and urban intellectuals in New Delhi argued that the landowning cultivators, especially the rich peasants, were gaining vast benefits for which they paid virtually nothing in taxes. These observers chose to ignore the facts that most inputs remained scarce, that the supplies of water, electricity, credit, diesel, and fertilizers were highly irregular, and that the peasants generally had to pay bribes to the operators of canals and tubewells, to the bankers for credit, and to the officers for every service provided by government, all of which constitute a very considerable financial burden on the farmers. The advantages to the peasantry even of institutional credit as opposed to resort to traditional moneylenders also may be exaggerated.[55]

What then are the realities of caste, class, and power in the Indian countryside? The first is that there are, indeed, sets of landed castes in every region of India who control most of the land and other economic resources and who are also politically powerful. The second is that these caste groups constitute politically solidary groups in relation to other castes, whether of elite, lower, or untouchable status. The third is that where there is a diversity of land-controlling castes, these relatively solidary caste groups are in strong competition with each other for favored access to scarce resources and political power. The fourth is that the landless and wage laborers at the bottom of the caste Hindu hierarchy are relatively powerless. The untouchable castes who form the largest numbers of the landless laborers live in separated hamlets where they and their families are vulnerable to attack by the landed caste men and their *goondas*.

In routine politics, the low castes who form the bulk of the landless are coopted by the factional and party leaders of the dominant castes in

[55] See, for example, the argument of Subrata Ghatak in *Rural Money Markets in India* (Delhi: Macmillan, 1976), p. 102, that interest rates charged by moneylenders are not as high as has commonly been assumed. When one weighs the ease of getting loans from the moneylender against the difficulties of gaining access to institutional credit, the difference between the effective rates of interests charged by the moneylenders, on the one hand, and the banks and cooperatives, on the other, appears less significant. As with most government policies for agriculture, the rich farmers get around these difficulties more easily than the ordinary peasants, but both are too often lumped by critics of the Green Revolution and its consequences as "rich peasants" benefiting from easy credit at low interest rates.

village, district, and state politics. When they attempt to mobilize for political agitations for higher wages against the landed castes, however, they generally meet strong resistance and their movements usually fail, except in states such as Kerala and West Bengal at times when the ruling Communist parties there support their demands. Since low caste movements tend to be local, it is usually sufficient for the members of one of the dominant castes immediately threatened by such movements to take action against the low castes without seeking any broader unity.

One strong element in the Marxist argument is that the various forces of change that have been in operation in India since Independence, particularly land reforms which benefited the so-called *kulaks* and the Green Revolution, have created class contradictions in the form of increasing inequalities between the rich farmers and the poorest, "depeasantization" and proletarianization of the marginal farmers, fundamental conflicts of interest between them and the rich farmers, and enhanced class consciousness on both sides tending toward class polarization which is preparing the ground for a major class struggle over land.[56] In fact, this scenario is far-fetched. The conflicts are greatest not in the Green Revolution areas, but in the more backward areas and the struggles are over wages not over land.

In fact, the landless and the poor are pawns both in the power struggles of the landed castes and in the intellectual exercises of the Marxist elites. Rather than seeing the bulk of the land-controlling castes as themselves in need of support through an agriculture-oriented plan with an emphasis on research, extension, and improved technology, they are all portrayed as *kulaks* or dominated by *kulaks* repressing and brutalizing the poor and landless below them. The lumping together of all the landed castes in India into a united body under the hegemony of its leading segments, the so-called *kulak*, reflects a deep anti-peasant bias rather than the realities of the Indian countryside.

In most states, particularly in north India, the Congress adopted the political strategy of aligning with the big farmers, the elite proprietary castes, and the poor, squeezing the bulk of the peasantry in the middle and denying them access to party nominations and local positions of power. The rise of the Lok Dal and recently of the Janata Dal in north

[56] Byres, "The Political Economy of Technological Innovation," pp. 39–46.

India have been largely consequences of that strategy, which drew the middle peasantry to these parties as alternatives to the Congress. The Communist parties – unlike many Marxist theoreticians – recognizing in fact the absence of class polarization in the countryside and the dangers of antagonizing the bulk of the peasantry, have attempted to counter the Congress strategy by mobilizing the poor and the middle segments of the peasantry together in pursuit of reformist goals of ameliorating the living conditions and wages of the landless and gaining secure rights for tenants and sharecroppers, without attacking fundamentally the control of the landed castes over their land. In practice, the Communist parties seek the support even of the bigger peasants.

Thus, the existence of similar structures of local power in most parts of India, based upon the predominance of the traditional land-controlling castes of elite and middle status, has consequences quite different from those that might be expected to flow from the Marxist notions of rich peasant hegemony and class polarization. On the contrary, one consequence has been the organization of political conflicts primarily along the lines of competition *among* land-controlling castes more than between the latter and the poor and landless. Second, political organization of the poor against the landed castes is, therefore, a risky enterprise even for the radical left parties because no stable power base can be built upon the poor and landless. Finally, it follows also that fundamental change in the agrarian order is not likely to come in the form of mass revolutionary action from below.

CHAPTER 10

CONCLUSION: PROBLEMS AND PROSPECTS

THE PROBLEM OF THE PERSISTENCE OF THE PARLIAMENTARY SYSTEM

India is virtually unique among contemporary post-colonial countries in having functioned since Independence, with the exception of the Emergency, with a parliamentary system modeled on the British form of government. India's parliamentary system has evolved from one in which the Cabinet and the Prime Minister were dominant and the President was a figurehead – though potentially important – into a form of prime ministerial government, in which both the Parliament and the Cabinet play a secondary role. The specific role of each Prime Minister and the relationship between the Prime Minister and other central government institutions and forces has varied somewhat, but one can also see an evolution over the past forty-five years. Nehru's period was one of prime ministerial government in which the Cabinet played an important role as well and Parliament was a place where opinions were expressed but little real power was exercised. Under Shastri, the influence of the Cabinet declined and that of the Prime Minister's Secretariat increased, a trend which continued under Mrs. Gandhi. However, there was a further shift under Mrs. Gandhi's leadership away from reliance upon any of the formal channels of authority in the system to dependency upon a narrow clique of personal advisers accountable only to the Prime Minister herself. Rajiv Gandhi continued his mother's pattern so that, in effect, prime ministerial government moved a further step toward a form of personal authority in which succession was dynastic and rulership was conducted with the counsel of a virtual princely court, and in which both Cabinet and senior bureaucrats were reduced in importance.

During the Janata period, an entirely different pattern, based on a form of coalition politics, developed in which the Prime Minister was only *primus inter pares* in a divided government, which ultimately fell in a Parliament that came to reflect the divisions within the Cabinet

336

and for a brief period exercised indirectly its ultimate power of granting or withholding confidence in the government of the day. That pattern was repeated in the rise and fall of the National Front government of V. P. Singh. The Congress government of Prime Minister P. V. Narasimha Rao, with his precarious hold upon a divided cabinet, is more similar to the previous non-Congress coalitions than to any previous Congress government.

Behind the adopted form of British prime ministerial government, therefore, there lie two indigenous adaptations: the patrimonial system of the Nehru family – predominant until the termination of the ruling dynasty by Rajiv Gandhi's assassination in May, 1991 – and the politics of personal ambition, personal conflict, and political opportunism of the Janata and National Front coalitions. Each of these indigenous adaptations is inherently unstable for the one depended upon the fate of a family and on the fragilities of personal leadership in general, while the second offers the prospect of the disintegration of any central authority in the system.

India's federal parliamentary system also presents some peculiarities and adaptations of a well-known form of government. Although politics in India are more regionalized than in any other federal polity in the world, reflecting the unrivaled cultural diversity of the country, the system has more unitary features than most federal systems including especially that of the United States. Residuary powers in the system rest with the Center, not with the states and the people. Virtually unique to India's federal system, moreover, has been the institution of President's Rule which allows the Center, either with or without the simultaneous exercise of constitutionally sanctioned emergency powers, to impose a unitary form of government upon a single state, a number of states, or the entire country.

Structurally, as in most federal systems, the institutions of the central government have been replicated in each state, with the governor playing the role of head of state and the chief minister the head of government, with a cabinet responsible to a popularly elected legislative assembly. In practice, however, state politics and government have functioned entirely differently from the Center and have evolved in different directions. The governors have become pliable instruments of central intervention in state politics, the state legislatures have been generally fragmented, unstable, and so opportunistically motivated that few governments can stay in power if a state legislature is allowed to remain in session for more than a few weeks. Consequently, once a chief minister has been appointed, the leader, for the sake of remaining in power, sees to it that the legislature meets as infrequently as possible. Much, often most, state legislation is in fact passed by ordinance rather than by the state legislative assemblies.

Though their positions are often unstable, the post of chief minister or any ministerial position in a state government is highly coveted, partly for conventional reasons of prestige and power, but increasingly because of the opportunities provided for the distribution of patronage and the acquisition of corrupt income. It is hardly surprising, therefore, that the performance of state governments, though it varies from state to state and from time to time within each state, has generally been poor.

In the Nehru period, there were some states which developed a sort of chief ministerial form of government comparable to the prime ministerial pattern at the Center, while other states developed more in the direction of an unstable factional and coalition politics of personal ambition, patronage, and corruption. During Mrs. Gandhi's period, most of the states in which the Congress ruled lost their autonomy and came directly under the control of the central leadership even without the use of President's Rule. However, underlying the overall pattern of Congress dominance in the states and increasing central control over the state governments was an alternative type of politics, involving the assertion of regional political and social forces and identities. Those tendencies have become increasingly powerful during the past decade. Where the central government has become directly involved in an effort to maintain Congress control and prevent the regionalization of politics, there has been instability and violence, most notably in the Punjab, in Assam, and at times in Kashmir. Where it has allowed or been unable to prevent the assertion of regional political forces and identities, the Congress has been displaced as the ruling party, as in West Bengal by the CPM and in Tamil Nadu by the AIADMK, among other cases.

While the struggles for power at the Center and between regionalizing and centralizing forces have produced singular adaptations of both parliamentarism and federalism in India, they have also created tensions that have from time to time aroused a desire among some of the participants to change the system to ensure continuity and authority at the Center and the primacy of the central government in relation to the states. Indeed, a general feeling has developed during the past two decades that the present system of parliamentary government is not working well. The apparent stability of leadership in the Nehru family at the head of the system did not prevent a widespread loss of authority in the country, manifested in its most extreme forms in increased disorder and violence in the countryside and new secessionist threats in the Punjab, Kashmir, and in the northeastern region of the country. Widespread corruption has undermined the legitimacy of all institutions: including the legislatures, whose members are often bought and sold in struggles for the votes necessary to sustain or bring down a government; the cabinets, whose ministers use their positions to aggrandize themselves; and the bureaucracy, whose members enrich themselves at the cost of the public and the health of the economy.

Although India has made considerable progress in economic development, particularly in the indigenous production of goods and services that were completely lacking at Independence, there is also a perception among many leaders of the country that the pace of economic development has been too slow to satisfy their desires for the rapid emergence of India as a modern, industrialized military power. Many leaders in politics, in the universities, and in business also feel that the pace of socio-economic change has been too slow, that India remains too agrarian, its population too illiterate, its social customs too backward. All these tendencies and ideas have converged in a current of opinion which favors the adoption of a new form of government of a presidential type which would enhance still further the authority of the central leaders and the Union government to restore order in troubled areas of the country, to eliminate corruption, and to increase the pace of economic and social change.

The presidential system most widely favored is not the American type, but the French system as it functioned in the Gaullist period, with its strong executive and unitary pattern of government. Although members of Mrs. Gandhi's government from time to time attempted to precipitate some public discussion of a shift toward a presidential regime – notably during the Emergency and again in 1984 – no sustained discussion of such an alternative has as yet taken place nor has a broad consensus developed in the country. The very problems which have produced a desire for stronger central authority have also produced a country-tendency in the form of demands for greater regional autonomy from several states and in somewhat more feeble, but recurrent proposals from politicians who continue to draw inspiration from the Gandhian tradition for greater decentralization of institutions in India down to the district and village level as well. In these recurring debates concerning the desirability of retaining or modifying the parliamentary system, there is a tacit recognition of the persistence of some structural problems in governing the country, in maintaining its unity, and in averting a descent into anomie, violence, and disintegration.

THE PROBLEM OF ESTABLISHING A STABLE STRUCTURE OF NATIONAL POWER: PARTIES, POLITICS, AND ELECTIONS

The Congress was the dominant, ruling party at the Center from Independence until 1977. However, its dominance was always somewhat deceptive, less secure than it often appeared. Even during the Nehru period, the Congress faced persistent problems in maintaining its dominance in and control over the several states. Moreover, in 1969, the Congress itself split nationwide, leading to speculation and fear on the part of its leaders that its power at the Center would soon be lost as well. Although Mrs. Gandhi succeeded on the face of things in reestablishing the overwhelming dominance of the Congress in the country and in virtually all the states by 1972, she knew very well that dominance was not secure in the states and that Congress power at the Center was always threatened by the potential disintegration of the party in important states in the Union.

Within two years of her overwhelming victories in 1971–72 in the parliamentary and legislative assembly elections, Mrs. Gandhi was confronted with widespread mass demonstrations against her party leaders in the states of Gujarat and Bihar, which caused her and other Congress leaders to fear loss of power in the country as a whole. When her own election was overturned by the judgment of the Allahabad High Court in 1975, Mrs. Gandhi was faced with the imminent prospect of loss of power, which she met with the imposition of the

Emergency regime in 1975. Although the imposition of the Emergency preserved her in power temporarily, the public reaction to various excesses committed by her government caused an unprecedented revulsion against Congress rule in north India that brought the Congress down and out of power in Delhi for the first time since Independence.

The Janata party, which displaced the Congress from power in 1977, itself proved unable to govern effectively and its disintegration in 1979 prepared the way for the return of Mrs. Gandhi and the Congress to power in the 1980 elections. By 1984, an accumulation of discontents with the ruling party, particularly focusing on the events in the Punjab, once again had threatened the power of the Congress to such an extent that Mrs. Gandhi delayed until virtually the eleventh hour the calling of the parliamentary elections, which she had not yet done when she was herself assassinated on October 31, 1984. The assassination and the Punjab crisis now converged in a new way to build support behind the new leader, Rajiv Gandhi, and the Congress won an unprecedented 80 percent majority in the parliamentary elections held in December, 1984.

Rajiv Gandhi's victory notwithstanding, it was evident that the political system had become more competitive at the national level with the central leadership of the Congress aware that power could be lost at the Center under certain conditions. Those conditions included the disintegration of the Congress and the rise of opposition forces within particular states, the occurrence of an incident or incidents that arouse widespread discontent in north India, such as the sterilization campaign during the Emergency and the Punjab crisis in the early 1980s, and the development of unity among the important non-Congress parties.

All these factors have since converged to weaken the Congress still further and to make the struggle for power at the Center more competitive than ever. The Bofors defense procurement corruption scandal and Muslim discontent in north India in the aftermath of major communal killings in Bhagalpur in Bihar and in connection with the movement to remove the mosque at Ayodhya provided the mobilizing bases while opposition alliances and electoral adjustments provided the organizational bases for the National Front victory over the Congress in 1989. The backward castes reservation issue and the intensification by the VHP and the BJP of the Ram Janmabhumi movement provided the issues which framed the 1991 election campaign, but opposition disunity and sympathy for the Congress in the aftermath of Rajiv Gandhi's assassination made it possible for the Congress to return to power with a minority government headed by P. V. Narasimha Rao. In the wake of the destruction of the mosque at Ayodhya and its association with a rising wave of Hindu nationalism in the north, extending also to other parts of the country, a reorganization of the entire basis of the party system and political practices appears imminent. All the secular political parties are in decline or disarray, factionalized and led by either incompetent or opportunist politicians while the BJP retains discipline and unity and is poised to ride the wave of Hindu nationalism to power at the Center.

Congress dominance has always been less secure in the states than at the Center, though the Congress under Nehru succeeded – after some initial problems in a few states – after Independence in establishing its preeminence in every state in the Union except Kerala until 1967. Between 1967 and 1972, however, when the Congress lost power in half the Indian states, a period of instability and coalition politics ensued in many states. Moreover, the Congress never regained ground lost during that period in some states such as West Bengal and Tamil Nadu. The delinking by Mrs. Gandhi of parliamentary and state legislative assembly elections in 1971 was designed both to free her from dependence on state party bosses for success in the parliamentary elections and to separate the parliamentary elections in general from the unstable conditions prevailing in many states. With the success of that strategy in 1971, the further pattern was developed of holding state assembly elections after the parliamentary elections to reinforce and stabilize a victory at the Center.

The new pattern introduced initially by Mrs. Gandhi has had three major results. The first was the destruction of the power of state party bosses in the Congress and the increased dependence of the Congress in the states upon the central leadership of the party and its ability to win national elections. The second was the isolation of regional political forces within the states, in some cases including specific alliances between the Congress and a regional party such as the AIADMK in which the Congress agreed to give up power in the state for the sake of the regional party's support in the parliamentary elections. The third consequence was a general nationalization of politics and political issues with a corresponding increased focus on power at the Center. Paradoxically, the increasing focus on power at the Center has been accompanied simultaneously by strong trends toward the regionalization of state politics and party systems.

The tension between these nationalizing and regionalizing tendencies in the post-Nehru period and especially since the delinking of parliamentary and legislative assembly elections in 1971, brought into being a new cycle of consolidation and disintegration of national power, which reproduces itself in a series of five steps. Each cycle begins with the call for parliamentary elections either by the ruling party or, as in 1979 and 1990, as a consequence of the disintegration of the governing coalition. Between 1971 and 1984, every parliamentary election led to a decisive result in favor of one party or another, that is, in favor either of the Congress or the Janata coalition in 1977. If the Congress won, it was clear who would be the new Prime Minister, for the party went to the country in each election with no doubts about its leadership. In the Janata and National Front cases, however, the electoral victories were followed by factional struggles over the selection of the Prime Minister. The installation of a Prime Minister by either of these methods concluded the second stage of the cycle. The new Prime Minister then introduced the third step, which was the dismissal of most state governments controlled by the opposition and the holding of fresh state legislative assembly elections, which invariably led to the victory of the ruling party or its allies in the several states. Step four involved the selection, with or without some struggle, of the chief ministers of the states in which elections had just been held. At this very point, when power was consolidated in Delhi and in nearly all the states, the fifth step in the cycle occured, namely, the beginning of a new cycle as a consequence of the disintegration of power in state after state either through factionalism in the Congress or through inter-party struggles in the non-Congress coalitions.

Herein has lain the great political dilemma at the heart of Indian politics, which has often caused national political leaders to long for the stability of a presidential system with fixed terms in office in a more centralized state. That dilemma is simply that it is impossible in such a diverse country within the framework of a federal

343

parliamentary system to maintain a stable structure of national power for long. It is an extremely difficult, prolonged, and absorbing task to build national power in the country and it begins to disintegrate at the very point when it appears to have been consolidated. The task is so absorbing that, even with the best will in the world, it is impossible for the national leaders to focus their attentions on the goals of economic development and the fulfillment of the basic needs of the people. Indeed, those goals themselves must be subordinated to the imperative need of maintaining the power so laboriously constructed.

At this fifth stage, therefore, the central leadership of the country faces an agonizing choice: either permit the disintegration of the power so painstakingly built up and face the possible loss of power in the next elections or even earlier, or impose an Emergency regime or use President's Rule and other extreme constitutional but politically ruthless measures to remain in power. At this point also, the third alternative must enter the minds of the leaders, namely, to try to change the system altogether to a presidential type. Thus, authoritarian solutions or alternative regimes as a possible resolution to the central political dilemma of Indian politics remain always lurking in the background and make it impossible to say, even 45 years after Independence, that a stable parliamentary regime of the Westminster type has been established in India.

This dilemma at the heart of Indian politics, surrounding the problems of building and maintaining a stable structure of national power, had to be faced by both Nehru and his successors, though they handled it differently. Under Nehru's leadership, the Government of India adopted a system of centralized economic planning which required centralized decision making and uniform national policies for optimal implementation. Nehru, however, was unwilling or unable to impose a centralized system of political control and preferred instead to attempt to bring along with him the powerful but independent-minded chief ministers who, he hoped, would support his policies for economic development if he supported them politically, or left them alone in their home states.

Under Mrs. Gandhi's leadership, quite in contrast, the struggle for political power at the Center became primary and centralized economic development planning, increasingly subordinated to political goals, began to disintegrate.[1] Plans and schemes such as the anti-poverty programs, however noble their intentions, were integrated more into designs for centralized political control than into a design for a new national economic order.

Since 1984, the Indian polity has been facing its second crisis of succession. The smooth transition to Rajiv Gandhi after Mrs. Gandhi's assassination and the overwhelming victory of the Congress in the election which followed provided only a brief respite before the beginning of the new succession crisis, which this time is a crisis of the system as a whole. The BJP now offers the country a new political order, ideology, and political practices. It proposes to replace the Congress as the dominant party, its ideology of secular nationalism with Hindu nationalism, its opportunistic, factional, and socially divisive political practices with idealism, united leadership, and social unity in a consolidated, politically dominant Hindu community in which caste divisions are overcome and minorities are shown their subordinate place.

However, the BJP's drive for power must confront three massive obstacles. The first is the persisting fragmentation – linguistically, socially, and in religious practices – of the Hindu community its leaders seek to unify. The second is the regionalizing political tendencies evident during the past twenty years. The third is the resurrection by its own efforts of a polarized divide between Hindus and Muslims. These three tendencies may not be sufficient to prevent the rise to power of the BJP at the Center for a time, but they will work against its consolidation as a new hegemonic force in the Indian political order. The BJP's militant tactics are likely also to precipitate new militant and terrorist movements among Muslims and other religious and regional minority groups which will threaten the very preservation of the Indian Union, whose unity its leaders claim to cherish above all.

THE PROBLEM OF MAINTAINING THE UNITY OF THE COUNTRY

Among the strongest reasons for the predominant consensus among

[1] The formulation of the argument in the previous two paragraphs was stimulated by the comments of an anonymous reader.

345

the top leaders of the country in favor of a strong centralized state has been not only the fear of losing power in Delhi but of the disintegration of all authority in Delhi and, therefore, of the unity of the country itself. Although a sense of the fragility of Indian unity has always been present among Indian political leaders in modern times, it was strongly reinforced by the bitter experience of partition of the country in 1947. For that reason, the national leaders have always moved cautiously and reluctantly in handling regional, linguistic, communal, and other ethnic conflicts which have developed in the post-Independence period.

Since Independence, the central leadership has, nevertheless, confronted several major challenges to the unity of the country with skill and success. These have included the integration of some 562 semi-autonomous princely states into the Indian Union in the years immediately after Independence, the linguistic reorganization of states, the resolution of the official language controversy, and the granting of partial official status in many states to minority languages, including Urdu among others. The resolution of most of these conflicts by the Center has been pluralist in form. Most of the major languages of India now have a federal unit – or units in the case of Hindi – in which their language is dominant and is the official language of the state or states. Bilingualism has become entrenched at the Center, with some multilingual features in some respects as well.

On the other hand, none of the resolutions has resolved all relevant problems. The integration of the princely states left Kashmir divided and three wars with Pakistan have been fought in which the unresolved international status of Kashmir figured. In the late 1980s and early 1990s, the Government of India was faced with a full-fledged secessionist movement with considerable popular support in this state and the routine political process was suspended and replaced by an all-out and brutal internal war. Within the linguistically reorganized states, minorities and minority language speakers sometimes experience varying degrees of discrimination. Demands for greater regional autonomy, at times bordering on secessionism, have emerged from time to time in many states besides Kashmir, most especially in the late 1980s and early 1990s, in Punjab and Assam.

Hindu–Muslim relations have remained tense and suspicion-ridden since Independence. Communal riots have been persistent, especially in north India, and have become an institutionalized feature in some towns in the north. In recent years, there has been an increasing polarization of communal hostilities and feelings and a great deepening of distrust between members of the two communities. The current state of Hindu–Muslim relations, exacerbated by the crisis at Ayodhya, the demolition of the Babari Masjid, the ghastly slaughter of several thousand persons, mostly Muslims, in cities and towns throughout northern and western India, is worse than at any time since 1947. The intensification and brutalization of Hindu nationalism under the RSS family of organizations, largely responsible for these events, constitute the gravest danger to the future of Indian unity, while those responsible proclaim the latter to be their most sacred trust.

Migrant problems also have intensified and added a new dimension to ethnic hostilities in some parts of the country, particularly in major cities and in several regions of the country where migrants have taken jobs desired by local residents. The problems in Assam have been the most serious in this regard, where migrants from neighboring states and from Bangladesh have come in large numbers and threatened both the dominance of the Assamese people in the region they consider their own and the displacement of tribal peoples from their lands. Agitations and violent incidents were widespread in the 1980s and 1990s on these issues. The demands of Assamese leaders for the removal of large numbers of foreign migrants from the electoral rolls were partly conceded by Rajiv Gandhi's government in an accord with the Asom Gana Parishad, which restored peace and parliamentary politics to that state in 1985. However, like most of Rajiv Gandhi's accords, its terms were not implemented and the peace of Assam was again shattered by a splinter militant force of former AGP and AASU leaders demanding the secession of Assam from India.

In 1993, the bitter, violent and prolonged struggle in the Punjab also remained unresolved. The accord between Rajiv Gandhi and the Akali Dal, reached in August, 1985, had still not been implemented. Repeated attempts to resolve the crisis through negotiations or to suppress it through massive force failed for a decade. However, in 1992, the authorities and the media were congratulating police chief K. P. S. Gill on having gained the upper hand over militant forces, which made possible the peaceful holding of village *panchayat* elections with a high voter turnout.[2] At the same time, the press expressed concern that the popular fear of the militants, whose leadership had been decimated and ranks depleted, was now replaced by fear of a police force harassing the people, extorting them, and taking revenge with no restraint in a state where civil liberties remained suspended.

Despite numerous successes, therefore, in resolving some of the major problems threatening the unity of the Indian state since Independence, some of the problems that remain are so severe as to cast doubts on the ability of the central government under a centralized parliamentary system to maintain the unity of the country. Moreover, the remaining problems cannot be considered to be merely the unresolved remnants of old conflicts but reflect a fundamental structural tension in the Indian political system between forces seeking to strengthen further and centralize more decisively the Indian state and regional and other forces demanding further decentralization. The predominant tendencies since Independence have been towards pluralism, regionalism, decentralization, and interdependence between the Center and the states. The counter-tendencies, however, became quite strong during the period of Mrs. Gandhi's dominance of Indian politics and her efforts to centralize power and nationalize issues.

The centralizing and nationalizing measures taken by Mrs. Gandhi included: the political destruction of the state political bosses; the selection of the chief ministers of the Congress-dominated states by Mrs. Gandhi herself in consultation with her small clique of advisers; the increased use of President's Rule in the states; the increased use of central police and intelligence forces to monitor and control regional opposition; populist, demagogic appeals to national categories of voters, such as the poor, the landless, and the minorities; and some manipulation of xenophobic and paranoiac nationalism against Pakistan and the American CIA. After coming to power on a wave of sympathy and Hindu nationalism, Rajiv Gandhi alternated between the policies and tactics of his grandfather and his mother. He came to power in an election campaign which went beyond even his mother's tactics in manipulating xenophobic nationalism and arousing Hindu nationalism. He then changed his stance to the non-confrontational,

[2] *India Today*, February 15, 1993 and *Spokesman*, February 1, 1993.

mediating posture of his grandfather and sought peaceful and pluralist accommodations to resolve the unresolved problems of Punjab, Assam, and other regions of the country as well as those of India's neighbor, Sri Lanka. Few of Rajiv Gandhi's efforts bore fruit and he began to revert to the more confrontational and xenophobic style of his mother, seeking to blame the problems of the country upon foreign forces, notably the U.S.A. and Pakistan.

In the meantime, the non-implementation of the Punjab and Assam accords was followed by new waves of violence in those states. The participation of the Congress in a rigged election in Kashmir in 1987 provoked already disaffected militant Kashmiri youth to take to arms and demand secession from India. The manipulation of the Ayodhya dispute to gain Hindu votes for the Congress began the process of transformation of that dispute into a national polarization of Hindu-Muslim relations and a crisis of national unity.

The primary dangers in Mrs. Gandhi's strategy and its revival by Rajiv Gandhi lay in the collisions that inevitably resulted between these centralizing, nationalizing, and militantly nationalist tendencies and the predominant tendencies toward regionalism, pluralism, and decentralization. With the assassination of the last two leaders from the Nehru family and the fractionalization of the Congress at the leadership level, its organizational disintegration at the local level, and its loss of electoral support in the major north Indian states, the Congress is no longer in a position to sustain the centralizing drives of the past.

The ardor to transform India into a strong, centralized state now comes from reinvigorated Hindu nationalism and the BJP. The pluralist policies of the period of Nehru's dominance have few effective spokesmen left for them. However, the BJP drive for national power may provoke a further drastic strengthening of the powers of the central government as the Congress leaders seek to thwart it by using state police powers. Should the BJP come to power in the face of such efforts, it will inherit those powers. However, the Indian state may yet disintegrate in this clash between secular opportunists and chauvinist nationalists equally tied to the pursuit of illusions and chimeras, "symbols and shadows"[3] of national unity and

---

[3] This phrase comes from a 1975 University of Wisconsin, South Asia Center Film, "Bangladesh Nationhood: Symbols and Shadows."

greatness pursued by all the tyrannical regimes of the twentieth century.

THE PROBLEMS OF ORDER, DISORDER, AND VIOLENCE

The previous two decades have been marked by a decline of authoritative institutions in Indian politics, of which the most threatening to the future stability and peace of the country have been the disintegration of the Congress organization, the ever-declining effectiveness of and the ever-increasing corruption of the bureaucracy, and the demoralization of the police and other state security forces and their direct involvement at times in the perpetration rather than control of violence.

The disintegration of the Congress is manifested particularly in four respects. First, the Congress was turned into a Nehru family patrimony by Mrs. Gandhi, dominated by her and a narrow personal and family clique. That patrimony was transmitted by what amounted to a form of dynastic succession to her son, Rajiv, whose style of rulership increasingly came to resemble his mother's. In the aftermath of Rajiv's assassination, the Congress has become leaderless, fragmented, and divided. The Prime Minister, P. V. Narasimha Rao, is an old man without authority in the party or the country, marking time as the head of a party facing its greatest challenge since Independence.

Second, the old state party bosses were effectively destroyed by Mrs. Gandhi, blocking the rise of a new generation of independent state leadership within the Congress. The state leaders became primarily dependents, sycophants, or corrupt politicians vying for the favor of the central leadership to maintain themselves in power rather than building political support bases in their states. Third, the Congress has disintegrated as a functioning organization. The party's formal institutions either do not exist any longer at the state and district level or they function only sporadically or at the call of the central leadership. Party organization elections were not held for two decades until P. V. Narasimha Rao revived them as part of his strategy to secure his own power base. Finally, despite the ability of Mrs. Gandhi and Rajiv to win parliamentary elections for the Congress through the force of their popular image, there were major erosions of electoral support for the Congress in whole states and regions and among social groups within other states. The Congress is no longer the dominant party in West Bengal, Tamil Nadu, and Uttar Pradesh and has lost much ground in most other states as well.

The second great authoritative institution in the Indian political order at Independence was the bureaucracy, with the efficient and largely incorruptible ICS officers at its head. Since Independence, corruption in the bureaucracy has reached the highest levels of the IAS. Although many IAS officers remain honest and effective and present a facade of efficiency, intelligence, and honesty at the top of the administrative hierarchies in Delhi, the state capital, and the districts, there is a sharp break in the quality of personnel below the elite senior officers. Moreover, corruption below the elite levels has been institutionalized and affects virtually all departments such that few services can be expected by right and little can be done without payment.

The spread of police violence also has eroded public confidence in the legitimacy of state institutions and in the ability of the Indian state to fulfill the elemental function assigned to it by Hobbes of ensuring the basic security of the people from the fear of violent death. Time after time in major disturbances and riots, the press and civil liberties groups have noted that the police often either stand aside or take sides. As with the IAS, the senior IPS officers in the district headquarters and in the state capitals are often highly educated, efficient, and honest. At the local level, however, the police constables and station officers are uneducated and underpaid. For many, if not most, of them a police job is a way to make illegal income. Investigations and other police "work" are undertaken upon payment of money by private citizens. The victim of a crime has to pay to get his grievance attended to. "Suspects," often selected without serious evidence against them, have to pay to get released. The guilty also can pay to get released irrespective of the evidence against them.

Since everybody knows very well the methods of police work, people increasingly have taken the law into their own hands. This latter tendency is manifested in the increased display of guns by locally powerful persons, especially politicians, the increased use of violence against one's opponents in politics or otherwise, and the increased incidence of confrontations between police and people.

The decline and partial discrediting of the two preeminent institutions of the early post-Independence political order, Congress and the IAS, has been associated with the increasing tendency for local political conflicts to be expressed violently. With a few exceptions, the old Congress system has not been replaced at the regional and local levels by a new party order dominated by other well-organized parties or by stable competition between two or more parties, but by populist leadership in some cases or ineffective leadership and political instability in others. Gandhian methods of calling attention to the alleged injustices committed by the authorities through peaceful demonstrations have increasingly been displaced by movements at both the national and local levels to foment violent disturbances to embarrass or bring down governments.[4] In the districts, political ruffians and criminal elements play increasingly important roles in local struggles for access to state resources.[5] Simultaneously, as local groups tend to resort more easily and quickly to solving their conflicts by violent means, the central importance of the District Magistrate as the upholder of civil order has declined and the Senior Superintendent of Police has become his equal in authority and, in the eyes of many people at the local level, the more important of the two.

As India's authoritative institutions have declined in effectiveness while public protests, mass movements, and lately violent insurrectionary movements have remained pervasive, the authorities have come to rely ever more on laws which infringe upon the civil liberties of the people, on the coercive powers of the state security forces, and on police violence. Most of the laws which violate the standard protections for civil liberties guaranteed in Western democracies have been enacted and used when the Congress has been in power. They include the Preventive Detention Act of 1950, the Maintenance of Internal Security Act of 1980, the 59th Amendment to the Constitution, and the Terrorist and Disruptive Activities (Prevention) Act of 1985. All these acts in various ways restrict the rights of citizens to protest state actions, some leave them defenseless against arbitrary arrest, imprisonment, and police violence – including murder – and

---

[4] Atul Kohli gives numerous examples, but see especially his analyses of the Gujarat riots of 1981 and 1985; *Democracy and Discontent: India's Growing Crisis of Governability* (Cambridge: Cambridge University Press, 1990), pp. 252–266.

[5] Kohli, *Democracy and Discontent*, Part II.

increase the powers of the police and other state security forces to deal with both non-violent and violent acts of individual citizens and organized groups.[6] The use and abuse of police violence – including well-documented and widespread incidents of torture and well-known and also widespread, if not legally proven, incidents of the killing of suspects in staged or false encounters with the police – have become grave enough in recent years to warrant the attention and criticism of respected international rights groups such as Amnesty International and Human Rights Watch.[7]

Most ominous of all has been the rise and spread before and after the demolition of the mosque at Ayodhya of what are loosely called communal violence and riots. These so-called riots are often deliberately fomented by political parties and other interested persons seeking local political advantage or economic gain. Since criminal and *lumpen* elements are recruited from the filthy slums of urban India and its outskirts to initiate and carry out these acts of murder, rape, and arson, the violence also reflects in part the economic crisis of India, the failure of the Indian state to provide for the minimum basic needs of its people, some of whom find "employment" in so-called riots.

As noted above, institutionalized riot systems have come into existence in several cities and towns in northern and western India, in which local political activists, students, ruffians, and others are always alert for the potential of converting isolated incidents involving Hindus and Muslims into communal disturbances which can be put to political and economic advantage. During the past few years, elements from the RSS family of organizations and the Shiv Sena in Bombay have been used as storm trooper bands setting out to kill and otherwise harass Muslims to intimidate them or force them to leave sites where they are concentrated. These aspects of the rise of Hindu nationalism have been equated by some observers in the press and elsewhere with the events associated with the rise of Nazism in Germany. While such a comparison poses the danger of minimizing the enormity of the evils perpetrated in Germany before and after the rise of Hitler, it is past time to note that Indian politics and society display many of the

---

[6] Kuldeep Mathur, "The State and the Use of Coercive Power in India," *Asian Survey*, XXXII, No. 4 (April, 1992), 340–343.

[7] These groups in turn have been alerted to police abuses in India by civil liberties organizations such as the People's Union for Democratic Rights.

symptoms of a murderous pre-fascist stage which has already produced a multiplicity of localized *Kristallnachts* in numerous urban sites.

INDUSTRIALIZATION IN A PEASANT SOCIETY

Development policy changes

At Independence, though it was by no means a classical tropical economy, the Indian market economy was, nevertheless, oriented primarily to external markets, was weak in the capital goods industries, and agriculturally stagnant. Since Independence, there have been significant changes in these and other respects. The dependence of Indian industry and agriculture on foreign trade declined in the first few decades after Independence and both sectors became oriented increasingly to the home market and toward inter-sectoral exchange between town and country. Foreign investment declined as a proportion of total GNP. Indian agriculture became a dynamic growth sector of the economy, with an average annual rate of growth of output of 3.5 percent.[8]

The major achievement of the early decades of planning was the development of "a diversified capital goods sector."[9] However, in a high technology century, many of the machines installed in the industries in this sector in the 1960s are already obsolete. Indian industries also lack significant research and development capabilities, "the ability to respond to market changes, or to put up new plants."[10] Moreover, industrial planning failed to achieve industrial output targets in all plans except the Seventh or to prevent "concentration of economic power in the industrial sector" and concentration of industries in states and regions which were already relatively "industrially developed."[11] The central emphasis of the Government of India's economic

[8] Aditya Mukherjee and Mridula Mukherjee, "Imperialism and Growth of Indian Capitalism in Twentieth Century," *EPW*, xxiii, No. 11 (March 12, 1988), 536–538.

[9] Ranjit Sau, "The Green Revolution and Industrial Growth in India: A Tale of Two Paradoxes and a Half," *EPW*, xxiii, No. 16 (April 16, 1988), 793; Vinod Vyasulu et al., "Towards a Political Economy of the Economic Policy Changes," *EPW*, xxvi, No. 38 (September 21, 1991), 2206.

[10] Vyasulu et al., "Towards a Political Economy of the Economic Policy Changes," p. 2206.

[11] Sunil Mani, "New Industrial Policy: Barriers to Entry, Foreign Investment and Privatisation," *EPW*, xxvii, No. 35 (August 29, 1992), M-86 to M-87; see also T. N. Srinivasan, "Reform of Industrial and Trade Policies," *EPW*, xxvi, No. 37 (September 14, 1991), 2144 on the failure of the regulatory system to prevent "industrial concentration."

development planning under Rajiv Gandhi shifted toward technological modernization of the Indian economy and the capital goods sector. Import restrictions were reduced significantly in relation to items of technological importance to the modernization of Indian industry. The policy rubric under which these changes took place was "liberalization" of the import and export control regime, which represented the most consistent set of policies of any sort followed by Rajiv Gandhi after his assumption of power in 1985.

A further force antagonistic to the Mahalanobis model of planning with its emphasis on the development of the capital goods industries in the public sector has been the enormous growth in the urban middle class, now estimated to comprise approximately 80 million people with the resources and desire to have a life style comparable to the middle class in the West, with its orientation toward consumer goods, including luxury goods such as air conditioners, color television and video sets, and stereo systems.[12] It is now being argued, therefore, that the demand for consumer goods should be allowed to lead the rest of the economy and that restrictions on the development of the consumer goods industries, including luxury goods, should be reduced or eliminated.[13]

The changes in Indian economic development under Rajiv Gandhi were made without a comprehensive statement from the government, which introduced them bit by bit, through the announcement of measures to liberalize imports, through new emphases in the annual budget statements presented to Parliament, and through the inauguration of new "centrally-sponsored schemes." The Planning Commission as such, however, ceased to provide a coherent, integrated statement of the goals and directions for the Indian economy, with detailed guidelines for their implementation.

In contrast to the halting and piecemeal moves toward liberalization made by Rajiv Gandhi, the government of P. V. Narasimha Rao has pursued "measures of economic liberalisation" since the middle of 1991 that are "revolutionarily daring."[14] These measures as of February, 1993 included: an initial two-step devaluation of the rupee in

---

[12] Bhabani Sen Gupta, "Crisis of the Indian State," *EPW*, xxiii, No. 16 (April 16, 1988), 765.
[13] Sau, "The Green Revolution and Industrial Growth in India," p. 791.
[14] *EPW*, xxvii, No. 42 (October 17, 1992), 2271. For a contrary view, see Mani, "New Industrial Policy," M-86 to M-94.

July, 1991 followed by the announcement of the change to full convertibility in February, 1993, liberalization of the import–export regime restrictions, and elimination of restrictions on industrial capacity for most industries. They are rightly characterized as revolutionary because they foretell the final casting aside of the Nehruvian model of economic development through state-directed capital-intensive industrialization emphasizing heavy industry, the further downgrading of the Planning Commission to an advisory role at best,[15] and the displacement of the import-substitution strategy in favor of an import-intensive one to promote "export-oriented industries" while simultaneously favoring the development of the consumer durable goods industries.[16] All these measures are designed to integrate India fully into the world economy.

The second great success often claimed for the Indian economy since Independence is the "green revolution" in agriculture. Aggregate production of foodgrains continued to increase in the country in the decade of the 1980s, from "129.6 million tons in 1980–81 to 170.6 million tons in 1989–90."[17] However, it needs to be reiterated in the face of the tall claims often made for it that while the "green revolution" has transformed agriculture in a small region of the country and has had considerable effects on the cropping patterns and productivity in other parts of the country as well, it has merely kept pace with the food consumption needs of an ever-expanding population.[18]

There has been talk in recent years of introducing another "new agricultural strategy" to produce a "second green revolution."[19] The new strategy is supposed to extend the green revolution to other crops, particularly rice, maize, gram, and arhar, and into other regions of the country, especially the eastern rice-producing states.[20] The potential for a "second green revolution" in India is quite high. Even in the areas most affected by the first green revolution, there remains considerable

---

[15] Arun Gosh, "Planning versus Market-Oriented Investment and Production," *EPW*, xxvii, No. 42 (October 17, 1992), 2283; see also B.M., "Charade of Plan Making," *EPW*, xxvi, No. 35 (August 31, 1991), 2037–2038.
[16] Vyasulu *et al.*, "Towards a Political Economy of the Economic Policy Changes," pp. 2207–2208.
[17] Vyasulu, p. 2205.
[18] Sau, "The Green Revolution and Industrial Growth in India," p. 789.
[19] *EPW*, xiii, No. 12 (March 19, 1988), 560.
[20] Nilakantha Rath, "A Budget for Farmers!" *EPW*, xxiii, Nos. 14 and 15 (April 2–9, 1988), 739.

potential for further increases in agricultural output through increased fertilizer applications and other means.[21] The potential of many of the so-called "backward districts" in eastern U.P. and Bihar and elsewhere, which were half a century ago ahead of the western green revolution districts, has hardly been explored. However, there has so far been no indication that the NEP includes a new strategy for agriculture which will reverse the declining public investment in that sector in the 1980s, the declining rate of development of irrigation projects, and the likely consequence of a declining rate of growth in agriculture.[22]

Neither the old nor the new development goals promise solutions to the persisting problems of poverty, hunger, and malnutrition in the foreseeable future for "the mass of the poor" population of the country, urban and rural, who have become not only a burden but a stigma and an eyesore.[23] It is increasingly the policy of the government to project an international image in which India's poor have no place and to keep them away from foreign eyes by restricting the access of foreign scholars to the countryside. Since, however, the rural population, including the poor, countinue to comprise the bulk of the population and the votes in India's representative system, their problems and needs continue to obtrude into public view.

Not only do the rural population and the poor continue to comprise a majority of India's population, their numbers also continue to increase. The rate of growth of the Indian population has been between approximately 2.00 and 2.25 percent.[24] A very large proportion of this ever-increasing population, whose numbers will reach a billion by the turn of the century, remains poor, illiterate, and without modern health care, and a substantial minority are malnourished as well.[25]

[21] Kirit S. Parikh, "A Development Strategy for the 1990s," *EPW*, xxiii, No. 12 (March 19, 1988), 598.

[22] A. Ganesh Kumar, "Falling Agricultural Investment and Its Consequences," *EPW*, xxvii, No. 42 (October 17, 1992), 2307–2312.

[23] Sen Gupta, "Crisis of the Indian State," p. 765.

[24] Arun Ghosh, "The Plan versus Departmental Prerogatives," *EPW*, xxiii, Nos. 14 and 15 (April 2–9, 1988), 677, and V. M. Dandekar, "Population Front of India's Economic Development," *EPW*, xxiii, No. 17 (April 23, 1988), 837.

[25] According to the 1991 census, literacy of the population above seven years of age at last passed the half-way mark, reaching 52 percent. The latest National Sample Survey results for the year 1987–88 showed 43 percent of the population still below the poverty line. *EPW*, xxvii, Nos. 31 & 32 (August 1–8, 1992), 1640.

The politicization of the peasantry

One of the arguments of this book is that the main responsibility for the development within India of an economy based on rural–urban disparities and gross inequalities in income and resource control has been the insistent drives of the Indian political leadership for equality with the advanced industrial countries, but an equality of the Indian state measured in terms of the output of iron and steel, the size of the GDP, possession of modern weaponry, and the assertion of regional hegemony. Since, however, the main intellectual critics and self-appointed watchdogs of the planning process in India have come primarily from the Marxist Left, who retain an unshakable faith in centrally directed planning, huge public investments, and heavy industrialization, the failures of Indian economic development planning have been attributed to inequalities in society rather than to the inherent deficiencies of the approach itself. Despite the dominance of Nehru and of socialist thinking during this era of leadership and despite the Mahalanobis plans themselves, it is contended that the Indian bourgeoisie has established and extended its "ideological hegemony" in Indian society and that the recent changes in Indian development goals reflect their influence rather than the failures of the previous policies.

The second great enemy of Indian development planning in the eyes of the Marxist Left are the rich and middle peasant castes and classes. They are variously categorized as "*kulaks*" or "big peasants" or new "provincial rich." Evidence is marshalled to show the pervasive influence of this class as one member of either a triple (bourgeoisie-bureaucrats-rich farmers) or dual alliance (bourgeoisie-rich farmers).

Such evidence includes especially the setting of support prices for the procurement of foodgrains by the government, which the left critics invariably consider too high. It is noted that the state governments are generally dominated by the rich farmer lobbies and that their power is evidenced in such widespread state practices as the raising of procurement prices above the prices set by the central Agricultural Prices and Costs Commission (APCC)[26] or in practices such as that of former Lok Dal chief minister Devi Lal in Haryana of

[26] B. M., "Government Helping Rich Farmers Profit from Drought," *EPW*, xxii, No. 44 (October 31, 1987), 1848.

writing off farmers' loans. Further evidence of the increasing power of the rich farmers is provided by the fact that the central government and Congress leaders have taken to vying with opposition state governments and even with rival Congress factions in adopting pro-farmer stances.[27]

The supporters of the old planning process use such evidences as these to identify this class even more than the capitalists as the chief "enemy of the masses." Some left critics even argue that the leaders of this rural class are not peasants at all, but a class of capitalist farmers or "provincial rich" leading even the rich peasantry, using caste to link them in turn with the "better-off sections of the peasantry" and recruiting "an army of foot soldiers from out of the middle peasantry to put down the poor."[28]

This left critique greatly exaggerates the influence of the rich and/or middle peasants in the Indian political order and misinterprets and maligns genuinely popular mass peasant movements. Despite the alleged inordinate influence of the rich peasants over policy, agriculture continues to be neglected in the plans and in the new economic policies.[29] The continuing neglect of agriculture, efforts to introduce new agricultural strategies without providing adequate resources for the widespread and equitable dissemination of the new technologies associated with them, the inefficiencies and corruption associated with the distribution of new agricultural inputs and credit, and the like have contributed to a rising tide of disaffection among the most dynamic middle sectors of the peasantry and to their increasing politicization.

The strongest counter-argument to the Marxist attack on the undue influence of the "better-off" peasantry comes from the middle peasant farmers' movements themselves, which have acquired increasing prominence in recent years, notably in Maharashtra and western U. P. The very rise of such mass movements directed against state policies and which identify "urban capitalists and the state" as "the main exploiters" of the peasantry must lead one to wonder how its participants, even the "better-off" segments among them, can be members of a dominant class or of a dual alliance with the urban capitalists they are

[27] *India Today*, March 15, 1988, p. 32 and April 15, 1988, p. 15.
[28] K. Balagopal, "An Ideology for the Provincial Propertied Class," *EPW*, xxii, No. 50 (December 12, 1987), 2178.
[29] Rath, "A Budget for Farmers!", p. 739.

attacking. It also stretches the imagination to believe that hundreds of thousands of peasants can be mobilized to agitate for an increase in farm prices if the prices are already pegged high enough to provide secure and reasonable profits for them.

The most impressive peasant movement in recent times in India was that led by Tikait, an ordinary Jat middle peasant from western U. P. who was clearly drawing upon the ideas and building upon the work of Chaudhury Charan Singh, who died in 1987. Tikait's demand was not simply for an arbitrary increase in farm prices but for "fair prices" for farm produce, measured in part at least in terms of a balance between the cost of inputs and the price of the produce. He also called for policy changes which would make available to the ordinary peasantry some of the opportunities and amenities of urban life, such as "improved educational facilities and more jobs for children of farmers" and for "narrowing the ... gap between the standard of living in towns and villages" generally.[30]

The ruling Congress adjusted to peasant discontent in several different ways in the different regional contexts of Indian politics. One adjustment was to coopt through caste appeals segments of the rich and middle peasantry into the ruling coalition and to give them preferential access to the scarce resources made available in the countryside. A second strategy used especially in the north was to squeeze the middle peasantry politically between the old landed elites and the rural poor, providing political access and differential economic benefits to the former and ameliorative economic benefits to the poor while ignoring the needs and demands of the middle peasantry of middle caste status. A third approach has been to build a ruling political coalition from below, based on the non-dominant backward castes, Scheduled Castes, minorities, and tribals, notably in Gujarat.

There is also a tradition of more radical and even violent insurrectionary movements among the poor peasants and agricultural laborers in modern India, but it has been argued above that such movements have been local, sporadic, and heavily concentrated among tribal peoples. Moreover, since the *garibi hatao* campaign of 1971, organization of the poor by opposition parties and radical movements has been partly preempted by government patronage measures. Among the more bizarre efforts in this respect were the loan *melas* (fairs) in the

[30] *India Today*, February 29, 1988, pp. 5, 9, 36 and March 15, 1988, pp. 44–46.

late 1980s, in which tens of millions of rupees in "loan" money were distributed in public places to persons from poor and disadvantaged groups.[31]

It remains true that such power and wealth as exists in the Indian countryside belongs to the land-controlling castes. In some districts and localities in the country, particularly in north India, ex-landlords with extensive illegal holdings remain powerful and have even extended their sway politically over large segments of a district or even over an entire district. Where they are descendants of former princes or local rajas and especially where they maintain some of the traditions of local kingship by acting as the benefactors and protectors of the local populations, they draw upon traditional loyalties which cross both class and caste boundaries to a considerable extent.

The new "provincial rich," in contrast, are primarily interested in making money rather than in exercising a form of princely or semi-princely power. However, the opportunities available to the new rich class in the countryside with surplus profits to be invested are limited. Much of it, therefore, goes into politics and does provide a basis for the "provincial rich" to enter politics and to aggrandize themselves still further. Such politicians, however, are mostly in the Congress and are not the persons who lead the peasant movements condemned by the Left.

The contradictory interests of the urban middle classes and the urban and rural poor

Policies which favor urban industrial development also tend to bring ever-increasing numbers of the poor and landless to the cities, who crowd into urban slums more degraded than any the world has ever before seen. These vast populations entering the cities intrude into their centers seeking any kind of living as domestic servants, rickshaw pullers, messengers, peddlers, and the like. They also "squat" in village-like settlements or on the pavements sleeping or selling or begging.

During the Emergency, attempts were made to break up the ugliest and most intrusive of such settlements and squatters' stalls. The inevitable violence which accompanied these efforts caused a considerable backlash, however, which contributed to the rising tide of

[31] *India Today*, January 15, 1988, p. 41 and April 15, 1988, p. 13.

resentment against the Emergency regime and the displacement of the Congress from power at the Center by an opposition coalition in 1977. A major effort to prevent further urban degradation by removing the poor is, therefore, unlikely to be made in the future as long as the electoral and competitive party system is retained.

The long-term political danger of a policy which caters increasingly to the urban consuming middle classes is that it may threaten the persistence of the parliamentary system itself in which the votes of the rural peasantry and the rural and urban poor continue to far outweigh those of the urban middle classes. It is necessary, therefore, to revise the traditional view of the urban middle classes as the main supporters of systems of political democracy. In developing countries, their expanding consumption demands can be met only by ignoring or repressing the needs of the majority.[32]

Centralized economic development and center–state relations

A further danger to the maintenance of a competitive parliamentary system is the potential strain on center–state relations and on the maintenance of local institutions of self-government which arises from centralized distribution of economic resources and centralized political control of the entire country. For example, despite the fact that one of the major long-term goals of centralized economic development planning was to rectify regional economic imbalances, the latter have persisted and even become greater in some respects.

A further potential danger to center–state relations arises from the increasing use of the resources available to the Center for purposes of political patronage. Those resources include the distribution of food from the buffer stocks to food-deficit states, the siting of major centrally sponsored schemes for agricultural development, and the location of public sector enterprises, among others.

The persistence of centralized economic control over the most dynamic segments of the economy and the ability of the central

[32] The general argument here comes from Albert O. Hirshman, "The Turn to Authoritarianism in Latin America and the Search for its Economic Determinants," in D. Collier (ed.), *The New Authoritarianism in Latin America* (Princeton, N.J.: Princeton University Press, 1979), p. 80. It is applied to India in Ranjit Sau, "The Green Revolution and Industrial Growth in India: A Tale of Two Paradoxes and a Half," *EPW*, xxiii, No. 16 (April 16, 1988), 792.

government to intervene in individual states or to deny them resources has been an irritant in center–state relations, particularly in those which have been dominated for some time by non-Congress parties such as West Bengal, among other states. Central projects may be granted to particular states when the Congress rather than the opposition is in power or may be sited even in districts within particular states to reward loyal local leaders who have produced Congress victories. The figures on resource distribution, therefore, may not show systematic discrimination for or against particular states, but their timing and precise location often have much to do with state and local political alignments.

As the state governments came increasingly under central control and direction and the local Congress organizations disintegrated, the Congress-controlled state governments themselves became perpetual election machines, distributing patronage primarily with a view to consolidating the control of a political faction in the state government, whose performance was in turn judged by the central government solely by its leader's ability to influence the results of the next election and especially to prevent any major outbreaks such as caste wars in Gujarat, which would cause the Congress to lose political control over a state. As for local institutions of self-government, the Congress-dominated state and central governments deliberately dismantled these institutions or superseded them virtually everywhere because it was too difficult to control them and because they tended to fall into the hands of opposition leaders or even local Congress politicians or non-party persons who then used whatever patronage was available as *they* chose rather than as the central and state government leaders chose.

The Indian state and the armies of the discontented

The armies of the discontented continue to increase throughout the subcontinent. They include especially the middle peasants in the rural areas, to whom emphasis has been given in this volume. They also include especially students in urban areas seeking employment, who are concerned about their life chances, who express their fears and resentments in a variety of ethnic movements, and who play a considerable role in the initiation of violent agitations everywhere in South Asia. They include the urban poor crowded in slums whose numbers are increasing every year as municipal services continue to deteriorate.[33] They include also tribal groups and others in remote areas of the country who continue to be dispossessed of their lands without adequate compensation in the name of economic development.[34]

These groups are disparate, dispersed, and often unorganized. They will not coalesce into a movement which will overthrow the regime.[35] Rather, it is more likely that regime leaders will find the endless task of appeasing them too distracting, will take further measures to restrict the functioning of what is left of the democratic political process, and will use increasingly the instruments of state oppression and violence against them in order to get on with the transcendent goal of building the Indian state.

PROSPECTS

Most scholarly observers of contemporary Indian politics agree that since Independence there has been a considerable decay in the functioning of political institutions and in their public legitimacy. From a comparative perspective, however, India's political institutions appear quite differently. Despite the evident decay over time within India, the performance of India's political institutions compares favorably in many respects with those of her neighbors or with most other postcolonial societies. Indeed, the Indian political regime is one of the most democratic in the world by most conventional measures of political participation, electoral and party competition, and persistence of parliamentary institutions. It is also among the least repressive regimes in the world. With admittedly major exceptions such as the annihilation of Naxalites, terrorists, and those suspected or wrongly accused of being in those two categories and the repressive and brutal measures taken against presumed militant, insurrectionary, and secessionist groups in Punjab, Kashmir, and the northeast, opposition politicians

[33] *India Today*, January 31, 1988, p. 66.
[34] Satinath Sarangi and Ramesh Billorey, "The Nightmare Begins: Oustees of Indira Sagar Project," *EPW*, xxiii, No. 17 (April 23, 1988), 830.
[35] Since these lines were originally written, V. S. Naipaul has put matters more eloquently, describing India's "million mutinies" as products of "a general awakening." "But," he says, "everyone awakened first to his own group or community; every group thought itself unique in its awakening; and every group sought to separate its rage from the rage of other groups"; *India: A Million Mutinies Now* (New York: Viking, 1990), p. 420.

and students and others who engage in public demonstrations against the regime or the dominant party are not normally harassed or imprisoned without cause and are certainly not tortured. There is a free press and ordinary people are free to speak their minds in public and private.

It is sometimes argued that many of the deviations from accepted standards of parliamentary performance, bureaucratic probity, and police honesty which developing countries such as India have been undergoing are stages that every developing or modernizing country, including the United States and Great Britain, have undergone. This kind of argument, however, is a form of intellectual distortion. If conditions improve in a given society, one may say that the bad periods were a "stage," even a necessary stage in its development. However, conditions often do not improve in developing countries or take a long time in doing so and they can also get worse. One may equally argue that India's recent political difficulties are a pre-fascist stage as a stage on the road to institutionalized democracy or republicanism. The point is that India's political system is unique and has to be described in its own terms and its future is uncertain.

The Indian political system shows signs of disintegration, which can no longer be dismissed as prophecies of doom. The existence of outright secessionist movements are only part of the problem. The Center and the army remain strong enough to resist any such attempts. Nor are there any foreign powers who are in a position to support secessionism in India or who stand to benefit from its disintegration. Pakistan or China might be happy to see such a disintegration but are in no position to support secessionist movements in India effectively. The United States clearly has no wish to do so and would most likely ignore such movements or oppose them if supported by any other power. On the other hand, the disintegration of both the Soviet Union and Yugoslavia have at once removed the previous freezing of the existing state system in a bipolar world and created ominous precedents for India's own future.

A further danger for India is the spread of violence, lawlessness, and disorder at the local level. If such a spread continues, the Center may feel the necessity of a further assertion of its power and authority, possibly including another venture into authoritarian practices, which will have its own costs. Those costs, if the evidence from neighboring countries is any guide, would include a long-term threat of major violence from discontented segments of society, more insistent demands from the states for regional autonomy, and even the spread of terrorist movements to other groups in society and other states in the Union.

The demolition of the mosque at Ayodhya, the terrorization of the Muslim population of the country through pogroms, and the utter lack of sensible Muslim political leadership within existing organizations are causes for the gravest concern. It is out of such circumstances that terrorist groups arise. Already, some Muslims in U. P. and elsewhere have used small arms and crude bombs in recent riots and pogroms. The next obvious step would be the acquisition of the standard weaponry of modern terrorist groups, the AK-47. The results of such a development would very likely be further Hindu consolidation, but at the cost of the disintegration of U. P. into a state of civil war comparable to that in Kashmir, Punjab, or Assam. Such a development would also make India itself ungovernable for no government and no party can rule India which cannot rule U. P.

Alternative solutions to India's multiple crises are available within India's traditions and political philosophies. They would include a move, which would be sanctioned by Gandhian ideas, toward greater decentralization of power to the states, districts, and villages of India, a return to the pluralist policies of the Nehru period, and major reforms of the bureaucracy and the police. Proposals for decentralization of powers to the states range from the very modest recommendations of the Sarkaria Commission to more radical proposals which would transform the Indian Union into a more federal union such as that of the United States to the most radical proposals for changing the balance of powers between the Center and the states by limiting sharply the former and granting regional autonomy to all the states of the Union.[36] Reform of the civil and police bureaucracies would require a complete transformation in patterns of recruitment, pay, and promotion to foster career orientations, work satisfaction, and incentives to resist corruption. The overall size of the civil bureaucracy might also be reduced for it is overstaffed, inefficient, and a great drain on the resources of the country. The dismantling of state-directed

[36] Rasheedudin Khan, *Federal India: A Design for Change* (Delih: Vikas, 1992), ch. ix (pp. 47-57).

economic planning is itself a major step in the direction of decentralization, which is bound to have decentralizing political consequences as well if only by the very reduction in the ability of the Center to allocate significant economic resources to the states.

However, if representative government is to be preserved in India, decisive moves toward further decentralization and pluralism are required to stem a general collapse of authority in the Indian polity. The alternative, a move toward further centralization and authoritarianism under a regime of militant Hindu nationalism represents the gravest danger to the Indian state, civil society, and the ideology and practices of secularism.

BIBLIOGRAPHY

INDIAN PUBLIC DOCUMENTS

Ministry of Agriculture. *Indian Agriculture in Brief*. Delhi: Controller of Publications, 1985.

Ministry of Agriculture. Directorate of Economics and Statistics. *Bulletin on Rice Statistics in India (District-Wise)*. Delhi: Controller of Publications, 1974.

Ministry of Agriculture and Irrigation. *Report of the National Commission on Agriculture, 1976*, Pt. 1: *Review and Progress*. Delhi: Controller of Publications, 1976.

Census of India, 1981, Series 1: *India*, Pt. 11-B (iii), *Primary Census Abstract: Scheduled Tribes*, by P. Padmanabha. Delhi: Controller of Publications, 1983.

Census of India, 1981, Series 1: *India*, Paper 3 of 1984: *Household Population by Religion of Head of Household*, by V. S. Verma. Delhi: Controller of Publications, 1985.

Census of India, 1981, Series 1: *India*, Paper 1 of 1987: *Households and Household Population by Language Mainly Spoken in the Household*, by P. Padmanabha. Delhi: Controller of Publications, 1987.

Census of India, 1971, Series 3: *Assam*, Pt. 1-A: *General Population*, by K. S. Dey. Delhi: Controller of Publications, 1979.

Census of India, 1971, Series 3: *Assam*, Pt. 11-C (ii): *Social and Cultural Tables*. Delhi: Controller of Publications, 1981.

Communal Riots and Minorities, unpublished, undated, mimeo report.

Economic Survey of Indian Agriculture, 1966–67.

Election Commission of India. *Report on the General Elections to the Legislative Assemblies of Andhra Pradesh, Assam, Haryana, Himachal Pradesh, Jammu & Kashmir, Karnataka, Kerala, Meghalaya, Nagaland, Tripura, West Bengal and Delhi (Metropolitican Council) 1982–83*, vol. 11: *Statistical*. Delhi: Controller of Publications, 1983.

Third Annual Report, 1985. Delhi: Controller of Publications, 1985.

Report of the Ninth General Elections to the House of the People in India, 1989. New Delhi: Government of India Press, 1990.

Lok Sabha Poll: An A. I. R. Analysis. New Delhi: Government of India News Services Division, All India Radio, 1991.

Ministry of Finance (Economic Division). *Report of the Finance Commission, 1973*. Delhi: Controller of Publications, 1973.

Economic Survey, 1985–86. Delhi: Controller of Publications, 1986.

Ministry of Home Affairs. *Report, 1966–67.* New Delhi: Government of India Press, 1967.

Report, 1967–68. New Delhi: Government of India Press, 1968.

Report, 1982–83. New Delhi: Government of India Press, 1983.

Seventeenth Report of the Commissioner for Linguistic Minorities in India (For the period July 1974 to June 1975). Delhi: Controller of Publications, 1977.

The Twenty-Third Report by the Deputy Commissioner for Linguistic Minorities in India, for the Period July 1982 to June 1983. Delhi: Controller of Publications, 1985.

The Twenty-Fifth Report by the Deputy Commissioner for Linguistic Minorities in India, For the Period July 1984 to June 1985. Delhi: Controller of Publications, 1986.

Home Department. *Report of the States Reorganisation Commission, 1955.* New Delhi: Government of India Press, 1955.

Ministry of Information and Broadcasting. *Annual Report of the Registrar of Newspapers for India 1961,* 1. Delhi: Manager of Publications, 1961.

Press in India, 1971, 1. Delhi: Manager of Publications, 1971.

Press in India, 1981, 1. Delhi: Controller of Publications, 1981.

Press in India, 1984. Delhi: Controller of Publications, 1986.

Ministry of Planning, Department of Statistics, Central Statistical Organisation. *Monthly Abstract of Statistics,* December, 1990, Vol. XLIII, No. 12.

Planning Commission. *Report of Joint Study Team, Uttar Pradesh (Eastern Districts): Ghazipur, Azamgarh, Deoria, Jaunpur.* Delhi: Government of India Press, 1964.

The Seventh Five-Year Plan, 1985–90, Vol. I: *Perspectives, Objectives, Resources.* Delhi: Controller of Publications, 1985.

Planning Commission, *The Seventh Five-Year Plan, 1985–90,* Vol. II: *Sectoral Programmes of Development.* Delhi: Controller of Publications, 1985

Statistical Abstract of India, for the years 1987, 1975, 1967, 1955–56. New Delhi: Government of India Press,, 1988, 1976, 1968, 1957.

BOOKS, ARTICLES, AND DISSERTATIONS

Abdullah, Farooq (as told to Sati Sahni). *My Dismissal.* New Delhi: Vikas, 1985.

Acharya, Sarthi. "Rates of Return in Indian Agriculture," *EPW,* XXVII, No. 3 (January 18, 1992), 111–119.

A Correspondent. "The MDR Myth: An Appreciation," *EPW,* XXIII, Nos. 1 and 2 (January 2–9, 1988), 23–24.

Ahluwalia, Isher Judge. *Industrial Growth in India: Stagnation Since the Mid-Sixties.* Delhi: Oxford University Press, 1985.

Ahluwalia, Montek S. "Rural Poverty in India: 1956/57 to 1973/74," in Montek S. Ahluwalia et al., *India: Occasional Papers,* World Bank Staff Working Paper No. 279. Washington, D.C.: World Bank, 1978.

"Rural Poverty, Agricultural Production, and Prices: A Reexamination," in John W. Mellor and Gunvant M. Desai (eds.), *Agricultural Change and Rural Poverty: Variations on a Theme by Dharm Narain*. Delhi: Oxford University Press, 1986, pp. 59–75.

Ahuja, M. L. and Sharda Paul. *1989–1991 General Elections in India (Including November 1991 By-Elections)*. New Delhi: Associated Publishing, 1992.

Alavi, Hamza. "Peasants and Revolution," in Kathleen Gough and Hari P. Sharma (eds.), *Imperialism and Revolution in South Asia*. New York: Monthly Review Press, 1973, pp. 291–337.

Almond, Gabriel and G. Bingham Powell, Jr., *Comparative Politics: System, Process, and Policy*. 2nd edn. Boston: Little, Brown, 1978.

Amin, Shahid. "Gandhi as Mahatma: Gorakhpur District, Eastern UP, 1921–2," in Ranajit Guha (ed.), *Subaltern Studies III: Writings on South Asian History and Society*. Delhi: Oxford University Press, 1984, pp. 1–61.

Andersen, Walter K. "India's 1991 Elections: The Uncertain Verdict," *Asian Survey*, XXXI, No. 10 (October, 1991), 976–989.

Andersen, Walter K. and Shridhar D. Damle. *The Brotherhood in Saffron: The Rashtriya Swayamsevak Sangh and Hindu Revivalism*. New Delhi: Vistaar, 1987.

Anderson, Robert and Walter Huber, *The Hour of the Fox: Tropical Forests, the World Bank, and Indigenous People in Central India*. Seattle: University of Washington Press, 1988.

Anonymous. "The Problem," in The Punjab Tangle, *Seminar*, 294 (February, 1984), 12–14.

Ansari, M. M. "Financing of the States' Plans: A Perspective for Regional Development," *EPW*, XVIII, No. 49 (December 3, 1983), 2077–2082.

Antulay, A. R. "The Constitution, the Supreme Court and the Basic Structure," transcript of a talk broadcast in the Spotlight programme of All India Radio on October 28, 1976 by Shri A. R. Antulay, Member of Parliament.

Asia Watch Report. *Human Rights in India: Kashmir Under Siege, May, 1991*. New York: Human Rights Watch, 1991.

Human Rights in India: Punjab in Crisis. New York: Human Rights Watch, 1991.

Austin, Granville. *The Indian Constitution: Cornerstone of a Nation*. Oxford: Clarendon Press, 1966.

Azeem, Anwar. "Urdu – A Victim of Cultural Genocide?" in Zafar Imam (ed.), *Muslims in India*. New Delhi: Orient Longman, 1975, pp. 256–272.

B. M. "Sixth Plan in Limbo," *EPW*, XVIII, No. 24 (June 11, 1983), 1041–1042.
"Catch-words for Seventh Plan," *EPW*, XIX, No. 26 (June 30, 1984), 974–975.
"Selling the Seventh Plan," *EPW*, XIX, No. 35 (September 1, 1984), 1507–1509.
"Policy-Frame for Seventh Plan," *EPW*, XX, No. 28 (July 13, 1985), 1165–1167.
"Making the Plan Irrelevant," *EPW*, XXI, No. 2 (January 11, 1986), 60–61.
"Privatisation, Indian Style," *EPW*, XXII, No. 32 (August 8, 1987), 1325–1327.
"Government Helping Rich Farmers Profit from Drought," *EPW*, XXII, No. 44 (October 31, 1987), 1325–1848.
"Charade of Plan Making," *EPW*, XXVI, No. 35 (August 31, 1991), 2037–2038.

Bajpai, K. Shankar. "India in 1991: New Beginnings," *Asian Survey*, XXXII, No. 2 (February, 1992), 207–216.

Bailey, F. G. *Politics and Social Change: Orissa in 1959.* Berkeley, University of California Press, 1963.

Balagopal, K. "Congress (I) *vs* Telugu Desam Party: At Last a Lawful Means for Overthrowing a Lawfully Constituted Government," *EPW*, XXII, No. 41 (October 10, 1987), 1736–1738.

"An Ideology for the Provincial Propertied Class," *EPW*, XXII, No. 50 (December 12, 1987), 2177–2178.

"Meerut 1987: Reflections on an Inquiry," *EPW*, XXIII, No. 16 (April 16, 1988), 768–771.

"Post-Chunder and Other Chunders," *EPW*, XXVI, No. 42 (October 19, 1991), 2399–2405.

Balasubramanyam, V. N. *The Economy of India.* London: Weidenfeld and Nicolson, 1984.

Bardhan, Pranab. "On Class Relations in Indian Agriculture: A Comment," *EPW*, XIV, No. 19 (May 12, 1979), 857–860.

The Political Economy of Development in India. Delhi: Oxford University Press, 1984.

"Dominant Proprietary Classes and India's Democracy," in Atul Kohli (ed.), *India's Democracy: An Analysis of Changing State–Society Relations.* Princeton, N.J.: Princeton University Press, 1988.

Baruah, Sanjib. "Immigration, Ethnic Conflict, and Political Turmoil – Assam, 1979–1985," *Asian Survey*, XXVI, No. 11 (November, 1986), 1184–1206.

Baviskar, B. S. "Factional Conflict and the Congress Dilemma in Rural Maharashtra (1952–1975)," in Richard Sisson and Ramashray Roy (eds.), *Diversity and Dominance in Indian Politics*, Vol. I: *Changing Bases of Congress Support.* New Delhi: Sage, 1990.

Bayley, David H. *The Police and Political Development in India.* Princeton, N.J.: Princeton University Press, 1969.

"The Police and Political Order in India," *Asian Survey*, XXIII, No. 4 (April, 1983), 484–496.

Beller, Gerald, E. "Benevolent Illusions in a Developing Society: The Assertion of Supreme Court Authority in Democratic India," *The Western Political Quarterly*, XXXVI, No. 4 (December, 1983), 513–532.

Bernard, Jean-Alphonse. "A Maturation Crisis in India: The V. P. Singh Experiment," *Asian Survey*, XXVII, No. 4 (April, 1987), 408–426.

"The Presidential Idea in the Constitutions of South Asia," *Contemporary South Asia*, I, No. 1 (1992), 41–52.

Bharti, Indu. "The Bihar Formula," *EPW*, XXV, No. 44 (November 3, 1990), 2407.

Bhasin, Prem. *Riding the Wave.* New Delhi: Ashajanak Publications, 1972.

Bhat, L. S. *et al. Regional Inequalities in India: An Inter-State and Intra-State Analysis.* Papers presented at an all-India conference on Centre-State Relations and Regional Disparities in India at New Delhi in August, 1980. New Delhi: Society for the Study of Regional Disparities, 1982.

Bhowmik, Sharit Kumar. "Tripura Election and After," *EPW*, xxiii, No. 16 (April 16, 1988), 776–777.

"Development Perspectives for Tribals," *EPW*, xxiii, No. 20 (May 14, 1988), 1005–1077.

Bjorkman, James. "Public Law 480 and the Policies of Self-Help and Short-Tether: Indo-American Relations, 1965–68," in Lloyd I. Rudolph and Susanne H. Rudolph et al., *The Regional Imperative*. Atlantic Highlands, N.J.: Humanities Press, 1980, pp. 201–262.

Blair, Harry. "Electoral Support and Party Institutionalization in Bihar: Congress and the Opposition, 1977–1985," in Richard Sisson and Ramashray Roy (eds.), *Diversity and Dominance in Indian Politics*, Vol. I: *Changing Bases of Congress Support*. New Delhi: Sage, 1990.

Bose, Pradip Kumar. "Congress and the Tribal Communities in India," in Ramashray Roy and Richard Sisson (eds.), *Diversity and Dominance in Indian Politics*, Vol. ii: *Division, Deprivation and the Congress*. New Delhi: Sage, 1990.

Bouton, Marshall M. *Agrarian Radicalism in South India*. Princeton, N.J.: Princeton University Press, 1985.

Brass, Paul R. *Factional Politics in an Indian State: The Congress Party in Uttar Pradesh*. Berkeley: University of California Press, 1965.

"The Politics of Ayurvedic Education: A Case Study of Revivalism and Modernization in India," in Susanne H. and Lloyd I. Rudolph, *Education and Politics in India*. Cambridge, MA: Harvard University Press, 1972.

Language, Religion, and Politics in North India. London: Cambridge University Press, 1974.

"Class, Ethnic Group, and Party in Indian Politics," *World Politics*, xxxiii, No. 3 (April, 1981), 449–467.

"Pluralism, Regionalism, and Decentralizing Tendencies in Contemporary Indian Politics," in A. J. Wilson and Dennis Dalton (eds.), *The States of South Asia: Problems of National Integration*. London: C. Hurst, 1982, pp. 223–264.

Caste, Faction and Party in Indian Politics, Vol. i: *Faction and Party*. Delhi: Chanakya Publications, 1983.

"National Power and Local Politics in India: A Twenty-Year Perspective," *Modern Asian Studies*, xvii, No. 1 (February, 1984), 89–118.

Caste, Faction and Party in Indian Politics, Vol. ii: *Election Studies*. Delhi: Chanakya Publications, 1985.

"The Punjab Crisis and the Unity of India," in Atul Kohli (ed.), *India's Democracy: An Analysis of Changing State-Society Relations*. Princeton, N.J.: Princeton University Press, 1988.

"Socio-Economic Aspects of the Punjab Crisis," in S. W. R. de A. Samarasinghe and Reed Coughland (eds.), *Economic Dimensions of Ethnic Conflict*. London: Pinter Publishers, 1991.

"Democracy and Political Participation in India," in Myron L. Cohen (ed.), *Asia: Case Studies in the Social Sciences, A Guide for Teaching*. New York: M. E. Sharpe, 1992.

"The Rise of the BJP and the Future of Party Politics in Uttar Pradesh," in Harold A. Gould and Sumit Ganguly (eds.), *India Votes: Alliance Politics and Minority Governments in the Ninth and Tenth General Elections.* Boulder, CO: Westview Press, 1993.

Brass, Paul R. and Marcus F. Franda. *Radical Politics in South Asia.* Cambridge MA: MIT Press, 1973.

Brecher, Michael. *Succession in India: A Study in Decision-Making.* London: Oxford University Press, 1966.

"Succession in India 1967: The Routinization of Political Change," *Asian Survey*, VII, No. 7 (July, 1967), 423–443.

Bryce, James. "Preface," in M. Ostrogorski, *Democracy and the Organization of Political Parties*, trans. by Frederick Clarke, Vol. I. New York: Macmillan, 1922.

Butler, David *et al. India Decides: Elections 1952–1991.* New Delhi: LM Books, 1991.

Byres, T. J. "The Dialectic of India's Green Revolution," *South Asian Review*, V, No. 2 (January 1972), 99–116.

"The Political Economy of Technological Innovation in Indian Agriculture," in Robert S. Anderson *et al., Science, Politics, and the Agricultural Revolution in Asia.* Boulder, CO: Westview Press, 1982, pp. 19–75.

Calman, Leslie J. *Protest in Democratic India: Authority's Response to Challenge.* Boulder, CO: Westview Press, 1985.

Cashman, Richard I. *The Myth of the Lokmanya: Tilak and Mass Politics in Maharashtra.* Berkeley: University of California Press, 1975.

Centre for Research in Rural and Industrial Development. Communal Violence and Its Impact on Development and National Integration. Chandigarh: Mimeo, n.d.

Chatterjee, Partha. "Gandhi and the Critique of Civil Society,"in Ranajit Guha (ed.), *Subaltern Studies III: Writings on South Asian History and Society.* Delhi: Oxford University Press, 1984, pp. 153–195.

Chatterji, Rakahari. "Democracy and the Opposition in India," *EPW*, XXIII, No. 17 (April 23, 1988), 843–847.

Chaube, S. K. *Electoral Politics in Northeast India.* Madras: Universities Press, 1985.

Chibber, Pradeep K. *et al.* "Order and the Indian Electorate: For Whom Does Shiva Dance?" *Asian Survey*, XXXII, No. 7 (July, 1992), 606–616.

Chopra, R. N. *Evolution of Food Policy in India.* Delhi: Macmillan, 1981.

Cohen, Stephen P. *The Indian Army: Its Contribution to the Development of a Nation.* Berkeley: University of California Press, 1971.

"The Military," in Henry C. Hart (ed.), *Indira Gandhi's India: A Political System Reappraised.* Boulder, CO: Westview Press, 1976, pp. 207–240.

"The Military and Indian Democracy," in Atul Kohli (ed.), *India's Democracy: An Analysis of Changing State–Society Relations.* Princeton, N.J.: Princeton University Press, 1987, pp. 99–143.

Dandekar, V. M. "Unitary Elements in a Federal Constitution," *EPW*, XXII, No. 44 (October 31, 1987), 1865–1870.

"Indian Economy Since Independence," *EPW*, xxiii, Nos. 1 and 2 (January 2–9, 1988), 41–50.

"Population Front of India's Economic Development," *EPW*, xxiii, No. 17 (April 23, 1988), 837–842.

Dandekar, V. M. and N. Rath. "Poverty in India: Dimensions and Trends," *EPW*, vi, No. 1 (January 2, 1971), 25–48, and No. 2 (January 9, 1971), 106–146.

Das, Arvind N. *Agrarian Unrest and Socio-Economic Change in Bihar, 1900–1980*. New Delhi: Manohar, 1983.

"Bihar: Landowners' Armies Take Over 'Law and Order'," *EPW*, xxi, No. 1 (January 4, 1986), 15–18.

Das Gupta, Jyotirindra. "The Janata Phase: Reorganization and Redirection in Indian Politics," *Asian Survey*, xix, No. 4 (April, 1979), 390–403.

Dasgupta, Biplab. *Agrarian Change and the New Technology in India*. Geneva: United Nations Research Institute for Social Development, 1977.

Dayal, Edison, "Regional Response to High Yield Varieties of Rice in India," *Singapore Journal of Tropical Geography*, iv, No. 2 (1983), 87–98.

Deka, K. N. "Assam: The Challenge of Political Integration and Congress Leadership," in Iqbal Narain (ed.), *State Politics in India*. Meerut: Meenakshi Prakashan, 1976, pp. 30–50.

Desai, A. R. (ed.), *Peasant Struggles in India*. Delhi: Oxford University Press, 1979.

Dhanagare, D. N. "Agrarian Reforms and Rural Development in India: Some Observations," offprint from *Research in Social Movements, Conflict and Change*, Vol. vii (JAI Press, 1984), pp. 177–201.

Dua, Bhagwan D. "A Study in Executive–Judicial Conflict: The Indian Case," *Asian Survey*, xxiii, No. 4 (April, 1983), 463–483.

"Federalism or Patrimonialism: The Making and Unmaking of Chief Ministers in India," *Asian Survey*, xxv, No. 8 (August, 1985), 793–804.

"India: Federal Leadership and Secessionist Movements on the Periphery," in Ramashray Roy and Richard Sisson (eds.), *Diversity and Dominance in Indian Politics*, Vol. ii: *Division, Deprivation and the Congress*. New Delhi: Sage, 1990.

Dutt, V. P. "The Emergency in India: Background and Rationale," *Asian Survey*, xvi, No. 12 (December, 1976), 1124–1138.

Engineer, Asghar Ali. "The Causes of Communal Riots in the Post-Partition Period in India," in Ashgar Ali Engineer (ed.), *Communal Riots in Post-Independence India*. Hyderabad: Sangam Books, 1984, pp. 33–41.

"Old Delhi in Grip of Communal Frenzy," *EPW*, xxii, No. 26 (June 27, 1987), 1020–1021.

Farmer, B. H. "The 'Green Revolution' in South Asian Ricefields: Environment and Production," *Journal of Development Studies*, xv (1979), 304–319.

"Perspectives on the 'Green Revolution' in South Asia," *Modern Asian Studies*, xx No. 1 (February, 1986), 175–199.

Franda, Marcus F. *West Bengal and the Federalizing Process in India*. Princeton, N.J.: Princeton University Press, 1968.

Radical Politics in West Bengal. Cambridge, MA: MIT Press, 1971.

Small is Politics: Organizational Alternatives in India's Rural Development. New Delhi: Wiley Eastern, 1979.

Frankel, Francine R. *India's Green Revolution: Economic Gains and Political Costs.* Princeton, N.J.: Princeton University Press, 1971.

India's Political Economy, 1947–1977: The Gradual Revolution, Princeton, N.J.: Princeton University Press, 1978.

Friedmann, Yohanan. "The Attitude of the JAM'IYYAT-'ULAMA'-HIND to the Indian National Movement and the Establishment of Pakistan," *Asian and African Studies,* VII (1971), 157–180.

Frykenberg, Robert Eric. "The Emergence of Modern 'Hinduism' as a Concept and as an Institution: A Reappraisal with Special Reference to South India," in Gunther Sontheimer and Herman Kulke (eds.), *Hinduism Reconsidered.* Heidelberg: South Asia Institute, 1988, pp. 1–29.

Galanter, Marc. *Competing Equalities: Law and the Backward Classes in India.* Delhi: Oxford University Press, 1984.

Gangal, S. C. *Prime Minister and the Cabinet in India.* New Delhi: Navachetna Prakashan, 1972.

Ganguly, Sumit. "Avoiding War in Kashmir," *Foreign Affairs,* LXIX, No. 5 (Winter, 1990–91), 57–73.

Ghatak, Subrata. *Rural Money Markets in India.* Delhi: Macmillan, 1976.

Ghosh, Anjan. "Caste Idiom for Class Conflict: Case of Khananjawala," *EPW,* XIV, Nos. 5 and 6 (February 3–10, 1979), 184–186.

Ghosh, Arun. "The Plan versus Departmental Prerogatives," *EPW,* XXIII, Nos. 14 and 15 (April 2–9, 1988), 675–678.

"Self-Reliance, Recent Economic Policies and Neo-Colonialism," *EPW,* XXVII, No. 17 (April 25, 1992), 865–868.

"New Economic Policy: A Review," *EPW,* XXVII, No. 23 (June 6, 1992), 1175–1178.

"Planning versus Market-Oriented Investment and Production," *EPW,* XXVII, No. 42 (October 17, 1992), 2281–2283.

Gill, Sucha Singh and K. C. Singhal. "The Punjab Problem: Its Historical Roots," *EPW,* XIX, No. 14 (April 7, 1984), 603–608.

Gohain, Hiren, "Bodo Stir in Perspective," *EPW,* XXIV, No. 25 (June 24, 1989), 1377–1379.

Goswami, Atul and Jayanta K. Gogoi. "Migration and Demographic Transformation of Assam: 1901–1971," in B. L. Abbi (ed.), *Northeast Region: Problems and Prospects of Development.* Chandigarh: Centre for Research in Rural and Industrial Development, 1984, pp. 60–80.

Gough, Kathleen, "Indian Peasant Uprisings," *Bulletin of Concerned Asian Scholars,* VIII, No. 3 (July–September, 1976), 2–18.

Gould, Harold A. "A Sociologial Perspective on the Eighth General Election in India," *Asian Survey,* XXVI, No. 6 (June, 1986), 630–652.

Graff, Violette. "La Jamaat-i-Islami en Inde," in Olivier Carré and Paul Dumont (eds.), *Radicalismes Islamiques.* Vol. II. Paris: L'Harmattan, 1986, pp. 59–72.

"The Muslim Vote in the Indian General Election of December 1984," in Paul R. Brass and Francis Robinson (eds.), *The Indian National Congress and Indian Society, 1885–1985: Ideology, Social Structure and Political Dominance*. Delhi: Chanakya Publications, 1987.

Grewal, B. S. *Centre-State Financial Relations in India*. Patiala: Punjabi University, 1975.

Grierson, G. A. (ed.), *Linguistic Survey of India*, Vol. I, pt. i: *Introductory*; Vol. v, *Indo-Aryan Family, Eastern Group*, pt. ii: *Specimens of the Bihari and Oriya Languages*; Vol. IX, *Indo-Aryan Family, Central Group*, pt. i: *Specimens of Western Hindi and Punjabi*. Delhi: Motilal Banarsidass, 1967–68.

Gujha, S. "Comprehending Equalities," review of *Competing Equalities: Law and the Backward Classes in India* by Marc Galanter, in *EPW*, XXVII, Nos. 31 and 32 (August 1–8, 1992), 1657–1662.

Gujal, I. K. "The Sequence," in The Punjab Tangle, *Seminar*, 294 (February, 1984), 14–17.

Gupta, Dipankar. "The Communalising of Punjab, 1980–1985," *EPW*, xx, No. 28 (July, 1985), 1185–1190.

"Religion, Politics, and the DMK," in Donald E. Smith (ed.), *South Asian Politics and Religion* (Princeton, N.J.: Princeton University Press, 1966), p. 227.

Hardgrave, Robert L., Jr. "Religion, Politics, and the DMK," in Donald & Smith (ed.) *South Asian Politics and Religion* (Princeton, N.J.: Princeton University Press, 1966).

"The Congress in India – Crisis and Split," *Asian Survey*, x, No. 3 (March, 1970), 256–262.

"India in 1984: Confrontation, Assassination, and Succession," *Asian Survey*, xxv, No. 2 (February, 1985), 131–144.

Hardgrave, Robert L., Jr. and Stanley A. Kochanek. *India: Government and Politics in a Developing Nation*. 4th edn. San Diego: Harcourt Brace Jovanovich, 1986.

Hart, Henry C. "Introduction," in Henry C. Hart (ed.), *Indira Gandhi's India: A Political System Reappraised*. Boulder, CO: Westview Press, 1976.

"The Indian Constitution: Political Development and Decay," *Asian Survey*, xx, No. 4 (April, 1980), 428–451.

Hauser, Walter and Wendy Singer. "The Democratic Rite: Celebration and Participation in the Indian Elections," *Asian Survey*, xxvi, No. 9 (September, 1986), 941–958.

Heginbotham, Stanley J. *Cultures in Conflict: The Four Faces of Indian Bureaucracy*. New York: Columbia University Press, 1975.

Henderson, Michael. "Setting India's Democratic House in Order: Constitutional Amendments," *Asian Survey*, XIX, No. 10 (October, 1979), 946–956.

Hirway, Indira. "Direct Attacks on Rural Poverty," review of *Direct Attack on Rural Poverty: Policy, Programmes and Implementation* by Prabhu Ghate (New Delhi: Concept Publishing Company, 1984), *EPW*, xxi, No. 1 (January 4, 1986), 22–23.

Huntington, Samuel P. *Political Order in Changing Societies*. New Haven: Yale University Press, 1968.

Hussain, Monirul. "Tribal Movement for Autonomous State in Assam," *EPW*, xxii, No. 32 (August 8, 1987), 1329–1332.

"Tribal Question in Assam," *EPW*, xxvii, Nos. 20 and 21 (May 16–23, 1992), 1047–1050.

Jagmohan. *My Frozen Turbulence in Kashmir*. New Delhi: Allied Publishers, 1991.

Jha, Prem Shankar. *India: A Political Economy of Stagnation*. Bombay: Oxford University Press, 1980.

Jones, Kenneth W. *Arya Dharm: Hindu-Consciousness in 19th-Century Punjab*. Berkeley: University of California Press, 1976.

Joshi, P. C. "Land Reform and Agrarian Change in India and Pakistan since 1947: 1," *Journal of Peasant Studies*, i, No. 2 (January, 1974), 164–185.

Kamalakar, Jaya. "Ethnic Politics in Municipal Corporations," *EPW*, xxiii, No. 19 (May 7, 1988), 945–946.

Kamarupee [Kamaroopi]. "AGP Facing Multiple Challenges," *EPW*, xxiv, No. 46 (November 18, 1989), 2533–2534.

"Congress Returns to Brahmaputra Valley," *EPW*, xxvi, No. 25 (June 22, 1991), 1510–1511.

"Enigma of ULFA," *EPW*, xxvi, No. 30 (July 27, 1991), 1786–1787.

Kamath, P. M. "Politics of Defection in India in the 1980s," *Asian Survey*, xxv, No. 10 (October, 1985), 1039–1054.

Kaur, Amarjit. "Akali Dal: The Enemy Within," in Amarjit Kaur *et al.*, *The Punjab Story*. New Delhi: Roli Books International, 1984, pp. 14–28.

Khan, Rasheedudin. *Federal India: A Design for Change*. Delhi: Vikas, 1992.

Kochanek, Stanley A. "Post Nehru India: The Emergence of the New Leadership," *Asian Survey*, vi, No. 5 (May, 1966), 288–299.

The Congress Party of India: The Dynamics of One-Party Democracy. Princeton, N.J.: Princeton University Press, 1968.

Business and Politics in India. Berkeley: University of California Press, 1974.

"Mrs. Gandhi's Pyramid: The New Congress," in Henry C. Hart (ed.), *Indira Gandhi's India: A Political System Reappraised*. Boulder, CO: Westview Press, 1976, pp. 93–124.

"The Politics of Regulation: Rajiv's New Mantras," *Journal of Commonwealth & Comparative Politics*, xxiii, No. 3 (November, 1985), 189–211.

"Regulation and Liberalization Theology in India," *Asian Survey*, xxvi, No. 12 (December, 1986), 1284–1308.

"Briefcase Politics in India: The Congress Party and the Business Elite," *Asian Survey*, xxvii, No. 12 (December, 1987), 1278–1301.

Kohli, Atul. "Democracy, Economic Growth, and Inequality in India's Development," *World Politics*, xxxii, No. 4 (July, 1980), 623–638.

"Parliamentary Communism and Agrarian Reform: The Evidence from India's Bengal," *Asian Survey*, xxiii, No. 7 (July, 1983), 783–809.

The State and Poverty in India: The Politics of Reform. Cambridge: Cambridge University Press, 1987.

Democracy and Discontent: India's Growing Crisis of Governability. Cambridge: Cambridge University Press, 1990.

Kothari, Rajni. "India: The Congress System on Trial," *Asian Survey*, VII, No. 2 (February, 1967), 83–96.

Krishna, Raj. "Growth, Investment and Poverty in Mid-Term Appraisal of Sixth Plan," *EPW*, XVII, No. 47 (November 19, 1983), 1972–1977.

Krishnaswamy, K. S. "Which Direction and What Atmosphere?" *EPW*, XXVII, No. 28 (July 11, 1992), 1471–1472.

Kulkarni, Sharad. "Forest Legislation and Tribals: Comments on Forest Policy Resolution," *EPW*, XXII, No. 50 (December 12, 1987), 2143–2148.

Kumar, Arun. "Punjab: Wages of Past Sins," *EPW*, XIX, No. 28 (July 14, 1984), 1076–1077.

Kumar, A. Ganesh. "Falling Agricultural Investment and Its Consequences," *EPW*, XXVII, No. 42 (October 17, 1992), 2307–2312.

Lakdawala, D. T. "Budget and the Plan," *EPW*, XVIII, No. 12 (March 19, 1983), 449–450.

"Eighth Finance Commission's Recommendations," *EPW*, XIX, No. 35 (September 1, 1984), 1529–1534.

LaPalombara, Joseph. "Penetration: A Crisis of Governmental Capacity," in Leonard Binder *et al.*, *Crises and Sequences in Political Development*. Princeton, N.J.: Princeton University Press, 1971, pp. 205–232.

Lele, Jayant. *Elite Pluralism and Class Rule: Political Development in Maharashtra*. Bombay: Popular Prakashan, 1982.

Lipton, Michael. "The Technology, the System and the Poor: The Case of the New Cereal Varieties," offprint, Hague, Institute of Social Studies, 1977, pp. 121–135.

Why Poor People Stay Poor: A Study of Urban Bias in World Development. New Delhi: Heritage, 1980.

M. T. "The God that Died: The MGR Phenomenon," *EPW*, XXIII, Nos. 1 and 2 (January 2–9, 1988), 21–22.

Madan, T. N. "Secularism in Its Place," *Journal of Asian Studies*, XLVI, No. 4 (November, 1987), 747–760.

Mahajan, O. P. "Balanced Regional Development: An Evaluation of Planning Strategy in India," in L. S. Bhat *et al.*, *Regional Inequalities in India*, pp. 35–55.

Mahendra Dev, S. "Direction of Change in Performance of All Crops in Indian Agriculture in Late 1970s: A Look at the Level of Districts and Agro-Climatic Regions," *EPW*, XX, Nos. 51 and 52 (December 21–28, 1985), A-130–136.

Maheshwari, Shriram. *Rural Development in India: A Public Policy Approach*. New Delhi: Sage Publications, 1985.

Majumdar, Grace. "Trends in Inter-State Inequalities in Income and Expenditure in India," in L. S. Bhat *et al.*, *Regional Inequalities in India*, pp. 24–34.

Malik, Harji, "A Punjab Report," *EPW*, XIX, No. 37 (September 15, 1984), 1607–1608.

Malik, Yogendra K. and V. B. Singh. "Bharatiya Janata Party: An Alternative to the Congress (I)?" *Asian Survey*, XXXII, No. 4 (April, 1992), 318–336.

Mani, Sunil. "New Industrial Policy: Barriers to Entry, Foreign Investment and Privatisation," *EPW*, xxvii, No. 35 (August 29, 1992), M-86 to M-94.

Manor, James. "BJP in South India: 1991 General Election," *EPW*, xxvii, Nos. 24 and 25 (June 13–20, 1992), 1268–1727.

Mathur, Kuldeep. "The State and the Use of Coercive Power in India," *Asian Survey*, xxxii, No. 4 (April, 1992), 337–349.

Mehta, Asoka. *A Decade of Indian Politics, 1966–77*. New Delhi: S. Chand & Co., 1979.

Mehta, Pratap Bhanu. "India's Disordered Democracy: Review Article," *Pacific Affairs*, lxiv, No. 4 (Winter, 1991–92), 536–548.

Mellor, John W. *The New Economics of Growth: A Strategy for India and the Developing World*. Ithaca: Cornell University Press, 1976.

Mies, Maria. "The Shahada Movement: a Peasant Movement in Maharashtra (India) – its Development and its Perspectives," *Journal of Peasant Studies*, iii, No. 4 (July, 1976), 472–482.

Minault, Gail. "Some Reflections on Islamic Revivalism vs. Assimilation Among Muslims in India," *Contributions to Indian Sociology*, xviii, No. 2 (1984), 301–305.

Misra, B. B. *Government and Bureaucracy in India, 1947–1976*. Delhi: Oxford University Press, 1986.

Misra, Udayon. "Bodo Stir: Complex Issues, Unattainable Demands," *EPW*, xxiv, No. 21 (May 27, 1989), 1146–1149.

Mitra, Subrata. "The Perils of Promoting Equality: The Latent Significance of the Anti-Reservation Movement in India," *Journal of Commonwealth and Comparative Politics*, xxv, No. 3 (November, 1987), 292–312.

Morris-Jones, W. H. *The Government and Politics of India*. London: Hutchinson University Library, 1964.

"India: Under New Management, Business as Usual," *Asian Survey*, v, No. 2 (February, 1965), 63–73.

"India: The Trial of Leadership," *Asian Survey*, vi, No. 2 (February, 1966), 67–75.

"India Elects for Change – and Stability," *Asian Survey*, xi, No. 8 (August, 1971), 719–741.

"India – More Questions Than Answers," *Asian Survey*, xxiv, No. 8 (August, 1984), 809–816.

Morrison, Barrie M. "The Persistent Rural Crisis in Asia: A Shift in Conception," *Pacific Affairs*, lii, No. 4 (Winter, 1979–80), 631–646.

Mukherjee, Aditya and Mridula Mukherjee. "Imperialism and Growth of Indian Capitalism in Twentieth Century," *EPW*, xxiii, No. 11 (March 12, 1988), 531–546.

Naipaul, V. S. *India: A Million Mutinies Now*. New York: Viking, 1990.

Nambiar, K. V. "Criteria for Federal Resource Transfers," *EPW*, xviii, No. 22 (May 28, 1983), 965–968. (Book reviews)

Nandy, Ashish. *At the Edge of Psychology: Essays in Politics and Culture*. Delhi: Oxford University Press, 1980.

379

"The Politics of Secularism and the Recovery of Religious Tolerance," *Alternatives*, XIII (1988), 177–194.

Narain, Iqbal. "India 1977: From Promise to Disenchantment?" *Asian Survey*, XVIII, No. 2 (February, 1978), 103–116.

"India in 1985: Triumph of Democracy," *Asian Survey*, XXVI, No. 2 (February, 1986), 253–269.

Nauriya, Anil. "Reservations in Public Employment: Modified Mandal Scheme," *EPW*, XXVI, No. 43 (October 26, 1991), 2454–2456.

Nayar, Baldev Raj. *The Modernisation Imperative and Indian Planning*. Delhi: Vikas, 1972.

Nicholson, Norman K. *Rural Development Policy in India: Elite Differentiation and the Decision Making Process*. DeKalb, Illinois: Center for Governmental Studies, Northern Illinois University, 1974.

Nigam, Aditya. "Mandal Commission and the Left," *EPW*, XXV, Nos. 48 and 49 (December 1–8, 1990), 2652–2653.

Nishtar. "Time for a Political Initiative in Punjab," *EPW*, XXII, No. 41 (October 10, 1987), 1731–1732.

Noorani, A. G. "Civil Liberties: Supreme Court and Punjab Crisis," *EPW*, XIX, No. 38 (September 22, 1984), 1654.

"Amnesty Report in Meerut Killings," *EPW*, XXII, No. 50 (December 12, 1987), 2139–2140.

Oldenburg, Philip. "Middlemen in Third-World Corruption: Implications of an Indian Case," *World Politics*, XXXIX, No. 4 (July, 1987), 508–535.

Omvedt, Gail and Chetna Galla. "Ideology for Provincial Propertied Class?" *EPW*, XXII, No. 45 (November 7, 1987), 1925–1926.

Paranjpe, H. K. "Centre–State Relations in Planning," in S. N. Jain *et al.*, *The Union and the States*. Delhi: National, 1972, pp. 207–241.

Parikh, Kirit S. "A Development Strategy for the 1990s," *EPW*, XXIII, No. 12 (March 19, 1988), 597–601.

Park, Richard. "Political Crisis in India, 1975," *Asian Survey*, XV, No. 11 (November, 1975), 996–1013.

Patel, Sujata. "Legitimacy Crisis and Growing Authoritarianism," *EPW*, XXIII, No. 19 (May 7, 1988), 946–948.

Patel, Surendra J. "India's Regression in the World Economy," *EPW*, XX, No. 39 (September 28, 1985), 1651–1659.

Paul, Samuel. "Mid-Term Appraisal of the Sixth Plan: Why Poverty Alleviation Lags Behind," *EPW*, XIX, No. 18 (May 5, 1984), 760–766.

Pettigrew, Joyce. "Take Not Arms Against Thy Sovereign," *South Asia Research*, IX, No. 2 (November, 1984), 102–123.

Potter, David C. *India's Political Administrators: 1919–1983*. Oxford: Clarendon Press, 1986.

Prakasa, Sri. *State Governors in India*. Meerut: Meenakshi Prakashan, 1966.

Prasad, Pradhan H. "Poverty and Agricultural Development," *EPW*, XX, No. 50 (December 14, 1985), 2221–2224.

Presler, Franklin A. "Studying India's Political Culture," *Journal of Commonwealth & Comparative Politics*, XXII, No. 3 (November, 1984), 224–234.

Pylee, M. V. *Constitutional Government in India*. New York: Asia Publishing House, 1965.

Radhakrishnan, P. "Ambasankar and Backward Classes," *EPW*, XXIV, No. 23 (June 10, 1989), 1265–1268.

"Karnataka Backward Classes," *EPW*, XXV, No. 32 (August 11, 1990), 1749–1754.

Ram, Mohan. "The Communist Movement in Andhra," in Paul R. Brass and Marcus Franda (eds.), *Radical Politics in South Asia*. Cambridge, MA: MIT Press, 1973.

"The Communist Movement in India," in Gough, *Imperialism and Revolution in South Asia*. New York: Monthly Review Press, 1973.

Ram Reddy, G. and G. Haragopal. "The Pyraveekar: 'The Fixer' in Rural India," *Asian Survey*, XXV, No. 11 (November, 1985), 1148–1162.

Ramaiah, A. "Identifying Other Backward Classes," *EPW*, XXVII, No. 23 (June 6, 1992), 1203–1207.

Rao, V. M. "Fixing Agricultural Prices: Issues and Experiences," review of *Agricultural Price Policy in India* by A. S. Kahlon and D. S. Tyagi, Allied, 1989, in *EPW*, XXVII, No. 12 (March 28, 1992), 639–645.

"Land Reform Experiences: Perspective for Strategy and Programmes," *EPW*, XXVII, No. 26 (June 27, 1992), A-50 to A-64.

Rath, Nilakantha. "'Garibi Hatao': Can IRDP Do It?" *EPW*, XX, No. 6 (February 9, 1985), 238–246.

"A Budget for Farmers!" *EPW*, XXIII, Nos. 14 and 15 (April 2–9, 1988), 739–744.

Ray, Amal and Jayalakshmi Kumpatla. "Zilla Parishad Presidents in Karnataka: Their Social Background and Implications for Development," *EPW*, XXII, Nos. 42 and 43 (October 17–24, 1987), 1825–1830.

Robinson, Francis. "Islam and Muslim Society in South Asia: A Reply to Das and Minault," *Contributions to Indian Sociology*, XX, No. 1 (January–June, 1986), 97–104.

Rosenthal, Donald B. *The Expansive Elite: District Politics and State Policy-Making in India*. Berkeley: University of California Press, 1977.

Roy, Ajit. "Darjeeling: Hopeful Turn and Remaining Obstacles," *EPW*, XXIII, No. 30 (July 23, 1988), 1511.

Roy, K. C. and A. L. Lougheed. "The Green Revolution in India: Progress and Problems," *World Review*, XVI, No. 2 (July, 1977), 16–27.

Rubin, Barnett R. "The Civil Liberties Movement in India: New Approaches to the State and Social Change," *Asian Survey*, XXVII, No. 3 (March 1987), 371–392.

Rubinoff, Arthur G. "Goa's Attainment of Statehood," *Asian Survey*, XXXII, No. 5 (May, 1992), 471–487.

Rudolph, Lloyd I. and Susanne H. Rudolph. *In Pursuit of Lakshmi: The Political Economy of the Indian State*. Chicago: University of Chicago Press, 1987.

Rudra, Ashok. "Political Economy of Indian Non-Development," review of *The Political Economy of Development in India* by Pranab Bardhan, *EPW*, xx, No. 21 (May 25, 1985), 914–916.

Sarangi, Satinath and Ramesh Billorey. "The Nightmare Begins: Oustees of Indira Sagar Project," *EPW*, xxiii, No. 17 (April 23, 1988), 838.

Sarkar, Sumit. *Modern India: 1885–1947*. Madras: Macmillan, 1983.

Sartori, Giovanni. *Parties and Party Systems: A Framework for Analysis*, Vol. i. Cambridge: Cambridge University Press, 1976.

Sau, Ranjit. "The Green Revolution and Industrial Growth in India: A Tale of Two Paradoxes and a Half," *EPW*, xxiii, No. 16 (April 16, 1988), 789–796.

Saxena, N. C. "Caste and Zamindari Abolition in U. P.," *Mainstream* (June 15, 1985), 15–19.

Schlesinger, Lee I. "Agriculture and Community in Maharashtra, India," in George Dalton (ed.), *Research in Economic Anthropology*, Vol. iv. JAI Press, 1981, pp. 233–274.

Sen, Amartya. "Poverty, Inequality, Unemployment: Some Conceptual Issues in Measurement," *EPW*, viii, Special Number (August, 1973).

Sen Gupta, Bhabani. "Communism Further Divided," in Henry C. Hart (ed.), *Indira Gandhi's India: A Political System Reappraised*. Boulder, CO: Westview Press, 1976, pp. 153–180.

"The Fourth Year," *EPW*, xxii, No. 50 (December 12, 1987), 2135–2136.

"Crisis of the Indian State," *EPW*, xxiii, No. 16 (April 16, 1988), 764–766.

Sengupta, Barun. *Last Days of the Morarji Raj*. Calcutta: Ananda Publishers, 1979.

Sethi, J. D. "Secularism, Communalism and Nationalism," in Amrik Singh (ed.), *Punjab in Indian Politics: Issues and Trends*. Delhi: Ajanta Books, 1985, pp. 434–446.

Shah, Ghanshyam. "Grass-Roots Mobilization in Indian Politics," in Atul Kohli (ed.), *India's Democracy: An Analysis of Changing State-Society Relations*. Princeton, N.J.: Princeton University Press, 1988, pp. 263–304.

"Strategies of Social Engineering: Reservation and Mobility of Backward Communities in Gujarat," in Ramashray Roy and Richard Sisson (eds.), *Diversity and Dominance in Indian Politics*, Vol. ii: *Division, Deprivation and the Congress*. New Delhi: Sage, 1990.

"Social Backwardness and Politics of Reservations," *EPW*, xxvi, Nos. 11 and 12 (Annual Number, March, 1991), 601–610.

Sidhu, D. S. and Derek Byerlee. "Technical Change and Wheat Productivity in Post-Green Revolution Punjab," *EPW*, xxvi, No. 52 (December 28, 1991), A-159 to A-166.

Singh, B. P. "North-East India: Demography, Culture and Identity Crisis," *Modern Asian Studies*, xxi, No. 2 (1987), 257–282.

Singh, Charan. *Joint-Farming X-Rayed: The Problem and its Solution*. Bombay: Bharatiya Vidya Bhavan, 1959.

Economic Nightmare of India: Its Cause and Cure. New Delhi: National, 1981.

Singh, Iqbal. *Punjab under Siege: A Critical Analysis*. New York: Allen, McMillan and Enderson, 1986.

Singh, Mahendra Prasad. "The Dilemma of the New Indian Party System: To Govern or Not to Govern?" *Asian Survey*, xxxii, No. 4 (April, 1992), 303–317.

Singh, Pritam. "Punjab: Lessons of Panchayat Elections," *EPW*, xviii, No. 43 (October 22, 1983), 1822–1823.

"Akali Agitation: Growing Separatist Trend," *EPW*, xix, No. 5 (February 4, 1984), 195–196.

Singh, Rajendra. "Agrarian Social Structure and Peasant Unrest: A Study of Land-Grab Movement in District Basti, East U. P.," *Sociological Bulletin*, xxiii, No. 1 (March, 1974), 44–70.

Singh, Ranbhir. "Changing Social Bases of Congress' Political Support in Haryana," in Richard Sisson and Ramashray Roy (eds.), *Diversity and Dominance in Indian Politics*, Vol. 1: *Changing Bases of Congress Support*. New Delhi: Sage, 1990.

Singh, V. B. and Shankar Bose. *Elections in India: Data Handbook on Lok Sabha Elections, 1952–85*, 2nd edn. New Delhi: Sage Publications, 1984.

State Elections in India: Data Handbook on Vidhan Sabha Elections, 1952–85, vols. i, ii, iii, iv – Pt. ii and v. New Delhi: Sage Publications, 1987–88.

Sinha, Arun. "Bihar: Bajitpur: Landlord's Violence," *EPW*, xiii, No. 50 (December 16, 1978), 2031–2032.

"Recurrent Pattern of Jharkhand Politics," *EPW*, xxii, No. 45 (November 7, 1987), 1887–1889.

Sisson, Richard. "Prime Ministerial Power and the Selection of Ministers in India: Three Decades of Change," *International Political Science Review*, ii, No. 2 (1981), 137–157.

Sivaraman, B. "This Mandalist Myopia," *EPW*, xxvi, No. 6 (February 9, 1991), 314–315.

Srinivasan, T. N. "Reform of Industrial and Trade Policies," *EPW*, xxvi, No. 37 (September 14, 1991), 2143–2145.

Srivastava, Arun. "Landlords' Mafias in Bhojpur," *EPW*, xvi, Nos. 1 and 2 (January 3–10, 1981), 17–18.

Stokes, Eric. *The Peasant and the Raj*. Cambridge: Cambridge University Press, 1978.

Subba Reddy, N. "Depriving Tribals of Land: Andhra Move to Amend Land Transfer Laws," *EPW*, xxiii, No. 29 (July 16, 1988), 1458–1461.

Tandon, Prakash. "Another Angle," *Seminar*, 294 (February, 1984), 35–37.

Taub, Richard P. *Bureaucrats Under Stress: Administrators and Administration is an Indian State*. Berkeley: University of California Press, 1969.

Thakur, Ramesh C. "The Fate of India's Parliamentary Democracy," *Pacific Affairs*, xlix, No. 2 (Summer, 1976), 263–293.

Thimmaiah, G. and Abdul Aziz. "The Political Economy of Land Reforms in Karnataka, a South Indian State," *Asian Survey*, xxiii, No. 7 (July, 1983), 810–829.

Toye, John. *Public Expenditure and Indian Development Policy: 1960–1970*. Cambridge: Cambridge University Press, 1981.

Trinque, Brian M. "The New Economics of Growth: An Assessment after 15 Years," *Contemporary South Asia*, I, No. 1 (1992), 67–91.

Tummala, Krishna K. "Democracy Triumphant in India: The Case of Andhra Pradesh," *Asian Survey*, XXVI, No. 3 (March 1986), 378–395.

"India's Federalism Under Stress," *Asian Survey*, XXXII, No. 6 (June, 1992), 538–553.

Vakil, F. D. "Patterns of Electoral Performance in Andhra Pradesh and Karnataka," in Richard Sisson and Ramashray Roy (eds.), *Diversity and Dominance in Indian Politics*, Vol. I: *Changing Bases of Congress Support*. New Delhi: Sage, 1990, pp. 249–275.

Van der Veer, Peter. "'God must be Liberated!' A Hindu Liberation Movement in Ayodhya," *Modern Asian Studies*, XXI, No. 2 (1987), 283–301.

Varshney, Ashutosh. "India, Pakistan, and Kashmir: Antinomies of Nationalism," *Asian Survey*, XXXI, No. 11 (November, 1991), 997–1019.

Vyasulu, Vinod *et al.* "Towards a Political Economy of the Economic Policy Changes," *EPW*, XXVI, No. 38 (September 21, 1991), 2205–2212.

Wade, Robert. "The System of Administrative and Political Corruption: Canal Irrigation in South India," *Journal of Development Studies*, XVIII, No. 3 (April, 1982), 287–328.

"The Market for Public Office: Why the Indian State Is Not Better at Development," *World Development*, XIII, No. 4 (April, 1985), 467–497.

Wariavwalla, Bharat. "India in 1987: Democracy on Trial," *Asian Survey*, XXVIII, No. 2 (February, 1988), 119–125.

"India in 1988: Drift, Disarray, or Pattern," *Asian Survey*, XXIX, No. 2 (February, 1989), 189–198.

Weiner, Myron. "India's Two Political Cultures," in Myron Weiner, *Political Change in South Asia*. Calcutta: Firma K. L. Mukhapadhyay, 1963.

Party Building in a New Nation: The Indian National Congress. Chicago: University of Chicago Press, 1967.

"Political Participation: Crisis of the Political Process," in Leonard Binder *et al.*, *Crises and Sequences in Political Development*. Princeton, N.J.: Princeton University Press, 1971, pp. 159–204.

"India's New Political Institutions," *Asian Survey*, XVI, No. 9 (September, 1976), 898–901.

India at the Polls: The Parliamentary Elections of 1977. Washington, D.C.: American Enterprise Institute, 1978.

Sons of the Soil: Migration and Ethnic Conflict in India. Princeton, N.J.: Princeton University Press, 1978.

"Congress Restored: Continuities and Discontinuities in Indian Politics," *Asian Survey*, XXII, No. 4 (April, 1982), 339–355.

India at the Polls, 1980: A Study of the Parliamentary Elections. Washington, D.C.: American Enterprise Institute, 1983.

"The Political Consequences of Preferential Policies: A Comparative Perspective," *Comparative Politics*, XVI, No. 1 (October, 1983), 35–52.

"Ancient Indian Political Theory and Contemporary Indian Politics," in S. N. Eisenstadt *et al.*, *Orthodoxy, Heterodoxy and Dissent in India.* Berlin: Mouton, 1984, pp. 111–130.

"The Political Economy of Industrial Growth in India," *World Politics*, XXXVIII, No. 4 (July, 1986), 596–610.

"Rajiv Gandhi: A Mid-Term Assessment," in Marshall M. Bouton (ed.), *India Briefing, 1987.* Boulder, CO: Westview Press, 1987, pp. 1–23.

The Indian Paradox: Essays in Indian Politics. New Delhi: Sage, 1989.

Weiner, Myron and Mary F. Katzenstein. *India's Preferential Policies: Migrants, the Middle Classes, and Ethnic Equality.* Chicago: University of Chicago Press, 1981.

Wood, John R. "Extra-Parliamentary Opposition in India: An Analysis of Populist Agitations in Gujarat and Bihar," *Pacific Affairs*, XLVIII, No. 3 (Fall, 1975), 313–334.

"Reservations in Doubt: The Backlash Against Affirmative Action in Gujarat," in Ramashray Roy and Richard Sisson (eds.), *Diversity and Dominance in Indian Politics*, Vol. II: *Division, Deprivation and the Congress.* New Delhi: Sage, 1990.

Wood, John R. (ed.). *State Politics in Contemporary India: Crisis or Continuity?* Boulder, CO: Westview Press, 1984.

World Bank. *World Development Report 1984.* New York: Oxford University Press, 1984.

India: Poverty, Employment, and Social Services. Washington, D.C.: World Bank, 1989.

World Development Report 1990. Oxford: Oxford University Press, 1990.

World Development Report, 1992: Development and the Environment. New York: Oxford University Press, 1992.

NEWSPAPERS AND PERIODICALS

Asian Recorder

Congress Bulletin

Economic and Political Weekly (EPW)

India: Economic Information Year Book, 1990–91. New Delhi: National, 1991.

India Today

Mainstream

The Military Balance, 1991–1992. London: The International Institute for Strategic Studies, 1991.

Muslim India

Seminar

Spokesman

Statistical Outline of India, 1989–90. Bombay: Tata Services, 1989.

UNPUBLISHED PAPERS AND DOCUMENTS

Davis, Richard H. The Iconography of Ram's Chariot, prepared for the Social Science Research Council Conference on South Asian Cultural Studies and the Subject of Representation, Durham, NC, February 4–6, 1993.

Duncan, Ian. Party Politics and the North Indian Peasantry: The Rise of the Bharatiya Kranti Dal in Uttar Pradesh. School of African and Asian Studies, University of Sussex, 1987.

Krishna, Gopal. The Problem of Integration in the Indian Political Community – Muslim Minority and the Political Process. No date.

Spodek, Howard. From Gandhi to Violence: Ahmedabad's 1985 Riots in Historical Perspective. 1987.

Van der Veer. Riots and Rituals: The Construction of Violence and Public Space in Hindu Nationalism, prepared for volume by Paul R. Brass (ed.), Riots and Pogroms, forthcoming.

INDEX

387

Khilafat movement, 26
Kilvenmani incident, 326, 328, 331
Kisan Sammelan (Peasant Association), 112
Kolis, 259
Konkani language, 160
Konyak language, 176
Korea, 288, 310
Krishna, 241
Krishna, Raj, 298
Kristalnacht, 354
Kshatriyas, 259–60
Kulaks , 271, 332, 334
Kumauni language, 161
Kunbis, 259
Kurmis, 258, 306
Kurukh/Oraon language, 160

Ladakh, 217
Laldenga, L. C., 203
Land ceilings, 8, 18, 64, 82, 142, 278–79, 296, 299–300, 302, 305, 331
Land ownership, 270, 305
Land reforms, 259, 270, 279, 291, 294, 305, 327, 331, 334
Left Democratic Front (LDF), 235
Left Front, 78
Lepcha, 176
Linguistic Survey of India, 183
Lohia, Rammanohar, 22, 80, 258
Lok Dal, 83, 85–86, 100, 104, 112, 136, 238, 258, 334, 358
Lok Dal (A), 85
Lok Dal (B), 83, 85, 102
Lok Sabha, 39, 43, 46, 76, 87, 94–95, 109, 128, 134, 165; 1991 elections by state, 126–32; elections in Punjab, 197–98; elections, 1952–91, 74–75, 83–84, 93–95, 101–04; role and powers of, 49–51; *see also* Parliament

Madhya Pradesh, 73, 87, 90, 102, 127–28, 176, 183, 185, 231, 243, 294, 304
Magahi language, 159, 183–84
Mahalanobis, P. C., 270, 275
Maharashtra, 73–74, 78, 89–90, 94, 102, 127, 143, 294, 306, 315; creation of, 169; industrialization in, 285; languages in, 160–61; Muslims in, 231; non-Brahman movement in, 6, 253, 259; official language of, 159, 176; *panchayati raj* in, 139; party system in, 94, 126–27, 129; peasant movement in, 113, 317, 359; per capita income in, 284; spread of Hindi in, 165; sugar factories in, 142; Urdu in, 180

Maharashtrawadi Gomantak, 90
Maintenance of Internal Security Act, 1980 (MISA), 352
Maithili language, 159, 173, 175, 177–78, 183–84
Majlis-i-Ittehad-i-Muslimeen, 236
Malabar, 234
Malayalam, 159, 176, 177
Mandal Commission, 88, 127, 252, 253, 258; agitations against recommendations of, 115; Report, 252
Manifestoes, party, 18, 19, 84, 97
Manipur, 90, 102, 176, 205
Manipur People's Party, 90
Marathas, 127, 259, 306
Marathi language, 159, 173, 176–77
Marginal Farmer and Agricultural Labor (MFAL) program, 296
Meghalaya, 90, 102, 176, 202
Mehta, Asoka, 139
Mellor, John, 288
MGR, *see* Ramachandran, M. G.
Mizo Hills district, 204
Mizo National Front (MNF), 90, 203, 204
Mizoram, 90, 176, 202, 204–05
Mizos, 172, 202
Montagu-Chelmsford Reforms, 1
Moore, Barrington, 320
Morley–Minto Reforms, 1
Munda language family, 185
Muslim India, 237
Muslim League, 5, 10, 128, 218, 234–35
Muslim Personal Law, 231, 233, 236
Muslim United Front, 221
Muslim Women (Protection of Rights on Divorce), Bill, 233
Muslims, 5, 7, 15, 151, 158, 228–32, 237–38, 246–47; and Babari Masjid issue, 236, 241–42; and communal riots, 353; and communal violence, 264; and Hindu nationalism, 265; and Hindus, 230, 241, 246, 266, 345; and Pakistan, 21; and Shah Bano case, 233; and Urdu, 179, 182, 184, 186; Bengali, in Assam, 134; Congress policy toward, 231, 233, 265; discontent among, during Emergency, 42–43; illegal immigration of, from Bangladesh to Assam, 134; in Assam, 201, 206, 226; in Gujarat, 260; in Jammu, 218; in Jammu & Kashmir, 222, 224–25, 234; in Kashmir Valley, 218; in Kerala, 235; in Punjab, 107; in Tebhaga movement, 322; in Telangana movement, 322; in U. P., 366; killed in riots, 239–40, 347; in political parties and government service,

THE NEW CAMBRIDGE HISTORY OF INDIA

I The Mughals and their contemporaries

II Indian states and the transition to colonialism

III The Indian empire and the beginnings of modern society

IV The evolution of contemporary South Asia

* Already published
† Available in paperback